C000133106

ALF MORRIS

PEOPLE'S PARLIAMENTARIAN

Scenes from the life of
Lord Morris of Manchester

by

DEREK KINRADE

First published in the UK in September 2007 by
National Information Forum
in association with the following charities:
Royal National Institute of the Blind
Arthritis Care
Deafax
Royal Association for Disability and Rehabilitation
Disabled Living Foundation

© National Information Forum

All rights reserved. No part of this publication may be
reproduced, stored in a retrieval system, or transmitted
in any form or by any means, electronic, mechanical
photocopying, recording or otherwise, without the prior
written permission of the publishers.

The Author asserts the moral right to
be identified as the author of this work.

Text typeset in 12pt on 16pt Palatino

ISBN No 978-0-9557515-0-9

Printed and bound in Great Britain by
Greenaways a member of the Ormolu Group

Xerox have supplied the paper for this biography which has been
printed on Igen and Nuvera machines that have recently been
installed in Greenaways' London office

DEDICATION

To my GP, Dr C. McColl

and the Cardiac Team at Kings College Hospital

who enabled me to finish this biography

THE PARLIAMENTARY PRAYER

LORD, the God of righteousness and truth, grant to our Queen and her government, to members of Parliament and all in positions of responsibility, the guidance of your Spirit. May they never lead the nation wrongly through love of power, desire to please, or unworthy ideals; but laying aside all private interests and prejudices keep in mind their responsibility to seek to improve the condition of all mankind; so may your kingdom come and your name be hallowed. **Amen.**

LIST OF ILLUSTRATIONS

CONTENTS

ACKNOWLEDGEMENTS

Many people have contributed or helped in shaping this memoir. I am particularly grateful to Shorayne Fairweather at the Library of the House of Lords who has been consistently diligent, unfailingly helpful and amiable in searching out obscure references and texts and guiding me through the Library's magnificent archives. Then to Barbara Tremewan, who has proof read the entire text with a combination of assiduity and common sense to reflect the perspective of the ordinary reader, and to Ann Darnbrough and Marion Janner for their perceptive suggestions, encouragement and wisdom.

I have had invaluable comments from Alf's contemporaries: in particular Frank White on the early years in Manchester and especially in Newton Heath which he shared with Alf; the political journalist Arthur Butler on Alf's work in Parliament; the late Dr Gordon Piller, father of a thalidomide daughter, on Alf's role in addressing that tragedy; Lt. Col. Ray Holland on Alf's association with the ex-service community and, in particular, with BLESMA; Karen Buck, now the MP for Regent's Park and Kensington North, who helped Alf with research and in campaigning for full implementation of the Chronically Sick and Disabled Persons Act; the late Sir Peter Large on his collaboration with Alf in researching and reporting the extent of discrimination against disabled people and in chairing for him the Committee on Restrictions Against Disabled People; David Watters, Karin Pappenheim, Sue Rocks, John Morris and Chris Hodgson of the Haemophilia Society; Maria Eagle MP, one of Alf's successors as Minister for Disabled People, for an overview of his work with and for disabled people; Colonel Terry English and Brigadier Ian Townsend of the Royal British Legion, among others, for their helpful comments on the campaigns to assist war disabled people, including the long hard battle for recognition that the illnesses of Gulf War veterans are war related.

I am also profoundly grateful to the Ormolu Group and Bob Hodgson, its Chairman and Chief Executive, who, in a spirit of co-operation, have designed and printed this not-for-profit biography free of charge and to Tom Holland and Steve Dewing of

Greenaways for their amazing patience in the face of last-minute amendments.

But the paramount acknowledgement belongs with the person closest to Alf over the last 57 years: his wife Irene. This is no trite tribute, made for what Mancunians call 'the sake of appearances'. Irene does not want recognition, nor does she ever seek public attention, but it would be impossible to overestimate her contribution. Alf knows that anything worthwhile he has ever done has been done with and usually because of Irene. She sees things with clarity and is always on the side of right. People who know Alf best recognise that they are not dealing with an individual, but with a partnership.

And, of course, Alf himself, who has kept me honest and on track.

Derek Kinrade, September 2007

FOREWORD

by Sir Harold Evans

It is 1939. England will be at war very soon. Crowded round the factories in Newton Heath, Manchester, that will make Lancaster bombers and machine guns and tank engines, are the streets where the workers live, thousands in slums without bathrooms, some in decent little council houses with a patch of garden. If we zoom in we see scruffy school kids running wild round the asphalt playground of Brookdale Park School. The trajectory of their lives is already determined. At 14, they will leave school for the factories, the majority in dead end jobs. None of them can expect to go to university. When the war reaches them, they will serve in the ranks as their fathers did so grievously.

I can see Alf Morris in short pants, a new boy who comes to Brookdale from Briscoe Lane Junior School with the reputation of being the cleverest boy in the school. I am there on the playground, a thin boy of eleven wearing a pullover knitted by my mother. I never overlap in classes – thank heavens – but apparently I made an impression on him because my father, a railway man, had saved enough from night work to buy a second hand car, so Alf dubbed me "Posh" Evans. For a working class family to have a car was, in truth, a phenomenal event. None of the families, of course, had phones, or refrigerators, or televisions, and quite a number at school didn't have baths; families thought they were blessed when they could put a meal on the table and didn't have to run to pawn grand-dad's watch when the rent collector was due. It is a relief to learn from this vivid biography that Alf regarded his sister's boy friend, Tom, as posh, too, because he had a suit. Alf's family was so very poor almost everybody else must have seemed posh. However hard his widowed mother tried to dress him well, Alf was identified as one of the poorest kids because he had vouchers for school meals and ate separately with other kids whose parents could not afford school "dinners": an odd name for lunches. Also it was known Alf had come from the worst of the slums in Ancoats.

Alf was clever enough to pass the 11–plus examinations to win a place at North Manchester High School – I guess only about one in ten qualified – but he never got there. His family would have been

x

hard pressed to afford the school uniform but the outbreak of war in 1939 impelled the evacuation of all the Manchester schools. He was decanted to a miserable old couple in Ramsbottom; I went to relatives on a farm in Wales. Both of us were called into the Armed Forces just after war ended. Both of us married very bright working class young women who should have known better: Irene, like Alf, was deprived by family circumstances of the higher education for which she was amply qualified.

In short, we lived parallel lives, but they began to diverge. Alf joined the allied Labour and Co-operative parties at a time when my mother, who had opened a small grocery shop, was battling competition from the local Co-op (successfully!). My family was solid Labour. We applauded Harry Thorneycroft, the Labour MP for the district, as did Alf's family, and we cheered Clement Attlee's election in 1945, but I did not follow Alf (and his brother Charles) into politics. I made the self conscious decision that if I was to have a career as a newspaper reporter I had to be non-partisan and seen to be non-partisan. But there was less difference in our lives at this point than from the lives of all the other kids in the playground. Somehow or other we both got into our heads to go to a university. He graduated from Oxford, I graduated from Durham. Neither of us would have had that benefit without the benevolence of the Butler Education Act of 1944 which awarded grants to "ex-servicemen" and we just about qualified. The parallel lives, though, persisted in the tendency to converge. Some years later, reporting politics for the Manchester Evening News, I found myself covering the election for MP for Wythenshawe, Manchester, and there I encountered candidate Morris, M.A. (Oxon) trying to whittle down a solid Tory majority. Well, as a reporter I had met and interviewed many aspiring candidates of all three parties. None of them was as deceptive as Alf in that his unassuming, humorous manner, his very soft voice, and his personal warmth, altogether belied a determination and a persistence to remedy social injustice equal to any I was to encounter in public life. The perceptive author of this book is surely right to attribute the formation of Alf's character to his nurturing family, his war-wounded father denied a pension and his wise loving mother. "Never forget you are as good as any", she told her nine children, "and better than none."

You didn't have to be told to know that Alf felt he had debts to pay for the chances he had been given – no, seized – after such an unpromising beginning. What was remarkable to me was that the energy was fuelled by empathy, not by bitterness. He was proud of his family and his background. I never heard him make a single vicious remark about an opponent, and I heard plenty from all the party men. But then Alf, while loyal to the party, remained very much his own man, never a party hack. He was not interested in class warfare; he was interested in class welfare.

As I moved from reporting into editing, I found that the MP for Wythenshawe kept forcing those parallel lines to converge again and again. I recall how distressed I was when an illiterate youth called Derek Bentley went to the gallows for a murder he did not commit. It was no surprise that the MP acting as teller for the veteran Sidney Silverman, the leading campaigner against the death penalty, was Alf Morris. As editor of The Northern Echo in the sixties, I became appalled by the government's abandonment of its responsibility for children badly damaged by thalidomide, taken by their mothers in pregnancy on National Health prescriptions. Around the same time Alf sent me a letter about a Manchester boy who had been afflicted. At the Sunday Times, when I became editor, I was determined to win proper compensation for them (and investigate the cause of the disaster). Alf was an instant ally and with the valiant Jack Ashley, the Cambridge graduate who had left his Widnes elementary school at the age of 14, Brookdale Park and Widnes formed a successful triumvirate of press and Parliament.

But these parallels of mine are only part of the story of Alf Morris. He is renowned for his work for disabled people, the less fortunate as he would say, but his civic endeavour has been as varied as it has been continuous. Derek Kinrade has marvellously evoked the origins of Alf's insistent drive. This is a rewarding – and very entertaining – biography and a fascinating social history.

Sir Harold Evans
editor of The Sunday Times (1967–81) and of The Times (1981–2)

©Harold Evans Associates

INTRODUCTION

"Mr Speaker, if we could bequeath one precious gift to posterity, I would choose a society in which there is genuine compassion for long-term sick and disabled people; where understanding is unostentatious and sincere; where needs come before means; where if years cannot be added to their lives, at least life can be added to their years; where the mobility of disabled people is restricted only by the bounds of technical progress and discovery; where they have the fundamental right to participate in industry and society according to ability; where socially preventable distress is unknown; and where no one has cause to be ill at ease because of her or his disability."

From Alf's speech introducing the second reading of his Chronically Sick and Disabled Persons Bill, 5 December 1969

In an unbroken and unfinished parliamentary career of over forty years, Alf Morris has reshaped the social map of Britain and wrought a sea change in attitudes to disabled people in ways that still resonate across the world, making him one of the foremost reformers of our age. And this from the poorest of beginnings, born as he was during the industrial depression of the 1920s into a family impoverished by the war disability of his father and living in one of the most squalid of Manchester's slums.

This memoir of scenes from his life and work is based on weekly tape-recorded interviews at the House of Lords from 2003–06, supplemented by written records and the recollections of his contemporaries. The recording sessions were fitted in around, and often interrupted by, Alf's still exacting schedule. For he is in every sense a working peer. He still travels to Manchester at week-ends as he did for 33 years as the MP for Wythenshawe, still pulled in innumerable directions at Westminster by involvement in widely ranging parliamentary questions and debates, division bells and relentless demands on his time from the many organisations he supports as patron, president, trustee or honorary advisor.

The process of recall has been a fascinating and rewarding one. Things remembered in outline in one session have prompted deeper recall later on, colouring in an absorbing picture of the past. We tried to focus on one or two episodes at a time, but memory cannot easily be constrained within a rigid framework and we jumped about and dipped in and out of Alf's life. My task has been to give these recollections shape and chronology, with Alf as a scrupulous collaborator. I should make clear that unattributed quotations in italics are Alf's own words, and that in all quotations I have sought to regularise language in line with modern usage.

Alf insists that his has been a "fortunate" life. Fortune, he says, smiled on him from his first school in Ancoats and his early employment in a Newton Heath brewery on to his National Service in the Middle East, through to Oxford University and an LLD from Manchester, and at almost every turn in his parliamentary life. Yet while luck plays a part in all our lives, for better or worse, in my view Alf's conspicuous personal qualities have been the primary source of everything he has achieved: dedication, application, sincerity, a lifelong belief in co-operation, endurance and, above all else, integrity. In his recent book *Downing Street Diary* (Jonathon Cape, 2006), Bernard Donoughue, chief policy advisor to both Harold Wilson and Jim Callaghan, sums up his qualities as a Member of Parliament:

> "Morris is absolutely genuine and devoted to his life passion of helping disabled people. Most MPs are partly cynical, partly phoney, often interested only in self-publicity without any deep principles at all, just loving being MPs and making the necessary noises. Alf is totally genuine."

The same can be said of Alf's life outside politics. It is no accident that all of his personal ties – family, marriage and friendships – have remained rock solid and that he remains in close touch with his boyhood friends from Newton Heath, notably Frank White and Harold Evans.

Alf is now widely and rightly regarded as the champion of disabled people. But it would be a gross error, and a misrepresentation of the parliamentary record, to imply that disability has been the sole focus of his 42 years at Westminster. Within a year of his election to

Parliament he was chosen by Michael Stewart, then the Foreign Secretary, to join Britain's delegation to the General Assembly of the United Nations. Since then, he has been a member of the Council of the Royal College of Veterinary Surgeons, representing the Privy Council (1968–74), chairman of the Co-operative Parliamentary Group (1970–71 and 1983–85) and President of the Co-operative Congress, the highest elective office in the British Co-operative Movement (1995); adviser to the Police Federation (1971–74); founder chair of the ANZAC Group (1972–97, president 1997); chair of the Managing Trustees of the Parliamentary Contributory Pension Scheme and of the House of Commons Members' Fund (1983–97); chair of the Parliamentary and Scientific Committee (1988–1992); honorary adviser to The Royal British Legion (from 1989); Honorary Associate of the British Veterinary Association (1991–); Member of the House of Commons Privileges Committee (1992–97); Honorary Fellow of the Association of Building Engineers (2000–) and, most recently (and uniquely for a non-American), a co-opted member of a US Congressional Committee of Inquiry. From 1968 to 1997, excluding his years as a Government Minister, he enjoyed a particularly long commitment in membership of the General Advisory Council of the BBC representing, with Jack Ashley, his side of Parliament. He was made a Privy Counsellor in 1979, received the Queen's Service Order of New Zealand (QSO) in 1989, the Order of Australia (AO) in 1991 and a life peerage in 1997. He is the only Briton outside the Royal Household ever to have been awarded both the QSO and AO.

The currents that have guided Alf through his long career at Westminster have also taken him into the deepest waters of parliamentary procedure, arming him with an expertise that is surprisingly rare among MPs and which has frequently been deployed to the considerable advantage of the causes he works to advance. His interests and legislative achievements in the Chambers of both Houses have ranged far and wide, beginning with agriculture, through principled opposition to Britain's accession to the Treaty of Rome – securing protection of access to Britain of Commonwealth cane sugar and of New Zealand's dairy exports, among other achievements – to the repatriation to Australia of its 'birth certificate': the Constitution of Australia Act 1900.

Many of the events of his political life have been without precedent. He is believed to be the first Oxford undergraduate to stand for Parliament. While the likes of Robin Day, Jeremy Thorpe, and Shirley Williams were involved in university student debating and spoken of there as possible future parliamentary candidates, Alf had already *stood* for Parliament. In 1970, he was the first Member of the House of Commons, or indeed any other legislature, to enact wide-ranging legislation to address the needs of disabled people, and within that legislation the first to provide for the special educational needs of children with autism, dyslexia or those at once blind and deaf, as well as access to the built environment for physically disabled people. On the same day he successfully took the second reading of the Food and Drugs (Milk) Act through the House of Commons – the first and still the only Member to secure, on the same day, second readings for two private member's bills, both of which became law. He followed this up in 1971 by again breaking new ground for a back bench MP when he introduced a private member's bill to relax the prohibition on external associations until then imposed upon Britain's police.

In the same year, he was the first recipient of the prestigious Field Marshal Lord Harding Award for distinguished service to disabled people and received the Louis Braille Memorial Award for outstanding service to blind people in the following year. In 1974, he became the world's first Minister for Disabled People. In this capacity, alongside responsibilities as Minister for War Pensions, he led the way in legislating for an income as of right for disabled people, revolutionising their opportunities for travel, and appointing in 1979 a Government committee of inquiry 'CORAD' into restrictions against disabled people. This began the process that led to them gaining legal protection against discrimination and securing basic civil rights. In the years leading up to 1980 and 2000 he chaired the World Council appointed to draft the first international charters for disabled people, both recognised by the UN as providing a consensus on global priorities. And in the millennium year he was awarded both Britain's People of the Year Award for lifetime achievement and Rehabilitation International's Henry H Kessler Prize "for inspired leadership and historic achievements for disabled people around the world".

More recently, when repeatedly refused a public inquiry into the medically unexplained illnesses of thousands of veterans of the 1990–91 Gulf War, he transformed the balance of power between executive government and the citizen by the groundbreaking masterstroke of setting up one on his own initiative.

Both as an MP and as a working peer, Alf's life has necessarily been split between Manchester and London. But he remains essentially a Mancunian, maintaining a home there and upholding many precious connections. He became an Honorary Doctor of Law of the University of Manchester in 1998 and an Honorary Fellow of Manchester Metropolitan University in 1998.

His gentle kindness is legendary. Yet when faced, as he often has been, with policies that negate social justice, the determination of his opposition has been extraordinary, even fiercely combative, in keeping always with an immutable political philosophy. In 1996, he greeted the launch of *South Manchester News* with the Oriental quotation "Let every flower bloom". The more outlets for public opinion to express itself, he wrote, the healthier our democracy. And he reminded its readers of the words of Aneurin Bevan that "any society must be judged by how it treats those most in need". Alf's test of progress and political success is not whether the United Kingdom is the enterprise capital of Europe, but how our most vulnerable people are faring: the defining test, he dryly remarks, by which Labour could once be distinguished from the Conservative Party.

His abiding concern has been the cause of full citizenship for disabled people, driven partly by pressure from those who have espoused him as their champion but also by a strong personal conviction born of childhood experience. This account of his life and work, therefore, has two objectives: one purely biographical (for his is a rich, varied and remarkable story); the other to record something of the historical, though still incomplete, emancipation of disabled people throughout the world that he has led. The story of Alf has inevitably become the story of the disabled people he has served and it will surely be the touchstone by which he is remembered. Along every step of the way he has remained unshakeably true to his democratic socialist and co-operative principles.

It has not been easy. Spending on the needs of disabled people has inevitably risen dramatically as a direct result of his initiatives and not everyone – least of all every Minister and department of state – has shared his zeal for expensive social change. Frequently in Whitehall, Ministers and officials with other priorities have solemnly warned that his proposals "would burst the floodgates". Which is why, when he was once asked to describe what his principal role at Westminster had been, he responded "that of a serial floodgate saboteur". Lord Filkin, in a Ministerial speech on 23 September 2003, summed up Alf's lifetime achievement when he referred to him as one of the most doughty campaigners in society, whether legislating as a Minister or as a back-bencher:

> "He has been amazing. Frequently, Government Ministers and civil servants have said, 'don't be silly, it's not possible, it can never happen, it can't be done'. But the only thing that seems to be in dispute is how long it takes before Alf gets his way. Sometimes, it's very short, sometimes a bit longer, but it always happens."

This biography unashamedly proclaims itself as a tribute to its subject. The fact is that in acres of research and countless interviews I have yet to find anyone, even among his political opponents, who has a bad word to say about Alf Morris.

Derek Kinrade, September 2007

Chapter 1

ANCOATS

1928–1935 (with a look back to earlier times)

The childhood shows the man, as morning shows the day.

John Milton: Paradise Regained

– History – Home – Fond memories – Designated for slum clearance

History

Ancoats, where Alf Morris lived for the first seven years of his life, is a district of Manchester lying within a half a mile or so of the city centre and now being developed as a 'heritage site' – unrecognisably transformed by the building of executive flats and lauded as the 'first industrial suburb in the world'. This was the historic starting place of Britain's industrial revolution; but for those who then lived and worked there Ancoats had no such mystique. They were among the first to suffer the social evils, the savage exploitation and the human misery that went with the new order.

During the second half of the eighteenth century, on the bank of a river, a cotton-spinning factory was built there. Within viewing distance at that time was the manor house that was home to the Mosley family. Other factories quickly followed and around them a large assemblage of dwellings was thrown up to house their workers. These set the pattern for most of the industrial, working class ghettoes that were later to be seen throughout Britain – a rigid grid of narrow, cobbled streets across which cheaply built terraces of homes looked directly into one another's tiny front windows.

To these insanitary hovels swarmed hundreds of hungry families, often with relief and renewed hope at the prospect of finding work: people dispossessed of tied cottages during the agricultural upheavals and, later, Irish immigrants escaping from their torments at home. With them came sad refugees from villages throughout Lancashire, remnants of the old cottage industry of handloom

1

weavers, whose way of life had been destroyed by the arrival of the huge, dark, satanic cotton mills in which they now had no option but to toil to survive.

At the hands of speculative builders, who often named their streets after members of their own families or sometimes after famous politicians, Ancoats rapidly developed. And as more and more potential workers came there, pressure on jobs became intense, especially so since, until the 1830s, whole families were available for hire. Children as young as six or seven worked alongside their parents, gathering waste from under the spinning machines or stacking bobbins. With this surfeit of labour, wages were abysmally low and savage exploitation grew. The cotton industry was helping to make Britain rich and powerful, while Ancoats and places like it were degenerating into slums, infamous for their squalor and deprivation. In his study, *Conditions of the Working Class in England in 1844*[1], Friedrich Engels, himself born into a mill-owning family with a cotton mill in Ancoats, described at first hand the appalling realities of life there in the mid-19th century. He not only observed but closely engaged with the social misery of its working and workless people, and was particularly well placed to comment on the squalid, insanitary conditions in which they lived. A recurring theme for Engels was the contrast between the greed of mill owners and the conditions in which their employees, paid as little as possible, lived and all too often died young. It was even said that the area was sited so that in the prevailing wind its fetid smell blew away from better-off neighbourhoods! Four years later, Elisabeth Gaskell set her classic *Mary Barton*[2] in Ancoats, aptly calling one of its chapters 'Poverty and Death' and movingly describing the extremities of human destitution to be seen there.

Over time, public conscience was aroused and social provision slowly improved the quality of life in Ancoats. A local hospital was built, together with a bathhouse and washhouse. Other desperately needed amenities followed. Eventually, gas was installed, and a primary school and child nursery appeared. Child welfare services

---

[1] First published (in German) in 1844. It did not appear in England until 1892. A modern edition is available in Penguin Classics.
[2] First published in 1848. A modern edition is available in Penguin Classics.

were established. Visiting nurses weighed babies, examined children for skin diseases and scuffed through their hair in search of lice.

Nevertheless, when Alf Morris was born there in 1928, Ancoats was still blighted by abject poverty. The General Strike of 1926 had signalled widespread industrial malaise throughout Britain. Wage cuts, social decay, strikes and industrial chaos had created a situation that no single political party seemed to have either the ability or the authority to control. The economic vitality of the whole nation was on a downward road to the Great Depression with unemployment on a sharply upward curve. By 1931 the numbers out of work had rocketed to over three million. Lancashire's world supremacy in the manufacture of cotton textiles was over. By now the industrial landscape of Ancoats was bleak and there was nothing quaint or endearing about it. Most of the old housing remained and had become a mouldering mess aching for demolition. The majority of the two-up, two-down dwellings were in gross disrepair. Lavatories were still outside across the yard, not even one per family but one per terrace. Walls were damp and roofs leaked.

Most of the adult population of Ancoats was out of work, doing their best to survive on the meagre hand-outs they received after queuing for hours at the dole office. Always over the area dense clouds of smoke hovered, dripping showers of soot and filtering sunlight down to a pale watercolour wash. Tuberculosis, bronchitis, and other diseases brought on by social deprivation and industrial pollution were endemic.

But children born into such conditions, unaware of what might exist elsewhere, had no option other than to accept life as they found it. For them, the sight of unemployed men aimlessly hanging about at street corners, or an invasion of black beetles into the kitchen, mothers sitting on their doorsteps breast feeding the latest additions to already large families, overcrowding and sickness, could only be the natural elements of their world. Kids being kids the world over, they fit into their local communities as best they can, and children in Ancoats were as busy and boisterous as anywhere else. Sometimes under-nourished and thin as Lowry's stick-children, ragged and sooty-faced, sometimes barefoot, they darted here and there over the dusty cobbles, past the local pawn shop and the Pineapple Arms and hooted in their games down echoing back entries.

A similar resilience pervaded the district as a whole. The people of Ancoats, like people in other such districts, had welded themselves into a close-knit and caring community. A family newly arriving in the district would find a cup of sugar and a bottle of milk waiting for them on their doorstep, put there by their neighbours as a gesture of welcome. From morning till night, through the thin walls that separated their houses, and indeed through their parlour windows, they could hear and see one another's lives being lived. They could follow conversations, listen to sudden flare ups and quiet reconciliations, hear babies being born, see the doctor arriving at a neighbour's house, and know when there was no money for food in the house across the street.

This was a shared intimacy that ensured family mingling with family. People helped each other through bad times in all kinds of ways and there was a powerful cohesion, bringing with it the emotional and social reassurance that only crowded living conditions can engender, and which vanished from the world when slum clearances and misguided municipal planning transplanted large numbers of families into the social isolation of high rise blocks of flats.

There was also in Ancoats in the 1920s and 30s a stoical determination to preserve as much human dignity (in local parlance 'respectability') as possible. Cleanliness was thus of high importance, in most homes coming not next to but before Godliness. The communal bathing and washing facilities were always busy, and hanging behind the back door was a galvanized tin tub into which the kids were dipped, usually on Friday evenings. Windows were kept clean and donkey-stoned doorsteps and windowsills glowed white or cream from one end of a row to the other. Poverty does not necessarily destroy personal pride. If a pawnbroker failed to return redeemed clothing in the same condition as he had received it, he confronted both outrage and threats to "bring in the law", not that pawnshop patrons were ever likely to be able to do so.

4

Suffusing everything was that comradely humour that underpins human endurance through even the most persistent tribulations. Lancashire people seemed particularly blessed with it. Walking the maze of streets that was Ancoats, amidst the ever-present noise and bustle, notwithstanding all the deprivation and anxiety, you would more often than not hear the sound of laughter.

Home

George Morris and his family lived at 34 Grace Street. Like Frank Owen in Robert Tressell's 'The Ragged Trousered Philanthropists', Alf's father George had been a sign writer and in most respects had shared a similar fate. Tressell depicted workmen as philanthropists because, working intermittently for a pittance, they consented to donating the fruits of their labour to the profit of their employers and the greater comfort and convenience of their affluent clients. George, however, was not only a victim of economic exploitation: he had sacrificed his health in the service of his country in a 'Great' War, in which human lives were the currency of supremacy. When the bloodshed was finally over, David Lloyd George famously identified the post-war task as one of making Britain "a fit country for heroes to live in". Nearly a decade later, Ancoats was short on fitness for anyone to live in and George Morris did not feel like a hero. His lungs irrevocably damaged, one of his legs shattered and blind in one eye, he became unemployable when Alf was only two years old. Existing on a meagre war pension and small contributions that his older children could make if and when they were in work, he and his family were among the poorest of Manchester's poor.

When George's sixth son, Alfred, was born on 23 March 1928, child mortality was still appallingly high. Alf now considers himself lucky to have survived. Many of the children he lived among died from diphtheria, consumption and scarlet fever, while numerous others were disabled by rickets and other deficiency diseases. Nevertheless, large families were not at all unusual. There in 34 Grace Street (long since demolished), Jessie Morris mothered nine children, by no means a local record. Children necessarily slept several to a bed, an arrangement which, however undesirable and unhealthy, did tend to knit a family together, if only because they shared the same discomforts. When one turned over, all in the bed did. If one caught a cold, all began to sneeze. Over dressing of a morning there could be confusion as to whose clothes each of them was putting on, and during the night much nudging and protest took place should one or other resort to loud snoring. Alf went on sharing a bed with his brother Charles right up to their being called-up for the army.

With Alf's arrival there were now seven mouths to feed. It would have been nine, but for the loss, shortly after birth, of the twin sister of Alf's elder brother Charles, and the fact that his brother Fred was a long-stay patient in Pendlebury Hospital for Children until 1934, when he was discharged and met Alf for the first time. In descending order, there were three girls, Ivy, Winifred and Vera, and six boys, George, Fred, John, William, Charles (the father of Estelle Morris, now Baroness Morris of Yardley) and Alf. As with most large families, the older ones, especially Ivy, shared in the care of the younger. But, of course, the bigger the family the greater the pressure both on income and on space. It was, in Alf's own words, "very tight". Meals were usually eaten standing up. Few could afford to buy tables large enough to accommodate everyone in the family (old, newspaper-covered tea chests were more common) and in any case conventional tables could barely be fitted into those crumbling hovels. In the absence of a bathroom, the children had to be washed in a tin bath in front of the fire, when coal could be afforded. More often than not it was a case of 'cat licks' and tide marks. One of Alf's earliest memories (along with the tin bath) is that of having to learn when and where to move a bucket or a basin to catch rain leaking through the roof, sometimes on to the bed on which he slept with some of his brothers. And just as it was tricky to keep dry, so food was hard to come by, reduced as they often were to bread and dripping or 'sugar butties'. When they could afford jam, poor families bought it by the two-penny cup, rather than the jar.

Alf thus spent the most formative years of his life in a landscape coloured by all shades of struggling humanity, their problems and emotions in full public view. It is hardly surprising that such experience can inspire and shape talented and sensitive people. In Alf's case there was an extra dimension. His father's plight made him acutely conscious of the disastrous effects that physical disability can bring upon a family, an awareness that was to prove one of the mainsprings of his political life.

Fond memories

Yet Alf emerged, not soured by the deprivation of his early years but with enduring pride in his family and an inner well of spontaneous humour. Many of his memories of Ancoats are indelibly happy. The boundaries of his world, up to the age of seven, were confined to the area around the Pineapple Arms in Palmerston Street, named after the longest-serving Foreign Secretary in our history, the main thoroughfare with its dozens of corner shops, beer houses, pawnbrokers and busy pavements, its energetically gossiping women in their head-shawls and its artfully scavenging dogs. The Pineapple was a navigational landmark from which all directions were given and taken: a kind of pole star for local people, often virtually empty and forlorn apart from one or two dedicated regulars, but on dole days and Saturday nights, with their wage packets, reverberating to the sound of exuberant singing and music from a long-suffering upright piano. As elsewhere, drunkenness in Ancoats, often at the expense of the family, was too often the only escape for poor workmen.

The local junior school, in Every Street, one of the first to be built for the 'working classes' under the Education Act 1870, had the distinction of having its playground on the roof. In more than a century many generations of children passed through its classrooms. Many of them, conditioned to the complacent fatalism, submissiveness and low expectations their background could easily induce, were destined to spend their lives in and out of low-paid, unskilled work in factories. But occasionally some pupils manifested a determined aspiration and a vigorous drive towards something better. Out of Ancoats and Every Street school came people successful in all walks of life from industry and the arts to medicine and politics. Alf, who was there from 1933 to 1935, particularly remembers the view from its playground: that wide view of the sky otherwise seen merely as strips of blue or grey between the eaves of the houses. He also recalls that it was warmer in school than at home and that he won, when he was five, a 'golden penny' for reading a poem out loud: a prize that he took home with pride. And not least the daily half-pint of milk that every child received as, in his case, an important supplement to a meagre diet.

Much charitable work was done by the local churches and the Salvation Army, whose band paraded the streets on Sunday afternoons, marching past the houses and rattling windowpanes with its forthright music. Sunday schools, intended to educate youngsters in their faith, tempted potential pupils by awarding a star for every attendance. A given number of stars would entitle the child to a place at that church's Christmas party, and children soon realised that by astute manoeuvring they could claim a seat at several. Alf recalls that in the weeks before mid-December, attendance at Sunday school was on a multi-faith plan. Some children soon realised that by moving between Sunday schools – with a facility that would have left the Vicar of Bray lost in admiration – they could go to more than one party! So their allegiance subtly shifted from Anglican to Free Church or Salvation Army. Of course, and much to their credit, the churches knew exactly what was going on. Christians could turn not only the other cheek but an ecumenical blind eye. Nor did beneficence stop there. It was not unknown for children winning entry to these parties to smuggle out goodies to their younger siblings outside. One of Alf's most treasured memories is standing outside Star Hall in Great Ancoats Street and being passed samples of the "absolutely marvellous" delicacies by his brother Bill!

He remembers, too, the Whit Walks and the problems they could inflict. These spectacular parades, designed as a witness of faith and organised by Sunday schools, were and remain a cherished tradition of churches in Manchester – and indeed in several other northern towns. Procession after procession of children, each following the banner of its church, marching in step to the music of a brass band, wound their way along the streets of the city centre: Protestants on Whit Monday and Catholics on Whit Friday. It all went on for so long and monopolised the streets so completely that the city was virtually taken over on both days. It was then the only place in the country to enjoy the privilege of having two 'bank holidays' at

Whitsun. To have one's children seen in these parades was important to the pride of any churchgoing family, and pride also demanded that new clothes must be worn. Over the years this crucial requirement of new clothes for Whit established itself throughout the area. Whether a child paraded or not, whether he or she belonged to a church or never saw the inside of one, they would be a pariah if, at Whitsuntide, they did not appear resplendent in something new – or at least in something that had never been seen on them before.

All this gave rise to much bustle and desperate resourcefulness. There were savings clubs a mother could join, providing she could save at all. But there weren't many such mothers about. More often, they had no option but to go into debt and borrow money either from a better off neighbour or from local moneylenders who were then even more predatory than their 'loan shark' counterparts of today. Short of that – and this was how Alf's mother and other mothers usually coped with the problem – there was the pawnshop. In went ornaments, odd bits of furniture and anything that could raise a shilling or two. Sometimes, she pawned enough of the family's existing clothes to raise the necessary funds and then walked along the road to buy new. Older brothers and sisters, and Jessie herself, might thus be short of a few garments to wear, but at least Whit fell at a time of year when the weather was fairly kind, and new clothes could always be pawned later. Outgrown clothes were passed down, mended and renovated until with a bit of pressing they could, at a pinch, pass muster.

Another tradition, one associated with New Year's Day, was that some local shops paid out threepenny bits to the children of their regular customers until noon. From shop opening times onwards, the streets would be a blur of children buzzing about like eager flies. Alf still frowns with disappointment to recollect the dread words from the shopkeeper, "You're too late, I've already given out what I had".

Early one Sunday afternoon Alf was playing in Cocky Wynn's entry, near his home in Grace Street. This had a sharp incline, ideal for the hair-flying sport of 'wheeled sledging' – roaring down the hill on the

9

converted chassis of an old pram. A nail projected from a wheel over which Alf's right leg hung. Whizzing round it tore a great gash in his calf. He bears the scars to this day, but also retains the vivid memory of being rushed to the casualty ward of Ancoats Hospital, wondering what might be going to happen to him. Someone with admirably prescient taste in fine art had gifted the hospital, to hang on one of its walls, one of L. S. Lowry's early paintings, long before the artist became universally known. It was of that same casualty department into which Alf was now taken, with his bleeding leg. Patients sat on rows of benches outside the open door of what would now be called the accident and emergency treatment room, moving up slowly one by one as they were treated. *"It was not a pretty sight; you could see and hear not only what was happening in the treatment room, but in other wards where longer stay patients lay dying"*. Alf was stitched up, borne home to Grace Street and – it being Sunday afternoon when most Ancoats families had home-made apple pie – given four pieces from sympathetic neighbours.

Sickness in Ancoats was ministered to by a remarkably caring, beloved and extremely busy doctor whose name must surely have reflected his disposition: Dr Faith. Alf's mother and others certainly had boundless faith in him, just as they held in admiration Hope hospital to which his patients were referred, and were grateful for the charity he often showed towards the poorest of them. "The doctor's man," responsible for garnering his client's income, knocked at patients' doors and collected small amounts weekly, but if it was clear that the family could not afford his fee, Dr Faith would waive payment and act purely on the basis of medical need.

Manchester was among the most heavily polluted and congested cities in Britain, and one of Dr Faith's great remedies to combat the environmental hazards was the wearing of a camphor block, contained in a muslin bag, tied round the neck with a piece of string or ribbon and worn under dress or shirt, all winter long, so that the menthol fumes could work their wonders. The results were probably at best patchy, but Dr Faith's advocacy was total. Some of his other remedies might seem equally quaint today, but this does not lessen Alf's admiration of his humanity and willingness to go to any lengths in the interests of his patients. *"The whole community respected him, and relied on him, personifying as he did caring at its most humane. I still think of him now with affection."*

Designated for slum clearance

In 1935, Ancoats was designated a slum clearance area, a privilege reserved for only the worst of the city's slum areas. By this time – at last – some signs of economic improvement were appearing – most notably in the provision of municipal housing. In the first years of the thirties, Manchester City Council began to build estates of rented houses in areas outside the inner city.

But there were restrictions as to who could apply for a tenancy. First priority went to the families of ex-servicemen, for which Alf's family qualified. But even an ex-serviceman had to show that he was employed and capable of paying the rent, and it was this restriction that ruled out the Morris family. Alf's most poignant memory of Ancoats was the wintry afternoon when all this was explained to his mother. She had gone, taking Alf with her, to the Round House, a building used for communal activities near to the junction of Every Street and Great Ancoats Street, there to see someone in authority – perhaps a local councillor – about what would happen when, fairly soon now, Grace Street would be demolished. Holding Alf's hand and crying inconsolably as they walked back home, she said, "there's no future for us now" and that "they" would put him in a home. Alf's father was now seriously and terminally ill and certainly would never work again, making any chance of re-housing by the council hopeless and family break-up inevitable. This had seemed of no concern to the man she had gone to see. Jessie, though she did not say so, knew that she faced life in a workhouse. Alf found it very hard to understand what 'being put in a home' meant. He accepted from his mother's grief that it must be too awful for him to be told.

Yet there was still hope. Their saviour was Canon Shimwell, of All Souls Church in Ancoats, who showed that Christianity could have a practical face. Whereas the municipal authority worked along strictly bureaucratic lines, Shimwell reached out to people who could not be relied upon to pay the rent: people from Moss Side, from Hulme and especially from Ancoats. He raised funds to launch a housing project in Newton Heath to sit alongside the newly-built

municipal housing indistinguishable from it and of equal standard but reserved for people of good character with large families and too poor to qualify for a 'corporation' property. The Morrises were among the first to qualify and in 1935 they left Grace Street for ever.

An Ancoats lad, circa. 1933: Alf aged 5 (this is the only photograph that Alf has from his Ancoats days).

c.1930: Varley Street, Miles Platting. The Labour Party's meeting rooms, where Alf and Irene's wedding reception was held, were above the Co-op butchers in the centre of the picture.

Chapter 2

NEWTON HEATH

1935–1945

To-morrow to fresh woods and pastures new

John Milton, Lycidas

– A new beginning – Death of Alf's father and its consequences – Family
– A new school – Threats to health – War clouds – A job opportunity
– Friends – Into politics

A new beginning

The transition to Newton Heath was nothing short of a metamorphosis. In place of a slum dwelling the Morris family enjoyed a newly-built house. Instead of living in an industrial wasteland, they were now not so much in a new district but a new world. In Ancoats, Alf had never been further than Hilkirk Street, less than half a mile from his home in Grace Street. He had never seen grass grow or flowers, except through cracks in pavements and at harvest festivals or, but not always, at funerals. Newton Heath had both. Their new home was at 14 Halliday Road, an airy cul-de-sac of well-built houses, each with three bedrooms, a bathroom, hot and cold water, gas and electricity. No damp, no leaks, no vermin – nirvana. The rent was 11s 3d per week, compared with 10s 0d for 34 Grace Street. For the extra 1s 3d they not only had a weatherproof home and modern conveniences, but even a small garden at front and back. Before the summer was out, flowers bloomed and vegetables were grown and dug up.

Most of the new residents found the contrast between these houses and their former homes in Ancoats and other slum areas deeply affecting. Jessie Morris told a neighbour that as she crossed the threshold of number 14, passed into its bright and comparatively spacious living room, and felt new floorboards under her feet – instead of cold flag-stones – she sank down on the staircase and gave thanks. Beyond the houses at the inner end of Halliday Road

13

there was a large recreation ground, well used by local children who had never before enjoyed such an amenity. It was surfaced with crushed brick and known to all as the 'red rec'. At its other end, Halliday Road opened on to Briscoe Lane, the neighbourhood's main thoroughfare.

Britain was at last beginning to emerge from a sequence of economic depressions that for a decade had played havoc with international trade, undermined currencies and put millions out of work. By the time of the Morris family's arrival in Newton Heath conditions had at last begun to improve. Textile, engineering and chemical factories in Manchester were again beginning to take employees on. Across Briscoe Lane from Halliday Road lay Newton Heath council estate, again only recently built, whose carefully laid out streets, all named from a map of the home counties – Lewisham and Bayswater Avenues, Ascot and Crayford Roads – were interspersed with green spaces newly planted with trees. Five years before, the area had been farmland, pasturage. Indeed, the farmstead itself, red brick, with barn and old cow-shed, all surrounded by a high fence, still stood like a forlorn relic in the middle of the estate. The farmer, with his dog at his heels and his staff in his hand, looking a little lost, still strolled daily into places, now occupied by houses and their gardens built on the fields where he had once rounded up his cattle for milking.

These were the council houses reserved largely for ex-servicemen from the First World War who were in work – and both qualifications could easily be noted. A number of the men on Newton Heath estate had limbs missing or disabilities of some other kind, or perpetual coughs from gassing, and the children of the estate, as they played their games and went chattering to school, were generally better dressed and fed than those of their workless neighbours.

For those able to work there were several employers in the area. To the south, the district was bordered by two large factories belonging respectively to A. V. Roe & Co, which designed and built the Lancaster bomber – to be among the most famous and successful aircraft of the Second World War – and the engineering firm Mather & Platt Ltd., known locally as 'Mathers'. The majority of workers there were fitters or turners, draughtsmen or mechanics – skilled and comparatively well-paid men. The firm was the patent holder of the overhead sprinkler system of fire protection that was exported with great success. Its cast iron plaque declaring 'Sprinkler Stop Valve Inside. Mather & Platt Ltd., Manchester' was to be seen fixed to the walls of buildings from Sydney and Hong Kong to New York and Cape Town. It also produced finely engineered parts of marine engines that were to be highly important in the Second World War. Large numbers of men marched along Briscoe Lane every morning to earn their living at one or other of these factories, and elsewhere in Newton Heath, as conditions got better, work was available on the railways, in food processing and a number of small businesses.

Usually, men were the only breadwinners. Married women with children rarely went out to work and the earnings of the men in the family were generally the only source of household income. A typical wage for the times in Manchester was around two pounds a week, barely enough for luxuries, but enough to keep afloat. Bank accounts and credit cards were unknown. Houses were furnished on hire purchase at monstrous interest rates, but for everything else people paid as they went. Most shopped for food at the local Co-operative store, and the yearly 'divi' on their purchases helped with the savings that might take them on holiday to Blackpool or North Wales. If a car was to be seen parked outside a house it almost certainly meant that the doctor had called, or perhaps a better-off relative had decided to pay a visit.

It was a time when quiet, almost complacent, pride and respectability distinguished those working class people who enjoyed the dignity of employment, visible in Newton Heath in its well-tended gardens and a common concern to maintain standards. Divorce was scandalous. Children were disciplined. Scruffiness let the side down.

Along Halliday Road, early alarm clocks could be heard ringing out, people could be seen setting off for work, and neighbours who had spent years on the edge of destitution could now invite friends to listen to their new wireless set, admire a new bit of carpet or sit in a new easy chair.

Death of Alf's father and its consequences

But this brave new world was far from universal. There were still over two million people of working age on the dole, and Alf's father was one of them. So ill as to be almost immobile and hardly able to breathe, he died on 11 November 1935 at the age of 44, a few months after the move to Newton Heath, as one of Manchester's "tubercular poor". There was a strange irony in the date, sixteen years to the day from the end of the savage and mindless war that had so damaged him. Alf's memory is of him sitting immovable in a chair in front of the fire unable, vitally important to him as it was, to bear the weight of the blanket around his shoulders, in Alf's words, "striving to keep warm, while waiting to die". Still only seven years old, Alf had already learned the hard way that when one member of the family is disabled, the whole family can be involved in the problems of disability; in families like his disability was synonymous with poverty. And as he grew up he saw that countless other families lived in circumstances similar to his own. He discovered that the quickest way to find a deprived child was to find a disabled father. Even if a disabled father could find employment, it would usually be in menial, low-paid work. If unemployed, he and his family would in most cases be living at or near subsistence level. State benefits to meet the extra costs of disability did not exist and had never even been contemplated.

Among the most distressing realities of life for working class families in Manchester's poorest areas was the incidence, not just of infant mortality, but of mortality generally. The whole environment was hostile to healthy living, and the threat of serious illness was ever present. Stuck on the margins of society they were always conscious of the dangers surrounding them. The harshness of the Poor Law persisted well into the twentieth century, and the fear of committal to the rigours and degradation of the workhouse remained a constant worry for those without income. Alf has never been able to forget his mother's dread of what might happen to her family after the death of his father. The ultimate humiliation was not to be able to escape a pauper's grave for one of the family. Although there was scant money for insurance policies, they were seen as a necessity. One of the questions asked by neighbours, as soon as it was decent to do so, was "how much did you have on him?" The answer would usually be a relatively small sum of money, only rarely more than sixpence a week. "Well," it would be said, "you won't be able to afford much of a funeral then". Today, very few people can understand the depth of anguish felt by people unable to afford a 'decent' funeral, or the lengths they went to in order to insure members of the family: perhaps a penny a week on a child, that would be increased as soon as possible as he or she grew older. Alf's mother had been able to afford only three pence a week, not really enough for her to be able to pay the expenses for her husband's funeral. The response of a public official at the hospital where he died – Manchester's Withington Hospital – was to suggest that she could economise by having him buried 'direct' from the hospital. Instead of her arranging the funeral from home with a private undertaker, he could be taken from the hospital to nearby Southern Cemetery. "What do you want to take him home for?" she was asked. Jessie found this insensitivity deeply wounding: something that for the rest of her life she would recount with a mixture of anguish and anger. To make matters worse, the War Office, as it then was, ruled that the cause of his death – which was put down to "heart failure" – was not war-related and thus, although her husband had been a war pensioner, Alf's mother did not qualify for a war widow's pension, even although in his final weeks, in the words of the sister on his hospital ward, he had to "fight for his breath", due to his lungs having been cut to pieces by gassing.

It was this injustice that would eventually bring Alf into the Labour Party. His mother, left with eight children and the unjust denial of a war widow's pension still rankling, wrote a despairing letter to her local MP, Harry Thorneycroft, who lived only about a mile away. It was, Alf supposes, a "rough and ready looking letter", of the kind that later, when he became a Member of Parliament, he knew was probably worthy of special attention, written with difficulty by someone who could barely afford the postage and who would write only in *extremis*.[1] Harry Thorneycroft evidently also thought along

---

[1] A view reinforced by Herbert Morrison, who advised Alf to give very careful attention to what people say when they write to their Members of Parliament and give their opinions in scruffy and semi-literate letters. It will not have been easy for them to have afforded the stamp and the stationery, he said, and they mean a lot.

these lines, because he promptly came round to see Mrs Morris. He had served as a councillor in that part of Manchester for many years, understood the problems that poor people faced and was well aware that Halliday Road abounded with them. He said that he would take the matter up, and was true to his word. He pegged away for three years, keeping in regular touch, until the day arrived in 1938 when he came round to tell Jessie: "We've won. You're now a war widow and there is quite a bit due to you in back pay".[2] Such was her abiding gratitude to her advocate, that there and then she turned to Alf, now nearly ten, and told him, "you'll be taking Mr Thorneycroft's leaflets when you're old enough". As he now reflects, he did not volunteer to join the Labour Party: he was volunteered!

The death of Alf's father, although a bitter blow, brought the Morris family even more closely together: close-knit in adversity. Nor were they alone or without friends. Although their surroundings were new, several of the families around them were old friends. They too were refugees from Ancoats, re-housed under Canon Shimwell's scheme and bound by ties of extreme poverty. They shared a common disadvantage, a unity of indigent equality. Achievement was not something to be vaunted over others, but a matter of universal rejoicing. Some of Alf's friends, like Arthur and Billy Gibbons, Charlie Shufflebottom, Frank White and Cliff Wright were among those who would go on to better things from the worst of beginnings.

Significantly, in all this and throughout his childhood, Alf was not burdened by any keen sense of underprivilege. 'Woe is me' never came into it. But what he did find very difficult to accept was being treated differently from others, of suffering, as we would now say, hurtful discrimination. While some families were able to pay for what they bought in the shops, when his mother was widowed his family had to rely on food tickets given by way of public assistance. Those using food tickets would be made to stand to one side, while paying customers were served. This even to his young mind was

---

[2] In 1974, as Minister for War Pensions, Alf Morris was able to introduce legislation to amend the War Pensions Act 1921 and the Pensions Appeal Tribunals Act 1943, both to speed and simplify pensions procedures for disabled ex-service personnel. Crucially, he amended the War Pensions Regulations to provide that any person who died from a cardio-thoracic illness, having served in a theatre of war where gas was used as a weapon of war, would be judged to have died from a war-related illness.

very wrong, since food tickets were worth just as much as coins when cashed by shopkeepers. Alf came to realise that the rationale for this practice was a distinction, in the perception of traders steeped in outdated values, between industrious taxpayers and those whom they saw as the undeserving poor. It simply made him feel treated like a wrongdoer, and rankled.

Alf would sometimes go to the local public washhouse after school with his mother and, when he was old enough, work the mangle. There, too, such were the conditions in which his mother worked, he was conscious of what he would later call unmerited suffering, and this even in a neighbourhood where the generality of people were looked down upon: *"My mother was quite as good as, if not better than, those who humiliated her, but even as a child I knew that such was the hand she had been dealt she could never win."*

Alf felt a similar apartheid throughout most of his school life. He and other pupils who received free school dinners were identified in the classroom and in the school canteen. They would eat separately from their classmates who paid for their dinners: *"I took examinations with everyone else and I was top of the class, but as far as meals were concerned I was bottom of the school. Had I known then about Oliver Twist, I would have thought him comparatively lucky, because at least he dined in a one-class environment!"*

There were around 200 children in Halliday Road, all from families rehoused under slum clearance orders. Although the development looked much the same as nearby municipal housing, it had a very different reputation. When, years later, Alf was invited as a Member of Parliament and former pupil to present prizes at his old school at Brookdale Park, the official whose job it had been to check on truants asked Alf where he had lived. Might it have been Culcheth Lane or Droylsden Road? Or on Briscoe Lane, perhaps? "Oh no," said Alf, "I lived in Halliday Road". Taken aback, the former School Board official gasped, "You're not saying *Halliday Road* are you?" He revealed that it had been one of his busiest areas, with scores of "problem children" who played truant. Probably, Alf thinks, most of them were too busy supplementing the family income.

By contrast, Alf's abiding memory of Halliday Road is that of good neighbours. His mother Jessie was one of these. Alf remarks that her achievements as a widow, with so many children and living in poverty, would need to have been witnessed to have been fully understood. She had diabetes, but those around her would never have known; she never complained about it, nor indeed about anything else that troubled her. Her concern was for other people, helping, in any small way she could, anyone in greater need than herself and even some in less need. She was regarded as a good neighbour, and Alf believes that his family was fortunate in this respect, because people who are themselves good neighbours generally find that they are among good neighbours: that one good neighbour deserves another. There is a story about a man climbing from one Pennine village to another who asked a passer-by what the people were like in the next village. The reply was, "What were they like in the last village?" "Quite nice," said the traveller. "Then," he was told, "that's what they will be like in the next village". Alf's mother exemplified this philosophy: as a good neighbour herself, she found her kindness and amity reciprocated.

Family

Alf was devoted to his mother and speaks of her today with great admiration. She worked tirelessly for her many children, preparing their meals, keeping a busy and boisterous household as comfortable as possible, and managing to maintain a family atmosphere marked by both affection and optimism. She was an intelligent woman who understood the world around her. To encourage Alf she would say, "Never forget: you're as good as any". But then, to discourage any hint of arrogance, she would add, "but better than none". She had keen insights into human nature. After their move to Newton Heath, Alf had an uncle and an aunt still living in Ancoats. If they fell out with each other, which they did from time to time, his aunt would arrive on the doorstep of 14 Halliday Road – a very poor doorstep on which to arrive – bringing with her the most essential of her personal effects. She would sit brooding near the fire and make some strong remarks about her husband. On such occasions, Jessie would say, "Whatever any of you do, don't ever agree with her; they'll be all in all to each other by this time next week," which always proved to be true. Jessie had to be something of a diplomat, as well as liaising with the pawnbroker and as manager of insurance policies and spreader out of debts. But it was the diplomacy of a deeper reality in her circumstances: the necessity to protect the assumption that if you were in trouble, you could turn to a relative and expect to be helped. She had her own rules in most things. Alf would often listen to her talking to a neighbour in the kitchen. They would almost always be asking after each other's relatives: "How's your Betty?" his mother would say. Should Betty be sick, there would be a further question: "What are you giving her?" To call in a doctor, who would expect to be paid, was a last resort. Working class people generally shifted for themselves, relying on a range of "tried and trusted" but rudimentary medicaments. "Have you tried a spoonful of vinegar in hot water with lemon juice? Or syrup of figs?" If both had been unsuccessful, she would ask, "A black draft?" This was a purgative, the ingredients of which still remain a mystery to Alf, though to this day he can recall its repulsive taste and smell. Constipation was a particular source of trouble, usually due to poor diet. Jessie, faced with the problem, would say, "The main thing is to get a road through her". If all else failed, her final solution was comfrey, a ditch plant that the Morris family had in abundance in their back garden. Alf's mother had tremendous faith in comfrey. He recalls hearing her say to a neighbour, whose daughter was not responding to other remedies, "Well it will have to be comfrey!" It has since been discovered to Alf's horror that comfrey, far from being therapeutically beneficial, can be quite dangerous.

Ivy, Alf's eldest sister, was Jessie's unflagging helper. Businesslike, even quite managerial, very attractive, energetic and as dedicated to the welfare of her brothers and sisters as Jessie herself, she stayed at her mother's side and was pivotal to the family's welfare. She was a good deal older than Alf and in his mind had something akin to a parental role. She gave up on the idea of marriage in order to keep the family together. Alf remembers a 'young man' who unsuccessfully courted her for nine years. Every Sunday, during Alf's childhood, he came to see Ivy at their two-up, two down Grace Street home. *"He was a teacher and very, very 'posh', always dressed in a smart suit. If apparel proclaims the man, he was in the context of Ancoats the man of the hour. He took Ivy out, and proposed marriage several times, but eventually the relationship fell apart by mutual consent.''* Some years later, Ivy met her future husband, Tom, but did not marry him until her late twenties, continuing meanwhile to live with and serve her mother, brothers and sisters with unrivalled devotion.

Ivy gained a place at the Manchester Central High School for Girls in Whitworth Street at the age of 11, but left three years later simply because the family needed every penny that could be earned. Canon Shimwell, who had rescued the family from Ancoats, is also remembered for his earlier advice to Ivy that when applying for a job she should on no account describe herself as living in Ancoats, much less Lower Ancoats: Manchester 4 would suffice. Heeding this warning, Ivy was appointed to her first job in the office of Clibran's, a well-known florist in Oldham Street, close to Manchester's Piccadilly. From there, she went to work at the nearby branch of Woolworth's, a huge, landmark, four-storey store on the corner of Oldham Street and Piccadilly, where she eventually became head cashier. The General Manager there was very senior in the Woolworth's hierarchy, but many shoppers came to think that Ivy headed the organisation. When the store was open she would be there. Alf well remembers her routine: up at 5.30 a.m., cooking breakfast for everyone before leaving to work around the clock from eight in the morning to eight in the evening, returning home at the end of the day to change out of her smart suit and help with the household chores. Withal she retained a sense of humour that could enliven the gloomiest moments and a smile that could enchant any stranger to the house.

Alf's eldest brother, George, passed his scholarship examination and was therefore entitled to go to a grammar school, but like so many children in those days, was denied the opportunity by the necessity for him to go to work at the age of fourteen. Emulating his father, he became an accomplished sign-writer, preparing posters and expertly decorating shop fascias and commercial vehicles.

Alf was very attached to all his brothers and sisters and is full of stories about them. His brother Fred triumphed over the serious illness that confined him to Pendlebury Hospital for several years. He returned to Ancoats in his teens when Alf was only five, clad in a smart new suit provided by the hospital's charitable fund, and found work only a few weeks after his discharge. Alf also remembers his brother Billy as someone who had a considerable influence on him, always concerned to try to ensure that Alf would not make the mistakes that he had made and giving him the protection and companionship that only an older brother can offer to a younger. A joiner by trade, Billy became a union organiser with the Amalgamated Society of Woodworkers, hugely respected for his commitment, integrity and principled support of the Society's members. During the war, Bill was called into the Royal Navy and served on H. M. S. Kimberley. This was part of the fifth destroyer flotilla and saw distinguished service both in the North Sea and the Mediterranean. The story of one of the flotilla's ships, H. M. S. Kelly, was made into the classic film, *In which we serve*. Kimberley herself, after sailing with the most dangerous of the Malta convoys, had her stern blown off by a torpedo from U77 with severe loss of life. She was repaired and survived to see action again in the Channel on D-Day. Billy had, in Alf's words, "a hard war" and died "before his time". When Jessie heard of the torpedoing of Kimberley, she said with typical optimism, "Our Billy will be alright, he's a really good swimmer".

Another brother, Charles, Alf's senior by less that two years, and father of Estelle, was also very close to him. Charles was a clever, quietly spoken, very likeable boy. He was somewhat underweight for his age and it was always thought in the family that this was because he was the survivor of twins. Despite this, ever genuine and without guile, he went on to have an outstanding career. At fourteen, he found work as a telegram boy and later as a counter clerk at Newton Heath Post Office on Oldham Road (within 100 yards from the ground where Manchester United Football Club began). In his early twenties, after National Service with the British Army of the Rhine, Charles became the youngest-ever chairman of the Union of Post Office Workers' National Executive Committee. He was elected to Manchester City Council and became Chairman of its Transport Committee. In 1963, he was adopted as Labour candidate to fight a by-election in the Openshaw Division of Manchester and became a well-liked and highly effective MP. He served – for most of the time alongside Alf – for nineteen years, first as a Parliamentary Private Secretary and then as a Minister, impressing everyone with his intelligence and infectious good humour.

A new school

In the family's new home in Newton Heath, Alf was sent to a new school, a walk of two hundred yards from the corner of Halliday Road. Only a year or two old, Briscoe Lane Junior was an 'open air' school, designed to incorporate the latest ideas in healthy education. Single-storey classrooms formed a square around a large patch of lawn. All its inner walls faced the lawn and consisted of floor-to-ceiling folding windows, so that on suitable – and now and again unsuitable – days pupils sat at their desks bathed whether they liked it or not in fresh air. Tuberculosis, diphtheria and scarlet fever were still prevalent in the 30s and perhaps this exposure to the elements, chilly though it was at times, helped to ward off infection.

The standard of teaching at the school was high. A significant proportion of its pupils, after passing the 'scholarship' examinations, went on to the city's grammar schools, and, like Every Street, Briscoe Lane gave their first lessons to several youngsters who later achieved considerable success, not least cricketer Michael Atherton and journalist Harold Evans. Harold, then one of Alf's friends, was to become, via the *Ashton under Lyne Reporter* and of the *Manchester Evening News*, editor of the *Sunday Times* and later *The Times*. They have kept in close and continuous contact ever since and are believed to be then the only two people in their locality ever to have gone to university. It was quite unusual, whatever the result of examinations, even to go on to secondary school, let alone university; and to go to university without having been to secondary school was unprecedented. Some pupils might go to a technical college or an art college, but 'cap and gown' was a remote mystery. In later years, Harold was to cover the election at which Alf became the MP for Wythenshawe, and they were to share common ground in pressing for an end to capital punishment and in campaigning for thalidomide children.

24

At school, Harold was sometimes referred to as 'Posh', possibly because his family had an old 'tin Lizzie'. His father was a train driver on the former LMS line between Manchester and London, an elevated status that enabled him to run a second-hand car. To have a car in Alf's part of Newton Heath was virtually unknown. Indeed, even to see one on the streets was something to behold. Harold paid for his school dinners and was more tidily dressed than most of his classmates.

Alf's memory of Briscoe Lane Junior is not one of harsh discipline and repression, although a strap was sometimes employed. He has a dim recollection that one blow – intended for a friend – missed its intended victim and hit him on the back. Obedience and compliance were axiomatic. Alf has a particular recollection of one afternoon, immediately before the summer holiday, when all the children had been given their reports to take home. The class teacher, having to finish off her – end of school year – returns, told the children to fold their arms and keep quiet. But from somewhere in the room there was a sound. "Who said that?" asked the teacher. She stared at a girl who lived across the road from Alf and said, "Come out, and bring your report with you". She put some words on the report that the rest of the class didn't know about until later, after they had all gone home. It was a hot July day and the front doors were open in Halliday Road. Suddenly, Alf heard something like a scream from the girl's house. Her mother came out, and crossed the road to where Alf's mother stood on the doorstep. "Look at this, Jessie, what they've said about our Agnes," shrieked the agitated neighbour. Mrs Morris read the comment on the report: "This girl is abominable". "What does that mean?" asked the neighbour. "I don't know," admitted Alf's mother. Other neighbours were consulted. "It means terrible, disgraceful, very, very bad," said one. So there was a collective anger and a resolution to go and sort this out with the teacher. Agnes, who Alf knew was not the girl who had spoken, was heartbroken, and the reaction of those around her was typical of the solidarity of working class people. They were not docile, nor prepared to accept injustice. They would be just as unlikely to go quietly if the Public Assistance Committee turned down a just claim. So Agnes was comforted, and then avenged by a posse of mothers deputed to express their anger direct on the teacher's doorstep. Justifying their sense of moral outrage, the 'abominable' Agnes went on to become the convenor – the top shop steward – at one of Manchester's biggest manufacturing enterprises, the first woman to be elected.

Threats to health

In the 1930s diphtheria was still one of the great scourges of childhood, more feared than the typhoid fever outbreaks of the previous century. If you had diphtheria in Manchester you went to Monsall Hospital, and all too often that was the last that anyone saw of you. Alf particularly remembers a time in 1938 when he had a painfully sore throat and a very high temperature, two of the classic symptoms of the merciless disease. His mother called the doctor, who took a swab for analysis, telling Jessie that if the results were positive Alf either had scarlet fever or diphtheria, and an ambulance would arrive to take him to hospital in about an hour's time. An hour later an ambulance did indeed turn into Halliday Road and came to a halt outside the gate of number 14. Alf, who was in bed upstairs, heard his mother say, "They're here. They've come for him". She answered the dreaded knock on the door, only to be asked "Is this the Finches?" They had come to the wrong address. Bernard Finch, a boy of about Alf's own age, lived on the other side of the road. They watched as Bernard was carried from the house and driven to Monsall where he died the next day. "That's how things were," Alf reflects. "Nowadays, children don't expect their pals to die – we always did. Many a time I was taken to the homes of school friends to pay my 'last respects' before their burial".

Alf's sore throat and high temperature turned out to have been infected tonsils. Shortly afterwards it was decided, despite Alf's nervous questioning, that his tonsils should be removed. For this he had to go far across the city to Booth Hall Children's Hospital, where he would stay for a full two weeks. This was located in Blackley, on the edge of Manchester, and it wasn't easy for his mother to get there, or to afford the two long bus rides involved. Then, unless a child was dangerously ill, visitors were allowed only half an hour on Wednesday afternoon and half an hour on Sunday. The regime, which compounded illness with the stress of separation, gave both children and their parents a great deal of anxiety. Alf never forgot it. One of the first things he set his mind to on entering Parliament was to campaign, with the National Association for the Welfare of Children in Hospital, to liberalise visiting in all children's hospitals in the country.

War clouds

Such problems, however, were soon overtaken as the threat of war increased following the Anschluss – Germany's annexation of Austria in 1938. Hitler had been in power for five years, half of Alf's childhood. But children, on the whole, were scarcely aware of the terrorism and brutality that marked the Third Reich. After Chamberlain's return from Munich, it was the issue in 1939 of gas masks and the distribution of the corrugated-iron, nuts and bolts needed to construct an air raid shelter – the so-called Anderson shelter – that brought home the reality of the threat that Germany posed. And even this, for high-spirited young people, invoked a sense of adventure rather than dread. Most boys in Newton Heath were looking forward to helping to dig the necessary hole and erect the shelters in their back gardens. Not so in the Morris household. The parts for their 'Anderson' were delivered on a day when the front page of the *Manchester Evening News* was headlined "War Threat Grows". Alf's mother was sceptical. She had never been out of Lancashire and regarded the south of England as foreign territory; nowhere more so than London, a remote citadel of alien culture that she had no desire to visit. After seeing the headline, Jessie gave her verdict. "That's just London talk," she said, "don't worry about that; there won't be any war and all that corrugated iron and the rest of it can stay against the back wall". Alf was disappointed. But Jessie's decision was firm and it seemed final. During the summer of 1939, shelters went up day by day in neighbouring gardens, while hers stayed unassembled against the back wall. Then one night in August she saw another headline in the *Manchester Evening News* announcing a pact between Germany and the Soviet Union. Jessie put the paper down and turned to Alf: "You'd better start putting the air raid shelter up".

Meanwhile, Alf had progressed at Briscoe Lane Junior School. On passing the equivalent of the '11–Plus' examination at the age of 10, he was allocated a place at North Manchester High School for Boys. The debate in the Morris household was on whether the family could afford to buy the uniform and other things that went with a high school education. But this was in August 1939, and the problem was overshadowed and eventually overtaken by events in Europe. War was becoming more and more likely and the evacuation of the nation's children – especially from places like Manchester – was already being actively discussed. In Newton Heath it would mean the relocation of two schools and their staff. Briscoe Lane and nearby Brookdale Park Secondary School were to go to Ramsbottom, a small Lancashire town midway between Bury and Rawtenstall. Alf, now 11, had concluded his final year at Briscoe Lane. His elder brother, Charles, was 12 and in his second year at Brookdale Park, and their younger sister Vera was at Briscoe Lane. Their mother's first principle was that they should stick together. Alf ought to have been evacuated to Blackpool with North Manchester High School; but this would mean separating the children and was out of the question. Jessie Morris's concern was that she would find it hard enough to afford visits to one destination, let alone two. So on 1 September 1939, Alf was packed off with the Briscoe Lane/ Brookdale Park Secondary contingent. As the train pulled out of Manchester Central Station his mother's words rang in his ears: "whatever happens stick together; don't let them split you up".

The evacuation officer in charge of receiving evacuees in Ramsbottom had booked the Non-conformist church hall, and the forlorn evacuees sat on row after row of wooden benches, there to be inspected by potential foster families. Local people came in, looked the apprehensive children over, mused over their choice before saying, "I want her" or "I'll have him". Almost all were willing to accommodate one evacuee and a few took two. But nobody wanted three. Five hours later, long after most of the others had been selected, the Morris children were still there. One or two more people came in during the evening, including the local vicar and a couple who lived near to him in Dundee Lane who were quite well to do. After speaking to the evacuation officer, they said, "We'll take two, so it had better be the older boy and the younger sister. We're sorry, but we can't possibly take three". So Alf was left on his own.

It was late and the problem had to be resolved. Earlier, the Evacuation Officer had rejected as potential foster parents an elderly couple by the name of Ellis. But they had not given up hope. By taking an evacuee, their income would go up by seven shillings and sixpence a week – more than their state pension – and they were still doggedly hanging about. Alf was the last green bottle on the wall and, under extreme pressure of time, it was finally agreed that they could take him.

The couple sold firewood to supplement their income. The old man chopped it up, his wife would bind it up in bundles with twine and go out and sell it around the streets for three ha'pence a bundle. When Alf came, they quickly made him sales executive. But the evacuation officer had been right in his judgement of the Ellis couple. Perhaps they were too poor and altogether too old. Conditions in the house were no better than those Alf had known in the worst parts of Ancoats, and less clean. He was often hungry, seldom miserable, but remembers poignantly a moment when, while out hawking his firewood on a rainy morning, ill-clad, wet through, looking down-hearted and badly done by, when a passing car showered him with water from the gutter. He looked up to see his brother Charles and his sister Vera sitting on the back seat, happy and bright-faced, waving to him vigorously. They were on their way to a day out at Blackpool with their foster parents from 'the other side of the tracks'.

After four or five weeks, Jessie got on the train and came to survey the situation in Ramsbottom. First she saw Charles and Vera at their new home on Dundee Lane and came away delighted. Then she came down to see Alf, below Bolton Road and 'well below the salt'. He and the elderly couple lived mainly on fish and chips, with mushy peas if the firewood sales were good. They were doing their best, trying to cope in very difficult circumstances, but Alf's mother was very worried about what she saw. The bed he was using had a hole in it, and then, looking behind his ears, declared "That's impetigo. I'm taking you home".

So there he was, back home in Manchester, living within 300 yards of A. V. Roe's factory and of neighbouring Mather & Platt, both of them prime targets for the Luftwaffe. There were now no schools, all of them having been closed and most of their teachers evacuated with the children. It was as though the Pied Piper of Hamlyn had been through the city. Alf felt like Rousseau's Emile – free and at large. Although he was an avid reader, his formal education went into abeyance and his days extended before him to do with as he wished. He now had many opportunities to supplement the family income. He had two newspaper rounds and his lively face and shock of hair soon became familiar to people all over Newton Heath. In between times, he ran errands for housebound pensioners, getting to know something of the difficulties they faced in the early years of the war. He also had a shelf-stacking job at a local Co-op store at the junction of Briscoe Lane and Ten Acres Lane. Many years later this boy was to hold the highest elective office in the British Co-operative Movement as President of the Co-operative Congress. He had begun at its very grass roots!

Taken together, his various jobs provided him with quite a little income, rather more in fact than when he later found formal employment. One of his tasks was to collect weekly payments for newspapers he had delivered during the week, a system that sometimes led to acrimonious disagreements with the collector if people suspected that they were being overcharged. Nevertheless, these weekly collection arrangements meant that all sorts of people came knocking on the door week by week: milkman, rent man, coalman, doctor's collector and insurance man. And, of course, the knocker-up, paper boy and rag and bone man, although the latter could be good for raising a shilling or two. Customers could not always pay every caller, and would say "Can you leave it till next week"? Those habitually in default would spread their bad debts around, so that no one service provider would refuse to supply them. Alf remembers one occasion when there was a knock on his own front door, which as usual was ajar, and his mother calling out to Alf, "Tell him we're not in".

On the night of 22 December 1940 came the devastating 'Manchester Blitz'. Luftwaffe bombers, flying along their efficient Knickebein beams, were able to target the centre of the city with great accuracy. Newton Heath, two and a half miles from the city centre, escaped unscathed, though the fury of the raids that could be seen in the winter sky was alarming. While never hit on the scale of that first raid, Newton Heath's turn was yet to come. Alf's paper rounds were for a newsagent in Briscoe Lane, and covered an area that was often bombed by night. Every morning, at the end of his second round, he returned to the shop and told the newsagent if and which houses on his round had been hit the night before. The newsagent's response was not to ask the extent of the damage or if anyone had been killed but to inquire, with manifest concern, "Did they pay you last Sunday?" (this being the collection day). Alf wonders what might have been his response had 14 Halliday Road been hit! The Anderson shelter would have afforded scant protection, for they hardly ever used it. In the worst weather it was often flooded or covered in snow. Alf's mother would say, "I'm not going out there", and stay under the stairs hugging her rent book, purse, and insurance policies.

A job opportunity

Eventually, as the bombing eased, children filtered back to Manchester. By this time, Alf was within eighteen months of the school leaving age (14) and he went with his brother Charles to Brookdale Park Secondary School to resume his formal education. He had grown into a self-possessed and confident youth who enjoyed his studies and made rapid progress. Even before leaving school, he was presented with his first job opportunity. Wilson's Brewery, an old established company based in Newton Heath, was seeking a 'smart lad' to work in their office, which in Mancunian terms meant clean and presentable, bright and hardworking. It was the third year of the war and, as in other firms, men were leaving all the time for service in the armed forces. Frank Welburn, the Company Secretary, decided to approach the head teacher of Brookdale Park Secondary, asking him to send three boys who might be suitable for the job. F. H. Turner, the head, chose his three star pupils, Eric Bloor, Wilfred Kirkland and Alfred Morris. This was regarded in Newton Heath as the perfect employment opportunity – a job for life. *"Archangel Gabriel's moral advisor, in the local view, had no better job."*

Moreover, Wilson's was a very important institution, supplying beer not only all over Manchester and into Cheshire, but also across the Pennines, into North Staffordshire and as far as North Wales. Most crucially it supplied most of the people making Lancaster bombers at A. V. Roe, and the workers at Mather & Platt and in Trafford Park, which, in 1942, was one of the main centres for manufacturing munitions in Britain. Alf was once asked what, in his opinion, was the greatest strategic error made by the Germans during the war. Was it failure to follow through after Dunkirk and invade Britain, or was it the timing of their disastrous decision to invade Russia? "No," he said, "despite the fact that they could no doubt smell the hops from fifteen thousand feet, they failed to bomb Wilson's Brewery".

When Bloor, Kirkland and Morris turned up at this immensely important site, missed by the Nazis, they found that they were facing a stern test. Welburn was both a Fellow of the Chartered Institute of Secretaries and a chartered accountant. He set the boys a two and a half hour examination that included arithmetical problems, general knowledge questions, an essay and writing to his dictation as he read the country diary from the *Manchester Guardian*. They were seated with him, in the firm's boardroom, for the test, until finally he told them "whichever boy I am thinking of appointing will know because I will also be writing to ask his parents to come for interview". Two days later, Alf's mother received a letter. Everybody in the street helped to rig her out in the smartest clothes they had for the interview. *"She had Mrs Murphy's hat, Mrs Brady's best scarf, and so on"* and can't have looked too bad because Alf's appointment to work in the office was confirmed.

He was still only 13, but Manchester Education Committee's rule was that if you were passing the age of 14 during one of the school holidays, you could leave before the holiday. So that when he began, he was barely 14. Wilson's Brewery was a very paternalistic employer. They paid the tuition costs and bought all the textbooks Alf needed to matriculate at night school. Nor was that the only fringe benefit. Every Tuesday night, four dozen bottles of 'Wembley'- Wilson's widely celebrated light ale – arrived at his home. Nobody drank in Alf's home, so they went all round the road: *"four for Mrs Murphy, two for Mrs Shaw and so on"*, with a plea for the empties to be back for collection by the following Monday evening.

Even in the finest job in Newton Heath and bottled largesse by the case full, Alf at first found his working conditions almost unbearable. In the brewery yard, there was a pyramid of spent hops, shovelled there after use in the brewing process. The office windows had to be open from time to time, admitting fumes from the sweating pile, and the new recruit was physically sick every day. After six or seven weeks of suffering in silence, he told his mother "I'm going to have to pack this job in, I can't carry on". She exploded, "Pack it in? You've got the best job anyone could have". Alf explained what the problem was, but was told that he would just have to persevere. Otherwise what about Mrs Murphy, Mrs Shaw and the rest? It seemed that the whole neighbourhood was dependent on him, the provider of an essential resource in wartime Manchester. So he gritted his teeth, soldiered on and gradually became inured to the fumes.

Friends

During the next few years, Alf gathered around himself three very close friends, all with similar interests, all just beginning, like Alf himself, to develop their personal responses to the world. First was John Bates, a thoughtful youngster with extraordinary intellect, a year or two older than Alf, who later became a Chartered Accountant and a university lecturer before an early death struck him down. From him, Alf acquired a lifelong enthusiasm for chess. This mild and gentle boy's father was Jackie Bates, a professional boxing trainer, whose stable produced three famous champions of the day, Johnny King, Jock McEvoy and Jackie Brown, and for being in Joe Louis's corner when he fought Max Schmeling for the world title in Berlin. Jackie Bates' name is still remembered in Manchester, and articles about him still appear in newspapers.

Another of this quartet of friends was Clifford Wright, ebullient, bright and exceptionally warm hearted – a wonderful companion. Cliff's father had lost his right arm at Passchendaele. Then there was Frank White, Alf's closest friend and one with whom he maintains contact down to the present time. Frank's father had been a regular soldier, one of the first to go to France with the original British Expeditionary Force in August, 1914. He had happened to be in the trenches at Festubert in 1915 when, despite the fact that the wind was blowing in completely the wrong direction, the British for the first time used poison gas. Of course, it blew back into their own lines. Now, having been laid low by it, Frank's father was three-quarters blind. Alf, already acquainted with the problems of disabled living in his own home, also found them in the homes of his friends.

These four pals, as interested as any other teenage boys in girls, allowed one another time off to do a bit of courting. But they were more often together. They tramped for miles, talking endlessly, educating each other, maturing as they went along. Such was the intensity of these conversations, these debates and arguments about everything under the sun, that Alf and Frank would suddenly find themselves far away beyond their normal horizons. On one occasion, having missed the last connection home, they sat overnight in a distant railway station, still talking, waiting for the first gasping steam train of the morning to turn up and take them home.

But as the son of an ex-professional soldier and the brother of a young man who had recently been killed while serving with the 8th Army in North Africa, Frank was impatient to get into the war himself. At seventeen and a quarter, as soon as the services were prepared to accept him, he volunteered for the Royal Navy and joined the British Pacific Fleet. For more than two years he and Alf exchanged lively letters until they were able to meet again in their old stamping grounds.

Into politics

Meanwhile, Alf had joined the Labour Party. True to his mother's wishes, he had begun to help to distribute Mr Thorneycroft's leaflets, and was soon taking leaflets out not just for him but for Labour Councillors as well. It brought him into contact with the Newton Heath ward branch of the Labour Party, part of the then Clayton constituency. You had to be sixteen to join the Party, but from the age of fourteen Alf was nevertheless allowed to attend meetings, held in the Co-operative Hall over the Daisy Bank store of the Failsworth Industrial Co-operative Society. From below wafted the wholesome smell of comestibles, food rations for the district, kept safe behind iron-barred windows. Alf was, of course, the youngest person there, but now in long trousers and in secure employment he felt quite adult. It was 1942, the low point of British fortunes in the war; before El Alamein, before Stalingrad, before any of the great turning points in the conflict. Party politics were in suspense. At Westminster, there was a coalition government, which was to persist until 1945. Clement Attlee was deputy to Winston Churchill, Herbert Morrison was Home Secretary and Ernest Bevin was Minister of Labour, all with seats in the Cabinet. This accord was reflected at local level: though the members firmly belonged to the Labour movement, party rivalries had been set aside. Apart from purely local issues – like the state of the washhouse which people like Alf's mother still relied on for the family's laundry – the talk was all about what was happening to people's sons and daughters. Harry Thorneycroft would come to some of the meetings, but it was to report on what was happening at Westminster and on the progress of the war. Manchester was still being bombed day and night as the Luftwaffe sought to destroy the city's strategic targets. It was the time of Michael Foot's 'The Guilty Men'. Everyone knew it from back to front and there was a common opinion that the Tories had caused the war through their policy of appeasement. People who had been bereaved felt the need to pin down responsibility for the slaughter and their personal suffering.

By his sixteenth birthday Alf was already dedicated to the cause, and his full membership was a formality. Charlie Fenton, a joiner who was chairman of the ward, had two daughters who were also quite active, and with some others a youth section developed – part of the Labour League of Youth. As the war moved into its final phase, Alf became its chairman, and as such had a place on Clayton's general management committee. Soon he was elected chairman of the constituency's divisional youth section. His political career had begun.

1936: Alf at Halliday Road before a street cricket match. Far left, back row, in the suit he wore at his father's funeral.

1944: Newton Heath Brass band. Alf, with his euphonium, is fourth from left of back row. To his right is his friend Frank White, and to his left Eric Bloor, one of the competitors for the job at Wilson's Brewery. The other competitor, Wilfred Kirkland, is on the front row on the far right of the photograph.

1944: A day out in Blackpool. Alf with his mother, Jessie.

1946: Army hospital at Geneifa, Egypt. Alf recovering from temporary blindness (the only photograph during his service with Middle East Land Forces).

Chapter 3

SOLDIER,
SWAIN AND STUDENT

1946–1950

Pressed into service, means pressed out of shape.

Robert Frost: The Self Seeker.

– Called up – Service in the Middle East
– Violence between Palestinians and Jewish settlers
– Return to Newton Heath; Labour people remembered
– A special friend and associate – Friendship turns to romance – Social activities
– Ruskin College – Vacation work – Wedlock and a new start in Oxford
– An unexpected invitation; – In hot water at St Catherine's

Called up

Alf Morris remained at Wilson's Brewery until, just after his eighteenth birthday, he was conscripted to the colours. Not to war, at least not to a declared war, although soon he was to be very much on what the army calls 'active service'. He had celebrated with everyone else Britain's victory in Europe and then in Japan, when Manchester shared the delirium of relief that swept the whole country. Now it was time to relieve the troops who had brought this victory, to allow them to come home.

Alf served with Middle East Land Forces, mainly in Egypt and Palestine, as it then was. Britain still had responsibility for Palestine and, while rival terrorist groups were at war over its future, he remembers it now as a hugely important part of his education, both literally (for he continued to study) and in terms of new horizons. This was a young man whose experience of foreign parts had been limited to day excursions to Blackpool and, on one occasion, three days at Red Wharf Bay in Anglesey. He left with a few cautionary words from his mother: "Just keep yourself to yourself", difficult advice to follow in the army, save that what she really intended was that he should stay away from bad company.

Alf first reported to Carlisle to be kitted out, before being sent on to Stranraer. From there he crossed the sea to Larne in Northern Ireland and finally south, through Belfast to Ballykinlar in County Down, for six weeks intensive training. Alf remembers his basic training as a soldier with gratitude, for without it he would not have survived his army service. It taught him what to do under sniper fire, a lesson that was later, in the Middle East, to save his life.

Northern Ireland in 1946 was not yet the cauldron it was later to become. Alf fondly recalls one particular weekend, when he was given a 48–hour pass. It was too short a time to return to Manchester; so instead a fellow army recruit and friend, Patrick, invited him to his home in Ballynahinch. Patrick's parents had a pub in a strong Catholic area, and it seemed entirely natural for them to ask their son and his friend to let them have a night off. The remarkable thing was not that Alf and Patrick should spend Saturday evening pulling pints in the bar, but that they did so in their British army uniforms! In later years, Alf told this story to Field Marshal Lord Inge, then Chief of the Defence Staff, who simply could not imagine such a thing. "Incredible, no impossible," was the astonished response, but then Alf Morris was in the army many years before Peter Inge.

Alf's army pay was 14 shillings a week. Out of this, he made an allotment to his mother of ten of those shillings, but didn't feel badly done by. For one thing, there was really no point in regretting one's lot – there was no alternative. And there was much to be said on the positive side: he had his keep, clothes on his back, a rainproof roof and a bed. By Ancoats standards this was luxury. It was, moreover, a new and fascinating experience to be in the company of other young people from all over the country and all sorts of backgrounds, and to be facilitating the homecoming of people who, with a little help, had prevailed against the armed might of Hitler, Mussolini and Hirohito.

Alf must have been a good soldier, for within a few months he was sent, on the recommendation of his Commanding Officer, to the army camp at Catterick to face a War Office Selection Board. The purpose, by means of close observation, interviews, written examinations and wide-ranging tests of competence as a soldier, was to identify young men who had the potential to become officers. After three days of this the point came when Alf was told, "Let's be clear. If you are going to be an officer, you will have to sign on for at least three years from being commissioned". At that stage of Alf's life, well upwards of three more years seemed like an eternity. So he told them, "thank you, but no," and went instead to the Middle East as a private soldier. From Aldershot, he travelled to Southampton to board the troopship Arundel Castle, bound for Port Said, along with 3,000 other troops.

Service in the Middle East

Egypt was then in firm alliance with the United Kingdom, having enjoyed the protection of British troops throughout the war. King Farouk was on the throne, and the Suez Canal, with substantial British financial holdings, remained a vital link between the Mediterranean and the Red Sea. Alf served in Ismailia on the Canal and at Fayid on the Great Bitter Lake, then the GHQ of Middle East Land Forces. He found Egyptians both friendly and hospitable, and retains many happy memories of friendship with them. But poverty was at levels that made his own experience fortunate by comparison. The average life span was 21 years, a statistic deriving from an appalling rate of infant mortality. The climate too could be insufferably hot for a Mancunian.

Even in this exotic, unfamiliar country, Alf did his best to maintain his links with his friends from home. One of those with whom he corresponded was Cliff Wright, a companion from his school days in Manchester. Cliff, like Alf, was by this time serving in the army but, under the code of secrecy imposed by the War Office, mail could only be addressed to a British Forces Post Office (BFPO) code number that gave no hint of the person's location. The closest bonds were thus inevitably remote. And nowhere seemed more remote to Alf than Fayid, where everyone slept in lines of tents pitched on the sand. In the heat of the day, off-duty soldiers would leave the flaps of the tent open. One day, shortly after his arrival, while making his way to his own billet, Alf glanced inside one of the open tents. To his utter astonishment, there was his pal, Staff Sergeant Cliff Wright, stretched out on a bed. It was a joyous reunion and from then on the two Manchester pals spent as much time as possible with each other, swimming together in the Great Bitter Lake, one of the great compensations of life at Fayid. Cliff and Alf remained firm friends and would both, after their service, link up as members of the Newton Heath Labour League of Youth.

During his service in the Middle East, Alf not only learned more about grinding poverty, but also what it is like to be blind. Caught up in a Khamsin, one of the desert's swirling sandstorms that William Woodruff has described as coming out of the desert "like a rolling cloud, blotting out sight and sound, so powerful as to give the impression of being the only thing in the world"[1], Alf's eyes filled with sand, and conjunctivitis swiftly followed. His pupils had to be dilated, so he could not see to read or to write his regular letters to his mother and a friend had to write for him. Alf was admitted to an army hospital at Geneifa, where he was reassured that it was only a temporary problem and, after three weeks when the sand had been removed, his sight was fully restored. Nevertheless, the experience gave him some idea of what blindness was like.

Alf neither smoked nor drank and, apart from long-distance swimming, his leisure time was devoted to learning: something that he regarded as a hobby. The army encouraged soldiers to pursue their education and he was able to study through correspondence courses and was already focusing on higher education. Alf acquired more than a smattering of Arabic and when the opportunity came for him to spend a week's leave in Cairo, along with another army friend from Manchester who was deeply interested in and knowledgeable about Egyptology, his interest was not only in the beauty of the Nile and the splendour of the pyramids, but in learning all he could about the country.

Violence between Palestinians and Jewish settlers

The responsibilities of Middle East Land Forces extended to a far less friendly territory. In 1947 Palestine was still a protectorate, under a British mandate established by the League of Nations after the First World War. Governance had become, in the words of Harold

---

[1] *Shadows of Glory* (William Woodruff, Little, Brown 2003)

Macmillan, "a painful and hideous problem". The Palestinians deeply resented the growing influx of Jewish settlers, while the Jews were eager to press on with the creation of the homeland Lord Balfour had heralded in 1917. By November 1947, the United Nations General Assembly had resolved to partition the country and three months later the British Government announced that it would terminate its mandate on 15 May 1948. Britain was unwilling to impose by force any plan that was not acceptable to both Jews and Arabs. But it was becoming more and more clear that, in the face of a dramatic escalation of mutual hostility and violence in the region, we were unable to do so.

This was the unhappy state of affairs when Alf was sent to Jerusalem and Tel Aviv in 1948. Enmity between Arab and Jew had become endemic and irreconcilable. Daily it was increasingly more difficult to keep order, and less realistic to think of doing so. The clash between the warring groups was for the prize of inheriting Palestine when, as would shortly be happening, the British mandate came to an end. Arabs fought Jews, and Jews fought Arabs. Both fought the British. Our troops were in the middle and the target of continuous guerrilla attacks by paramilitaries from both sides, and casualties mounted in what the British press rightly described as non-stop atrocities. Our service men and women felt that they could not do right for doing wrong. Nor could British politicians. If they had simply pulled the troops out, they would have been attacked for making it easy for the more powerful and ruthless groups to take control. So the Attlee government opted for a phased withdrawal, attempting, as best it could, to carry out its contractual duty and to leave Palestine, as far as possible, with some semblance of order. But by staying put after the end of the mandate, our troops earned and had to endure resentment as an occupying power. In Alf's view, the situation was even more difficult than the later troubles in Northern Ireland and involved far more terrorists than ever operated there. It was war in all but name. Our troops were charged with backing up the Palestine Police, helping where civil authority, such as it was, could no longer cope. In this role, they were a prime target, and the British headquarters in Jerusalem's King David Hotel was the scene of several savage attacks. As in other conflicts, the

43

sense of outrage was most keenly felt when one of the victims was a young woman serving with the Auxiliary Territorial Service. Her murder, more than other casualties suffered every day, shocked public opinion in Britain. There was widespread feeling that British involvement wasn't worth its cost in lives and the well-being of our service personnel.

Alf himself came close to being added to the list of those killed when, on overnight patrol near the border with Egypt, he was fired at from a moving vehicle. He was some forty yards from the road when shots rang out. Throwing himself head first to the ground, as he had been trained to do at Ballykinlar, the bullets passed over him. He often thinks of himself as having been fortunate in life, and this was certainly the most crucial and dramatic of such godsends.

Return to Newton Heath; Labour people remembered

Alf left the Middle East, as a sergeant, in October 1948 and returned to civilian life and to Wilson's Brewery. It was equally predictable that he would resume active membership of his Constituency Labour Party (CLP) in Manchester's Clayton division. The senior officers of the general management committee at that time were Alderman Bob Malcolm, its chairman, and Arthur Stevenson, the secretary. Alf remembers both of them with great affection: *"'Old' Bob Malcolm (to distinguish him from his son of the same name) was chairman of the city council's Baths and Washhouses Committee, a very much more important role at that time than it may sound now, since civic baths and washhouses were then integral to tens of thousands of families who had no such facilities at home. He never meant to be dictatorial; he was too benign for that, but typically he would say 'Arthur will read out the correspondence'. And Arthur would begin, 'Well the first letter is from the North West Regional Council of the Labour Party and it's about a weekend conference in Blackpool', whereupon Bob would interpose, 'Me and Arthur will be going there. Next one Arthur.'*

"Arthur Stevenson, known as Stevie, was a councillor in Manchester. He was an engineering worker, very able and well read. He was one of those who had a major influence on me as a young person. A fine orator himself, he used to say that the only way to learn public speaking is to speak publicly. In those days most CLPs had a kind of mobile rostrum, and local

public representatives and their active supporters would go from street to street addressing meetings. This is what Arthur did, and I went with him. We also did a lot of doorstep canvassing in an area of tightly packed terraced housing, and Arthur encouraged me to speak both there and in Labour Clubs on a Sunday evening. They would be crowded with club members but, as Arthur pointed out, that was where you could learn to speak. He was also instrumental in me becoming editor of the constituency's newspaper, 'The Clarion'. Each month I used to invite one of the local councillors to contribute an article about her or his role on the council. They would usually say to me, 'well yes, but I assume that you're going to write it', since most of them were in mortal fear of writing."

There were several other fondly remembered party members: *"Councillor Bill Onions (which he had us pronounce Oh-nigh-ens), who later became Lord Mayor of Manchester; Councillor Alf Logan, a highly regarded Methodist lay preacher in Newton Heath, clerical in manner and always very right and proper, who made you feel you were in the presence of the highest respectability; Bill Winstanley, another councillor in the constituency, the proprietor of a herbalist corner shop on Ashton New Road in the Beswick ward, who ought to have been a happy man because he had a very thriving little business. Yet he often looked glum and had a certain reputation. Arthur said, 'You know what's upsetting Bill don't you? He charges three pence a time for a glass of Vimto. It costs him about a farthing, so he only makes two pence three farthings profit a glass, and he's distraught because it's not the whole three pence'. Harry Frankland, another local councillor, and then a city alderman, was an insurance collector (and therefore also a man of some standing). He habitually wore a red bow tie and spoke in a very learned voice. He loved beer, and whisky even more, and would say after he had had a few, 'Never forget circumstances alter cases'. To prove the point, he became chairman of the Housing Committee, and quickly changed his attitude to some of the applications he had been making for council housing tenancies."*

A special friend and associate

At this time, a number of boundary changes were in process, one of which would involve merging the Labour League of Youth branches of the Clayton and Miles Platting constituencies. This was confirmed in November 1948 at an inaugural meeting of the combined branches in a room over the Co-op butcher's shop in Varley Street in Miles

Platting. Nineteen-years-old Irene Jones, who was later to become Alf's wife, was one of those who came to that meeting. She was one of eight girls who had left Manchester Central High School for Girls in 1945 and who, together with five other local girls, constituted the Miles Platting branch of the League of Youth. She recalls that her admission to the Labour Party had been less than encouraging. She had gone to the party's Manchester headquarters with her friend Audrey, both brimming with idealism and eager to join. They thought that they would be welcomed with open arms, but instead were met with jaundiced indifference. "They simply didn't want to know". Nevertheless, the girls located and got involved in the Labour League of Youth in their areas. The Miles Platting branch had been going for only about four weeks when the decision to merge was decided "on high". Like most of her companions, Irene had never met any of the members of the Newton Heath branch, most of whom, propitiously, were young men who had just finished their period of conscription and had not long been demobbed.

The inaugural meeting of the newly merged branch was opened by Jack Hill, the Assistant Regional Organiser for Northwest England. It was decided to elect the branch officers alternately from each of the two former branches. First Alf was elected chairman and went into the chair, then Irene was made secretary. At first, their relationship was simply that of colleagues, albeit in ways that brought them quite closely together. They came from similar backgrounds and were intellectually well matched. Irene's infancy began in Moston where her mother and father shared a decaying house with her mother's sister and her children. Irene's earliest memory is that of "flitting" to Collyhurst, just a mile or so down Rochdale Road, with her father and uncle Jim pushing a handcart laden with a couple of mattresses, a dresser, an old table and four-years-old Irene perched on top of it all as they trundled down the bumpy cobbled road to their new home: a two-up, two-down slum terraced house reminiscent of the Morris's home in Ancoats, and hardly less dilapidated. They had no electricity, one gas light in the living room-cum-kitchen (elsewhere they relied on oil lamps and candles) and one cold tap and an old iron stove in a tiny scullery off the back yard, an outside lavatory and a prodigiously-leaking roof.

Irene especially remembers "a daily battle with bed bugs and black beetles".

When Irene and Alf first met, this mean house in Laverack Street was still her home. Her father, Abel Jones, a railway worker, was in poor health from the combined effects of gassing while serving with the Manchester Regiment in the First World War and working in the dense sulphuric fogs of industrial Manchester. Her mother was severely disabled by rheumatoid arthritis, and could move about only if pushed in her wheelchair. She was a deeply religious woman, but it was a daunting struggle for her even to attend the Anglican church some eighty yards from her home. Irene has her own memories of the Second World War, when the winters were often bitter and cold and fuel in short supply. On Saturday mornings hundreds of people went to the gas works, where old coke was sold off at sixpence for 28 lbs. You had to be there by 6 a.m. and even then the queue would seem unending as you stood waiting in the cold. Everyone had their little cart, but the narrow entrance door to the yard would only admit only one cart at a time and everyone would push and shove to get in. "You couldn't give an inch if you wanted to get through, so that your legs would end up battered, bruised and sometimes bleeding from people ramming their carts against you". Irene and her father would each get 28 lbs and this, augmented by pieces of old creosoted sleepers scrapped at the railway depot from which he worked, kept the home fires burning.

Saturday night was bath night for Irene and her sister, using an old tin bath in front of the fire, painstakingly filled from kettles of boiling water. They never knew that scented soap existed. "It was carbolic for your body and Thom's Castile soft brown soap for your hair". Then their father might give them a small bar of Aero chocolate, a new and quite sensational treat.

But despite this primitive lifestyle, Irene was both highly talented and energetic. She had gained the School Certificate with flying colours and, at the age of 16, passed with distinction what was called the Town Hall examination. There could be no question of her going on to Higher School Certificate, because her family's circumstances made it essential for her to start work as soon as possible. She was taken on as a trainee secretary by Imperial Chemical Industries, and was to become a private secretary in ICI's dyestuffs division in Blackley, north Manchester. Later she moved to F.H.Wheelers, electrical engineers, who serviced RAF depots throughout the country.

These positions rivalled even Alf's 'job of jobs' at Wilson's Brewery. But in the Labour League of Youth they were not in competition. The first item on the agenda at the inaugural meeting had been to deal with correspondence that included an invitation – which was accepted – to attend a Christmas social arranged by the Withington League of Youth at Chorlton Town Hall, which took two tram rides across the city to reach. The social began with everyone joining in games that would be thought juvenile today: things like 'spinning the bottle', 'pass the plate' and even 'postman's knock' – very daring! Every guest had a number and most games hinged on guessing the number of someone of the opposite sex. Irene was tipped off that Alf was trying to get her number and she unscrupulously changed it whenever he got it right. But eventually Alf and Irene danced together for the first time that night.

Friendship turns to romance

They all went home on the same trams and Alf and Irene got talking. They discussed P.G.Wodehouse and the music they liked and before they separated they made a date to meet again a week later at 6.45 p.m. at the Playhouse cinema at the corner of Oldham Road and Queen's Road. After eagerly rushing home from work, Irene expectantly turned up on time, in her best coat and all dressed up because she thought they were going to a Hallé concert. But Alf had found himself inescapably involved in the final stage of striking a balance in the brewery's accounts, in which all hands were on deck at Wilson's brewery office. When he at last got away, he ran down to the Playhouse, three quarters of an hour late. Remarkably, Irene was still there. It was too late for the concert, and Alf asked her where they should go instead. Irene's response was that she thought he had it all organised! Reluctantly they agreed to go to The Ceylon, a cinema a bit further up Oldham Road, whose chief claim to fame was that it had many double seats designed to help social cohesion. Irene recalls that a horror film was showing – not at all her cup of tea. However, cohesion survived and they caught the bus home, back down Oldham Road. Alf began searching his pockets, unsuccessfully, for the bus fare and was beginning to get seriously embarrassed when at last he found a ten shilling note (a lot of money then) screwed up in his top pocket. It had not been a promising start, but by such precarious patience are true bonds sealed.

As secretary of the new branch, Irene arranged a programme of activities which included going down a coal mine; visiting the northern office and works of the *Daily Herald* (where Frank Allaun, who was to become Labour MP for Salford East, was then a journalist); rambles round some of Derbyshire's beauty spots, particularly from Mottram to Marple; even the odd – very odd – cricket match, debates, discussions and some other "daft" things not always received with universal acclaim. These led to particular hilarity when linked to elocution and public speaking techniques.

As well as tentatively beginning 'a relationship', Alf and Irene worked closely together. Their roles as chairman and secretary were complementary. Alf edited the Constituency Party's monthly newspaper 'The Clarion', costing two pence a copy, Irene was its film correspondent, Cliff, his army pal, the football correspondent and his brother Charles, writing under the pseudonym of PUG, the boxing correspondent. The first issue appeared in April 1949, with articles by Alderman Harry Thorneycroft JP, MP, the Rt. Hon. Herbert Morrison MP, Lord President of the Council, and a young Michael Foot MP. The latter taken from the *Daily Herald*. Foot, responding to a question about the impact of foreign workers on British industry, pointed out that we needed them and counselled readers not to blame all foreign workers because a few misbehaved. "Sometimes British people misbehave themselves too," he remarked. "Give the foreigner who has come here, sometimes on our invitation and sometimes to escape persecution, a fair deal, and they will usually give a fair return". That was more than half a century ago, yet the same issues still arise.

Alf and Irene inevitably liaised with each other between meetings. Like most people then, neither of them had a telephone at home and although in their particular jobs they had access to phones at work, personal calls were permitted only in emergencies.

Social activities

One League of Youth activity was a Sunday outing to the Peak District. Fourteen members left Manchester's London Road station (now Piccadilly) on the 7.15 a.m. train to Hayfield. The plan was to climb Kinderscout – England's highest peak – and for sustenance everyone brought sandwiches. The weather was exhilarating, perfect for walking, and by 9.30 a.m. they had reached the foothills of Kinder, three-quarters of an hour out of Hayfield, but three hours since breakfast. Alf said to Irene, "I wouldn't mind having a sandwich now". Irene said, "Me too". One thing led on to another and by 10.15 a.m. all their sandwiches had gone. For the rest of the day all they had was spring water from the mountain streams. The party toiled right over the top of Kinder and down to Edale, getting back to Hayfield around 6 p.m. They'd had more fresh air in one day than most Mancunians have in their lives, but correspondingly less food. Thankfully, they found a little café in Hayfield and had egg and chips with bread and butter, and a cup of tea. It cost only seven-pence, but Alf still counts it the best meal of his life. He knew then that the true measure of what we consume is not always its quality but how hungry we are and the company shared. Once again, things had not gone entirely according to plan – indeed there was no plan – but it was a decisive stage in their courtship.

There was an even more remarkable adventure over the Easter weekend of 1949. He and Irene were joined by Frank White, one of his few companions in Newton Heath during the wartime post-evacuation period, and Frank's girlfriend June Bates to visit the Falls of Lodore, south of Keswick. It stemmed from Alf's interest in the Lakeland poets. He was particularly fond of Robert Southey's famous onomatopoeic poem about the falls, itself a cascade of almost every conceivable verb in the language. The quartet had booked two rooms in a boarding house in Keswick from where they planned to visit the falls. On arrival, they seemed to be viewed with some circumspection by the two ultra-respectable maiden ladies who ran the house and in keeping with the proprieties of the age, Alf and Frank were allocated one room, and Irene and June shared another. As they set out on the following morning to catch the ferry across to

Lodore, they were told that lunch was strictly, **very strictly**, at one o'clock which seemed to present no problem.

The falls proved something of a disappointment. While spectacular after heavy rain, the 'cataract' is but a trickle in dry weather. Viewed from the boulders below, there was nothing of the "pouring and roaring" described by Southey. Nor, indeed, any "shaking and quaking" or "quivering and shivering"; not, at least, until the tranquillity of the scene was suddenly broken by a mighty crash. A man had fallen from the top of the falls on to the rocks at their feet and was terribly injured. Coats and woollens were quickly discarded to keep him warm and make him comfortable. Still conscious, he told them that he was a doctor and needed morphine. Alf swiftly ran up the side of the falls to seek help from a hotel about a mile away, leaving Irene, June and Frank to do all they could to comfort the injured man. People at the hotel reacted very quickly and a mountain rescue team was summoned and quickly despatched to the falls to give the doctor morphine, strap him to a stretcher and rush him to hospital. All this took time, resulting in their missing the return ferry. So that when the travellers finally did get back to the boarding house it was a quarter to two. The landladies were hugely sceptical and dismissed their explanations. Alf and his friends were firmly told to settle up and leave. They were out!

They began to make their way home to Manchester, staying overnight in Kendal. Next morning they bought a national daily paper and saw the headline "Distinguished doctor badly injured at the Falls of Lodore". The story ran that four young climbers had rescued and saved the life of the well-known cardiothoracic consultant from Leeds. When they got back to Manchester, Alf's mother told him that they were all over the *Manchester Evening News* as a fine example for the city! Alf reflected "well that's one in the eye for the prim ladies of Keswick".

Ruskin College

Alf continued to study. He had (and has) a remarkable facility with figures, and many people told him that he should have been trained as a mathematician. However, he focused on history and English, and in 1949 an opportunity came for him to apply for a place at Ruskin College, Oxford. This college, named after John Ruskin and funded partly by trade unions, was founded primarily to help young people of ability who, because of social deprivation or, as in Alf's case, the disruptive effect of war, had been unable to gain all the qualifications necessary to enter higher education. One of the principal tests required him to submit a thesis. He chose the Lakeland poets, especially Wordsworth, and Irene typed it for him at work in her own time, after consulting her boss. Initially hostile (as bosses then usually were), he reluctantly agreed on condition that it did not interfere with her work. This and other tests were ultimately assessed by the Principal of Ruskin College, Lionel Elvin, a very distinguished scholar whose speciality was English. The outcome was an invitation to spend a weekend at the college.

It was Alf's first sighting of the university spires and elegant, cathedral-like architecture, and like most first-time visitors he was at once captivated. Welcomed at the station by a Ruskin student, he was taken to see the great Lionel Elvin on Saturday afternoon. Elvin went over a whole range of things, before introducing Alf to other members of staff. This was another world, and an alluring, seductive one. He was back at the brewery on Monday morning, but a few days later a magical card arrived from Elvin. It simply said "Yes"!

In October 1949, Alf took his place in Ruskin College, where he made rapid progress. So much so that he was told at the end of the first year that in the view of his tutors – and of Lionel Elvin – he was already well able to start on an Honours Degree course at one of the Oxford colleges. And after various further tests and, examinations, that view was confirmed.

Vacation work

In the meantime, Alf had to earn a living. An opportunity to do so was chanced upon by his friend Stan Carter[2], also at Ruskin and approaching his summer vacation, who happened to see a letter on the notice board to the Principal from Fred Henry, General Secretary of the Waterproof Garment Workers Union, based in Manchester. The Union wanted two people to work as temporary trade union

---

[2] Stan Carter, who hailed from the Gorton district of Manchester, subsequently became Assistant General Secretary of the Printing and Kindred Trades Association, Mayor of the London Borough of Enfield and personnel officer of *The Times*.

organisers. Stan and Alf applied and were selected at a wage of £7.50 a week. Their task was to increase membership by unionising waterproof garment factories, which then had no union members.

Among other stratagems they leafleted people going into work in the morning to tell them the advantages that would accrue from trade union membership and to announce lunch-time meetings, at which they would often use loudspeakers. In this way Alf learned a lot more about public speaking. He particularly remembers leafleting and addressing the workers at one quite big waterproof garment factory in Stalybridge, just across the Cheshire border. Their efforts bore fruit and they recruited quite a lot of members. One of them, who appeared to have the makings of a good shop steward, suggested that everyone should meet in a local hostelry the following evening after work and try to build on the membership that had already been gained, prior to launching a union branch. Stan and Alf thought this was a great idea and arranged for Fred Henry to come from the Union's HQ in Miller Street, Manchester to address the meeting. A goodly number of people came to hear him. He spoke in a very gentlemanly way, the antithesis of what you would expect from a trade union official. Alf was chairing the meeting when the shop steward designate rose to his feet to ask the first question. Fred Henry responded, "That was a very pertinent question", whereupon the questioner became incandescent with rage. Alf had thought it was quite a coup to get the General Secretary to the meeting, but had not reckoned on this kind of misunderstanding. Fred searched for another word, assuring the questioner that he was saying that it was a good question, a timely and appropriate question. "That's not what you said," the questioner rejoined, as his feathers slowly unruffled. They concluded that they would have to think twice about whether this man would indeed make an ideal shop steward.

On another occasion they visited a factory where the union had long been fighting for recognition. Alf recalls: "The management knew that we had been leafleting the workers, and we were intrigued when invited to the manager's office, up a flight of stairs. I was a little behind Stan, and as I reached the foot of the stairs, Stan had already been bundled down them, colliding with me on the bottom step. I asked Stan to dust himself down and that I would go up. The managing director was very aggressive and we had quite a tussle, but in the end we organised union recognition at the factory".

Wedlock and a new start in Oxford

Knowing that the university course would last for three years, Alf and Irene decided to marry and live in Oxford. They 'tied the knot' on Saturday, 30 September 1950, little more than a week before the commencement of the academic year. The marriage ceremony was conducted by Reverend Henson, the vicar at St. James's Church, Collyhurst. Irene's mother thought the world of her vicar and wouldn't hear a word of criticism against him. Alf was rather more circumspect, knowing him to be partial to a 'wee dram' or two after officiating at funerals, and thinking him inclined to make rather too much of the 'MA (Oxon)' after his name. Of a political persuasion, Alf believes, to the right of centre, Rev. Henson seemed amazed that anyone from Collyhurst could be about to enter the hallowed precincts of Oxford University. Nevertheless, the service went well and was followed by a splendid reception in what had been Johnny Clynes's[3] committee rooms over the Co-op butcher's shop in Varley Street, Miles Platting. This book-lined room had never before been used for such a purpose, and had to be scoured and cleaned to get rid of the dust and accumulated debris of thirty years of Labour Party meetings. It was none the less an entirely fitting venue to celebrate the union of the national Chairman of the Labour League of Youth and the Secretary of its Miles Platting branch, toasted by their political friends not with champagne but with 'British Empire' wine at one shilling and sixpence a bottle! Whether it was the wine or the comfort of having Alf as a partner it is a fact that the migraines that Irene had previously suffered disappeared upon her marriage.

Stan Carter asked them not to worry about accommodation in Oxford. The Ruskin academic year started earlier than the university's and he would have a week there to find them somewhere to live. He wished them well on their way to their honeymoon on a farm at Red Wharf Bay in Anglesey, where they had both been before.

---

[3] J. R. Clynes, a Cabinet Minister in both the first and second Labour Governments, and appointed Home Secretary in 1929, was the MP for Miles Platting (then called Platting).

They returned on the following Saturday, two days before the start of term, to learn that Stan had found it no easy task to find a place for a married couple, something that was, to say the least, unusual among the undergraduate fraternity. Nevertheless, he had taken an option on a room with an old lady, Mrs Phipps, in one of the Rookery Cottages at Headington. "It isn't ideal," he said, "but there really was no alternative." Alf and Irene took a bus there, and found the formidable figure of Mrs Phipps, well over 80, waiting for them. She looked at them with some suspicion, while the young newly-weds felt correspondingly apprehensive. Both they and Mrs Phipps, however, needed each other. The rent (like the heating) was minimal and the room would suffice.

The next morning, 8 October, while Alf was matriculating into St Catherine's College, Irene sought work. Wages in Oxford were far lower than in Manchester, where she had been earning £4.50 a week. In Oxford £3.00 was as much as you could hope for. She worked for a time at Pressed Steel in Cowley and later as secretary to the social secretary at Morris Motors, a job that she found interesting and a lot of fun. Generally working conditions were very strict. To be late three times could get you fired.

An unexpected invitation

Alf saw no merit in telling the college authorities that their new student[4] was just married; indeed it might be unwise to do so. Nor when, less than two weeks later, an unexpected letter arrived with a Liverpool postmark, did he think it wise to reveal its contents other than to Irene. It was from Bill Sefton[5], inviting him to the Garston constituency of Liverpool, where Bill was Labour's Secretary/Agent, to be considered for selection as the prospective Labour parliamentary candidate for the next general election. Garston was then a Tory stronghold, as were most of the Liverpool constituencies: places like Toxteth, Walton and West Derby were safe Conservative seats[6]. But Clement Attlee had said after the February 1950 general election, when Labour's majority had been

---

[4] Like most other young ex-servicemen.
[5] Later Lord Sefton, and before that Leader of both Liverpool City and the Greater Merseyside County Councils.
[6] Alf's recollection is that only Exchange (Bessie Braddock), Scotland (David Logan) and Edge Hill (Arthur Irvine) then held by Labour.

reduced to six at most, that he wanted a prospective Labour candidate in every constituency by mid-November. Alf knew that, even if chosen, he would have no real chance of being elected, and felt no less certain that neither did he have any realistic hope of being selected. When had a Mancunian ever been chosen to stand for election in Liverpool? He thought, however, that to enter the selection process would be a fascinating experience of which it would be foolish not to take advantage. He decided that he could slip away at midday on the day of selection and be back in college on the following day, without anyone being any the wiser. There not only seemed to be no chance of being selected, but even of being detected! In this he was sadly mistaken. The selection committee at Garston, which included Jack Jones, then a transport workers' union official in Liverpool, and Pat Wall, a very active member of Garston's Labour League of Youth[7], chose him as their candidate. The *Oxford Mail* received the story via the Press Association and reported on its next day's front page: 'Oxford Undergraduate to Stand for Parliament'.

In hot water at St. Catherine's

Soon after Alf got back, he was told "the Censor (The Very Reverend Victor John Knight Brook, head of the college) wants to see you". That morning, like William Woodruff twelve years earlier[8], but in even less happy circumstances, he was called to the presence of the austere Brook, who was holding the *Oxford Mail* in a shaking hand. "Never was a Censor more censorious;" Alf recalls, "had he also known I was national chairman of Labour Youth, incandescence would have been out of control". Instead, Alf took the offensive. "Are you speaking to me as head of this college or president of the Oxford City Conservative Association?" he asked the Censor. "How do you know that?" exploded Brook, by now very angry. Alf did not explain his source, which had been no more than the chance reading of an Association leaflet, but the revelation cut the interview short.

---

[7] In later years Pat ('Paddy') Wall was associated with the Militant Tendency and was said to have infiltrated the Labour Party. Alf, on the contrary, remembers him back in the 1950s as a very hard working and straightforward Labour Party member.

[8] 'Beyond Nab End' (William Woodruff, Abacus, 2003)

Chapter 4

OXFORD

1950–1953

"Ah'll tell thee sumthin'. It's for thee own good. When tha famous, don't forget me or where tha's cum frae".

Harold Watkins to William Woodruffe in 'Beyond Nab End'

– Formidable figures – Shattering news – A miraculous achievement
– Austrian adventures – Alf's luck changes
– Called to contest the Garston constituency – An honourable but sad defeat
– Studies intensify – More foreign missions – A move to Wythenshawe
– Final examinations

Formidable figures

Even in retrospect it is difficult for Alf to say, in contemplating The Very Reverend V. J. K. Brook and Mrs Phipps, which of them was the more forbidding. But whereas contact with the head of college was rare, the presence of Mrs Phipps was a daily challenge. Her living room was full of clocks, on the walls, cabinets and tables that ticked and tolled throughout the day and night – but none agreeing with the others. She used to say, " 'em keeps me company". They also granted her the freedom of deciding the time: she could choose whichever she wanted. There was Greenwich Mean Time, but at Rookery Cottage there was only Phipps Time.

She always wore black and her demeanour was that of another and stricter era. Having spent most of her life in service, her domestic standards were quite rigid and, especially for Irene, intimidating and demoralising. Her value judgements had become as the laws of the Medes and Persians and two of her cardinal principles were obsessive prudence and thrift at its thriftiest. She kept hens and a pig in her small back garden and every bit of kitchen waste was recycled for their nutriment. She felt it was her bounden duty to warn Alf of Irene's profligacy, often prefacing her remarks with the comment, "'Er'll ruin thee". And then detailing Irene's latest extravagance, such as using a new match "every toime er loits the stove". Mrs Phipps, by contrast, boasted that a box of matches "lass's me months". She would indeed make a single match last all day. Having lit the fire in the morning, for the rest of the day she would rely on a taper of rolled up newspaper to ignite anything else. Despite this, Mrs Phipps was ever willing to partake of whatever modest cuisine Irene managed to concoct in her living room-cum-kitchen, always under her eagle eye. She was especially partial to Irene's Lancashire hot-pot and would hover around spoon in hand. Her only outing was a weekly visit to the Women's Institute on Wednesdays, something that both Alf and Irene anticipated with pleasure.

It was altogether a constrictive place, with inflexible rules. Not least when Alf wished to invite his friend Albert Hyndman, who was at Christchurch College, to tea one Sunday afternoon. When she was first approached about this Mrs Phipps was visibly excited by the prospect of two undergraduates in the house at the same time; but when she opened the door her immediate reaction was to blurt out, "Oh, we're having no blackies in here". Alf had not thought to mention that his friend came from Trinidad. With some persuasion, Albert was admitted, Mrs Phipps retired to her living room and afternoon tea was served in the parlour. Mrs Phipps had said, before she knew that Albert was black, that they could use her favourite tea set. This was displayed, like a trophy, in a cabinet, rarely if ever used. On the fatal day of Albert Hyndman's visit, however, as tea was being taken, one cup from the aged and fragile set audibly cracked. If there was anything capable of rousing Mrs Phipps' ire, it was to mark, let alone break, any part of her prized tea set. So Irene, Alf and Albert had this terrible problem of finding a way to stick it together, at least temporarily. They put it back in its place, hoping that their quick-fix would not be noticed. Fortunately, Mrs Phipps was none the wiser, and on the following morning Irene discretely took the cup into Oxford to be repaired properly.

Mrs Phipps had a long memory. She could recall, for example, throwing pigswill over Randolph Churchill during an election in the 1880's. She read the *Oxford Mail* from cover to cover, not missing a word, and the headline 'Oxford Undergraduate to Stand for Parliament' did not escape her. Like The Very Reverend Brook, she thought it sensational, but was rather more inclined to see it as an honour for her young lodger. In her book it was an achievement to win any mention in the *Oxford Mail* and Alf's standing rose vertically.

Shattering news

These were difficult days. From Irene's weekly wage of £3.00 there was £1.00 for Mrs Phipps, £1.00 to send home and £1.00 to live on until Alf's grant came through. Through that first winter they shared one navy gabardine raincoat, and even that was a hand down from Alf's brother Bill, who had had it as part of his Navy issue. Nevertheless, Alf applied himself assiduously to his studies, content that his brush with the Censor was a thing of the past. But in the seventh of the eight weeks of his first term, towards the end of November 1950, a message came inviting him to see his principal tutor, Wilfrid Knapp[1]. He conveyed the shattering news that the University's Hebdomadal Council, which comprised the head of each of the Oxford colleges, had decided that Alf would have to submit himself for examination in French the following March in addition to his existing six other subjects. So late a decision would have been devastating even for a student with a grounding in French, but for Alf, who had never studied French, it seemed that a great chasm was opening up beneath him and Wilfrid Knapp clearly thought it unlikely that he could possibly get across it. The First Public Examination, at intermediate degree level, was less than four months away, in which time he would have to get from zero to the required high standard in French. Moreover, he would be examined in the same room as undergraduates who had been to colleges such as Eton, Harrow and Rugby, all of them having been in full-time education up to the age of 18 and having studied French at least to Higher School Certificate level even before coming to Oxford.

It was obviously bad and shocking news and Alf responded that it also seemed wholly unreasonable, as he had been preparing himself in a wide range of other subjects and was now to be examined in one that he had never touched before. Taken aback, Knapp said, "You

[1] Knapp later became Dean of the college.

don't have any French?" "None at all," replied Alf, "but surely there is some right of appeal? It seems so unfair". His principal tutor told him there was no point in appealing to the Hebdomadal Council[2]. Nevertheless if Alf accepted the challenge, said Knapp, he would coach him for two hours every day, including Saturday and Sunday, without charge. Having survived Ancoats, with its staggering rate of infant mortality, and having made it to Oxford from the poorest of beginnings, there was no way Alf could turn back now. He agreed to go for it, and Knapp, whom he held in the highest regard, was true to his word.

Irene's old schoolbooks on French grammar were retrieved and these, together with *Teach Yourself French*, were his starting point. Deciding that he could get by in his other subjects with minimal extra study, Alf gave his time almost exclusively to the French examination. There were several set books, the main one being Alexis De Tocqueville's *L'Ancien Régime* (as it had been for Woodruff twelve years earlier, and despite an intervening world war). Approaching this great text in a language in which Alf was initially word blind, and to get to know it almost by heart, was a formidable undertaking. He had first to master the language in order to be able to read the required books in French at all. He could, however, read the texts in English translation and was able to discuss them from time to time with a friend of his, Geoffrey Gough, a mature student at Balliol who, though not starting from scratch, was also taking French in his First Public Examination. Meeting in the Cornmarket one morning, Gough, carrying a copy of *L'Ancien Régime*, said to Alf: "Look at this," pointing to and reading out in French De Toquerville's assertion that feudalism in France was never so much hated as when in the 1780s its final remnants were about to disappear. "That's certainly going in," said Geoffrey. They decided it was a possible response to almost any question they might have to confront on *L'Ancien Régime*.

For months on end, Alf studied little else but French and often far into the night. He would read until 5 a.m. before sleeping for a few hours. Through this, and his daily afternoon sessions with Wilfrid Knapp, Alf gained sufficient proficiency to convince his tutor that he

---

[2] St. Catherine's was represented on the Hebdomadal Council by The Very Rev. V. J. K. Brook

could have a shot at the examination. The results when they came were posted up at the University's Schools building in the High Street, during the vacation that followed the exam, and students would go to look for their names on the lists. Alf had to be back in Manchester to work and earn, as he did throughout all his vacations, so Knapp conveyed the result to him by letter. He had passed in all other subjects, but not in French.

A miraculous achievement

Knapp's letter, however, also explained that Alf had the right to a further – and final – chance to retake the French paper at the end of the following term. Again the challenge was accepted. After re-sitting the exam in late June, Knapp again contacted Alf in Manchester about the outcome. This time he telegraphed as well as wrote to Alf. He had got through – and with flying colours – something that had seemed like a miracle to them both.

This further period of intense study meant that Alf had lost another full university term doing almost nothing but French which, taking into account the handicaps his background imposed, was not easy for him to bear. Nevertheless he had now bridged the chasm and meanwhile could enjoy some respite from the grindstone of interminable French studies.

Alf spent his Oxford vacations with Irene and her family at their home in Collyhurst. She worked as a 'temp' – something new at the time – but Alf had to find vacation employment to help them make ends meet. One job during the long summer vacation of 1951 was in the market and consumer research department of the Co-operative Wholesale Society in Manchester. Under the tutelage of Fred Lambert, his role was to study consumer protection both in Britain and in other countries, particularly in Scandinavia and the United States. (It is commonly thought that innovations in retail trade have occurred through the enterprise of private firms. In fact, it was the Co-operative Movement that introduced the first supermarket to this country and which has, since its founding, taken the lead in promoting consumer protection).

The house at 10 Laverack Street to which Alf returned each evening was in a poor state of repair. In the bedroom that he and Irene shared there was a large gap between the walls and floors. For lighting, they relied on a gaslight, oil lamps and candles. There was no bathroom; in fact no bath, no hot water, just one cold tap and an outside lavatory in the back yard. Alf went to the public 'slipper' baths in Osborne Street, where if you were immersed for more than five minutes, the attendant would shout "Come out, or I'll scald you out". Collyhurst was much as Thomas Hood had depicted urban desolation:

> "No warmth, no cheerfulness, no healthful ease,
> No comfortable feel in any member
> No shade, no shine, no butterflies, no bees,
> No fruits, no flowers, no leaves, no birds
> November!"

Towards the end of Alf's second term, Irene had returned to this desolate family home. She was expecting their first child and her father's health was deteriorating fast. Later that year he died. Alf recalls that even while his father-in-law was awaiting admission to Crumpsall Hospital, his bed, which was then on the ground floor in the living room of the house, was sometimes soaked by rain from the leaking roof. "As well as being one of the most intelligent men I have known," Alf wrote later, "he was also one of the most calm, gentle and considerate. He knew that he would never return home from hospital, but was much more concerned for his wife than for himself".[3] After this, Irene stayed at home to work until her confinement and to help care for her mother who was becoming increasingly disabled.

Austrian adventures

Also in the 1951 summer vacation, at the instigation of Socialist International, Alf attended a coming together in Austria of representatives of the youth organisations of democratic socialist parties from all over the world. Even the United States and Canada, Australia and New Zealand were represented and there was a most impressive international programme of speakers. Those from Britain

---

[3] *No Feet to Drag*, Alfred Morris and Arthur Butler (Sidgwick & Jackson, 1972)

included Aneurin Bevan and Dr Shirley Summerskill (unsurprisingly the two didn't see eye to eye). There were no fewer than 150 participants from the Labour League of Youth alone, all to camp for a little over a week under canvas in the Sugar Loaf Mountains on the outskirts of Vienna. To reach the camp it was necessary to enter the Russian zone of Austria which, like Germany, was then under the control of the four occupying powers: UK, United States, France and Russia. As national chairman of the Labour League of Youth, Alf led the British delegation, travelling from London to the Austrian capital by train to Linz, and crossing from the American zone to the Russian zone at the Enns canal. Each delegate had to have a 'grey card' (a visa) arranged by Denis Healey, then International Secretary of the Labour Party (not yet a Member of Parliament). As leader, Alf had all the grey cards, which were quickly examined and approved by the Soviet border guards.

But soon after their arrival at the camp it became clear to everybody that the Russians regarded the whole event as a provocation. Indeed they commenced army manoeuvres around the camp, and often the sound of gunfire could be heard in the near distance. The siege of Berlin was not long past and it was not a happy moment in East-West relations.

On their return journey, when they reached the Enns Canal border crossing into the American zone, the train was stopped and Russian troops again went through the train. Having cursorily examined the grey cards handed over by Alf, they pointed at him and said just one peremptory word: "Ausgang", then escorted him off the train. As it pulled out of the station to cross the canal, the rest of the delegation, among whom were several future MPs, saw Alf being directed off the platform by two Russian guards, both armed with machine guns. It was an especially evocative moment for Reg Freeson and other Jewish members of the delegation, for whom the sight they were witnessing from the train's windows recalled only too vividly what this had come to mean for people escorted off trains by armed troops. For it was then only six years after the discovery of Auschwitz and Treblinka.

After the canal crossing – it was then late morning – the train's first stop was at Linz, six or seven miles further on, and from there Reg Freeson phoned Morgan Phillips, General Secretary of the Labour Party, at Transport House. In turn, Morgan quickly contacted the Foreign Office. Meanwhile, Alf was taken by the guards to their border guard room and later invited to play chess with a young Russian officer, who spoke enough English for them to converse. They gave him black cigarettes which in order to seem sociable he quarter-heartedly tried to smoke. Even more shocking, and challenging to sociability, was the Russian coffee he was given. *"If they had added poison it could not have tasted more vile."* But again their captive expressed his appreciation.

It became quite clear to Alf that strong protest had been made about his detention. They found a qualified English interpreter. It appeared that there had been contact from Vienna and that probably the officer in charge had been told to be careful with him. Eventually they released him with travel documents to return to Vienna for a new visa in order to leave the Russian Zone. Alf then returned to the station, where he asked Austrian railway staff if there was any alternative to going back to Vienna. They said that there was just one possible way, but it was very risky. A goods train would be going through to cross the canal in about a quarter of an hour. It was then pitch dark and the train would be thoroughly searched at the border, but if they could negotiate it with the driver Alf could be concealed under his cabin. Of course, if he were to be found there would probably be dire consequences. But if not, they could ask the driver to slow down after crossing the canal, allowing him to jump off in an unploughed field and make his way to Linz on foot. Alf said he would take the chance, and that's what he did, surviving the search and jumping off the train, his luggage thrown after him, reaching Linz around dawn. From there, after breakfast and a cat nap, he caught the train to London corresponding to the one he had been taken off the day before. He showed up at Transport House the following day, where there had been great concern about his well being. But according to the records, he is still back in Austria, with no stamp on his passport to say that he ever left.

His delayed return to Manchester was met with great relief all round, particularly as the birth of Cathy, their first child, was expected soon. However, Alf was back in good time to become the proud father of a beautiful daughter.

Alf's luck changes

When in Oxford, Alf was left alone with Mrs Phipps. But here too Wilfrid Knapp proved a very good friend. As an undergraduate at New College, Knapp had lived in the home of Philip Andrews[4], a distinguished academic and writer and a Fellow of both New College and Nuffield. It was just possible, Knapp told Alf, that he could get 'digs' for him with Andrews and his wife Mary at their home at 64 Sandford Road in Headington. Alf took the bus there, but when he saw the very grand, detached property he thought that this could hardly be for him. Andrews answered his knock and was obviously expecting him. He showed Alf the accommodation on the second floor: a marvellous bedroom, a spacious study, a private bathroom and a separate toilet. Breakfast would be available, and Alf could join the family for Sunday lunch and possibly also from time to time for an evening meal. Alf said that everything was fine, but he doubted if he could afford such accommodation. How much would it be? Andrews paused to draw breath and asked whether twenty-five shillings would be too much. This seemed unbelievable even in 1951. The breakfasts alone would be worth 25 shillings a week! Yet Andrews said that would be the rent, so, of course, Alf moved in. In public, Philip Andrews, whose university lectures were invariably packed, was an advocate of fairly harsh economic doctrines. But his private persona was in sharp contrast. It could not have been more kindly. Perhaps he had heard from Wilfrid Knapp something of Alf's background and the problems that he had experienced in getting to university. His new landlord's own upbringing had not been particularly grand; while not nearly so impoverished as that of Alf, it had been sufficiently down to earth for him to have gained some understanding of the barriers faced by poorer young people in search of higher education. What can

[4] Philip Walter Sawford Andrews (1914-1971), then Professor of Economics at Nuffield College. His publications included *The Life of Lord Nuffield: a study in enterprise and benevolence* (1955) and the classic *Manufacturing Business*.

certainly be said is that he was manifestly attracted by and sympathetic toward the young student. He asked Alf on which day of the week he would like to pay. This was a courtesy entirely foreign to Alf's experience. In the tough territory of Ancoats and Newton Heath, suppliers of any kind of service – not to mention the rent man – would tell you in no uncertain terms when payment was to be made. In the middle class environment of Headington, however, this was something politely to be agreed, and it was amicably settled that Alf's weekly rent would be paid on a Friday. But even this was not insisted upon. When, at the end of the first week, the new tenant tried to pay his 25 shillings, Andrews said, "Oh no, let's go out and have a drink at the Black Horse". Alf knew that in his lectures Andrews was a passionate supporter of Ricardian[5] principles, especially of the critical importance of charging people the full cost of the property, goods and services they used. Whatever else it meant this must, of course, mean the necessity, if society was not to fall apart, for landlords to charge a rent for their property that represented the full economic cost. So as they sat in the Black Horse, Alf half jocularly suggested that his host's practice was not very close to his precepts, to the point of him being a complete fraud: commending Ricardo's principles, while here was his tenant, in the best possible student accommodation in Oxford, not paying anything like an economic rent; indeed finding it hard to pay anything! "Well," responded Andrews, "this is different!" He knew full well that Alf was a member of the Labour Party and had been selected to stand at Garston, but his kindness transcended any such political divide.

The fact was that Alf had entered a new world, several steps up from anything that had gone before. Andrews, who had purchased the house from none other than Richard Crossman (who will enter these pages again in 1969), was removing the last traces of the former owner, including some murals that had not been appreciated. On Saturday evenings, friends and colleagues of Andrews, many of them highly distinguished academic figures, were invited over and Alf was often included in these fascinating soirees. He recalls with particular fondness that Mary Andrews was just as warm,

---

[5] David Ricardo (1772-1823), chiefly remembered for his theory of rent.

hospitable and generous as her husband. Sometimes, after he had been studying in the Bodleian Library all day, he would return to Sandford Road in the late evening, to find Mary waiting for him, anxious to ensure that he had something to eat.

Called to contest the Garston constituency

With this support, Alf's studies could not but go well. But, just into the first term of his second year, in the autumn of 1951, Clement Attlee, bowing to the inevitable, decided to call a General Election, to be held on 25 October, only 18 months after Labour's narrow victory in 1950. So Alf was called to Liverpool to contest the Garston constituency in a three-week campaign. He was the youngest Labour candidate in Britain.[6] This time he did not travel alone. Alf having blazed the trail, Fred Jarvis[7], a student in his final year at St Catherine's, had also been adopted to stand as Labour candidate for the Wallasey constituency, just across the Mersey from his home city of Liverpool. A year on, The Very Reverend V. J. K. Brook raised no objection to them standing in the General Election. It was understood that they would be expected to make up any lost ground upon their inevitable return (for neither had any expectation of being elected). They left on the night train together for their adoption meetings in Liverpool, travelling third class only because there was no fourth class. Their plan was that they would take off their shoes and raincoats and sleep on opposite sides of the compartment. Fred was carrying humbugs with him, a so-called 'everlasting' sweet of impenetrable hardness. Both had settled down for the night, when Alf heard an almighty crack from Fred's direction. It transpired that Fred had broken a front tooth eating a humbug and was badly shaken, less by the damage to his appearance than because he was to have his election photograph taken next morning.

A week or so later, Alf, Irene and baby Cathy travelled from Manchester to Garston for the campaign. Apart from his army demob suit, Alf had only the clothes he stood up in. The trousers from his suit had been carefully pressed and placed under the pram mattress that was then packed with essential baby clothes and

---

[6] But not the youngest candidate. The Conservative candidate Norman St John Stevas, then an undergraduate from Cambridge, was even younger (born 1929).

[7] Later to become the General Secretary of the National Union of Teachers.

nappies and the pram left in the guard's van for the hour-long journey to Lime Street. But on reclaiming the pram on arrival there, they discovered to their mutual horror that whatever else was still there, the trousers were not. To use the vernacular, they had 'walked'. Clothing was still rationed, but in any case they had no money for new clothes. Bill Sefton, Alf's election agent, came to the rescue with a pair of his trousers – they took much the same size, were immediately needed and proved a fair match. Alf, Irene and Cathy stayed with Bill and his wife Phil at their home in Station Road, Garston throughout the campaign, where all three of their guests could not have wished for a more congenial and welcoming environment.

Alf and Fred Jarvis had agreed to speak in each other's constituencies, which were not too far apart, and they fulfilled that promise. Alf particularly recalls speaking in Wallasey. In 1953, many people bought television sets to view the Coronation of Her Majesty Queen Elizabeth, but in 1951 access to such luxuries was very limited and public meetings were big occasions. Fred's chances of success in Wallasey were no rosier than Alf's in Garston. Even so, at the meeting Alf attended, Mrs 'Bessie' Braddock[8], who had been the MP for Exchange Division in the two previous parliaments, was also to speak, along with a bevy of local Labour councillors. The attendance was so huge that there was a large overflow and Alf remembers having to be lifted into the meeting and out again when he left.

It was a similar scene when Fred came to Garston, packed meetings being the order of the day, with keen public participation by way of heckling and very lively questioning. A candidate would often speak at several meetings most evenings. They had no cars at their disposal. Indeed, when Bill Sefton and Alf went to St George's Hall to pay the £150.00 deposit for his candidature, they did so by train from Garston station to the centre of Liverpool, counting out the notes and coins on the journey to make sure they had the right money! The local party could not afford a lot of literature and most of the canvassing was done by door to door visits.

---

[8] She was a Liverpool legend, 'large' in every sense of the word, first as a city councillor and then, for 24 years from 1945, as Labour MP for Liverpool Exchange. Her forthright campaigning frequently shocked the 'Establishment', but among the city's underprivileged people earned her the title 'our Bessie'. She was made a freeman of the city shortly before her death in 1970.

On the eve of poll, the candidate had to attend meetings in all the wards of the constituency. In the case of Garston this involved meetings at Childwall, Aigburth, Allerton, Hunts Cross, Speke and Garston itself. So, Bill Sefton, as Alf's agent, developed a strategy for a very strict timetable on the candidate's movements. This would be copied to everyone concerned with arrangements for the meetings. In particular it indicated the candidate's time of arrival and instructed the chairmen of meetings that he must not be kept at any meeting for more than twenty minutes. The instruction ran that when the candidate arrived, whoever was on his feet would be asked to wind up, so that he could speak, answer some questions and be off to the next meeting as rapidly as possible. This could have surprising results. When Alf arrived at Childwall, Mrs Braddock's husband, Jack, who was Labour's Council Leader in Liverpool, had just risen to speak. Almost immediately quite a row broke out. In fact all that Jack had done was to start his speech with "Com....". But that was as far as he got before there was a flurry of interruptions. "Don't you call us comrades! Not you!" The Chairman interjected to calm people down, but was cut short by spotting Alf's arrival. So that Jack never got beyond "Com", making it perhaps the shortest ever public address. "Not so much a case of dot.com," Alf now says, "but one of com.dot".

Fortunately, Alf's experience of public speaking as national chairman of the League of Labour Youth was to prove invaluable. He recalls one enormous Sunday afternoon meeting, with many thousands of people, at the Liverpool Stadium, a venue normally used for boxing. Even that great venue was full, with an overflow, to hear three speakers: a young parliamentarian called Harold Wilson, who had been President of the Board of Trade in the outgoing government, Aneurin Bevan, as the main speaker, and a fresh-faced young student from Oxford. Alf especially remembers one heckler. This man had a towel around his neck as though he was a leftover from the last fight there, shouting something that was incomprehensible to those on the platform. Turning to him, Bevan's response was to say, "And Mademoiselle from Armentieres to you!". Richard Cobden famously said that the small meeting was to inform, the big meeting to excite. And this was a monster example of the truth of the latter part of that dictum, as it was when Alf also spoke with Attlee when he came to Liverpool two nights before polling day and addressed another huge meeting at St George's Hall.

Throughout the campaign, Bill Sefton was a guide and an inspiration. He told Alf that the best way to find out about the problems and needs of working people in Liverpool would be for him to arrange for Alf to sit in with Mrs Braddock at her weekly advice bureaux, held every Sunday morning. Alf remembers her as "a transparently honest and frank person in her politics". She would always make it clear that she could only deal with Parliamentary matters such as pensions and national insurance, not local issues like housing. "Some MPs try to give the impression that they can deal more effectively with housing problems than their local councils, which doesn't do relationships with them much good". It was a huge privilege for Labour's youngest candidate to be sitting with Mrs Braddock, a very seasoned Member of Parliament, and he learned a very great deal from her. She and Alf became very close, and he could always count on her support in all the elections he contested during her lifetime.

Bill had also arranged for Alf to speak to the Liverpool Trades and Labour Council, who had invited all the Labour candidates selected to stand for Merseyside constituencies to come in turn to their meetings. These meetings had the reputation of being 'never-ending' affairs that could go on well into the night. Alf was still on vacation when his turn came up in September and he had to be back in Manchester to work on the following day. The chairman reassured him that he was down as number three on the agenda, after apologies for absence and the minutes of the previous meeting, so that he could be away by 9 p.m. at the latest. However, when they came to the minutes, they had a complete re-run of the last meeting, with people challenging every syllable, dot and comma of exactly what they had said, minute by minute. Whereas it is normal in many organisations for the minutes to be disposed of quickly, often being approved as a formality, this was not acceptable there, where disputes went on, and on, and on. Alf missed the last train, and ended up walking to Bill's home.

Bill Sefton worked at the 'bobbin' works at Garston, close by his home. He started work at half-past-five in the morning, but then had a half-hour break when he came home for breakfast. The Labour Party HQ was in his cellar, replete with an in-tray, an out-tray and a waste paper basket. Religion was then a particularly divisive issue in Liverpool. In some respects it was a second Belfast, with ingrained enmity between Protestant and Catholic. An annual Orange Day march almost invariably finished up with fighting. There was even a Protestant Party, with something like seventeen Protestant councillors on the Liverpool City Council, one of them – Reverend Henderson – representing a Garston ward. Bill cautioned Alf at the beginning of the campaign that whatever else happened they must not get involved in the sectarian divide. One day, during one of his breakfast breaks, Bill looked at the waste paper basket (as all great generals will) and spotted a letter from Archbishop Heenan, then Roman Catholic Archbishop of Liverpool (and later, of course, of Westminster) inviting groups of candidates and agents from each party to see him at his residence to discuss issues of importance. Alf, following Bill's dictum, had dutifully filed the letter. "No," Bill told him, "that's not religion, that's politics. We've got to go there".

The visit was arranged, and upon their arrival the Archbishop's secretary approached Alf and asked him what he would like to drink. Bearing in mind that Bill Sefton was a strict teetotaller, Alf replied, "could I have a soft drink?" Bill turned to Alf and whispered, "You've just lost us 5,000 votes. They don't drink that sort of stuff here". The Monsignor returned with lemonade, just as Bill was explaining the gravity of Alf's *faux-pas*, and said to Bill, "Would you like something different?" "Yes," replied teetotaller Bill, "I'd like a large Hennessey with ice and soda", which he later quietly swapped with Alf's lemonade.

Sir Victor Raikes was Garston's Conservative Member of Parliament, while Lionel Blease, a Professor of History at Liverpool University, had been selected to stand for the Liberals. Blease, however, had to pull out during the campaign and the Liberals called a membership meeting to question the other two candidates and then advise their supporters for whom they should vote. They opted for Alf. Nor did Alf lack support from his own Labour roots. One of the things he found very moving was that his old friends from Clayton, including Arthur Stevenson and Alf Logan, came regularly by charabanc from Manchester to encourage him.

The *Liverpool Echo* represented the contest as one between "youth and experience"[9]. Alf's message beneath this headline, however, was to invite the electorate to choose between war and peace. On 6 October, the USSR had admitted exploding an atomic bomb and two days later Egypt had denounced the Anglo-Egyptian Treaty of 1936. It was little more than six years after the end of the Second World War and peace was a precious commodity. Alf wrote: "As a young person, I have a vested interest in peace, for it is youth that suffers first in the event of war... the return of a Tory Government would gravely increase the risk of war... the Tory reaction in a crisis is to threaten force; but the people of this city would rightly shudder at the prospect of another war. Labour will ensure that reason, not force, is used in solving international problems".

He could also point to an unprecedented period of social change since 1945: "Labour has the finest record of service to the people of any Government in our history. Mass unemployment is banished. Under Labour, even local unemployment will soon be unknown. We have the finest social services in the world. The health and welfare of our people have never been better. Our housing problem has been tackled humanely and successfully". He therefore urged the voters of Garston: "For the continuance of peace and a standard of values based on human needs, it is absolutely necessary to vote Labour on October 25".

An honourable but sad defeat

80 per cent of the electorate turned out on polling day. It is tempting to say 'remarkably', except that in the fifties this was by no means remarkable. Alf gained 34.8 per cent (19,025) of the vote, against his opponent's 65.2 per cent (35,650). Alf could reflect on an exciting campaign and a strong showing. It had been anything but a fruitless exercise, rather an experience from which he gained enormously and which had brought him to a much closer understanding of the realities of political life than any previous Oxford undergraduate

---

[9] 17 October 1951.

could ever hope to have had. The fact that he had not been elected came as no surprise; indeed, personal success would have been disastrous to his progress at St Catherine's. Nevertheless, he returned to Oxford disconsolate that Labour, in spite of recording the biggest total vote ever achieved by any party, had narrowly failed to retain office.[10] The beacon of democratic socialism, which had shone so brightly after the six years of war, had been dimmed, and Winston Churchill would now form the next government.

Studies intensify

This was no time, however, for prolonged depression. The rest of his degree course awaited him at Oxford and three weeks' absence had to be made up. The course was very demanding and nothing was more challenging than Oxford's way of defining modern history. Usage there ruled that it started in 55BC! The first of the three periods into which it was divided went through to 1307, the second on to 1660 and the third to 1914 (not 1939 as it became later). Other papers required specialist knowledge of constitutional documents over a lengthy period of British history and of World history (in Alf's case from 1870–1939). Among other papers there was one on historiography and examinees also had to offer a special subject. The choice was wide-ranging and included John O'Gaunt, the Cromwellian period and the American Civil War. The subject Alf selected was the financial and economic policy of the Peel administration from 1841–1846, a period in which he was already deeply interested, and which was to become increasingly important to him in the world of politics.

His tutor for this special subject was Asa Briggs, the author of *Eminent Victorians*, who was a foremost authority on the 1840's. There were to be two papers on the special subject, and the student would be examined meticulously on everything of significance that happened, not least on every statute enacted in the five years. The social history of the period was to prove integral to Alf's political thinking. Engels' *The Condition of the Working Class in England* was a primary text, linking directly with Ancoats, while the Chartist movement, which between 1840–1848 had taken on the character of

---

[10] The Conservative majority over Labour was 26, and 17 over all other parties combined.

a socialistic crusade, also featured prominently in Alf's studies. The modern Co-operative movement, with which Alf was to be closely associated, was another product of the 1840s with the opening of the first co-operative store in Rochdale in 1844. The same period also spawned two great and inspirational legislative reforms that connected closely with Alf's political ideals. One was the Public Health Act 1848, inspired by the studies of Sir Edwin Chadwick[11]. Alf firmly believes that Chadwick's achievements in improving public health exceeded those that most widely-known politicians could hope to achieve in any field. He fearlessly took on the mill owners, like the widely admired John Bright, Rochdale's MP, whose involvement in cotton manufacturing made him hostile to the proposed legislation. A parliamentarian of the time much respected by Alf was John Fielden, a Radical MP who was elected to represent Oldham from 1832 to 1847. Himself a partner in his family's cotton mill in Todmorden, on the Yorkshire and Lancashire borders, Fielden nevertheless strenuously supported the Ten Hours Bill to limit the length of time that children and women could be required to work in any factory. The enactment of this reform, first espoused by Lord Ashley in 1833, was greatly protracted. It was eventually rejected in 1846, but carried by a majority of 63 in the following year. Alf finds parallels with the way that his Civil Rights (Disabled Persons) Bill was systematically obstructed over a period of four years (1991–95) before becoming the basis for the Disability Discrimination Act and the Disability Rights Commission.

More foreign missions

In the 1952 summer vacation, as well as being by then national chairman of the Labour League of Youth, Alf was elected as British Labour's nominee for election to the Bureau (executive committee) of the International Union of Socialist Youth (IUSY). He attended its Copenhagen Congress and was elected both to the Bureau and as chairman of the control commission that oversaw the International's finances. The secretary was Per Haekkerup, who later became

---

[11] Edwin Chadwick KCB (1800–1890) was born near Manchester. Appalled by the insanitary and degrading living conditions of working people, his vigorous and determined reports on both the Poor Law and public health, prompted, despite entrenched opposition, the Poor Law Amendment Act 1834, the Public Health Act 1848 and the Nuisances Removal and Diseases Prevention Act 1848. His three-volume report *Survey into the Sanitary Condition of the Labouring Classes in Great Britain* (1842) was a major catalyst for reform.

Minister for Foreign Affairs in Denmark. Other members included Franz Molinar from the Netherlands, who later became a distinguished EEC official; Peter Strasser who (although sadly he did not live for very long) became Foreign Secretary of Austria; and Heinz Westphal, who was to become Speaker of the Bundestag. His father Max Westphal, an honoured leader of the Labour movement in Germany, was executed almost immediately after Hitler's coming to power. Another representative was Francisco Matteotti, who was to become a Member of the Italian Parliament. He was the son of Giacomo Matteotti, leader of the Italian Socialist Party and another honoured name, whose verbal attacks on Mussolini are thought to have prompted his murder in 1924. Martinez Dazi, who represented Spanish Socialist Youth in Exile on the Bureau, was under sentence of death in Franco Spain and lived in France. Finally there was Franz Nilsson, a brilliant young socialist and editor in Stockholm of Sweden's leading social democratic paper. At one meeting of the Bureau, Alf travelled from London with Kofi Baku who was from Ghana and in his late twenties. He edited the *Accra Evening News* and was in Europe to address the Bureau. His political activities in Ghana later cost him his life at the hands of the military there.

Because Alf chaired the Control Commission of IUSY he was nominated by the Bureau to represent the IUSY as an observer at meetings in Strasbourg of the Council of Europe. He was also co-opted onto the Council of the Socialist International.

In the same year, as the representative of British Labour youth, Alf was also invited by the SPD in Germany – then under four power control – to speak at a torchlight rally in Hamburg. The city was still unrecognisable to people who had known it before the war – such had been the scale of Allied bombing in the final stages of the conflict. At the rally Alf spoke in German, in which language he was by no means fluent. But he knew enough for the occasion and it was carefully rehearsed, including a warning to avoid the word 'freundschaft' (friendship), because it had been commandeered by the Communist Party as their form of greeting. Tens of thousands of young people walking slowly past rejoiced to hear simply stated greetings from the British Labour movement.

A move to Wythenshawe

During his vacations in 1952, Alf continued to be based at Irene's home in Collyhurst. After his splendid accommodation in Oxford, this was just about as downwardly mobile as anyone could go. Not that it concerned Alf or diverted him from the tasks on hand, but they constantly had to do minor repairs. Whenever the question of major repairs was raised with the landlord he always reacted as though they were joking. Once again, however, a kindly fate stepped in. Just as had happened in Ancoats, eighteen years earlier, the house at 10 Laverack Street came under a slum clearance order. In 1953, a year after the death of her husband, Irene's mother was made the tenant of a brand-new ground floor flat at 94 Painswick Road, Wythenshawe on the southernmost edge of the city. In contrast to Collyhurst it was a green and pleasant land and the flat had more living room than Irene's family had ever known. There was a kitchen and bathroom, three bedrooms off a long lobby and a good-sized living room with a balcony and French window that overlooked open country as far as the eye could see. It was the first time that Irene's family – she was then 24 – had lived in a home with electricity, a bathroom, inside toilet and hot water. For her mother, the change was at first too much to take in. "Who else will be living here?" she asked, and was amazed to be told that it was all theirs. The offer of a council flat had had nothing to do with her severe disability. And even in this far more pleasant environment her problems were not at an end. Appliances such as ramps, handrails and a hoist to help her in and out of the bath were unthought of. If she wanted a bath, Alf and Irene had to lift her in an out. They had only a bike between them, so that her world was limited to the distance they could push her wheelchair. There were very few social buildings Esther Jones could ever hope to enter and even churchgoing had become too difficult. They attempted a family holiday only once. For her it proved to be not so much a holiday as a test of endurance. Her problems, of which Alf was acutely conscious, were to have a profound influence on his thinking when, sixteen years later, he won the opportunity to introduce his Chronically Sick and Disabled Persons Bill.

For Alf the move to Wythenshawe was a return journey, for it was there that he had been despatched when his father died in 1935. His Uncle Sam and Aunt Edith had moved there from Hulme, to a bungalow at Hollyhedge Road in the Benchill area. To give Alf's mother some breathing space immediately after her bereavement, they had volunteered to take one of the children, and young Alf was chosen. He remembers being taken from Newton Heath to Piccadilly in the centre of Manchester, and then by tram as far south as Barlow Moor Road, beyond which there was only horse-drawn transport. The Council would eventually expand housing in Wythenshawe to take more and more people out of Hulme, Moss Side, Ancoats and Miles Platting, but at that time it was relatively undeveloped and attracted very few visitors. It seemed to Alf that he was in another world, as indeed he was.

Uncle Sam had a steel plate in his head as a result of injuries in the Great War. Remarkably, he could take this out, so that you could see inside, something that Alf found weirdly fascinating as a young child. The stay could not have lasted more than a few days for Alf remembers returning home to Newton Heath, wearing a little black coat, on the morning of the funeral. Such was his introduction to Wythenshawe, which he would later represent in the House of Commons for thirty-three years.

Final examinations

Later in 1953, Alf took his finals. Unlike other universities, there were no examinations at Oxford between the end of the undergraduate's first year and the conclusion of the degree course two years later. It was widely seen as a cruel system. There was no thesis, but the examinations in the special subject were extremely rigorous. In every subject it wasn't enough to have a retentive memory for facts, you were also judged on your interpretation of events and their significance. Alf recalls that he took 13 or 14 three-hour papers in final 'schools' over ten days or so, one after another. There was very little time in between for reading, students were expected to be comprehensively ready to be examined in everything they had been studying. The ink was dry on the last paper by mid-June, and Alf returned to Manchester to await the results.

1956: Alf receiving his MA degree. Flanked by his mother Jessie and sister Ivy.

1951: Filey. Aneurin Bevan speaking to an audience of more than 1,800 Labour youth. Far left: Alf (co-speaker as Chairman of the National Committee of the Labour League of Youth), Mark Hewittson (John Prescott's predecessor as MP for Hull) and Morgan Phillips. On the right: Eirene White, Tom Driberg, Edwin Gooch, Barbara Castle and Ian Mikardo.

1950: Oxford. Left to right: Harry Holland, Alf, Harold Smith, Stan Carter, all Manchester pals.

30 September 1950: Alf and Irene's wedding day.

October 1951: Labour Party Conference, Scarborough, shortly before the General Election. From left: Edwin Gooch, Hugh Dalton, Alf, as national chairman of the Labour League of Youth, Herbert Morrison, Clement Attlee, Morgan Phillips, Alice Bacon, Harry Earnshaw and Edith Summerskill.

Chapter 5

PRELUDE TO PARLIAMENT

1953–1964

"Let us, then, be up and doing,
With a heart for any fate;
Still achieving, still pursuing,
Learn to labour and to wait".

Henry Wadsworth Longfellow, The Song of Hiawatha.

– A career in education? – Chosen as parliamentary candidate for Wythenshawe
– General Election 1959 – Walter Citrine – General Election 1964

A career in education

The results came through from Oxford in July 1953. The boy from Ancoats had become a Bachelor of Arts (Oxon). Keen to build on this achievement, Alf immediately embarked on a one-year post-graduate course at Manchester University towards a Diploma in Education. Philip Andrews, who had many influential friends, had asked him if he would welcome a recommendation to the *Manchester Guardian*. He knew the editor well and felt that Alf could soon become a leader writer. But Alf felt he would rather teach and that there would be more certainty in doing so. Norman Morris (not a relative), one of his postgraduate lecturers, arranged for him to gain some experience of teaching English and history at Manchester Grammar School. Dr Eric (later Lord) James, the High Master, was another friend of Philip Andrews and, like him, hailed from Southampton.[1] It was a deeply formative experience from which Alf learned much and which, though he did not know it at the time, was to ease his introduction into the House of Commons.

In his post-graduate year, as well as studying during the day, Alf gave a series of evening university extension lectures on English social history, a remarkable feature of which was that one of his

[1] In later years, Alf, as Minister for Disabled People, appointed Eric to chair the Personal Social Services Council, which worked to improve the well-being of disabled people and carers.

mature students was none other than Frank Welburn, the Company Secretary who had taken him on at Wilson's Brewery in 1942.

Alf went on to teach, again with help from Norman Morris, in entirely different settings at Manchester's Old Moat secondary modern school and at Baguley Hall Junior School in Wythenshawe. It was at Old Moat that he first taught children with what we now call 'learning difficulties' and he especially remembers an 11–year-old boy called Sam. He had asked the class to write down an extract from an English text he had been talking to them about. After those around him had begun to write, Sam raised his hand and came to Alf's desk, making horizontal movements and asking, "Sir, do you write dis way or dat?". Sam sat with his teacher and they talked about extra help he would need. He was, however, a very generous boy. One day, after the lunch-break, Alf found a lovely bunch of flowers on his desk. He was told it was thought Sam had put them there. Soon afterwards, however, there was an angry commotion outside in the corridor. The head teacher was there with a furious group of women. After staring, then glaring, through the classroom window, in they came, absolutely livid and demanding to know just where the flowers had come from. Further enquiries revealed that it was indeed the kind-hearted Sam. He had picked, from every garden he'd passed on his way back to school, the biggest, best, most beautiful and colourful blooms he could find for his teacher. Grasping the situation, Alf then apologised. This was something quite different from teaching at Manchester Grammar School and the need to help boys like Sam was ever to be a strong priority for him as a Member of Parliament.

After gaining his Diploma in Education, Alf also taught at St Columba's, a Catholic secondary school, at the suggestion of Father Murphy, the chairman of its governors and the priest at St John's Church in Wythenshawe. It was very unusual for anyone not of that faith to be welcomed into the school as a trainee teacher, but the experience was to prove a happy one. Tommy Fitzpatrick, the headmaster, was a brilliant practitioner in teaching children with special educational needs (then called 'handicapped' or 'backward'), and Alf counts him as one of the people who had a profound effect on his thinking about education and disability.

By this time, Alf and Irene had two children. His income as a teacher and university extension lecturer was not large and, while he enjoyed doing both, his young family was financially very much at the margin, living then in Woodhouse Park with Irene's mother as the tenant. In 1956 Alf applied for a job with the then Central Electricity Authority advertised in the *New Statesman*. Lord Citrine, who as Walter Citrine had been General Secretary of the TUC at the time of the General Strike in 1926 and now chaired the CEA, presided over the selection panel. They were making six regional appointments and, contrary to his expectation, Alf gained one of them, becoming at a stroke Assistant Secretary of the industry's District Joint Advisory Councils for the North West & Merseyside and North Wales. A car went with the job and his salary almost doubled, making things much easier. It was quite a memorable moment for the whole of Painswick Road when a little green Ford Anglia – TNB 135 – was parked outside no. 94! Alf had to learn to drive in a hurry and gained his driving licence in June 1956 with the help of his brother John.

Having a car gave Alf the chance to take his mother beyond the confines of Manchester and the first thing he did was to take her to Liverpool, her husband's birthplace. He had started life in Fazakerley, but Jessie was keen also to go to New Brighton, across the Mersey, where she could sit and overlook the sea.

The next trip was more adventurous. Alf was invited to go to Oxford to receive his MA. It was a purely ceremonial occasion, one that he would not normally even have thought of attending, but now, with his own car, it gave him the opportunity to take his mother and sister Ivy to the world-famous university city. Jessie had reservations about visiting the unknown territory of the deep south, and Ivy, who had been badly shaken by being in the centre of Manchester during the *blitzkrieg* of December 1940, was also very nervous about travel. Nevertheless she saw it as important to encourage and be with her mother to make it a family occasion to remember.

Chosen to stand as the parliamentary candidate for Wythenshawe

Within a year of leaving Oxford, Alf was short-listed for adoption as Labour's prospective parliamentary candidate for the Gorton constituency of Manchester. By the narrowest of margins the seat went to the far left candidate Konni Zilliacus,[2] a choice determined by his having been able to offer to finance the appointment of a full-time constituency agent; but after the election of May 1955 Alf's name was put forward for the Wythenshawe constituency, where he lived. While it had always been held by the Conservatives, the seat was thought winnable, and the Manchester & Salford Co-operative Society (M&S) was interested in nominating for the Labour candidature. To stand as a Co-operatively-sponsored candidate, you had to be on the parliamentary panel of the Co-operative Party nationally. Alf was put forward for the panel by the M&S, together with Manchester Councillor Walter Frost, then a member of the M&S board of directors and later its chairman. After travelling to London to be interviewed by Jack Bailey, the distinguished General Secretary of the Co-operative Party and Alderman Alf Ballard, its chairman, who was then Leader of Sheffield City Council, both Alf and Walter were admitted to the panel, but it was Alf who was finally chosen in December 1955 as the prospective 'Labour and Co-operative' parliamentary candidate for Wythenshawe. To be chosen to stand for his own 'native heath' and thus became 'a prophet in his own country' was highly unusual. Many politicians who have already contested one parliamentary election – as he had done in 1951 – then wait for a safe seat to become vacant in a constituency for which they might be considered or, as often happens, more now than then, get 'parachuted' into by party officials. So for him to stand in Wythenshawe, a constituency that had always been Conservative, was also unusual and certainly not the best career move. But he still feels it was the right thing to do, for all too few Members of Parliament represent the people among whom they live.

In the 1930s, Wythenshawe, on the southern tip of Manchester, had begun as a number of small settlements in the Benchill and Royal Oak localities there, but was much expanded in the 1950s to rehouse

[2] Who won the seat for Labour in the election of May 1955, but only by a slender majority of 300 votes

more and more families from Manchester's inner-city slums. The constituency straddled the border with Cheshire. As well as Wythenshawe's council estates – described by the city's planners as a 'garden city' – it included some of Manchester's wealthiest suburbs and pleasant villages in North Cheshire, where even parish councillors were generally of the bluest of hues.

The Wythenshawe estates owed their existence to the beneficence of Lord and Lady Simon, who donated land in the Wythenshawe area to Manchester Corporation to build houses for rent to re-house people from the city's slums. Lord Simon was later to become influential, with Bertrand Russell, in pressing the idea of an international 'non-nuclear club'. Lady (Sheena) Simon was very active in the Labour Party and was in fact one of the selection panel that chose Alf to contest Wythenshawe in 1955. She had been a city alderman for many years, had chaired the council's education committee and was recognised nationally as a leading and formidable pioneer of comprehensive education.

Her principal concern was to promote equality of educational opportunity; and soon after Alf's selection she was invited to speak in a Manchester University Union debate on a motion that equality of opportunity is in practice unrealistic. Knowing of Alf's background and current involvement in education, she asked him to join her in opposing the motion. Their case was a remarkable portent of Alf's future reforms. They argued that notwithstanding any difficulty there might be in defining equality of opportunity objectively and to everyone's total satisfaction, it was not difficult to point to manifest obstacles to equal opportunities, which clearly stood in their way. For example, the privilege of being able to buy the best education was clearly antagonistic to equality of opportunity by any definition. Another barrier was the grave lack of appropriate provision for severely disabled children.

Alf was convinced that if a child has a severe disability, he or she needs extra help to overcome its handicapping effects to compete on equal terms with other children. "If you want disabled children to be involved in a photo finish with other children of the same ability," he said, "you cannot submit them to a level start". Yet as things were then, much apart from reducing the handicapping effects of disability, the system multiplied them. One of the clearest examples of the denial of equal opportunities, he said, was the added educational deprivation inflicted on disabled children by segregating them from educational opportunities available to children generally. The task of any teacher, Alf argued, is to close the gap between a child's innate ability and his or her attainment. Education at its best was thus about providing all children with opportunities to enable them to perform in keeping with their abilities.

Alf soon found that there were some distinct challenges in living in the constituency. Even as a parliamentary candidate he ran weekly advice bureaux, but outside his working hours he was accessible either where he lived or by telephone and was approached constantly. He particularly recalls a visit from schoolteacher friend Bill Holland, a party member, calling while he was papering the ceiling, precariously holding a length of pasted paper in place with a broom. The result of Bill's visit was that the whole lot slowly unpeeled, came down and festooned itself on Alf's head.

But perhaps the most intrusive episode of all happened one night while Alf was in the bath after a long day's work. Irene answered a knock on the door, to find Bill Dyke, a member and active worker in the local Labour Party, standing outside. Irene explained that Alf was in the bath, but Bill said that there was a problem he would like to talk to him about and that he knew Alf wouldn't mind. Before Irene knew it, Bill was down the lobby, putting his head round the bathroom door. Having seated himself on the corner of the bath, he began explaining the problem, expecting Alf to take note. Helped by Irene with hand towel, pencil and paper, Alf finished up trying to write the details on a pad that became soggier by the minute. At the time, Bill's problem seemed more and more trivial than his own predicament, as Bill stayed and stayed until the water became decidedly chilly, before Irene succeeded in luring Bill away with tea and toast, allowing the shivering bather to escape to the bedroom from his now cold bath!

It was Alf's patience and sociability that helped gradually to win him the affection and respect of local people. They also recognised his integrity and kindness and the genuineness of his political ideals: qualities that then as now could not be taken for granted in politicians. Through the second half of the 50s, he and his supporters in Wythenshawe built up a solid base of trust. His mother Jessie had cause to be proud of her son, as he of her, and it was a matter of profound sadness when in February 1959 she died. Alf was still working for the Central Electricity Authority, but every Sunday he, Irene and the children travelled across the city from Wythenshawe to Newton Heath to have tea with her and the rest of the family. Two days after one such visit Alf suddenly became very anxious and felt that he must go to see her again. Something told him that she was not well. *"There was nothing other-worldly about it. I just realised that something about her on the previous Sunday had worried me, but had filtered through to me only gradually. I left my office in Sale and drove straight over to Newton Heath. When I arrived she was on oxygen, and died within half an hour."*

General Election 1959

Alf's mother could never be forgotten, but the same year brought the calling of a General Election. *The Manchester Evening News* – which then had Harold Evans on its reporting staff – commented that "hardly a corner of Wythenshawe would look out of place in a Conservative party political broadcast – new schools, smokeless factories, trim lawns, new old people's bungalows, new maternity clinics".[3] Alf, by contrast, was reported as pointing out that many of his neighbours were describing it as "a housing camp, without a civic centre and without a soul".

Politically, the constituency was a patchwork of contrasting support and hostility. Didsbury, for example, home to some of the richest people in the conurbation and pretty solidly Conservative, was a very much more prosperous part of Manchester than Wythenshawe itself and the Tory candidate there once had a five-to-one majority in a 92 per cent poll – an almost Muscovite turnout! Whereas in Alf's strongholds, such as Woodhouse Park, he not so much doorstepped voters as joined them for a cup of tea.

[3] 26 September 1959

But the Conservative and Labour candidates were not the only contestants. Originally, there was a strong challenge from the Liberals, whose candidate was campaigning quite vigorously and a force to be reckoned with. He came from a distinguished Manchester family, one of whose members, Oliver Heywood, is to this day remembered by a statue in Albert Square. It came as a surprise, therefore, when Alf's agent was approached by the Association of Jewish Ex-servicemen (AJEX), for a meeting about him. What they reported was that the Liberal candidate had until recently actively supported Oswald Mosley's black-shirted British Union of Fascists. Alf responded that if they could produce evidence he would raise it with Jo Grimond, the Liberal leader. The upshot was that Heywood had to withdraw. In Manchester, where Liberals were traditionally more likely to vote Tory than Labour in the absence of a Liberal candidate, this would almost certainly benefit the Conservatives. Alf knew all this just as well as other activists, but accepted the validity of AJEX's objection.

Heywood's departure left a straight fight between Alf and the incumbent Conservative candidate, Mrs Evelyn Hill. The seat was one that the Labour Party had never won, and Mrs Hill had a number of distinct advantages. Like Alf, she lived in the constituency, in her case in Didsbury, and had been the local MP since 1950, having last been returned in 1955 with a majority of 2,822. Having also been a respected Alderman she enjoyed a substantial popular following. Her line, which was certainly true around where she lived, was that the constituency "was 96,000 people for whom life had never been so good, and was getting better".[4]

Alf, however, also had considerable personal popularity and not merely because he lived locally. "Many of the old folk," commented the *Manchester Evening News*,[5] "whose pension problems are almost his daily work, see the friendly ex-school teacher as more of a Good Samaritan than a politician". It was said that since his adoption in 1955 he and his supporters had "conscientiously nursed the constituency".

---

[4] *Ibid.*
[5] *Ibid.*

Alf remembers with affection many of the local stalwarts who worked with him – day in, day out – to wrest the seat from the Conservatives. They were as much a fellowship as a political grouping, conspicuous for good humour but also a close-knit and dedicated team bent on social progress through a change in political representation. He specially remembers David Graham, active in the National Union of Railwaymen and a local magistrate, who chaired the Wythenshawe Constituency Labour Party, and his agent Jim Stuart-Cole, both of them dedicated in their support. Councillors Charlie Hall, Lloyd Griffiths, Ken Collis and Harry Reid were other steadfast supporters. It was Harry Reid who, when asked what his policy would be as the newly appointed chair of the City Council's Art Galleries Committee, responded "A Rubens in every council house". His wife tartly commented, "I'd be happy if he would just cut the grass, never mind about Rubens. He only ever goes out to snip a bit off if it appears above the window sill". Ken Collis, soon to become Lord Mayor of Manchester, typified the prodigious capacity for hard work among Alf's team. Quite apart from his council and election work, he had a little shop and a stall on the local market and was invariably up with the lark to go to Manchester's Smithfield Market for green groceries, fresh fruit and plants. Yet he and his wife Pat were often out canvassing for votes until nine in the evening. And come polling day, Ken, minus his mayoral chain, was at Alf's central committee rooms, making tea and 'bacon butties' and organising leafleting and canvassing.

Charlie Hall was quite badly hearing-impaired and heavily dependent on a powerful hearing aid. He would sometimes say to Alf, "I don't see how that motion was carried at all". To which Alf responded, "Isn't the truth, Charlie, that you always switch off if you don't like the speaker, or what he's saying, and switch on again when you like a speaker and know his views?"

Annie Shepherd, Harold Brown, Eddie McCulley and Ellen and 'Jock' Cooper are also fondly remembered, as are Sheila and Councillor Tony Burns (later to become Alf's longest-serving agent and abiding friend). Annie, like Charlie Hall, was an institution, having been in Wythenshawe Labour Party since its inception. Their great hope in life had always been that one day Labour would win the Wythenshawe seat.

Alf was also helped in that objective by the addition since the 1955 election of nearly 5,000 extra voters from Manchester's inner city areas, most of them people from localities like Ardwick, Beswick, Hulme, Gorton, New Cross and Chorlton-on-Medlock, with a long tradition of Labour support and much more likely to vote for Alf than for Mrs Hill.

Important too was the unflagging support of the formidable Bessie Braddock, *"the no-nonsense 'leading lady' of Liverpool's Labour movement"*, who spoke for Alf at no fewer than fourteen meetings all over Wythenshawe in 1959. Memorably, during the campaign, Bessie and her husband Jack had tea and cakes with Alf and Irene at their council flat in Woodhouse Park. Irene tells the story: "We had very little furniture and few other worldly goods, but neighbours from the nine flats that comprised our block helped out by bringing their best bits and pieces in honour of their guests, and out of respect for Bessie, a woman whom they greatly admired. All went well until the middle of the visit, when Bessie and Jack were sipping their tea. Our first-born, Cathy, then eight years old, came in from playing with other children in the block and looking round piped up, 'Mam, where did you get all this posh furniture from?' And then we all fell about laughing and Alf said it served me right for pretending to be what I wasn't!"

Another factor was television. The 1959 election campaign was only the second to reach voters through the screens in their living rooms. The commercial station Granada TV achieved a 'first' by deciding to give two minutes broadcasting time to all candidates in their catchment area, provided that every candidate for the seat took part. Most constituencies were covered in this way and Alf and Evelyn Hill each took their two minutes. Alf recalls standing in line with other candidates in the Manchester studio, awaiting his turn. When a candidate reached the head of the queue, he or she would sit in a chair and without further ado speak to the camera for two minutes. So those immediately behind the speakers could clearly hear what their opponents were saying. *"Granada was beside itself to keep strictly to the provisions of the Representation of the People Act 1949, and it was made clear that the allotted time could not be exceeded, on pain of being eased off camera."* Alf and Evelyn were immediately behind Leslie

Lever, a former Lord Mayor of Manchester, and his Conservative opponent Harry Sharp, the candidates for another Manchester constituency. Leslie went first and introduced himself as the Member of Parliament for Ardwick. Since 1950, he said, he had worked tirelessly to help everybody there regardless of their politics. "I don't mind if they're Liberals, Conservatives or Labour. All I want to do is to serve all my constituents". And he went on in this vein until the 120 seconds had long gone. Whereupon, Harry Sharp nudged Leslie off camera and took over. "The first thing I want to say," Harry began, "is that he is the Socialist candidate. He's not everybody's candidate. He's the Socialist candidate for the Ardwick constituency. I am the Conservative candidate. My people and many thousands of others no longer want to be represented by him. They want a man who stands in his true colours". And so on, until Harry too had to be pushed off. That was the very odd cue for Alf's maiden speech on television!

The election was, however, almost certainly decided not locally but nationally, not least by the avuncular charisma of the incumbent prime minister, Harold Macmillan, whose famous remark that "most of our people have never had it so good"[6] resonated among people who, in a consumer boom, were indeed enjoying unaccustomed affluence. In this climate, Wythenshawe was one of the key marginals. Its importance was certainly recognised by Hugh Gaitskell. On 1 October, in a speech at Manchester's Albert Hall, he declared "we must hold every seat we have – and win at the very least Wythenshawe and Blackley. This is our opportunity and we must grasp it". On the same occasion, Labour MP Frank Allaun was bold enough to claim, "We've got the Tories on the run".

The reality was different. There was dissension in the Labour ranks, even opposition in some quarters to Hugh Gaitskell's leadership of the party. An organisation called 'Victory for Socialism' had been formed which to some appeared to prefer losing the 1959 election rather than having Gaitskell as Prime Minister.[7] The party was also divided over the issue of nuclear disarmament, with the CND – backed by scores of Labour candidates at the election – campaigning

[6] First used in a speech at Bedford, 20 July 1957.
[7] *Life and Labour* (Michael Stewart, Sidgwick and Jackson, 1980, p.109).

vigorously for Britain to abandon nuclear weapons, a policy that would inevitably have involved leaving the NATO alliance. Such was the disunity that the election was, for Labour, "a drab, unhappy contest".[8] Alf believes that another difficulty was that Labour's manifesto pledges were widely seen as short on credibility. It was difficult to understand how their programmes for huge increases in public spending, not least on health and social security, could be delivered without increasing taxation, on which the manifesto was silent. People reasoned that you could have stable taxation or more expenditure on improved services, but not both. Increasingly, as polling day drew near, Labour was very much on the defensive, Gaitskell arguing that the increased resources needed to improve social provision as the Labour Government of 1945–51 had done could be found by increasing productivity, without increasing taxation. More people would be in work under Labour, he said, and reducing unemployment would increase the tax intake.

Voters were not convinced. From a good start when the campaign began, support was now ebbing away. Nevertheless, Alf's supporters still felt that they could win Wythenshawe. Unlike the contest at Garston, where it would have been fanciful to suppose that anyone could overturn a majority of 16,000, a modest swing at Wythenshawe would see Alf home. There was a sense of excitement as Labour's active constituency workers felt that they were in the front line. They were imbued with a spirit of hope that saw them through a demanding and tiring campaign in which there was a total canvass of the constituency and nothing was allowed to go by default. In the north-west, seen as the key region in the election, more and more political observers saw the election as too close to call. It was only eight years since the heady days of Attlee's post-war administration and Labour's manifesto pledged further major reforms. There was nothing to keep voters at home: for despite the time of year, the sun shone brightly, a heat wave showed no signs of abating and drought conditions persisted in many areas.

In the event, the tipsters were well wide the mark. On 8 October, the Tories romped to victory with a majority of 107. In the context of this sweeping Conservative victory, Alf's result was remarkably good.

---

[8] *Ibid*, p.110.

Indeed, many of his supporters felt that if the Liberals had remained in contention, largely drawing votes away from wavering Tories, Alf would have won. Even so, he had succeeded in reducing Mrs Hill's majority to 1,309 and thus established a strong platform for the future. The more immediate question at this point, however, was whether he could continue to combine his demanding work for the Central Electricity Authority with the responsibilities of running an effective campaign as Wythenshawe's candidate. And equally whether the constituency party would want him to carry on as their candidate. It was, of course, open to him to go anywhere else, but he was very attached to Wythenshawe.

Before he could take a decision on whether to stand again he was promoted within the electricity supply industry to a post in London. This complicated matters considerably, because it meant that he would have to travel up and down to fulfil his twin roles as candidate and a senior employee of one of Britain's biggest industries. As an MP, of course, travelling between Westminster and one's constituency in the service of constituents goes with the territory. But for Alf, who now had four children and a living to earn, the question of whether he should continue as a parliamentary candidate was not an easy one to decide. For their part, the membership of Wythenshawe Labour Party's management committee made it clear that, regardless of whether he moved to London, they still wanted Alf to carry on as their candidate.

As a result of the keenly fought 1959 election campaign, the Wythenshawe seat was now a classic marginal and an exciting challenge. Moreover, it was his home place and, in the end, Alf decided to keep going. It was, however, on the understanding that he would need to see how it worked out, bearing in mind not only the physical demands of travelling back and forth weekly between London and Manchester, necessarily at his own expense, since the constituency party's funds would not stretch to that kind of expenditure. Until he found somewhere to live in London, Irene and the children would remain in Wythenshawe, so he would in any case be returning there at weekends.

It was an exacting schedule: a demanding job at the headquarters of the Central Electricity Authority in Winsley Street, W1 and weekly journeys to and from Manchester. Alf was again helped out by Stan Carter, who had found the newly-weds their lodgings with Mrs Phipps in Oxford. Stan was now Assistant General Secretary of the Printing and Kindred Trades Federation, and lived with his wife Eileen and their children near Turnpike Lane in north London. They not only gave Alf a home, but Stan went with him house-hunting at the end of each working day.

One consideration was that Alf's family then lived in a very quiet area on the southern edge of Wythenshawe, where the children were free to play in safety. He was concerned that they should not have to move to a place where there was heavy traffic. Another constraint was that it was not easy to move from rented housing to a property of their own. By this time, Irene's mother had died and Alf and Irene had succeeded to the tenancy in Wythenshawe. Finding an affordable property to buy in the capital was, even then, a huge problem. House prices in London were typically £1,000 per bedroom and Alf, like many other first-time buyers, found it necessary to look beyond the borders of Greater London where prices were marginally cheaper.

It took eight or nine months to settle on a house in Whyteleafe, south of Croydon, and throughout this time Alf was commuting at weekends, mostly by car, back to Manchester. This could prove arduous, particularly on the return journeys when he needed to be back in good time on Monday mornings. This was before the M1 had been constructed and long before the M6 was even conceived: so a very different car journey than now. Alf would leave Wythenshawe at around 4 a.m. and drive on the A34 towards Kidsgrove, Newcastle under Lyme and Stoke on Trent, then along the A5 to London. One journey in February 1960 remains etched in his memory. His car, which was parked outside the house, had first to be de-iced. Then, shortly after he started out, snow began to fall. By the time he reached the Cheshire/Staffordshire border it was falling very heavily. Alf remembers one T-junction where he had to stop near the brow of a steep hill. It took what seemed an eternity to restart. But he kept on going, passing any number of vehicles turned over on the road, and arrived in Winsley Street at 5.20 p.m. in the afternoon. By then he was very cold and tired, but had to be back because he was editing an issue of the industry's journal, *Joint Consultation*, then about ready to go to the printer, but needing a few last-minute details. The person who designed the cover for each issue had waited on for it to be approved. Alf quickly did what was necessary before going back to Turnpike Lane and house-hunting with Stan Carter: a friend indeed!

Even after the move to Whyteleafe, since Alf was the candidate for a highly marginal seat, he continued regularly to commute back to Manchester at weekends and, whenever possible, *en famille* because his sister Ivy and his older brothers and their families lived there. He needed to address the General Management Committee of Wythenshawe Labour Party and to attend meetings of trade union branches in the constituency, of which there were a score or more. All of them liked to see their parliamentary candidate, for whose election many of their members were working in their spare time. Accommodating both his political work and his responsibilities in the electricity supply industry was quite a hard road.

Walter Citrine

At times, Alf's work for the Central Electricity Authority brought him close to Lord Citrine. Perhaps now most often remembered for his *The ABC of Chairmanship*, Alf knew that as a chairman Citrine was sometimes capable of being pragmatic enough to step outside his own guidance:

"I remember him saying to me on one occasion that he would need a chairman's note for a meeting the following day, but promising that it would then become the minutes of the meeting! Of course, there was nothing in his great classic on chairmanship to allow for that."

Alf's personal recollection of Citrine is one of a scholarly-looking and highly intelligent man, always immaculately clean and straightforward; in every sense a very remarkable leader of the highest integrity, who commanded respect throughout the industry.

"His leadership as a very young man at the time of the General Strike – as General Secretary of the Trades Union Congress – speaks for itself. He was

not 'left-wing' or 'right-wing' and neither a hothead nor a revolutionary. What he wanted was social improvement, not the overthrow of elected institutions, and his aim during the General Strike was a successful outcome in terms of making life better for working people. There were others, of course, who wanted the General Strike to end in general strife. That didn't happen, not least because of Citrine's central role.

"He was of a generation in which the abilities of working people were given recognition as never before: people like Ernest Bevin, George Tomlinson and Herbert Morrison, people who manifestly did not lack ability but who had lacked educational opportunities. I remember him as a restless innovator, forever turning stones over, always prepared to look at some better way of doing things: no worm would have had a peaceful life under Citrine.

"He also knew the shop floor, having been there as an electrician. Of course, that didn't qualify him to be the founder chairman of the Central Electricity Authority. What did qualify him were his management skills and leadership ability. But it gave him enormous respect for working people, not least manual workers, having been one himself. He wanted the industry to be informed by the abilities of everyone in the industry".

It was for this reason that Citrine involved Alf in what was then the very sophisticated concept of joint consultation, so that people working in the power stations or local distribution districts of area electricity boards could elect representatives to serve with management on local advisory committees, where a whole range of issues could be addressed. Employee members of them could also get issues on to the agenda of the district advisory council for their region and from there to the national advisory council, making it possible for them to have an impact nationwide. Suggestions made in local advisory committees not infrequently became national policy. Alf was closely involved in all this and frequently lectured on various aspects of industrial relations at the industry's educational establishments at Horsley Towers near Effingham in Surrey and at Buxton in Derbyshire. He also arranged lectures by distinguished trade union leaders and employers. This led to the publication of a book, *Human Relations in Industry*, offering a vision of harmonious links between management and workers.

Another of the key tasks entrusted to Alf was a study for Citrine of the quality of communication between management and the workforce at all levels of the industry.

"One important but frequently overlooked point that came out of the study was that it is often the failure to review decisions that leads to serious errors in decision-making. A well-taken decision is one where every relevant factor is taken into account and given proper weight, so that the decision once taken is fully defensible. But, of course, factors can quickly change. Quite often when people are asked about the effectiveness of this or that arrangement in a major industry, they will say that they looked into all the factors and took very great care in making the arrangement, failing to recognise that for one factor to change may have a crucially important effect. It also set in relief that there was a great deal of waste in the system: that people were copied into correspondence needlessly, something that was time-consuming and clogged up efficient working. The emphasis in my findings was that communication should be on the basis of 'need to know'. Citrine was also a great believer in making sure that a communication was received in the sense of it being fully understood. It was not enough to ensure that people were included: what was quite often never checked was whether its message was understood by them".

Alf's next assignment took him into the key area of the negotiation of pay and conditions of employment. Public sector pay negotiations usually began in the electricity industry as everyone recognised the fundamental importance of industrial peace there. Settlements in other public industries then followed the 'going rate' in the electricity supply sector, because its employees had maximum muscle and industrial power. It was a challenge that was to serve him very well later:[9]

"There is nothing like being responsible for drafting agreements on pay and conditions of employment – as I was for quite some time in an industry with upwards of 200,000 employees – to teach you the importance of writing English that is capable of only one interpretation. Skilled draftsmanship is a crucial necessity, for if what you write can be read two ways there will be people affected well capable of seeing and using both according to

[9] Specifically in drafting the Chronically Sick and Disabled Persons Bill, described in Chapter 8.

choice. Employers often badly underestimate the intelligence of working people, so many of whom have been educated well below their intelligence".

The co-signatory to these agreements was Frank Foulkes, at that time President of the Electrical Trades Union and secretary of the National Joint Industrial Council, representing the five manual workers' unions in the electricity supply industry. The drafting was Alf's, but it was subject to rigorous scrutiny by Foulkes and his trade union colleagues.

"The need for absolute clarity had never been more clear to me. Otherwise, there would be disputes over interpretation in power stations and other local units of employment up and down the industry. The ability to draft very tightly was a discipline I learned then and there. I never related it in any way to future parliamentary activity, but it was this training, prior to my entering the House of Commons, that was to be of the highest utility when I won the opportunity to promote a Private Member's Bill".

Alf's work also brought him close to the realities of life for the industry's manual workers and their families. In particular, he studied in case after case the consequences for them of industrial disease or injury, and the extent of the calamity it conjured up for the manual worker afraid of ending up on the scrap-heap. The enlightened employer, Alf knew, was one who realised the need for adequate compensation for the damage done to a worker's health by his employment. This affected many trades and industries: byssinosis among cotton workers, varicose veins in shop assistants required to stand up all day, pneumoconiosis among miners. Nor did one have to be very observant to notice such things. Alf had seen in his own family that his brother George, a signwriter, had developed as the years passed an arthritic condition in his right shoulder from having constantly to raise his arm painting signs. Today we know about repetitive strain injury among people constantly putting strain on one particular limb: people, such as television cameramen, continuously required to carry heavy equipment. Much less was then understood about the disabling effects of particular kinds of employment. But Alf's work in electricity supply made him all too aware that employers generally were not meeting the costs of the damage done by their work to the health and well-being of employees.

General Election, 1964

Alf had been eight years in the electricity supply industry when the 1964 election was called. This time the auguries for Labour were more favourable. Morale in Conservative ranks had plummeted following the defection of Burgess and Maclean to Moscow and the unfortunate Profumo scandal. In October 1963 the Tories were dealt another blow when Macmillan was forced by illness to resign his leadership of the party. His replacement, Lord Home (who began by failing to win the support of two key members of Macmillan's cabinet[10]) was faced with the forbidding task of attempting to restore party morale and public confidence in government with no more than a year left to him before a General Election. So low had Conservative morale fallen that the party chairman, Lord Blakenham, estimated that if the election were to be called in June 1964, they would lose by 60 or 70 seats, whereas by October there was "just an outside chance" of victory.[11] Home announced the October election date on 9 April 1964 in the belief that this would "steady confidence". He reckoned, however, without the misfortune of needing, shortly before the election, to ask the World Bank for a loan to meet a budget deficit. Harold Wilson, who had succeeded Gaitskell as leader of the Labour Party, was well equipped to exploit this revelation. Labour was helped too by Home's own admission that he did not present well and, both on television and at public meetings, was a ready target for his opponents.[12]

Even so, the election looked too close to call, and the marginals, as ever, were the key. Wilson famously said: "We will know the result of this election by the outcome in Wythenshawe". Alf's commitment to winning Wythenshawe was total. As the *Manchester Evening News* commented, it was a sore point with Labour that a division with about 23,000 council houses and flats should have returned Mrs Hill in four successive elections,[13] and all Labour activists were

---

[10] Ian Macleod and Enoch Powell.
[11] *The Way the Wind Blows* (Lord Home, Collins, 1976, p.190)
[12] *Ibid*, p. 214.
[13] 7 October 1964.

determined to redress this indignity. None more so than Frank Price, who was Alf's agent for more than a decade and is remembered by him with great affection. In wartime, Frank had been in the Navy, patrolling the South China seas. Returned to civilian life as an engineering worker at Trafford Park, he became, without study or academic qualification, a superb agent. Despite his war record, no one could have regarded Frank as remotely warlike. He was a great pacifier with whom it was very difficult, if not impossible, to fall out. As the election of 1964 approached, Frank's expectation of success was being expressed almost in terms of certainty, bolstered by the euphoria of passing his driving test and of Manchester City winning at Maine Road in the week before polling day. But as well as being an optimist, Frank was also a shrewd operator. Among many gifts, if he felt that a visiting speaker sent from Transport House would not go down well with the electorate, it was not unknown to arrange for him to lunch with his friend Father Joe Taggart. This was equivalent to shunting a train into the sidings.

The Conservatives were on the back foot, but perhaps the decisive factor was the candidature of Tom Armstrong for the Liberals, who had not contested the seat in 1955 or 1959, and who now took the votes of many wavering Tories. On 15 October 1964, Alf triumphed over Mrs Hill by 4,777 votes, remarkably one of two pairs of brothers to win seats in Manchester.[14] "While elsewhere," Alf remarked at the time, "Labour members talk of brotherhood, here in Manchester we practice it!"

Alf's victory, though not dreamt of at the time, heralded a continuous period of 33 years as Wythenshawe's Labour Member of Parliament. It had taken nine years to get there, fourteen since his candidature in Liverpool, but this was the summit of a crusade of commitment to Labour's cause and one, in Alf's case, in which principle came before personal benefit. As an MP in 1964, his annual salary of £1,750 (with no allowances, other than help with travel to and from his constituency, and no pension scheme)[15] would be much lower and his prospects for advancement greatly reduced. In the electricity

---

[14] Alf and Charles won the Wythenshawe and Openshaw seats, while Leslie Lever and his brother Harold won the Cheetham and Ardwick seats.

[15] His pension in the electricity industry was frozen. Happily for Alf, the first contributory pension scheme for MPs came with the Ministerial Salaries and Members' Pensions Act 1965.

industry he could reasonably have expected further promotion and a higher salary. Instead he now faced a tough, uncharted and probably brief career on the back benches of the House of Commons. Nationally, Labour had scraped in with a bare majority, effectively, of only three and at Westminster Alf was jocularly advised not to unpack his bags. Locally, he was also very much on trial in a constituency that had never before had any kind of Labour representation. The future was dramatically uncertain.

October 1964: Trafford Park, Manchester. Eve of poll rally attended by over 30,000 people. Harold Wilson with Alf (co-speaker) and Frank Allaun.

1963: The Morris family: Stephen, Irene, Gill, Cathy, Paul and Alf.

Chapter 6

THE NEW MP

1964–1969

"Each change of many-coloured life he drew, exhausted worlds, and then imagined new".

Dr Samuel Johnson,
Prologue at the opening of a theatre in Drury Lane.

– Unanticipated fortune – Churchill's old room – Working with Fred Peart
– Forging bonds with Commonwealth countries
– Improving parental hospital visiting – To speak or not to speak
– A visit to the UN – Another, extended visit to the USA
– A sour experience on home territory – A rising socialist star
– Joining the campaign to end capital punishment
– Objections to joining the Common Market – The foot and mouth outbreak
– Charles Morris
– Fred Peart takes on a new role, but keeps Alf as his right-hand-man
– At the hub of procedural issues

Unanticipated fortune

Alf says that his has been "a most fortunate life". None of his achievements was planned or expected; all of them were propelled by remarkable strokes of good fortune, not least, he says, becoming his own Member of Parliament! In a provocative maiden speech during the Budget debate on 12 November 1964, he began by recalling Aristotle's belief that it was "the essence of probability that some improbable things will happen". That, he contended, was certainly true of the election from which he had emerged as the first-ever Labour Member for his home place, the Wythenshawe constituency of Manchester. Much of the credit belonged to a "superb fellowship of natural supporters", he said; but he had also been helped by the speeches for his Conservative opponent by three visitors to the constituency: the arch-Conservative Selwyn Lloyd (dubbed 'Celluloid' by Churchill), then Leader of the House of Commons; Quintin Hogg, the Secretary of State for Education and Science; and Sir Alec Douglas-Home the Prime Minister who, incredibly in the working class environment of most of Wythenshawe, had remarked that its people lived in surroundings very much like his own home place. That trio, said Alf, had contributed in no small measure to his electoral success. His agent, he said, could not have chosen better.

Alf then described his constituency, made some sharp comments on the effects there of the thirteen years of Conservative rule now ended and on the need for a fair incomes policy, concluding with a heartfelt testimony to his own feelings: "Finally, one of my main impressions of the House so far was when, on the election of Mr Speaker, it was said that what unites the House is the love which all right hon. and hon. Members have for it as an institution". As a new Member, he had brought with him an enduring respect for a House of Commons that had been an instrument of revolutionary social change while providing the means for it to be carried through peacefully. As a life-long democratic Socialist and co-operator, he felt honoured to be there at a time when, he believed, the House would be seen to be acting in keeping with its finest traditions.

Alf cannot have known then, that with 'Lady Luck' still smiling on his endeavours, he would soon be the main instrument of further revolutionary social change, indeed one of the most significant, enduring – and global in its effects – of all social reforms during the entire twentieth century in Britain. But already he had received one entirely unforeseen benefit. Within three days of entering the House he was asked by Fred Peart, the new Minister for Agriculture, Fisheries and Food (MAFF) to be his Parliamentary Private Secretary and thus become a member of the Government. This was at a time when there was a great deal of grumbling among members about their conditions of work, not only brand-new members but also many who had been in Parliament for years. Scores of them still didn't have even a desk to call their own, and kept their papers in wall cupboards. Alf recalls his Labour colleague Tam Dalyell complaining that he had a shoebox for an office. The fact was that the building was not designed to accommodate over six hundred Members of Parliament. It had not been built as a representative assembly at all, but as a royal palace: the Palace of Westminster. Then as now there were not enough seats in the Chamber of the

House to accommodate all the MPs, which at its most crowded could seat only about 400 members. That meant that over 200 were unable to sit in the Chamber for the most important debates.

It was also a time when all-night sittings were commonplace. If the Government moved a guillotine to prevent further debate on a piece of legislation – a so-called 'gagging' motion – there would invariably be a big row in the House. The fact that Labour's majority was paper-thin made matters worse. It was an Opposition tactic to keep Ministers up all night, knowing that they would have to be at their departmental desks early the next morning. And, without a guillotine, debates could go on indefinitely. In these circumstances an Opposition spokesman, having tabled dozens of amendments to a Bill, might say to a Minister: "If you will accept this amendment, I will drop all the rest", a suggestion very tempting to someone who faces being kept up all night. Now, of course, things have changed – too far, Alf thinks – in the opposite direction. But in his first parliamentary session the arrangements seemed perverse and were exhausting for all concerned. When Members were kept at all-night sittings so, of course, were the Commons' staff. But when business finished, usually at around 10–10.30 p.m., whereas Members could go and rest, shower and change their clothes, staff could not. They were often working around the clock and it was clear to Alf, as a new MP, that they were very badly used. One of his first initiatives, using his experience in the electricity supply industry, was to put down questions about their pay and conditions, not least hours of work, and whether they were allowed sufficient rest. From that point on Alf could do no wrong in the eyes of the messengers, doorkeepers and other staff: the people whose working conditions at Westminster never seemed to be considered, despite the importance of their role. He admits to having been given special treatment from then on. Several attendants would go far beyond the calls of duty to make sure he received messages promptly and to make sure he had a peg for his coat in the lobby behind the Speaker's chair. There was no entitlement to a special peg, but if any Member was seen to be about to hang his coat on one a member of staff wanted to keep for Alf, you would hear "No, not there, that's committed" or words to that effect. Alf recalls that on one bitterly cold night, when he had to go to the Foreign Office, his coat was missing, inadvertently taken by a Treasury official whose coat was fairly similar. Immediately, the head doorkeeper came forward to lend him his own coat. Small things, perhaps, but indicative of how Alf was seen by those in the engine room of Parliament – with a respect that very obviously persists across the palace to this day.

Churchill's old room

The fact that Alf had become PPS to Fred Peart would mean that he had access to the Minister's room, something of enormous help. Better still, Fred told him that he would have the main use of the room, because for most of the day he would be at the Ministry. Thus room 56, on the Lower Ministerial Floor of the House, would to all intents and purposes be Alf's room.

The only disadvantage was that Alf had no experience at all of working in the Palace of Westminster. He had been there on a couple of occasions as a visitor, but knew very little about its geography or its procedures and administration. Fred told him how to go about securing the key for room 56. The system provided (and provides) that if there is a change of government, the incoming Minister will arrange for Commons' staff to have any belongings left by his or her predecessor placed in a little skip on the carpet outside the room. Fred therefore told Alf to phone the Sergeant at Arms to get the key to what, until the election, had been Christopher Soames's room. When he got in, Alf phoned Fred at the Ministry and told him that it didn't look like Soames's room, more that of his father-in-law, Sir Winston Churchill, who had left Parliament at the 1964 General Election. Asked why so, Alf said there was Churchilliana on every wall: a portrait of his father, Lord Randolph Churchill, a photograph of Churchill's wife Clementine, and others of his son Randolph, his daughter Mary and his grandchildren, along with one or two paintings which were, Alf thinks, by Churchill himself. Moreover, and conclusively, the drawers of the desk were groaning with Havana cigars, all bearing the legend 'W. S. Churchill'. It emerged that Soames had been given that room to help Churchill, who by then was over 90 and heavily disabled. On

Fred's advice, Alf later phoned Lady Churchill, having been given her number by Sir Martin Redmayne, the Conservative Chief Whip, and told her what was happening. She responded warmly: "How very kind! This has never happened to us before. We've been here since the back end of the last century, and every time there's been a change of government, our stuff has been put out on the carpet outside the room". Lady Churchill came in the afternoon and again said how very kind it was and how moved she had been, whereas to Fred and Alf it was the merest gesture they could possibly make.

So there was Alf, within a few days of coming into Parliament, sitting in Churchill's room at Churchill's desk, with a view through the window on to Star Chamber Court leading through to Westminster Hall. Churchill died in the following January and from his desk, through the open doors from the Court to the Hall, Alf could see the great man's coffin and the mourners filing through for the lying-in-state.

Working with Fred Peart

But there was much more to the relationship with Fred Peart than the bequest of a room. Alf was working with arguably the most kindly and widely respected of all MPs. Harold Wilson aptly described him as "one of the most popular ministers in the Commons",[1] and Edward Short, a close friend, was to write: "He was incapable of anger. He succeeded because of his good humour and charm...one of the very few [politicians] I have known who were without guile".[2] Alf himself remembers Fred as "a very frank person of abiding political cleanliness and courage, never arrogant but always prepared to stand his ground". He particularly recalls an altercation between Fred and his predecessor at MAFF. The dispute centred on one of Fred's first pieces of legislation, as the new Minister, on tied farm cottages, and the issue between them was whether Soames, by voting while Fred abstained on his own department's Bill, had broken a pairing agreement – something taken very seriously in the House. Soames went to see Fred at the Ministry in Whitehall Place to talk it out and arrived in a distinctly surly mood. By contrast Fred,

[1] *The Labour Government 1964-1970* (Harold Wilson, Weidenfeld and Nicolson and Michael Joseph Ltd, 1971), p.522.
[2] Obituary, The Independent, 29 August 1988.

although wronged by him, was superbly disarming. Having returned from war service in 1945 a more senior officer than his pair, he invited Soames to have a seat and immediately spiked his guns with a plea to "calm down *Captain Soames*". And the exchange ended with an apology from Soames for voting in Fred's absence.

Fred described himself, echoing Robert Blatchford, as a 'Merry England socialist', but this apparent *insouciance* concealed a resolute determination and outstanding skill as a negotiator. Alf warmed to his approach to life and the two became and remained very close to each other.

In the 1945–51 Labour Government, Fred had been appointed as Parliamentary Private Secretary to the then Minister of Agriculture, Tom Williams, with whom he developed an astonishing rapport and a notable reputation in the department. It came as no surprise, therefore, when thirteen years later he was chosen to take over responsibility for agriculture, fisheries and food in the Wilson government of 1964. But to this day Alf has no idea why he should have been chosen to inherit Fred's former role as the Minister of Agriculture's PPS. Ian Aitken, then one of *The Guardian's* lobby staff and highly regarded by the lobby as a whole, remarked that he was one of the luckiest new MPs there had ever been to be immediately appointed as a PPS, and to Fred Peart of all people.

Forging bonds with Commonwealth countries

The appointment to work with Fred Peart was to prove a cornerstone of Alf's parliamentary career. Fred gave him opportunities that would otherwise never conceivably have been available to a newly elected MP. From 1964 to 1966, Alf represented the Ministry on visits to Fiji and Mauritius, both cane sugar producing countries vitally dependent on the Commonwealth Sugar Agreement, and to New Zealand and Australia. The Anzac countries were among Britain's main suppliers of food, and bilateral trade with them was crucially important to them both. In Wellington, Alf addressed the chairmen of all New Zealand's producer boards. One of these was Sir James Lynton, then chairman of the Dairy Board, to whom Alf confided that the speech would be his first in New Zealand. Was there anything that he should know about the customary form of address as between there and the UK? Lynton replied that there was just one difference. In New Zealand speeches began with "Ladies, Gentlemen and Australians"! Australia was Alf's next stop. In Canberra he had talks with, among other federal ministers, 'Black Jack' McEwan, the legendary formidable Overseas Trade Minister, whom he found much more agreeable than his reputation.

At the time of these visits, promoting trade within the Commonwealth and most of all with Britain was a top Whitehall priority, more especially in agriculture. Under longstanding agreements preference was given to goods from Commonwealth countries, and there were annual price negotiations with New Zealand and Australia on agricultural goods. Alf recalls that when Lord Palmerston was asked who were Britain's closest friends in the world, he replied, "countries don't have friends, they have interests". A century later, friendship and interest coincided in respect not only of New Zealand and Australia, but of other Commonwealth countries more generally. Their contribution to our survival in the Second World War had from the outset been vital, not merely in military terms – in Europe, the Western Desert and the Far East – but also as our main lifeline for food supplies. Alf forged personal ties with New Zealand and Australia that have never been broken.

Improving parental hospital visiting

But his involvement in the work of the House as a fledgling MP was by no means confined to his role with Fred Peart. One of his first priorities was to raise the insensitive arrangements for parental visits to children in hospital, of which he still had vivid memories from his own stay in Booth Hall Hospital in 1938. This was the major concern of the National Association for the Welfare of Children in Hospital, founded specifically to humanise access both for parents and grandparents. One of the people nationally involved with NAWCH – Elizabeth Garland – lived in Wythenshawe Road in his own constituency and was, and long remained, one of Alf's strongest supporters. She was the catalyst for action in what was Alf's first parliamentary campaign. As a parent, she was deeply upset about the lack of access to her sick daughter and was seeking an extension and relaxation of visiting hours. She argued that parental visiting was important therapeutically as well as emotionally. Together they succeeded in bringing the traditional attitudes of hospitals into public focus and securing a more enlightened approach, which was to lead to revolutionary change: so much so that liberal visiting hours have become recognised as a vital factor in the health of child patients.

To speak or not to speak

There is ample evidence in *Hansard* to surprise those who now know Alf only as the champion of disabled people. As a new MP, he received emphatic advice from Leslie Lever, a seasoned Member of the House he very much liked and who had helped to secure his election in 1964. Leslie, who represented the Ardwick constituency of Manchester, took Alf aside soon afterwards and said in an avuncular tone, "the essential thing in Parliament is not to make speeches, but to become an expert questioner. Ask as many questions as you like but be very, very careful to keep speech-making down to an absolute minimum". He confided that he had made a speech just before the 1959 election at which his vote slumped by 2,000. And that a contemporary of his had made a speech, breaking the silence of years, and lost his seat altogether! Alf certainly complied with part of the advice he had been given. In his first year he put 58 questions on a wide diversity of subjects, including school milk and dental health; proposals for an international treaty to control the spread of nuclear weapons; Sunday trading; and the protection of trees in parks. He has remained a searching questioner throughout his parliamentary career.

But in late 1964 he was also bold enough to speak in a debate on secondary education, during which Leslie Lever was sitting in the Commons tea room when the parliamentary ticker tape showed that Alf had stood up to speak. According to Members who were there, Leslie recoiled in shock, pushed his tea away, went post-haste to the Chamber and stood watching from the Bar of the House. Eventually he came onto the floor, sat next to Alf and tugged at his coat. When Alf sat down, Leslie asked him for how long he had spoken, and it was explained that Michael Stewart, then Secretary of State for

Education, who knew that Alf had recent experience of teaching in a variety of schools – including for a time Manchester Grammar School, where Leslie himself had been educated – had asked him to say a few words. Leslie shook his head gravely and said quietly, "No, no, no", which Alf interpreted as the last rites on his parliamentary career.

A visit to the UN

Others felt differently. Notwithstanding his short time in Parliament, Alf's impact was such that he was selected to spend part of a summer parliamentary recess with the British delegation to the General Assembly of the United Nations in New York. Michael Stewart, who had moved from education to become Foreign Secretary in January 1965, had come up with the idea of giving two newish MPs from each side of Parliament the opportunity to form part of Britain's representation. Together with Chris Rowland, another new and by common consent highly promising Labour Member, Alf spent some weeks of the long recess of 1965 involved in everything that was happening in the General Assembly and meeting, on every hand, representatives from countries all over the world. He recalls that the 'cocktail belt' at the UN was one of the most intimidating challenges that he had ever faced, with one cocktail party after another, night after night. *"You ran the risk of choking on downtown New York's finest 'rubber chicken', not to mention the threat of liver failure for those unskilled in making a slimline tonic water, ice and lemon look like a dry Martini."* His programme also included a visit to hear the proceedings and debates of the first session of the 89th Congress, as well as the privilege of joining Britain's ambassador as an observer at a meeting of the UN Security Council, allowing Alf to experience the conduct of international parleying at the highest level. The world, it seems, is never without strife and conflict, but this was a particularly challenging period, dominated by "great questions of life and death, peace and war".[3] The Cuban crisis was over, but the 'Cold War' continued. The Americans and North Vietnamese were locked in horrific combat, Ian Smith was on the brink of making a unilateral declaration of independence in Rhodesia, and there were a myriad of 'North-South' problems and divisions. The UN itself, in danger of

---

[3] *Life and Labour: an autobiography* (Michael Stewart, published by Sidgwick & Jackson, 1980), p. 141.

bankruptcy, had been saved only by donations from Britain and some other countries.[4] It would be difficult to imagine a more informative and instructive experience for someone at the beginning of a parliamentary career.

Another, extended, visit to the USA

Within two years, the US Congress invited Michael Stewart to send four young parliamentarians for a month-long exchange visit to Amercia during the summer recess. He chose Alf and Gordon Bagier on the Labour side and Christopher Chataway and John Biffin from the Conservatives. *"It was fascinating. We didn't have to keep together. You could have your own programme and Congressional staff worked to arrange for you to meet whoever you wanted to see. I went first to see the British Ambassador and then to the State Department's offices in Massachusetts Avenue in Washington DC for a briefing, after which I was taken around Congress by Edward Kennedy, then a young Congressman, who was my host. The informality of it all amazed me. The rules of procedure are quite unlike those of the British Parliament. Everything was so much more relaxed. In the Senate, proceedings were adjourned so that we could be greeted by Senator Mansfield of the Democrats, then Floor leader, and introduced by him to other senators. There was no leader of our group, but because I was from the governing party and indeed a junior member of the Government I was asked to speak. I remember introducing Chris Chataway, who had been a contemporary of mine at Oxford, as runner-up in Roger Bannister's first-ever four-minute mile, and said, 'I think I can beat that today. My speech will be well within four minutes.' I might have added that I had been within earshot of the first four-minute mile. One of my tutors at Oxford was the Rev. Trefor Davies, whose home in Iffley Road overlooked the track where this historic breakthrough was achieved. My tutorial about Roman Britain was interrupted by the cheering as history was being made across the road.*

"I went from Washington down to Atlanta and then to New Orleans to see Bob Farbacher, a friend of Fred Peart, who served side by side with him in the epic battle for Monte Cassino. Bob's family owned the brewery where the most popular beer south of the Mason-Dixon line was made. He took me all round Basin Street where the family's beer was widely consumed, and other

[4] *Ibid*, p.148.

places of special interest, not least the levees that had been breached in 1927. From there I went to St. Louis and then to Los Angeles, where I had a morning with Walt Disney in Pasadena. Then on to San Francisco, Omaha in Nebraska, Cedar Rapids in Iowa, Chicago, Michigan – visiting two universities – and from there to Cornell University in New York State, before returning to Washington."

A sour experience on home territory

Not all visits were so rewarding. One of them remains the very opposite. Alf had been asked by Fred Blackburn, then the Labour MP for Stalybridge and Hyde, to address a constituency meeting he would be chairing. This was an evocative link with the past, for Fred was a former distinguished head teacher of North Manchester High School for Boys to which Alf would have gone when he was 11 but for the wartime evacuation. The meeting was to be held at Hyde Town Hall on a Saturday afternoon in May 1965 and Alf readily accepted. It so happened, however, that the Saturday came at the end of a week in which Alf had not been in bed from Monday until Friday. He had to stay at the House of Commons continuously for the Report Stage of the Wilson Government's first Finance Bill. He had left Manchester before 7 a.m. on Monday morning, arrived at the Members' Entrance of the House of Commons at 11.45 a.m. and did not leave the building again until 4.30 p.m. on Friday, over 100 hours later. Wilson had a theoretical majority of three but in practice was in a minority of one, because Desmond Donnelly and Woodrow Wyatt, although elected as Labour MPs only months before, seldom voted with the Labour Government. As a new MP, Alf had no chance of being paired with anyone. Fred Peart, as a Minister, and Fred Blackburn, as a senior MP, were allowed to pair for two nights that week, but Alf had only the benefit of occasional naps on a settee in room 56, to which changes of clothing were brought. There was no question of leaving the House as one parliamentary day merged into another through an exhausting week.

Even so he was determined to fulfil his commitment to Fred Blackburn. He got back to Manchester late on the Friday night, and had an advice bureau in his Wythenshawe constituency on Saturday morning. In the early afternoon, he travelled to Hyde Town Hall and spoke under the heading 'The Week in Westminster' for about half an hour. At the end of his address a young man stood up and said "Mr Chairman, what an astonishing speech! The speaker was billed as a new Labour Member of Parliament, yet did not even try to articulate the words 'overseas aid' or 'Third World'. How can any young Labour MP, worthy of the description, speak for half an hour without referring once to the problems of the world's poor?" Looking toward Fred Blackburn in the chair, Alf could see a widening red patch on the back of his neck as the question proceeded. When it had finished, Fred exploded, "This young man, my parliamentary colleague, has been in the House of Commons non-stop for 103 hours this week and still kept this engagement. I asked him to speak about the week in Westminster, and that is exactly what he has done. The week was about the Finance Bill, not overseas aid and the Third World". In an aside, Fred then whispered to Alf, "He's after my seat, this fellow". In this the interrogator – a university lecturer – was disappointed, but he did go on to become a Labour MP; tragically or happily according to taste. Not for long, though, and without Alf ever hearing him articulate the words 'overseas aid' or 'Third World'.

A rising socialist star

Alf's reputation was growing. So remarkable had been his energy that in November 1965 Robert Mellish, soon to be Government Chief Whip (*"as working class as they come and a parliamentary tough guy if ever there was one"*), paid him a most uncommon and, for him, extremely rare tribute: "He has been a member of the House for just over a year and, if I may say so without intending to be patronising in any form, he is a credit to this House and to his constituents".

In some of his early interventions Alf was remarkably ahead of his time. On 10 December 1964, he asked the Home Secretary whether he would "hold an inquiry into the cruelty involved in some field sports, with a view to the introduction of legislation". And on 18 November 1965, he demonstrated his interest in constitutional issues by questioning the Prime Minister as to whether he would introduce legislation to translate hereditary peerages into life peerages, thus eventually removing the hereditary factor from the legislature, or to exclude hereditary peers from the right to sit in the legislature.

But the most conspicuous characteristic of his early parliamentary years was that of calling attention to the need for social change related to and connecting with his own life experiences. Three examples must suffice:

22 November 1965, debating slum clearance in Manchester. Alf reminded the House that a report published earlier that year had remarked that the first and lasting impression of a visitor to the North West was "one of astonishment that the housing conditions he sees around him could still exist in a relatively prosperous part of an advanced industrial country". This was Alf's home territory: "I shall never forget my childhood days in Ancoats," he said, "nor shall I ever ignore the claims of those who live in such areas still".

29 November 1965, a question to the Minister of Health: "What further progress has been made in respect of unrestricted visiting by parents to children in hospital?"

18 February 1966, a speech in support of a Private Member's Bill introduced by William Hamling (who in 1951 had fought the Wavertree constituency of Liverpool alongside Alf's campaign in Garston). Hamling had moved, among other things, that "responsibility for the education and training of all mentally handicapped children should be transferred from the Ministry of Health to the Department of Education and Science", and that "improved educational opportunities are the key to the proper development of these children". In a telling speech, Alf drew on his own experience in teaching both very able children and those with severe learning disabilities, arguing that "the ideal of equality of opportunity is not enough". Anticipating his later campaigns, Alf argued that it was necessary to bias opportunities in favour of those who lacked the physical or mental powers to compete on the basis of equality of educational opportunity. He brought the attention of the House to the expert view of Dr Simon Rudkin that "all children need to be accepted in society as worthwhile people".

This, of course, was radical and socialist. More than once, Alf noticed, more was done to protect the interests of those in least need of protection, the affluent, than for those in greatest need, making the gap between them even wider and more indefensible. It was also an affirmation of his belief that social ends should take precedence over political expediency.

His views have not changed. Today he sees the word 'politician' more and more often used pejoratively, in some part to imply disingenuousness and even dishonesty: a readiness to trim, to be all things, if not to all people, then at least to most people. In his experience, one of the most distressing things about Parliament is that organisations tend to get noticed and win support in proportion to their strength. That doesn't leave much room for the least powerful, the least electorally significant. Survival at Westminster, he observes, is all about being re-elected, and to be re-elected one needs public support. It is thus unsurprising that most people in elective office will pursue what they feel is the most likely course to achieve their re-election. But, paradoxically, he asserts, this does not always work out as they expect, not least if they swing from one view to another to win the support of people who suspect them of changing their tune rather than their views.

"Simply to bend with the prevailing wind is to run the risk of losing respect, than which nothing is more important in public life. It is a mistake – and contemptuous of the electorate – to think that re-election can be assured by 'back-scratching' after weighing up the 'mileage' in taking a particular stance. Voting this way or that according to what you think might get you more votes is not wisdom. Respect founded on integrity and trust is what ultimately counts."

Joining the campaign to end capital punishment

All this was dramatically put to the acid test shortly after Alf took his seat in the House, when Sidney Silverman introduced a Private Member's Bill to abolish once and for all the death penalty for murder. Much progress had been made towards this by the Homicide Act 1957; but Silverman now saw the return of a Labour Government as an opportunity to secure "a final end of the last remnant of a grotesque barbarity". One of his earliest moves was to seek, as active colleagues for the campaign, two tellers: one from among those who had assisted him over many years in his campaign for abolition, the other from the intake of new MPs from the 1964 election: the 'new blood' who could change the balance of opinion. This honour fell to Alf who became actively involved in the campaign. He felt very strongly about the issue, and for him that was the only relevant consideration. He thought that one question those who favoured capital punishment should ask themselves was whether they would be prepared to undertake the execution; if not they were not entitled to pay somebody else to do it for them. Friends and colleagues alike immediately told Alf that by supporting Silverman so prominently he had committed political suicide. Feelings ran particularly high in Manchester where Tom Henry, probably among the world's most devout, militant supporters of capital punishment, was then editor of the *Evening News*. *"He wouldn't, it was said of him, go to bed at night without writing a leading article on the villainy of those supporting the Silverman Bill"*.

Nevertheless, on 21 December 1964, the second reading of the Murder (Abolition of Death Penalty) Bill was carried by a large majority on a free vote; and after overcoming mainly Tory manoeuvrings, cleared the Commons on 14 July 1965, albeit on a trial basis. The issue Alf now had to face was how his active role in producing this outcome would play in his Wythenshawe constituency, home to both (divorced) parents of Leslie Ann Downey, one of the child victims of the Moors murderers.

The question was soon to be put to the test. Harold Wilson, who had been governing on the slenderest of parliamentary majorities, decided to go to the country on 31 March 1966 and Alf's political future appeared to be in the gravest jeopardy. The issue of capital punishment resonated throughout the Manchester area, when Leslie Ann Downey's father announced that he would stand as an independent against Sidney Silverman in Nelson and Colne, a constituency not very far from Wythenshawe. Many of his constituents openly declared that by sponsoring the Silverman Bill Alf had signalled the end of his parliamentary career. Even close friends told him he had no chance at all of being re-elected. Labour canvassers came back from the doorsteps reporting that the only issue being raised was Alf's involvement in the campaign to end the death penalty.

The polling night was one he will never forget: *"Everyone that day had been saying I could not possibly survive having been – in the words of the then editor of the Manchester Evening News – "a ringleader" in the success of the Silverman Bill. Going by car down to the Town Hall for the counting of the votes, my agent Frank Price and I talked about the valedictory speech I would have to make after declaration of the result. In fact, I secured a majority of 8,937 votes over my Conservative opponent, nearly doubling that of 1964!"*

The moral of this "shock result", he reflected later, appeared to be that while they may not share a candidate's views on some issues, most voters are concerned more about trust and a readiness to stand by firmly-held convictions. Over many years, Alf had earned the respect of the people of Wythenshawe and, as their MP, they now knew not only that his concern for their problems was genuine, but that he represented their interests rather than feathering his own nest. He was in Wythenshawe, where he retained a home, as often as he could be – usually travelling between Westminster and Wythenshawe twice a week – and continued to maintain close links with local people.

Objections to joining the Common Market

Alf remained with Fred Peart until May 1967. It was then that a vote took place on whether Britain should move toward adherence to the Treaty of Rome. The question was one that had occupied Members on all sides of the House for years. Both Alf and Fred had strong reservations about the effect British membership of the European Economic Community would have not only on many of our own small farmers and less well off consumers, but also on Commonwealth countries and on the poorest of them most of all. Alf spoke passionately in a debate on 8 May, describing the issue as a serious test of the Community's willingness to adopt attitudes that looked outwards beyond the boundaries of Europe, taking account of the interests of countries whose historical and economic development had been closely linked to that of European countries. "Some of us," he said, "who have reservations about entering the Common Market are told that we are not internationalists. At one time I was Chairman of the Control Commission of the Socialist Youth International. Many of the people with whom these negotiations will now take place were my colleagues there and are now Ministers in European Governments. If people question my internationalism, my reply is that I do not believe that internationalism resides behind high tariff walls".

Both Alf and Fred Peart wanted strong guarantees to protect the poorer nations but saw it as inconceivable that they could be secured in the foreseeable future. They were concerned also about the very damaging impact Britain's entry into the Common Market could have on the interests of New Zealand and Australia, among other developed Commonwealth countries. As the minister at MAFF, Fred was duty-bound to support the Government, but Alf felt that, until the guarantees he was seeking were available, he could not do so and abstained when the main question was put to the House.[5] He was well aware that this was anything but a good career move. The weight of both press and parliamentary opinion was heavily against him. He was now widely seen as due for elevation to the next rung on the ladder as an Under Secretary. Alf saw, of course, as clearly as everyone else, that this would not happen if he failed to support the Government, but was less concerned about getting on, and more about doing what he felt to be right. His principled stand meant there would be no alternative to resigning his post as PPS and he did so.

Interviewed by *The Guardian* after attending an all-party group of MPs, at which Alf was the principal speaker, one of those present referred to him as having "seared the conscience of the listener" with his assessment of the consequences for the poorest Commonwealth countries – and particularly those dependent on producing sugar cane – of failing to protect them before adhering to the Treaty.

Fred Peart's response was extraordinary. He announced that he would not be appointing another PPS. Such was the strength of

[5] Ayes 488, Noes 62.

their bond that when they met after the vote Alf said jocularly that if he could no longer help Fred as his Parliamentary Private Secretary, he would try to do so as his Parliamentary Private Friend!

The foot and mouth outbreak

It was as such that he remained close to Fred throughout the most grievous outbreak of foot and mouth disease this country had ever known. The point almost came where Fred would have to opt for a policy of vaccination. He was under relentless pressure to do so as the number of cattle destroyed rose ever more grievously day by day. Fred and his wife Bette stayed with Alf and Irene for two days over Christmas 1967 and, on Boxing Day, they heard by telephone that the turning point had come when for the first time the rate of increase slackened. Fred's concern was that to vaccinate would be to concede that foot and mouth disease was endemic in the United Kingdom, with devastating effects on our pedigree livestock export industry. He stood his ground and saw the crisis through without resorting to vaccination.

The foot and mouth outbreak had originated in an abattoir in Argentina, leading to a ban on imports from Argentina. And this, combined with a drastic fall in home production, meant that Britain urgently needed to seek meat imports from new suppliers in countries that were free from the disease. In 1968, by which time Parliamentary Private 'Friend' had been restored to 'Secretary' – by a decision of the Prime Minister – Alf went to talks on the possibility of meat imports from Cuba. Castro was in office then as now, and on the outward journey it was necessary to fly to Havana via Madrid, returning via Prague. The flights had to keep clear of the US coastline, because they were in a state of virtual, if undeclared, war with Cuba. Once there, Alf remembers being driven from one meeting to another in a Cadillac, no doubt grabbed from its owner in the revolution and now in an advanced state of disrepair. The Americans wouldn't, of course, supply spare parts, so the Cubans had to resort to cannibalising vehicles that went back to the Batista regime. The United States had been Cuba's principal market and most of their cane sugar had gone there, but this ended when

Castro seized power. So new export opportunities were eagerly sought and, following Alf's visit, Cuban meat was indeed imported into Britain in exchange for the export of Leyland buses to Cuba.

Above all, the foot and mouth outbreak taught Alf just how vitally important our trade in agricultural goods was to the British economy. *"You had to be in MAFF to appreciate that its work is not just about farmers and farming: it's about food, consumers, public health and well-being, international trade and the national interest."*

Charles Morris

Alf's brother Charles, meanwhile, had a very different niche in the parliamentary hierarchy. He enjoyed the distinction of serving in three very disparate capacities: as Parliamentary Private Secretary to Tony Benn, then Minister of Technology, as a Government Whip and as Vice Chamberlain to the Royal Household, a post originally created to give parliamentarians access to the Court. The latter duty required him to write a daily report of proceedings in the House, to be "delivered to the Queen before dinner wherever she is in Britain".[6] In practice, whenever the Queen was in London, this meant a journey to Buckingham Palace to present the report in person. His other regular journeys, of course, were to his constituency in Manchester Openshaw, more often than not with Alf. Having slept together as boys, the brothers remained, despite their separate responsibilities, very close. After 1974, they were to become fellow Ministers in Harold Wilson's second administration and when Michael Foot became leader of the party and of the Opposition in 1980 Alf spoke from the front bench as Shadow Minister for Disabled People while Charles was made deputy to the then Shadow Leader of the House, John Silkin. No two members, Alf recalls, ever collaborated more. Indeed, because Charles lived in his Wythenshawe constituency, Alf was his Member of Parliament!

Fred Peart takes on a new role, but keeps Alf as his right-hand-man
In November 1968, Fred Peart replaced Richard Crossman as Lord President of the Council and Leader of the House of Commons. He promptly reappointed Alf as his PPS in his new role, a position he

---

[6] *The Reality of Monarchy* (Andrew Duncan, William Heinemann Ltd, 1970), p.2.

continued to hold until the General Election of June 1970. This was a crucial development. It brought him, less than four years after becoming an MP, to the very epicentre of the parliamentary institution. Notwithstanding his relative inexperience as an MP, he quickly got to know about the day-to-day working of the machinery of Parliament – not least the 'usual channels' – and found it deeply absorbing. Every week, while Parliament was sitting, Fred Peart met the Shadow Leader of the House and the Government and Opposition Chief Whips – the business managers from both sides involved in arranging parliamentary business – to discuss and often haggle over the allocation of parliamentary time for the week ahead. One of the duties of the Leader is to answer the 'Business Question' every Thursday, when he or she informs the House what the business managers have agreed will be debated, and when any MP who wants the programme to be reconsidered can raise questions. It now fell to Fred to field their questions and quite often this took more than an hour. Alf considers himself to have been immensely lucky to be involved, at such a formative stage of his parliamentary career, in these and other processes. It was an aspect of Alf's parliamentary life that was largely unseen within Parliament and little known outside, but it both fascinated him and proved of great importance to him in later years.

At the hub of procedural issues

In his new role, Alf became an ardent student of parliamentary procedure, not least as it affected the work of select committees. In May 1965, a study group of three learned professors of politics and government had been set up to examine the scope for expanding the work of select committees and to report their proposals to the strong and venerable Select Committee on Procedure. The report argued for procedural changes aimed at making parliamentary control more effective. Such control, they contended, should be founded on five principles: to influence executive government, but not direct; to advise, but not command; to criticise but not obstruct; to scrutinise but not initiate; to publicise, and not be secretive. The study group noticed, in particular, that the machinery of Parliament had failed to keep pace with the increasing range of government activity, making it ever more difficult for the House to obtain "the background facts and understanding essential to any detailed criticism of administration or any informed discussion of policy".

They said that government departments had come to rely on the "filtered" advice from committees external to Parliament (not yet called quangos) and argued that the remedy was the formation of a number of new-style "specialist" select committees, through which MPs could scrutinise in detail the work of one or other of the departments of state, more effectively exert influence on the executive and more fully inform the electorate. As an experiment they wanted specialist select committees of back-benchers covering five major departments. In the long-term the development of such committees was seen as extending to cover the whole field of administration.

Alf became privy to all ministerial and cross-party deliberations about select committees and closely monitored their outcome, aware that this would be an area of growing significance if Parliament and the executive were to conduct business on more equal terms and with mutual respect. In 1969 he embarked on a book to examine the issues in detail and discuss the divergent views surrounding them. This was to be *The Growth of Parliamentary Scrutiny by Committee*, published in 1970 (with a foreword by Fred Peart, as Leader of the House of Commons). It became a textbook in a number of universities and was the first ever work on select committees to be published by an MP. It makes fascinating reading in the light of subsequent events. The chairmen of all of the then long-established select committees contributed their views to the book, but they by no means converged. In a searching introduction, Alf presented the history of the experiment, inviting the readers to draw their own conclusions on the basis of all the viewpoints known to him.

He described how the proposals of the study group were dealt with by the House and the Government. To begin with, the Select Committee on Procedure was not willing to go as far as the study group had recommended. It came out in favour of only one committee – on Estimates – that would function through specialising sub-committees. Only four of the eighteen MPs on the Procedure Committee voted in favour of a wide range of specialist committees.

In their report, the committee stressed the need to provide *all* Members of Parliament with the means to carry out their responsibilities, rather than to elevate any new committees of the House to positions of special influence.

Notwithstanding this and other cautionary pleas, the Government decided on a wider experiment. Richard Crossman, who preceded Fred Peart as Leader of the House, had announced the formation of two, rather than one, new committees. One would have an ongoing 'subject' remit of science and technology; the other would scrutinise one Ministry at a time over a single parliamentary session, starting with MAFF. Crossman had moved even further towards the views of the study group of professors by deciding to create the office of Parliamentary Commissioner for Administration – an 'ombudsman' – and a specialist select committee to oversee his work. From this beginning, over a period of four years, the number of specialist select committees quickly increased.

But the arrangements were not without influential opposition. In particular, Michael Foot was *"a most thoroughgoing critic of the whole idea of increasing the amount of time spent by MPs in committees upstairs"*. He believed that such committees strengthened the "appalling" drift towards a consensus in politics, launching a withering attack on the entire notion that MPs can work more effectively for the electorate unseen on committees 'upstairs' than in conflict across the floor of the House. The cosier the atmosphere, argued Foot, the less likely it became that the clash between the parties would be seen and understood by the public.

Although he wrote impartially, Alf was no less concerned about the consequences that might arise from the Crossman experiment. He felt that one of the dangers was that members of the committees would become immersed in their own narrow speciality and detached from the general body of MPs. Looking back, he thinks that to a great extent this has now happened. By 1970 it was becoming increasingly evident that the people who spoke on their reports in debates on the floor of the House were themselves members of the select committees; hardly anybody else took part, so they were left debating their own report, and wider parliamentary scrutiny of the

Executive – among the most important functions of Parliament – was gravely impaired. Specialisation might begin with the promise of keeping to the study group's five principles, but it could easily develop into the exercise of power by small groups of MPs with rivalry supplanting co-operation. Even worse was the possibility that departmental select committees might move into too cosy a relationship with the civil service bureaucracies they were appointed to scrutinise, so that the scrutineers became, some said, more and more comfortably embedded in the pockets of departments of state.

Yet Alf recognised that it would be difficult for any government to turn back. The likelihood was that specialist select committees were there to stay as a check on executive government and would eventually be a permanent feature of the British parliamentary scene. His comments and the highly influential views brought together by his book reflected a deepening controversy on the issue. The success of select committees was, in his view, still a matter for "highly subjective judgement". What was certain, however, was that it would be decisions of the executive that would determine whether the new select committees were to be a permanent parliamentary institution and, if they were, for it to determine the relative merits of "departmental" and "subject" committees. The question was ultimately one of whether a formula that resolved the conflict could be found between Members who saw the select committee system as a panacea for most constitutional problems and those who saw its growth as a serious threat to the primacy of debate on the floor of the House.

Alf was in his element at the hub of procedural decision-making. What he did not know, as 1969 drew to its close, was that his grasp of the machinery of government, on which he was now a respected author, and his close ties with those most involved in that machinery, were suddenly and unexpectedly to be needed in a practical application that was to change for ever both his life and that of millions of others.

1971: with his Louis Braille Memorial Award, presented by the National Federation of the Blind for distinguished services to blind people.

THE HARDING AWARD PRESENTED

1971: Alf was the first-ever recipient of the Field Marshal Lord Harding Award, for outstanding services to disabled people. Designed by Garth Evans.

1969: Parliament. Visit of President Nixon. To his right: Dr Horace King (Speaker), Fred Peart, Alf, Speaker's Secretary.

March 1966: Crossacres, Manchester. Alf, already involved in advancing provision for disabled people, opens Woodside School, for disabled children.

1966: Manchester. Alf at a rally convened by Equity. Charles Morris third from left: James Callaghan, MP for Heywood and Middleton fourth from left.

October 1964: 10 Downing Street. With Harold Wilson, following Alf's appointment as Parliamentary Private Secretary to Fred Peart (then an office strictly confined to support members of the Cabinet).

October 1964: Alf and Charles upon their election success. Irene centre.

Chapter 7

DISABLED PEOPLE EMERGE FROM THE SHADOWS

1964–1969 (with a look back to earlier times)

"Nowadays many disabled people will have nothing to do with resignation as it used to be understood. Thriving in a climate of increasing public tolerance and kindness, and on a diet of pensions and welfare, we are becoming presumptuous. Now we reject any view of ourselves as being lucky to be allowed to live. We reject too all the myths and superstitions that have surrounded us in the past.

"We are challenging society to take account of us, to listen to what we say, to acknowledge us as an integral part of society itself. We do not want ourselves, or anyone else, treated as second-class citizens and put away out of sight and mind".

Paul Hunt
(severely disabled and a long-standing friend of Alf's) in Stigma:
The Experience of Disability (Geoffrey Chapman, 1966), chapter 12.

– The 60s: a turning point – A history of neglect – Beveridge and Bevan
– Disabled people left behind – The seeds of change
– Birth of the Disablement Income Group – Parliament begins to listen
– A Disability Commission proposed – A new voice and a new message
– Development of the 'social model' of disability
– The pressing need for practical help

The 60s: a turning point

Alf's introduction to Parliament in 1964 coincided with a major shift in the social mores of British society and the dawn of the swinging sixties. Despite the minefields of national and international problems and hot and cold wars, there was a perceptible change of gear in British society. In retrospect and in its totality, the swing was 'off with the old and on with the new'.

But for many life was unchanging and bleak. Not everyone was into 'flower power' and 'strawberry fields'. These flights of fancy barely touched the lives of disabled people. They were still rarely able to contribute to society – 'looked after' in institutions, or unseen and impotent in the privacy of family homes. It has been said that no disadvantaged group was so utterly neglected.[1]

Parliament continued largely to ignore the needs of disabled citizens. Such provision as existed was heavily disposed towards institutional care rather than the promotion of independence. The Statute Book was innocent of any specific requirement to help disabled people to lead more fulfilling lives. Guidance to local authorities issued by the Ministry of Health in 1951[2] was not revised during the whole of the following 19 years. Between 1945 and 1960, no mention whatever was made in the manifestos of any political party, other than in the context of war, of anything that could help disabled people. Between 1959 and 1964, there was not one single debate on disability in the House of Commons.[3] Within the Labour Movement, only the Co-operative Party, on Alf's initiative, had raised the issue of disability at its annual conferences.

A history of neglect

The roots of this unconcern lie deep in our history, embedded, one might almost say, in the British psyche. As far back as the 14th century, the demise of the feudal system and the emergence of a capitalistic society brought immediate and familiar problems. Those in economic danger could no longer look to the protection of their masters, however discretionary and limited this may have been. Wages, though they represented an escape from serfdom, also became an indispensable passport to survival and security. By and large, if you didn't work you didn't eat, and begging could be ferociously punished.

So what about those who could not work? By a statute of 1388, subject to severe restrictions, disabled people could be accepted as "impotent" to serve or labour and as such granted a special dispensation allowing them to beg. Though shocking to modern sensibilities, this was the first recognition that disabled people merited special treatment. In 1531, this dubious privilege was

---

[1] *As of Right* (Michael Meacher, Margaret Beckett and Alfred Morris, 1985).
[2] *Circular 32/1951.*
[3] *Disability, Legislation and Practice* (Ed. Duncan Guthrie, The Macmillan Press Ltd, 1981).

reinforced by the formal registration of all "poor and impotent persons" living "by alms of the charity of the people". Such persons were provided with a letter that authorised them to beg within a specified area.

These arrangements were short-lived. In 1536, a major development in social policy was introduced, with a package of measures that included the establishment of a comprehensive system of parish relief. Leading citizens of every parish were required to gather and procure "charitable voluntary alms" to provide for "the poor, impotent, lame, feeble, sick and diseased people, being not able to work" so that none of them "be suffered to go openly in begging".

In 1601, this development was taken a stage further by an Elizabethan Poor Law that abandoned the reliance upon voluntary contributions for the funding of parish relief. A system of local taxation on the inhabitants of every parish was substituted, with a view to more securely obtaining "money for and towards the necessary relief of the lame, impotent, old, blind and such other among them being poor and not able to work". At the same time it was decreed that families of people without means of support, who themselves had sufficient ability, should "at their own charges relieve and maintain every such poor person".

Redress for disability caused by wrongs or negligence was a feature of common law during the Middle Ages and by the 16th century there was a right to compensation for injuries sustained in military service. But in practice even those disabled in war were shamefully neglected. After the Napoleonic wars, thousands of disabled soldiers were forced to beg or to steal. It was in an attempt to sweep these men from the countryside that the vagrancy laws were amended so that it became an offence "to expose wounds or deformities" to seek alms.

Much as in our own times, taxation rose steadily year by year and the idea of providing relief for the poor found little favour. It was not until 1832 that the administration and practical operation of the Elizabethan Poor Law was called officially into question, with the appointment of a Royal Commission. It soon became clear, however, that its primary concern was to reduce expenditure. The thrust of the enquiry was directed, almost exclusively, at questioning the merits of providing relief to the able-bodied poor, and its conclusions were emphatic that such relief was morally destructive. In their report of 1834, the Commissioners stated that able-bodied paupers had everywhere demonstrated "idleness and vice" and that in most cases pauperism could have been averted by ordinary care and industry. They were thus held to be largely to blame for their own condition. The Commissioners concluded that the provision of relief encouraged a feckless mode of living and that the moral (as well as the economic) argument lay with the utmost restriction of relief.

On 14 August 1834, an Act for the Amendment and Better Administration of the Laws Relating to the Poor in England and Wales set the pattern for social security for the next 75 years. In addition to centralising the administration of the Poor Law, a key strategy was that relief should, wherever possible, be provided by admission into a network of local workhouses. Here was a system of relief that could be made so irksome and disagreeable that it would not be sought by anyone who could possibly do without it.

Although these draconian measures had not been directed against disabled people (the Commission having drawn a distinction between the "determined pauper" and the "infirm and deserving poor"), the effects of the New Poor Law of 1834 were inevitably regressive. By 1850, despite growing national wealth, total relief had been more than halved. Even the burgeoning of charitable philanthropy in the late nineteenth century, in response to the desperate plight of poor people, tended only to reinforce the policy of restraining the provision of public relief. Charity, it was argued, could not be anticipated by the individual with any certainty, and was therefore less likely to encourage improvidence than relief given by the state as a right.

The characteristics of the Poor Law were very deeply entrenched, namely an overriding concern to limit public expenditure and a reluctance to provide financial relief to people who could possibly fend for themselves. Provision was at once meagre and confined to people in extreme poverty. While disabled people were accepted as deserving of help, relief was inescapably linked with destitution and the stigma of poverty. Those in receipt of relief through the Poor Law were labelled "paupers" and were seen and treated as being of inferior status as citizens.

These attitudes persisted well into the twentieth century, resting on an inheritance of deeply rooted prejudice. In many respects things went from bad to worse. Huge increases in the population of urban areas put more and more pressure on the system and as the distinction between the deserving and undeserving poor eroded, disabled people inevitably endured the same misery as everyone else.

There was, nevertheless, some limited progress. Towards the end of the nineteenth century, with the expansion of industrialisation and the extension of the franchise to working men in 1870, pressure for compensation for industrial injury led to the Employers' Liability Act 1880 and the Workmen's (Compensation for Accidents) Act 1897. The latter Act made provision for compensation to be paid for death or incapacity suffered as a result of an accident in certain specially dangerous industries, and was subsequently extended to provide a comprehensive system of benefits for those disabled in the course of employment.

This was followed by the introduction of social insurance against sickness and unemployment. For people who built up a sufficient contribution record, the National Insurance Act 1911 provided a variety of benefits, including payment for sickness and disability. Although a notable advance, the scheme's reliance on the contributory principle excluded the vast majority of disabled people from benefit, setting a pattern that was to persist for many decades to come, with a growing gap between the working (and thus insured) population and unemployed (and thus uninsured) disabled people. Little further progress was made in social security provision for disabled people generally, apart from bits and pieces of legislation responding to the problems of people disabled through injury at work or in war: the Blind Persons Act 1920 – condescendingly referred to as providing "blind welfare" – and the largely ineffective Disabled Persons (Employment) Act 1944.

Beveridge and Bevan

But social policy moved nearer to centre stage among domestic policy issues when, in 1941, Arthur Greenwood, the Minister for post-war reconstruction, set up an Inter-departmental Committee on Social Insurance and Allied Services under the chairmanship of Sir William Beveridge. Its landmark report, *Social Insurance and Allied Services*, published in 1942, put forward plans for a 'Welfare State'. Government White Papers appeared in 1944, detailing Beveridge's main recommendations on which the Attlee Government's post-war legislation on social security and the National Health Service was largely based. The National Assistance Act 1948, incorporating proposals by Beveridge, ended the Poor Law, decreed the closure of workhouses and provided a new system for helping people whose needs could not be covered in other ways. Section 29 of the Act laid the task of promoting the welfare of disabled people on local authorities. It gave them power to extend services to "persons who are blind, deaf or dumb, and other persons who are substantially and permanently handicapped by illness, injury or congenital deformity or such other disabilities as may be prescribed by the Minister". The arrangements they could make under the Act included advice on available services, instruction in ways of overcoming the effects of disabilities, the provision of workshops and hostels for disabled workers, and the provision of work and recreational facilities for disabled people. Just how bad things had been up to then can be gauged from Aneurin Bevan's speech introducing the second reading of the National Assistance Bill on 24 November 1947. Despite substantial expansion of social services, he told the House, there were still 400,000 people on "outdoor relief" and 50,000 in institutions. The Bill marked "the end of a whole period of the social history of Great Britain". The workhouses would go, and not before time. Although many people had tried to humanise them they were, he said, "a very evil institution". Sidney and Beatrice Webb, to whom a great debt was owed, had written: "The young servant out of place, the prostitute recovering from disease, the feeble-minded woman of any age, the girl with the first baby, the unmarried mother coming to be confined of her third or fourth bastard, the paralytic, the epileptic, the respectable, deserted wife, the widow to whom outdoor relief has been refused, are all herded indiscriminately together".

Bevan, who is perhaps better known as the architect of the National Health Act, was well ahead of his time. He saw "bigness as the enemy of humanity" and legislated for the introduction of small residences for older people, run like hotels and accommodating people across a wide range of income groups, even suggesting names for them such as "The Limes". In the debate which followed there is evidence – for perhaps the first time – of a recognition that people incapacitated by mental or physical impairments were worthy of "dignified relief" and a hope that the Bill would "bring a great deal of help and hope to these disabled people". One speaker, Basil Neald (City of Chester), hoped that provision might be extended to cover "the supply of surgical appliances" and even suggested that people who, because of incapacity, could not do work of any kind "should not be dependent upon sickness grant and assistance, but should have an adequate national handicap allowance", thus anticipating the mission of the Disablement Income Group by more than 20 years. Bevan himself clearly recognised that money devoted to the welfare of disabled people was money well spent. Some years later, in 1955, he pointed out that the Treasury failed to appreciate that leaving disabled people to their own resources inevitably led to their decline. They became depressed and introspective and very often developed a diversity of mental disorders. Because they were not rehabilitated they became a permanent and unquantified cost to the social services, a figure that was not on the Treasury's balance sheet at all.[4]

Disabled people left behind

Revolutionary and seminal though the National Assistance Act undoubtedly was, however, it did little for the dignity of people with long-term illnesses and disabilities not occasioned at work and therefore outside the national insurance system. With the exception of war pensioners, the only source of income for disabled people living in poverty – 'national assistance' – was both minimal and strictly means-tested. Although the Act did away with the Poor Law

---

[4] *Aneurin Bevan* (Michael Foot, David-Poynter Ltd, 1973), vol.II, p.490.

it was its lineal descendant and was in many respects modelled upon it. The Supplementary Benefit Act that followed 18 years later, although intended to be more flexible, was also lineally descended from the Poor Law and in practice proved another parsimonious flop. Disabled people who could claim the limited benefit available had to plead and prove absolute poverty. Like Alf's father, they were unidentified and ignored by the authorities.

Local authority services under the National Assistance Act 1948 were largely discretionary and quite limited. The only mandatory requirement was the keeping of a register of disabled people who applied for assistance. Ursula Keeble has pointed out that until 1960 no pressure was put on local authorities to submit plans on how they proposed to implement the Act. By then, councils had become accustomed to making provision for disabled people, if any, in their own time and at their own pace. The result was that services varied greatly from area to area, with many authorities giving spending on disabled people such low priority that welfare officers frequently referred to their work as 'the Cinderella service".[5]

Such voluntary organisations for disabled people as existed also had little to offer. They were well intentioned and 'do-gooding' but tended to be patronising and generally uninformed about the realities of life for those they were created to help. Disabled people were expected to be grateful for small mercies; the smaller the mercy, the more grateful the beneficiary was expected to be. The concept of charity was one largely of almsgiving, with no thought of conferring independence. Nor was there ever any thought in the voluntary sector of seeking legislation to improve social provision. Society excluded disabled people – even from public sanitary facilities – and seemed hell-bent on continuing to do so. A 'disability movement' – a phrase first used by Alf – was still undreamt of and the question of rights never arose.

The seeds of change

But this parsimony was soon to be challenged. The catalyst was an article on 15 March 1965 in *The Guardian* by its women's editor, Mary Stott, a kindred spirit, close friend and fellow activist of Alf's

[5] *Disability: Legislation and Practice* (ed. Duncan Guthrie, Macmillan, 1981).

in the Co-operative Movement. His first speech at a Co-operative Congress – the 'annual parliament' of the movement – was in moving a motion on 'Dignity in Old Age' in 1951, and Mary was there with him helping to ensure that it was carried. Alf recalls her as *"a very ordinary person, without airs and graces. At the Congress you would have seen her as a run-of-the-mill delegate. She was a doer not a publicist, imbued with the spirit of the Co-operative Movement's founders. But her very ordinariness gave her social insights into difficulties faced by ordinary people of which other senior journalists were totally unaware."*

Mary's 1965 article included the following seminal passage: "Beveridge's foundation stone for our system of National Insurance was that when people could not maintain themselves and their families either temporarily, as in sickness or unemployment, or permanently, as in old age, the State must take over responsibility. But there are people who not only cannot work for a living, they cannot *live* without long-term, perhaps permanent care. All these should have a disability pension, whether their disability was due to industrial accident, war injury, innate defect, illness, or the infirmities of old age, and that pension should be enough to cover not only food and clothing and the essentials for a healthy person but payment for some care and attention".

Birth of the Disablement Income Group

Two disabled and dynamic women, Megan du Boisson and Berit Moore, both of whom had multiple sclerosis, backed Mary Stott's call for purposeful action to win new help for disabled people. Their immediate concern was personal need and this was rooted in their own experience of disability. They and other women like them had no entitlement to any financial help as of right. The social security benefits offered them no help as disabled housewives to enable them to meet either the costs of paid help to replace their economic contribution to their families or any of the other expenses of disabled living. Their response to Mary Stott's article suggested "the foundation of a group, to which all societies, such as those for people with muscular dystrophy, multiple sclerosis, poliomyelitis, and other long-term diseases would contribute their ideas and authority. This group could be called the Disablement Income Group – or DIG. It would exist only to correlate the work of the other groups in regard solely to getting recognition for the *right* of disabled persons, irrespective of the reason for that disablement, to pensions from the State to enable them to live in a reasonable degree of independence and dignity *in their own homes*''. This suggestion evoked around a thousand letters of support from disabled people from all over the country. On 10 September 1965, the Group – of which Alf was soon to be a patron – came formally into being.

The Group's first priority was to set about influencing the media, opening discussions with MPs and others and generally lobbying for parliamentary action. Benefiting from the extraordinary skills and vision of Mary Stott, DIG quickly gained a reputation for being thoroughly professional in the presentation of its case, beginning with a memorandum in September 1965 to The Rt. Hon. Douglas Houghton MP, Chancellor of the Duchy of Lancaster, a social policy co-ordinator in the Wilson Government. It affirmed that DIG existed to work in general for the improvement of the social and economic conditions of disabled people, and in particular "for the provision by the State of a modest basic income, with special supplementary allowances, for all disabled persons ordinarily resident in the United Kingdom, whatever the cause of disablement, and irrespective of previous national insurance contributions". It was then submitted "that legislation should speedily be introduced to provide for such a basic income known as the National Disability Income" of an amount related to that of the current retirement pension.

Megan du Boisson and Berit Moore, drawing on the evidence of the letters sent to them by other disabled people, showed themselves to be able advocates, as later did Mary Greaves and Peter Large. Their concern soon widened to embrace the plight of more and more other people with disabilities who were excluded from the rigidly circumscribed benefits system. They drew attention, as Mary Stott's *Guardian* article had done, to the fact that Beveridge's 'Welfare State' provided only for those with entitlement through National Insurance contributions or under the war pensions scheme. It did nothing for the vast majority of disabled people. It drew no distinction between long-term disability and short-term sickness, and totally ignored the need to provide an income as of right for disabled married women, people with severe congenital disabilities or who had become disabled early in their lives, very few of whom would have built up a National Insurance contribution record. The hated means-testing of the 1930s, thought by many to have disappeared, was still alive and well in the Welfare State, despite its claim to be providing "help with dignity from the cradle to the grave". The notion of non-contributory benefits as a basic right had not been contemplated by any of the political parties. Not only were there no such benefits, they were not even perceived as a desirable objective. Shoals of letters to DIG reflected the distress of disabled people for whom no economic provision had been made. Alf described them as "almost non-people in the eye of the state". Megan du Boisson called them "the forgotten poor".

In all DIG's activities at this time, Megan took the major role. In what she saw as an urgent mission she never underestimated the task that lay ahead. For disabled people in general, as well as from a personal perspective, there was no time to be wasted. Mary Stott later recalled that because Megan had multiple sclerosis she felt that her time was limited and this was one of the things that drove her on. The sense that she must do as much as possible in the shortest possible time gave her spiritual energy. Believing wholeheartedly in the cause for which she was working provided the additional strength to do what required to be done. She did, Mary Stott noticed, have periods when she was confined to bed, but this brought out her extraordinary shrewdness in gathering around her a number of people to take her place at short notice if she wasn't able to fulfil an appointment.[6]

DIG unleashed an outcry from many thousands of people around the country who were desperate to be heard. It had an impact out of all proportion to the size of the organisation. From the parliamentary session of 1964–65 onwards, there is evidence in *Hansard* of greater and better-organised pressure for the improvement of services. Much of that pressure was inspired by Megan. She regularly made contact and met a number of sympathetic MPs from each of the three main parties, some of whom became very supportive. She asked them to table repeated questions about provision for disabled

[6] *A Story of Our Time*, a programme about Megan Du Boisson broadcast on Woman's Hour, BBC Radio 4, 22 February 1973.

people, and Alf was one of those who responded, asking dozens of questions on the problems and needs of disabled people and speaking in a number of debates. The interest that Megan generated in the House of Commons was also an important factor in the later setting up of an All Party Parliamentary Disability Group.

Among the leading players from the outset were The Hon. John Astor, Conservative MP for Newbury, and Jack Ashley, Labour MP for Stoke on Trent South, who first met Megan in 1966 shortly after his election. Jack, like Alf, had risen from the poorest of Lancashire's poor through a scholarship to Ruskin College and from there to university – in Jack's case Cambridge – where he became President of the Union. In his second autobiography, *Acts of Defiance*, he recalled Megan du Boisson as having: "a certain magic, a gaiety, even frivolity, which enlivened conversation with her. Yet she was also deeply serious, dedicated to a cause which she espoused passionately and intelligently. People listened to Megan du Boisson".[7]

DIG organised successful, high profile rallies in Trafalgar Square in 1967 and 1968. At the first of these it was able to bring together a platform of speakers of diverse political persuasions. Introduced by Duncan Guthrie, then Director of the Central Council for the Disabled and Founder and Director of the National Fund for Crippling Diseases (now Action Research), speaker after speaker affirmed the need for economic justice for disabled people: the radio and television interviewer, Mary Dalison (who organised the rally), Dame Joan Vickers, Professor Michael Fogarty, Dr David Owen (then DIG's Vice-Chairman), Mervyn Pike, Bill Molloy and Rev. Austen Williams joined in one accord to proclaim the importance of DIG's aims. From Trafalgar Square they went in procession to Parliament. London had never seen its like. Hundreds of people from all over the country in wheelchairs, on crutches, in invalid cars and ambulances and, as best they could, on foot, with placards held high to tell the world about their cause, those heading the procession reaching the Cenotaph while others still waited to leave the Square.

[7] *Acts of Defiance* (Jack Ashley, Reinhardt Books, 1992), p.312.

The second Trafalgar Square rally coincided with the United Nations Year of Human Rights. This time Lord Soper was one of the speakers, forcefully quoting Article 25 of the Declaration of Human Rights: "Everyone has the right to a standard of living adequate for the health and well-being of himself and of his family, including food, clothing, housing, and medical care, and necessary social services, and the right to security in the event of unemployment, sickness, disability, widowhood, old age or other lack of livelihood or circumstances beyond his control".

Duncan Guthrie again introduced the speakers, who once more spanned a range of different political and religious beliefs. As well as Lord Soper, the meeting was addressed by Lord Balniel, then a Conservative MP, Rabbi Nemeth, Margaret Wingfield, the Right Reverend Patrick Casey, Michael Flanders, Megan du Boisson, and the Right Reverend G. D. Leonard. The issue, as Lord Balniel put it, transcended all political passions and political parties. It was one, to quote Rabbi Nemeth, that united "every shade of religious and political life in this country about the grave social injustice that is being allowed to continue in our midst".

In the first issue of DIG's magazine, *Progress*, in March 1968, the continued failure of the Government to address the needs of disabled people was again presented as a human rights issue. The assertion that disabled people should have equal rights with other citizens was to become the bedrock on which DIG's policy aims were shaped. Its leadership was championing universal human rights at a time when people with disabilities were still commonly treated as non-citizens. DIG was essentially an organisation *of* as well as *for* disabled people – perhaps the first of its kind – led by disabled people and uniting a wide diversity of disabled people as members who joined its campaigns and took an active part in policy-making. Significantly, however, it did not reject help and support from non-disabled people. Megan du Boisson strongly emphasised that her inspiration was the article by Mary Stott, not herself a disabled person, and her approach from the outset, like Mary's, was one of charming persuasion rather than angry confrontation, least of all with anyone willing to help. Disabled people were in control, but the value of partnership in achieving change was clearly recognised.

Parliament begins to listen

Megan du Boisson, Duncan Guthrie, Mary Greaves, Marsh Dickson and Mary Stott, among others, were leading activists in helping to start the parliamentary impetus for change. Their influence transformed the climate of both parliamentary and public opinion from one of, at best, benign charity to an acceptance that disabled people were entitled to live independent and dignified lives as full members of the community.

By now Jack Ashley had become particularly active on DIG's behalf. It was his association with Megan that first led him to "think seriously about disablement" and to recognise the need to "translate the wind of change into political action".[8] His first step, in October 1967 – shortly before he lost his hearing – was to initiate an adjournment debate to draw the attention of the House to the financial need of chronically sick and disabled people. Replying, Norman Pentland, then Joint Parliamentary Under Secretary at the DHSS, reassured his "Honourable Friend" that provision for chronically sick and disabled people was one of the Government's priorities.[9]

Later in that year, DIG initiated a significant exchange of correspondence with Judith Hart, the Minister of Social Security, and Michael Stewart, First Secretary of State. In their ministerial replies both expressed genuine concern. Judith Hart recognised that the financial problems of disabled people were not fully covered by a system that related benefits to contributions and said that she would "like to find a solution". Michael Stewart emphasised that it was a mistake to imagine that legislators and administrators failed "to understand the basic human problems which confront ordinary people", but that there were practical limits to what could be done at any given moment.[10]

---

[8] *Acts of Defiance* (Jack Ashley, Reinhardt Books, 1992), p.313.
[9] *Hansard*, Commons, vol. 751 23.10.67, col.1397.
[10] DIG archives.

On 15 March 1968, there was a second, and historically significant, debate on disability, led by Gordon Campbell, Conservative MP for Moray and Nairn. He had benefited from success in the private member's ballot, bringing a motion that urged the Government to give high priority to the task of identifying those with severe disabilities or chronic illness who were in need of special help because of their inability, or much reduced ability, to earn a living. During a four-hour debate attention was drawn to the hardship faced by all severely disabled people, not merely those disabled through war or industrial injuries and, in particular, the plight of the disabled housewife, then entirely excluded from benefit. The debate also pressed the essential need for the introduction of a constant attendance allowance outside the industrial injuries scheme. Among others, Paul Dean (Conservative, Somerset North) demonstrated a new understanding of the problems associated with disability. He perceptively identified three themes: lack of information about disability and its connected problems and, therefore, "a need to identify and define"; the inevitability of the numbers of people with disability and chronic sickness increasing as a consequence of longer life expectancy; and, finally, anomalies in public provision among such people. And he went on to notice that there had already been a strong development in care services – "away from care in institutions to care in the community". This, he said, was not only socially right but also better for the people concerned. The provision of supporting services must therefore be given the highest priority.

The response of Julian Snow, Parliamentary Secretary to the Ministry of Health, was lengthy and detailed but cautious and procrastinating, emphasising the many difficulties faced in meeting the problems faced by disabled people. Local authorities, in particular, needed "a great deal more information – information which takes years to compile". In the meantime, they would not be able to provide services as efficiently as everybody would wish. Those services, he said, would include people living in their own homes, remembering that "the chronic sick and disabled have the same basic needs, hopes, fears and need for personal relationships as the more fortunate of us". "Where they differ," he asserted, was that "handicap sets a barrier between aspiration and fulfilment, if indeed it does not weaken aspiration". Thus, "the aim of all services, should be to help remove that barrier, or lower it, so far as it stands between the individual and independent life for so long as he or she is able and willing". The possibilities that had been suggested were being studied, and the whole question of a constant attendance allowance was a matter of very earnest and urgent consideration.[11]

On 8 April 1968, John Astor pressed the matter again. Would the Minister of Social Security seek to make available allowances for constant attendance and other benefits, equivalent to those payable under the industrial injuries scheme, to all disabled people who were not eligible to receive benefit under existing schemes? Judith Hart confirmed that she was "anxious to find some way of helping people who are very severely disabled, irrespective of the cause of disablement", but that it was necessary to await the result of the Government's research as to the incidence of disability of differing degrees in the community outside those injured in industry or war and among groups of people like housewives, so that proper costings could be made.[12]

A Disability Commission proposed

A few months later, David Owen, who had just been appointed to ministerial office, invited Jack Ashley to present, under the 10–minute-rule, a Bill that he had prepared. It proposed the appointment of a commission to investigate a strategy for the introduction of a disablement income. Jack's total loss of hearing had been diagnosed only a few months earlier, and in his second autobiography, *Acts of Defiance*, he describes his anxiety. Unable to hear his own voice, he found it difficult to control its volume, modulation and pitch. He was conscious of the hazards of making a speech in Parliament in such circumstances. But on the weekend before his speech, he had attended DIG's second Trafalgar Square rally. He had been struck by the spirited way disabled people coped with the most severe handicaps. It gave him a new perspective and he decided that "it was clearly time to forget my problems and state an effective and persuasive case". Patient rehearsal ensured that the

[11] *Hansard*, Commons, 15 March 1968, cols.1905-73.
[12] *Hansard*, Commons, 8 April 1968, cols. 874-5.

speech was a triumph. An unusually quiet and packed House of Commons, including the Prime Minister and the Leader of the Opposition, listened intently as Jack told them of the Trafalgar Square demonstration and what it had meant to disabled people and of their need for financial assistance. Jack resumed his seat to cheers and applause. Though he could not hear the acclaim which came from all sides of the House, it signalled that the case for disabled people had been made more powerfully than ever before. On his way to present the Bill to the Speaker, Harold Wilson touched Jack's arm: "Well done, Jack" was the congratulation that he read on the Prime Minister's lips.[13]

The idea of a Disability Commission was not, however, acceptable to his government. They resisted both this Bill and a Disabled Persons Pensions and Miscellaneous Provisions Bill presented by the Conservative MP James Prior in February 1969. Richard Crossman, the Secretary of State for Social Services, had flatly declared in correspondence with DIG that he and his colleagues, and they alone, were "responsible for ensuring that the right things are done for the right people at the right time and in the right way".

He did, nevertheless, concede one item on Megan du Boisson's shopping list. She had lobbied him when the National Superannuation and Social Insurance Bill was being drafted. Her purpose was to get him to include in the legislation some provision for a pension for disabled people. Initially he rejected the idea, because the Act had been planned on the basis of a scheme for people who were in employment. Largely as a result of Megan's pressure, however, Crossman was persuaded to include a clause about an allowance for people who were so severely disabled that they needed constant attendance from another person. A White Paper published on 28 January 1969 outlined plans for a contributory social security scheme to be introduced in 1972 which would provide an invalidity benefit for those who fell sick or had an accident and whose absence from work lasted for more than 28 weeks. For those outside the contributory scheme, it proposed a new non-contributory benefit which went a long way towards meeting DIG's aspirations: the Attendance Allowance, payable to

---

[13] *Acts of Defiance* (Jack Ashley, Reinhardt Books, 1992), p.165-66.

those with a handicap so severe as to make them "wholly or largely dependent on help from other people in coping with the functions of daily living".

Sadly, this potential step forward was quickly followed in May 1969 by the devastating news of Megan du Boisson's death. Such had been her influence on Parliament that, within hours, ten MPs led a motion calling upon the House of Commons to pay tribute to her work. Letters poured in from both the Lords and the Commons and from MPs on all sides of the political divide. James Prior remarked upon the impact that she had managed to make on so many Members of Parliament and Ministers in such a short space of time: "Amongst her many great gifts she had the ability of exerting her pressure and authority without ever seeming to be doing so, without ever causing the slightest offence. To many Members, such as myself, she opened our eyes, not only to the problems posed by disablement itself, but also to the side effects of poverty and isolation".

Many others testified to Megan's outstanding achievement, but also pointed up the need for her work to be carried on. Lena Jeger MP captured the mood: "What can we do when a beautiful, talented, totally unselfish woman is taken away before her self-appointed task is done? There is only one answer. Finish it for her ... complete her work. That brave spirit will continue to disturb the consciences of us all".

DIG responded by reorganising itself, under the leadership of Mary Greaves, to intensify the campaign for a national disability income. "It is a tribute to Megan," wrote John Astor, "that those who remain to carry on the work she inspired are determined to do so with even greater enthusiasm". Little more than a month after the tragedy of Megan's death, DIG organised a mass lobby of Parliament, an event which its newsletter *Progress* described as a "mass plea for justice". David Ennals, Joint Minister of State for Health and Social Security, "bravely threw himself to the lions. They wheeled around him ... engaging him in lively debate on the shortcomings of State aid for the disabled, while ... other MPs both answered and asked questions of DIG lobbyists". On the following day, more than 100 MPs signed a special motion calling on the

Government to introduce an attendance allowance as a matter of urgency. DIG was inching its way towards its goal.

A new voice and a new message

One other, largely unsung, pioneer outside Parliament was to have a profound influence. In 1966, Paul Hunt, a wheelchair user who had lived for the previous ten years in a Cheshire foundation home in Hampshire, contributed a thoughtful essay, *A Critical Condition*, to a book published under the title *Stigma: the experience of disability*[14]. As a severely disabled young man, living among severely disabled people, paralysed and deformed (as he put it), Paul had pondered on the very meaning of life. He pointed out that being cheerful and keeping going was scarcely good enough when one had an illness that would end in an early death, dependent on others for daily needs, probably denied marriage and a family and forced to live out one's time in an institution. In these circumstances the most acute questions arose and the most radical answers were called for. Paul thought that what he called the "problem" of disability lay not only in the impairment of function and its effects on people individually, but also, more importantly, in the area of disabled people's relationship with "normal" people. He argued that a focus on the ways in which disabled people were set apart from the "ordinary" did not imply that they were separated from society: they shared their human nature with the rest of mankind.

Nevertheless, he contended, disabled people held a special position, distinguished by the challenges they presented in their relations with "ordinary society": particularly by being seen as "unfortunate, useless, different, oppressed and sick". In responding to these challenges in detail, Paul was at pains to reject "society's tendency to set up rigid standards of what is right and proper, to force the individual into a mould". This "pressure towards unthinking conformity" in some way related disabled people to "other obvious deviants and outcasts like the Jew in a gentile world, a Negro in a white world, homosexuals, the mentally handicapped" and "other subversive elements in society". But Paul and other disabled people could give witness to the truth that a person's dignity did not rest in

[14] Ed. Paul Hunt, London, Geoffrey Chapman, chapter 12.

beauty, age, intelligence or colour. Those with unimpaired minds but severely disabled bodies could show that their "big difference" from other people did not lessen their worth, nor do away with their right to be treated as fully human.

This, at the time, was totally at odds with conventional thinking. Paul was especially critical of the widely assumed perception of disabled people as being different and therefore having minority status. That he and others like him were "different" was not something that he sought to deny, but he rejected the implication that it justified their having to face prejudice, expressed "in discrimination and even oppression" from people assuming their superiority and authority over them.

Paul's closely reasoned conclusion was to challenge British society to take account of disabled people, to listen to what they had to say, to acknowledge them as an integral part of society itself. They did not want themselves, or anyone else, to be treated as second-class citizens and put away "out of sight and mind". Many disabled people, wrote Paul, were just beginning to refuse to be put away, insisting that they too were part of society. They were saying that being deformed and paralysed, blind or deaf – or old or mentally impaired – was not a crime, nor, in any meaningful sense of the term, a divine punishment. Illness and impairment were facts of existence; diminishment and death were there to be thought about and to be taken account of in any realistic view of the world. "We are perhaps also saying," he argued, "that society is itself sick if it can't face our sickness, if it does not overcome its natural fear and dislike of unpleasantness as manifested by disability".

It was no part of Paul's case to deny that his impairments were disabling. On the contrary, his essay stressed that he and other severely disabled people "naturally" wanted to get away from and forget the sickness, depression, pain, loneliness and poverty of which they had to endure more than their share. To repudiate this "special relation to the dark", he said, would mean that they had ceased to recognise their most important asset as disabled people in society: "the uncomfortable, subversive position from which we act as a living reproach to any scale of values that puts attributes or possessions before the person".

Development of the 'social model' of disability

There was nothing in this to prompt a rush to the barricades by non-disabled people, but ten years later Hunt's original views were taken up and developed – far beyond his original thinking – by the Union of the Physically Impaired Against Segregation (UPIAS). They came up with an assertion that disability was "the disadvantage or restriction of activity caused by a contemporary social organisation which takes little or no account of people who have physical impairments and thus excludes them from participation in the mainstream of social activities". From this was developed the so-called 'social model of disability', an ideology that has subsequently attracted remarkably wide acceptance, even emerging in a report of the Prime Minister Blair's Strategy Unit, *Improving the Life Chances of Disabled People*[15]. The concept rightly focuses upon the physical, attitudinal and communication barriers faced by people with impairments and in so doing allows any negative feelings they may have about their own disability to be displaced by a shared experience of external prejudice. But like all models, the 'social model of disability' predicates a one-rule-fits-all fundamentalist formula, underestimating the diversity of disability and the severity of its impact. The thrust for equality, self-determination and choice has its limits and the paradigm of disabled people held back only by society is not always appropriate.

Ann Darnbrough, herself disabled from childhood and a strenuous advocate of empowerment, recalls a visit she made to a class of profoundly disabled children some twenty-five years ago that is etched on her memory:

"There were about twelve children sitting in their wheelchairs in a semi-circle around their four teachers, so that they were being very well looked after. They had small desks and were being given work to do. They were working very hard, but it was the same thing over and over again. I had the opportunity to talk to the children and it was really a complete joy, although I was thinking all the time that

---
[15] January, 2005.

they were going to be very limited in what they could do. I had another experience at the same place of a young girl, aged about twelve, and I think it was quite clear that she was not able to join the class because of her very severe mental limitations. It was a lovely sunny day and she was sitting in the sunshine. I talked to her, but had no idea of whether she understood anything I said or whether she was deaf and perhaps blind. I didn't know. Her hand was hanging down outside her wheelchair and I took her hand and held it. She grasped it in a way, but I had no idea of whether she knew she did that or whether it was involuntary. I will always remember that. I can see it now and I can feel her little hand in mine, but it was so sad because she was never going to be able to do anything independently and she clearly couldn't learn in a classroom".[16]

The social model of disability is not, as lawyers say, 'case-sensitive', derogating from, if not entirely rejecting, the view the rest of the world has that impairments are themselves to a greater or lesser degree disabling.

The pressing need for practical help

In the late sixties, however, such controversy was still some way off. Parliament was only just beginning to respond to the weight of disadvantage suffered by disabled people. Alf Morris needed no persuading of the avoidable affliction heaped on disabled people. He knew from his own experience the importance of financial help as of right, but he also knew that the social exclusion of disabled people went deeper than poverty. His awareness had been heightened by seeing and working to help countless disabled constituents, among them children with special educational needs; young people incarcerated in long-stay hospitals, often in geriatric wards; people whose disabilities kept them off the pavements, let alone the roads; and older long-term sick and disabled people struggling against hopeless odds to preserve their independence.

Perhaps the worst indignity was that huge numbers of disabled people were simply forced out of society into institutions and abandoned there. One case brought Alf to challenge this by direct

---

[16] Interview, 5 February 2006.

action. He had run advice sessions at Wythenshawe well before his election to Parliament and at one of these, in 1958, Sarah Johnson came to see him. She told him that her brother Jim, to whom she was devoted, had been held at Calderstones, a barrack-like institution near Blackburn for people then described as mentally retarded, since 1928. As a child, Jim had been knocked down by a horse and cart and sustained brain damage, after which he was regarded as ineducable. Shortly after the accident, his mother's sister found that her gas meter had been raided and young Jim, who had been there at the time, was charged by the police. In the magistrate's court he was found unfit to plead and was sent, as were many others like him, to be detained in Calderstones, where he was incarcerated for the next thirty years. There had been no evidence that he had any involvement in the theft; indeed his elder sister Sarah was quite sure he was blameless. She was certain that she would have known had he been in any way involved. Every Saturday, over the thirty years, Sarah, herself severely disabled, travelled from Manchester to Calderstones, a return journey of over 40 miles, to visit her brother.

Alf wrote to Ministers and the Governor and a meeting with the governing body was arranged at Calderstones. It was a long meeting, held against a background of enormous press interest in the case. Alf secured Jim's release into a world transformed and entirely new to him, but to which he adapted well. In a couple of weeks, with Alf's help, he found a job as a dustman with Manchester's Cleansing Department, where he was a conscientious, eager and contented employee; a taxpayer rather than a dependant. His only quirk, Alf recalls, was his entrenched habit of arriving for work at 5.45 a.m., well before anyone else!

Alf knew that Jim was not the only disabled person to be treated as he had been. Their detestation of social exclusion – in Jim's case social expulsion – was the common thread that united most disabled people. They wanted independence, to be able to go where everyone else could go, and to achieve this they needed access to the built environment, state benefits as of right, social services appropriate to their individual needs and much else.

Yet the legislation to bring all this about was not even on the horizon. In fact no legislation on any aspect of disability was in prospect. Of suggestions there were for changes of policy Alf was well aware, but no-one had even considered drafting the wide-ranging legislation that would be needed. Marsh Dickson, founder of the National Campaign for the Young Chronic Sick, had prompted Alf to put parliamentary questions about the need for legislation or ministerial action to tackle the plight of young people locked away in the geriatric wards of hospitals. This was one of the issues in which Alf was also very much involved 'off the Order Paper' in detailed correspondence with Richard Crossman. He argued that current practice was morally wrong and ought not to be legally permissible. The predictable response was that there were many conflicting claims but, as Alf told Crossman, there could be few more pressing claims to priority than that of a young person with a lively mind who was being driven mad by having nobody to whom he or she could relate or even talk.

In 1967 and 1968, as we have seen, there were a number of limited attempts by backbench MPs to put disability issues on the legislative agenda, but these were gestures of parliamentary support rather than meaningful attempts with any realistic hope of legislating on the basis of well drafted bills and all were abortive. Parliamentary time for viable and wide-ranging legislation, with all-party support, was a precondition of any kind of legislation worth having. The opportunity for such an initiative, when it came, was unforeseen and entirely fortuitous.

Chapter 8

A MOST REMARKABLE ACT

1969— 1970

"When I find myself before St Peter in the near future, he may say to me, 'Did you do any good down there?' I shall be able to murmur a little bit about the honours I have received. And he will say, 'I do not want to know about that. I want to know did you do any good?' I shall be able to say, 'I played a small part in helping to carry the Alf Morris Bill through the House of Lords 30 years ago'. He will probably say, 'OK, you can take a day off purgatory for that'".

The Earl of Longford, House of Lords, 19 April 2000.

– Fortune favours an historic Bill – Resisting the easy option
– A clash with Crossman – Ready in time: the Second Reading
– Preparing for the Committee Stage – Not without opponents
– Saved on the brink of failure
– Extraordinary help in the hour of extraordinary need
– Practical solutions to practical problems – An informal support team
– Securing essential Treasury support – Twin committees
– Report Stage and Third Reading – Deliberation in the Lords: a race against time
– Harold Evans sounds the alarm – Harold Wilson to the rescue
– An Act of historic wide-ranging and lasting value

Fortune favours an historic Bill

In 1969, the annual ballot for Private Member's Bills was held on 6 November. At the time, Alf was away in New Delhi as a British delegate to the annual conference of the Commonwealth Parliamentary Association. He had, however, asked his brother Charles, the Member for Manchester Openshaw, to enter his name. As the Government's deputy chief whip, his brother was ineligible for the ballot, but was allowed by the rules to enter the name of another Member if authorised by her or him to do so. Flying home from India two days later, Alf discovered that he had won first place in the ballot.[1] He began at once to sketch out in an old

---

[1] Emanuel Shinwell complained, "It wasn't your turn Alf, you've only been here for five years!" Alf rejoined, "Manny, it wasn't your turn either. With some 550 people in the ballot the odds are around 549 to 1 against any Member coming top. On that basis we can only hope to top the ballot once every 550 years!"

address book his first thoughts for what was to become the Chronically Sick and Disabled Persons Bill.

Few people outside the Commons fully understand the processes surrounding Bills introduced by 'Private Members', that is to say MPs who are not Ministers. In every new parliamentary session, on the Thursday morning of the week following the Queen's Speech that marks its commencement, a ballot is held to allow twenty such Members, drawn from a hat by the Speaker, the opportunity to introduce a Bill of their own choosing. The first six have a reasonable chance of successfully completing the course, providing all other factors are favourable. The further down the list Members come, the lower are their chances of securing enough parliamentary time to get their Bills through both Houses of Parliament to Royal Assent. Even then, the chances of success for a Bill of the Member's own making are very slim indeed.[2]

As soon as the names of those successful in the ballot are announced, those at or near the top are pressurised by all and sundry: both Ministers whose intended legislation has not been included in the Queen's Speech and pressure groups all over the country, many of the most powerful of which always have a draft Bill on issues of importance to them ready and waiting. Highly attractive support goes with most of the Bills on offer: drafting and secretarial assistance, speech preparation, and much else. What is never seen by the public is the enormous pressure Ministers can exert on MPs who have won high places in the ballot. Although governments already have all the cream in terms of parliamentary time, individual Ministers often fail to get into the Queen's Speech Bills their departments want urgently to get onto the Statute Book. So they are in the hunt and theirs are the strongest inducements of all. What Ministers have on offer are Bills drafted by parliamentary counsel with legal advice to go with it and the full backing of their departments. As well as prepared speeches and secretarial support, there is also the guarantee of support from the government whips to

[2] Dr Horace King, the first-ever Labour Speaker in the House of Commons, underlined this when interviewed in 1971 by the Select Committee on Procedure set up to examine the problems faced by Private Members, entirely without resources, when seeking to introduce a Bill of their own making. Dr King commented that he is a very fortunate Member of Parliament who introduces a private Member's Bill in one year and sees even part of it become law ten years later.

make sure the private Member has a quorum in committee and sufficient votes on the floor of the House. This is the primrose path to the Statute Book and in 1969 it was a particularly seductive one. In those days, the parliamentary salary was but a fraction of what it is today, there were no office costs and other allowances, and there was no pension scheme.[3] Alf recalls one MP – who shall remain nameless – who was a miner when he entered Parliament at a by-election. He came straight from the pit face to the House of Commons. Walter Harrison, later to become Labour's Deputy Chief Whip, realising that the new Member would not receive any pay as an MP until the end of the month and, as a miner, used to being paid weekly, would be virtually penniless until then, organised a whip round to help him out. Later, when Walter's parliamentary career came to an end, he had money problems of his own. Although he counts himself luckier than many of his former colleagues of those days, his income is not a tenth of what his successors earn today.[4]

So in 1969 it was almost overwhelmingly tempting for an MP who was successful in the ballot to take a ready-made Bill. Then, as now, to succeed in the ballot only to see one's chosen Bill voted down or talked out is a matter not merely for disappointment, but for distress and even embarrassment. That is why Ministers or others who say, "here is a Bill, all prepared and with a good deal of public support, plus everything you need to help in taking it forward" are often the main beneficiaries of the annual Private Member's Ballot. Over the years, such have been the inducements on offer that most Bills presented by Private Members have not been in any real sense Private Members' Bills at all. An examination of the records will show that between two-thirds and three-quarters of them were government Bills masquerading as Private Members' Bills. Many of the rest died at birth or in their infancy because there wasn't a quorum at the committee stage.[5]

---

[3] Alf's annual salary was £1,700 when he entered Parliament in 1964. MPs now enjoy basic annual pay of £56,358, and (at February 2004) up to £96,784 can be claimed for office costs and secretarial help, with car mileage allowances of up to 56.1p a mile, or 7.2p-a-mile bicycle allowance. A pension scheme has been introduced and improved greatly with Alf as Chair of the Management Committee.
[4] Highlighted in an interview with Harrison featured in *The Times*, 9 February 2004.
[5] The committee must consist of 25 MPs, and for the meeting to be quorate nine of them, including the chairman, must be present.

Resisting the easy option

This was the challenge that faced Alf. He returned to Westminster to an enormous postbag. Over 450 proposals were put to him by a very wide variety of interests and pressure groups. Some offered ready-made parliamentary Bills on issues that ranged over licensing hours, betting, hare coursing, gypsy rights, environmental protection, animal welfare and Sunday trading to name but some. Having been so very controversially involved in the furore surrounding the Government's agonising decision over whether or not to join the Common Market, it was assumed by some in the media that Alf would use his luck in the Private Member's Ballot to address matters related to the interests of the less developed countries of the Commonwealth, whose trade with the UK in agricultural products was expected to suffer under the EEC's highly protective Common Agricultural Policy.

But Alf had a different aim. Scorning easier options, he determined to pursue his vision of a Bill radically to improve the quality of life of disabled people. Surprisingly, he quickly discovered that, unlike the countless pressure groups then seeking legislation from Parliament – on from bees to badgers and newts to nightingales – such disability organisations as existed had no united sense of purpose. They had neither coherent plans nor vision for the policy initiatives needed to achieve social change beyond their own limited aims. In 1969 the voluntary sector lacked the support it has today, nor was it organised in any meaningful sense of the word. Nobody had contemplated the opportunity to legislate, even to the extent of presenting 'wish-lists', and only the newly-formed Disablement Income Group had previously lobbied Parliament. So Alf was aiming to break entirely new ground. For most of what he wanted to achieve, there was nothing on which to model legislative provision nor indeed any existing law to amend. There was nothing whatever, for example, here or anywhere in the world, on access to the built environment. With considerable urgency Alf trawled the disability organisations, asking them for any specific proposals they wanted to make. The response was extremely limited but helpful. Mary Appleby, then General Secretary of MIND, said that the starting point must be to establish how many disabled people there were in contemporary Britain. Lady Hoare, founder of the Thalidomide Trust, urged provisions to allow the use, within strictly defined limits, of some 'invalid carriages' on footways, and Lady Hamilton, who chaired the Disabled Living Foundation, suggested two clauses: one to encourage the involvement of disabled people on housing advisory committees and another to further the training of disabled people for employment.

Another notable 'encourager' was The Hon. Dorothy Wedgwood OBE, who surely deserves a biography of her own. As Dorothy Mary Winser she had married the fifth Josiah Wedgwood in February 1919, only to contract polio in the following year. She was a natural and gifted campaigner 'against the grain' and as a notable disabled person she held an appropriate place on the executive committee of the Central Council for the Disabled, which had been founded on 11 December 1919.[6] Fifty years on, the idea of disability legislation came as a huge surprise to the CCD. After all, the chance of legislating had come by sheer luck and when the prospect of a Bill for chronically sick and disabled people was not on anybody's horizon, certainly not coming 'out of the blue' with a time-scale heavily restricted by the procedural arrangements of the House of Commons. Nevertheless, Alf remembers Dorothy Wedgwood as 'up for it', a resolute and formidable woman who quickly took up and exemplified, like Sir Harry Platt and Sue Masham, the need for action to meet any challenge that inspired her zealous support.

Also influential was Marsh Dickson, who had a strong personal experience of disability. For years he had looked after his severely disabled wife who but for him could not possibly have lived in the community. As a member of the Labour Party and President of the National Campaign for the Young Chronic Sick, he worked to draw public attention to the plight of young people with long-term illnesses and disabilities who were then routinely consigned to geriatric wards and old-people's homes. Alf, who had spoken at one of Marsh's constituency meetings, was able to include a clause in his

[6] First known as the Central Committee for the Care of Cripples. Alf joined its executive committee in 1969 and was later instrumental in its translation to the Royal Association for Disability and Rehabilitation (RADAR).

Bill requiring local authorities to advise the Secretary of State of the numbers of people under the age of 65 cared for in premises accommodating people over that age. This exposed the practice to scrutiny and made the case for the purpose-built provision of small residential units for the care of younger chronically sick and severely disabled people that ensued from the Bill's enactment.

A clash with Crossman

When Alf took his ideas on what was needed to Richard Crossman, then Secretary of State for Social Services, he 'hit the roof'. His response was to ask who Alf thought he was, after barely five years at Westminster, to be instructing him on social priorities. Had such a Bill been needed, he would already have put it on the Statute Book himself. His own department's National Superannuation and Social Insurance Bill (described as 'the half-pay on retirement Bill') might include some financial provision for severely disabled people, he told Alf, and it was ridiculous to start from scratch as he was proposing to do. There was not the slightest chance, said Crossman, of legislating on that basis. Alf should take a Bill that had some chance of reaching the Statute Book, such as his own department's Human Tissues Bill on the gifting of body parts for medical research, for which regrettably provision had not been included in the Queen's Speech.

Alf said that he had no doubt that this was a laudable Bill, but that he was never likely to win first place in the ballot again and so wanted to use his great good fortune for a cause of his choosing. He readily accepted that in introducing his intended Bill on long-term illness and disability he had no chance of reaching the Statute Book. His purpose and prospect was only that it would put down a marker of the need for such legislation. It would put the problems and needs of disabled people before Parliament, so that others, in future parliamentary sessions, could build on whatever was achieved by promoting his Bill.[7] This was a reasonable hope for a Private Member whose Bill was well founded and likely to attract support at least in principle. The alternative, of course, was that the Bill

---

[7] In this Alf was mindful of the example set by John Fielden in paving the way for the Ten Hours Act of 1847.

would be kicked out as irrelevant, unnecessary and derisory, and Alf was also prepared for that outcome. He said his intention was not as grandiose as Crossman had thought; he simply wanted to put "firmly on the parliamentary agenda" what he regarded as the most neglected area of social policy in this country and indeed across the world. His hope, he said, was that his Bill would help to "nudge things forward" for disabled people and he was prepared to take the hard and rocky and – some thought – mountainous road to try to achieve that limited objective.

Others sought to deflect Alf's purpose. His friend, the political journalist Arthur Butler, who was to become a totally committed supporter of his Bill, told him that, while his intentions were admirable, he could expect scant press or media support. Editors did not want to face their readers over breakfast with pictures and copy about badly disabled people. Butler, in his years as lobby correspondent for various national newspapers, had come to expect that MPs winning a high place in the annual ballot would hope and expect to get a lot of favourable personal publicity from piloting their bills through Parliament. When he gave his opinion to Alf that his proposed Bill, because of lack of media attention, would not win him much publicity and so not enhance his career, he found it very refreshing that his friend was not influenced by such considerations. His admiration for Alf rose higher as the ballot winner replied that if he did not get much publicity that would be too bad – but that he was going to push ahead with the measure anyway.

Encouraged by Fred Peart and other friends, Alf formally moved the First Reading of his Chronically Sick and Disabled Persons Bill in the House of Commons on 26 November 1969, supported by Jack Ashley, Dr Shirley Summerskill, Neil (later Sir Neil) Marten, Dr Michael Winstanley, Will Griffiths, the Hon. John Astor, Lena Jeger, George Darling, Lewis Carter-Jones, Sir Clive Bossom and Laurence Pavitt. Its long title sought to make further provision with respect to the well-being of chronically sick and disabled persons; and for connected purposes. Having been read a first time, it was ordered to be read a second time on Friday, 5 December.

Alf had already sketched out the main clauses of his Bill, but he now faced enormous technical difficulties in completing its preparation so as to have a full and viable Bill ready, as required by the rules of the House, by at least seven days before the Second Reading debate. Sir Peter Rawlinson, then Shadow Attorney General and Alf's 'pair' in the House of Commons at that time, had offered congratulations on winning first place in the ballot but had made it crystal clear that, if he was expecting any help in drafting his Bill, he would have to look elsewhere. "I have to tell you," he said, "that I may be an expensive lawyer and can argue all day about what the law means, but I really couldn't draft the sort of Bill you seek to save my life".

Fortunately, as we have seen, Alf was a very tight draftsman, already skilled in preparing agreements of legal effect. This helped him to turn what amounted to a series of propositions into the language of legislation. He also had, behind the scenes, most generous help from Giles Ecclestone, who worked in the Public Bill Office of the House of Commons,[8] and Sir John Fiennes, a senior civil servant in the Office of Parliamentary Counsel. Fiennes, who had a severely disabled daughter, worked unofficially behind the scenes at weekends to polish a number of the Bill's clauses. Alf today is unstinting in his admiration for those who work in the Office of Parliamentary Counsel: *"People think that lawyers can draft, but in fact the skill of parliamentary draftsmen is very, very, very uncommon among them"*. One lawyer, however, was to prove an exception. Alf was greatly assisted by being able to draw on the legal expertise of his colleague and friend David Weitzman QC MP, a devoted supporter of his Bill throughout and of Alf personally.

Another colleague who was involved was Jack Ashley, who, as we have noticed had lost his hearing following an unsuccessful operation on a perforated eardrum in December 1967. Jack had come close to ending his parliamentary career in the months that followed and Alf was one of those who urged him to carry on and helped him to do so. In his first autobiography, *Journey into Silence*, Jack commented: "Fortunately at that time there were a small number of people I could always rely on, no matter how great the

---

[8] Ecclestone went on to become the Secretary of the Social Responsibility Council of the Church of England.

difficulties. Alfred Morris stood out as the most considerate man in the House of Commons – and his unstinting generosity was to mean even more to me later".[9] "He proved to be a man with quite exceptional understanding of my problem; we soon formed a warm personal relationship which I value highly".[10] Alf's Bill was important to everyone concerned with it, but perhaps none more so than Jack Ashley, who later said that working on it pulled him out of the isolation of deafness; it was "a psychological tonic".[11] As the Bill passed through Parliament – in the words of Jack's second autobiography, *Acts of Defiance* – his "political reflexes returned".[12] He found that his views were wanted again and that to get them "people were willing to make the effort to communicate".[13] Such was the warmth of Alf's affection and regard for Jack Ashley that this outcome alone would have been reward enough for all his energy and commitment in promoting his Chronically Sick and Disabled Persons Bill.

Many local officials, steeped in a culture that emphasised 'welfare', with all the charitable 'do-gooding' connotations that went with it, had got wind of Alf's intention to legislate but were deeply perplexed as to what he hoped to achieve. None more so than a Chief Welfare Officer[14] who approached Alf at a meeting in Manchester shortly before the Second Reading. He and many of his colleagues were dubious at the prospects for a Private Member's Bill in this policy area and sceptical of him succeeding. What, he asked, was Alf trying to achieve? The questioner was a model of rubicund good health and prosperity. "What I want to do," Alf replied, "is to create a society where the recipients of welfare looked as well as the providers of welfare!"

Once the wheels started turning, Members on all sides, particularly the all-party signatories of his Bill, came forward to give whatever help they could. Fred Peart, now Leader of the House of Commons,

---

[9] *Journey into Silence* (Jack Ashley MP, The Bodley Head, 1973), p. 150.

[10] *Ibid*, p.175. See also Bernard Donoughue's *Downing Street Diary*, p.281: "The relationship between him [Jack Ashley] and Alf Morris is wonderful to watch – the latter full of affection and concern, and constantly bantering and joking at one another's expense."

[11] *Ibid*.

[12] *Acts of Defiance* (Jack Ashley MP, Reinhardt Books, 1992), p.178.

[13] *Ibid*.

[14] Following Alf's legislation, Chief Welfare Officers metamorphosed into Directors of Social Services.

arranged for an informal 'trawl' of Government departments to seek suggestions. Although very little came of this it would be difficult to exaggerate Fred Peart's importance to the Bill. He was then principally responsible for arranging the Government's parliamentary timetable and highly influential all across Whitehall. He and Bob Mellish, the Government Chief Whip, encouraged Ministerial support for the Bill from behind the scenes, notwithstanding the scale of its provisions and its very considerable potential cost.

Ready in time: the Second Reading

Remarkably, the Bill was published and available to all MPs on Friday 28th November, a week before the Second Reading debate. Alf rose to move its Second Reading at 11.05 a.m. on Friday 5th December 1969. It had no fewer than 33 clauses, all with a common purpose: to increase the well-being, improve the status and enhance the dignity of chronically sick and disabled people.

Of primary, not to say crucial, importance to the Bill was its first clause. Alf told the House that there was a near consensus among the organisations working to help people with disabilities "that the maintenance of a register of the names of disabled persons, regardless of whether they apply for assistance, should be mandatory on local authorities, subject only to a person's willingness to have his name included and the assurance of a reasonable degree of confidentiality". The services and information set out in clause 2 could not be delivered, he said, unless local authorities knew the whereabouts of the chronically sick and disabled people in their areas who needed help.

No less important was the need to communicate information, in whatever form was appropriate to the individual, along with the provision of key services, to empower disabled people, not constrain them. What most disabled people wanted more than anything else, he told the House, was to lessen their dependence on other people, to live their own lives as normally as possible in their own homes, with their own families, and to have the opportunity to contribute to industry and society as fully as their abilities allowed.

Some people, he acknowledged, might object to the Bill on grounds of cost. To them he said: "We still live in a society where more is heard of the complaints of the affluent and the strong than of the legitimate claims of those in special need". Many of the most vocal critics of increased public expenditure on health and welfare, he said, were people whose most daunting problems were trying to diet and knowing where to park their second car. And this while there was still a shortage of hospital beds for young people with chronic illnesses, many of whom had to spend the final years of their young lives incarcerated in geriatric wards.

It was a highly readable Bill with clearly stated aims, requiring specific services based on rights rather than charity. For too long, said its architect, disabled people had existed on the shifting sands of handouts. Any help that charities and local authorities provided had depended on haphazard benevolence. This had produced widely variable results: obtaining services depended on "geographical luck". One famous Lancashire resort – which Alf left nameless – spent more on its annual end-of-season illuminations than on its disabled citizens.

Alf ended his opening remarks with the paragraph that heads the introduction to this biography, a statement that has come to be recognised as a classic statement of the impulse towards equal opportunities. The Bill was welcomed, and its architect congratulated, from all sides of the House. Dr John Dunwoody, for the Government, said he had some reservations about detail: there was a lack of definition of chronic illness and disability and there could be problems with its impact on social security benefits. These would have to be considered in the light of the National Superannuation Bill that his department intended to introduce in the near future. He went on to remind the House that financial resources were finite and, speaking as Under Secretary of State in Richard Crossman's Department of Health and Social Security, Dr Dunwoody warned that some of the clauses would have to be carefully examined to ensure that they achieved a "practical" result. Nevertheless, and critically, he too welcomed the Bill and said he hoped that the House would give it a Second Reading.

Jack Ashley went further. This was not so much a Bill as a charter to transform public attitudes towards disabled people and transform their lives. Laurence Pavitt, chairman of Labour's back-bench Health Group, believed the Bill would provide the impetus to fetch into the mainstream of national life people who had been pushed to one side and too often forgotten. Sir Clive Bossom, from the Tory side, said it was one of the most sorely needed measures ever to be presented to Parliament during his ten years as an MP. Lewis Carter-Jones – a widely respected, humane and persistent ally of Alf's Bill – hoped for the support of the House as a whole for it to become law: it was one "of immeasurable value to countless thousands outside". Paul Dean, who was to become a Social Services Minister in the following Conservative Government, said that there was no Bill he could more have wanted to see first in the Private Member's Ballot. He hoped that there would not be too many amendments in committee and that it would speedily reach the Statute Book. So rare a unity of purpose heralded further progress, and the Bill, against all predictions, was given an unopposed Second Reading.[15]

Preparing for the Committee Stage

Alf's next task was to try to ensure the maximum possible co-operation between Members chosen by the House to undertake the committee stage of the Bill. A particular difficulty was that only two Ministers could be on the committee, whereas the Bill impacted on the work of at least twelve departments of state. Ministers are notoriously jealous of their own spheres of interest; yet here, long before the phrase 'joined-up government' had been coined, was a measure that ranged across the preserves of nearly all of them. The two Ministers selected to serve on the standing committee were Dr John Dunwoody (Health and Social Security) and Reg Freeson (Housing). They would be in the not merely awkward but

---

[15] On the same day, the second reading of another important bill was introduced by Alf, using procedures under what was then Commons Standing Order 68. This allowed an MP to submit a non-balloted bill for formal first reading and, when doing so, to nominate a date for the second reading. In practice, very few MPs take this route since, without any allocation of parliamentary time, they have scant hope of it going beyond a first reading. In the case of this bill, however, Alf was fulfilling a promise made to Cledwyn Hughes, then Minister of Agriculture, Fisheries and Food. The Food and Drugs (Milk) Bill, legalising the ultra high temperature (UHT) treatment of milk, was given a formal second reading and became law in 1970. For a Member to secure second readings for two private member's bills on the same day, both of which became law, is thought to be unique in parliamentary history.

unprecedented position of speaking for departments other than their own, something previously seen as totally unthinkable. Yet this was the reality that had to be faced and in facing it there were a number of steadfast supporters willing Alf and his Bill to succeed. They included Jack Ashley, John Astor, Lewis Carter-Jones, Maurice Macmillan, Fred Evans, Neil Marten, Bob Edwards, Laurie Pavitt, Jim Prior, John Golding, Dame Irene Ward, David Weitzman, Richard Body and Sir Clive Bossom. All played their part, but Alf particularly treasures the memory of Lewis Carter-Jones as crucial to the passing of the Bill: *"Just as, having been a navigator in the war, so too in Parliament he was a navigator, finding support in all parties. He was one of the few who thought the Bill would ever reach the Statute Book, and that it did so was due in no small part to his expertise in pinpointing the unmet needs of disabled people. He fought the good fight in Parliament with enormous energy and total commitment and was fearless in countering ministerial hostility."*[16]

Not without opponents

Nevertheless Alf recalls that opposition to the Bill was very strident on occasions, sometimes overtly, but more often behind the scenes. In the corridors of power – populated by Ministers and senior civil servants – the Bill was anything but universally welcomed. Several Ministers made no bones about their hostility to one or more of its clauses, while others were strongly against the Bill as a whole on the grounds that, if enacted, it would pre-empt resources they were seeking for their own departments.

It was necessary for Alf to try to soothe Ministers annoyed by having to brief Dunwoody or Freeson on parts of the Bill that affected their departments: for example, the clauses on dyslexia and autism (the first parliamentary recognition of the two conditions) and that for children who were both deaf and blind, in many cases also without speech. These were matters that fell to be addressed by the Department of Education and Science, which was one of the Ministries not represented on the committee. The then Minister of State for Education and Science, anguishing about the cost

---

[16] Lewis Carter-Jones died on 26 August 2004, steadfast in his advocacy of the cause of disabled people and universally respected; one of those politicians, said Tam Dalyell, who really wanted to do something, rather than be someone.

implications of the clause on dyslexia, told Alf that his department's finding, after very careful checking, was that the condition simply did not exist. To which Alf replied that if he was right, then at least the clause would not cost him anything! Yet he was not without sympathy for departments whose Ministers were excluded from the Standing Committee. Alf recalls that although some Ministers were unaffected or could be brought in to deal with issues of concern to their departments at the Bill's Report Stage when the committee reported back to the House, before then Ministers had for the most part to delegate their concerns to Ministers in other departments. Only people within Whitehall could even begin to appreciate just how sensitive that was.

Alf is on record as admitting that when the Bill reached its committee stage it was still "a pretty ramshackle affair"[17] At the beginning of each sitting of the Standing Committee he had to ask the Chairman to accept a procedure motion to enable him to take clauses out of order. This was because he was able to polish up only a few clauses at a time for detailed consideration by the committee.[18]

Saved on the brink of failure

It was also vitally important to ensure that all the meetings of the Standing Committee would be quorate. Any failure in this respect would kill the Bill and the responsibility for avoiding it was Alf's and his alone. The first meeting took place on 16 December 1969 and the second was held immediately after the House returned from the Christmas recess in darkest mid-January 1970, when extreme weather conditions made travelling arduous. One of the Members Alf phoned to encourage was Maurice Macmillan, son of Harold Macmillan and former Conservative Minister of Labour, who had a close and genuine interest in the employment problems faced by disabled people. Alf found he was struggling with a very difficult breathing problem at his home in far distant Haywards Heath, with black ice all around. He told Alf that he was not at all well and asked if he was really needed. Of course he was, but that was not Alf's response. He reassured Maurice that the first consideration was his

[17] *Teaching Politics: Private Member's Legislation — The Chronically Sick and Disabled Persons Act* (Rt. Hon. Alfred Morris MP with Bill Jones, Manchester University, December 1980).
[18] *Ibid.*

health. Maurice nevertheless told Alf that if he needed him he would come out. Well aware of the potential consequences, Alf said "Maurice, please don't".

On that fateful morning Alf got to the House at 8 a.m., to make final preparations for the meeting of the committee at 10.30 a.m. He was still waiting there at the appointed hour, unable to say anything because the committee was one short of a quorum, with a blizzard raging outside. At that point Maurice Macmillan walked slowly in. He was a very sick man, and was to die not long afterwards. It was a very fine example of parliamentary commitment on his part and Alf was visibly very deeply moved by it.

Extraordinary help in the hour of extraordinary need

The burden on Alf was very great and at times he, not to mention other MPs, wondered if he could cope with the enormous task he had set himself. Along with massive administrative difficulties and his continual struggle with many parts of Whitehall, "he was inundated with letters from all over Britain from people anxious to help or to unburden their personal problems on him"[19] At one stage he received over 1,100 letters in two days, which, while they reinforced the need for legislation, were hugely difficult to handle.

Arthur Butler, in *No Feet to Drag*, written only two years after the events, recounts how help came in the nick of time. Just before the Christmas recess in 1969, Alf was invited to a lunch at the House of Commons to celebrate the Golden Jubilee of the Central Council for the Disabled, attended by the current and six former Ministers of Health. Seated next to him were Enoch Powell and Duncan Guthrie, then the Central Council's Director. Duncan had invited Alf because he knew what he was trying to achieve and had arranged the seating plan to ensure that he would be placed next to him. He wanted to ask him about his plans and, if it were necessary, "undertake some indoctrination" of his neighbour. It was certainly not necessary.[20] Although they had corresponded, they were meeting for the first time. Duncan was himself, by any standard, a remarkable man: an activist *par excellence*. He had fought with the Finnish guerrilla

[19] *No Feet to Drag* (Arthur Butler and Alfred Morris, Sidgwick & Jackson, 1972).
[20] *Disability: Legislation and Practice* (ed. Duncan Guthrie, Macmillan, 1981), p.224.

Resistance against the Soviet Union in 1939 before the two countries signed a peace treaty in March 1940. Back in Britain, Duncan was seconded to Special Forces, parachuted behind enemy lines first with the Resistance in France and then in Burma. There, famously, he broke an ankle on landing – his parachute having been entangled in a tree – and was sheltered and nursed by the Karen people in a hiding place safe from the Japanese Army. Eventually, after transmitting a great deal of invaluable information on Japanese troop dispositions back to the Fourteenth Army, he reached the safety of the British lines on the back of an elephant. In spite of all this, he was not by nature a warlike man; rather one of exceptional determination, courage and steadfast resolve. These qualities came to the fore again when, a few years later, his 20–month-old daughter Janet was struck down and initially paralysed by polio. Adversity inspired Duncan to commit his life to eradicating the disease, first setting up the National Fund for Research into Poliomyelitis (now Action Medical Research), before extending his pioneering work to the needs of all disabled people.

Knowing none of this in 1969, Alf quickly recognised Duncan as a kindred spirit and a man of extraordinary vision and imagination. And hearing of Alf's difficulties Duncan immediately offered him administrative help, especially with much-needed secretarial support to cope with a surging torrent of correspondence. "No one," Alf said shortly after Duncan's death in 1994, "gave me more practical help. Flexible of mind, he was a man of transparent decency and inflexible integrity... mourned by everyone who had the privilege of knowing him".[21]

Practical solutions to practical problems

Some years later, Alf confessed that the central purpose of his Bill had been to challenge "the serene satisfaction then with the *status quo*".[22] But his more down to earth motive was a desire to solve the problems of people such as he had known and lived among in Manchester. He recalled, for example, the difficulties faced by a woman whom he saw day by day pushing her husband to the

---

[21] *Hansard*, Commons, 19 October 1995, col. 585.
[22] The Kenneth T. Jenkins oration, Canberra, 16 November 1979.

out-patient department at Wythenshawe Hospital. She stayed on the road, among the traffic, simply because she wasn't strong enough to push the wheelchair up and down the kerbs of the pavements. The kerbs were multiplying the handicapping effects of her husband's disability. Guthrie and Alf agreed that while preventing disability – saving people from becoming disabled or more disabled – was extremely important, so was the urgency of the task of social action to reduce the handicapping effects of disability and to remove the barriers that excluded disabled people from community involvement and the built environment.

Existing practice effectively did nothing to reduce their social exclusion. Hence the Public Health Act 1936 said that sanitary conveniences provided by local authorities must be accessible to all citizens, but in practice many of them were below ground, down stone steps, and statutory precept was thus totally divorced from social practice. It was such thinking that brought Alf to tackle head-on wide areas of British legislation that, far from reducing, cruelly increased the handicapping effects of disability.

An informal support team

In January 1970, at Guthrie's suggestion, Alf formed an *ad hoc* committee to consider with him his priorities in managing the Bill in Standing Committee. It included MPs – Jack Ashley, John Astor, Lewis Carter-Jones and Neil Marten – along with such distinguished experts from the voluntary sector as Guthrie himself, Mary Greaves[23] (who had taken over the leadership of DIG following the untimely death of Megan du Boisson), Peter Large, Oswald (Denny) Denly, Leonard Cheshire, Sir Harry Platt, Lady Hoare, Michael Flanders, James Loring of the Spastics Society and George Lee of Mencap. Harry Platt's involvement was particularly gratifying to Alf. A distinguished orthopaedic surgeon, held in high regard nationally and internationally, his professional expertise had been greatly in demand over many years. In 1918 he had operated on and cared for Alf's father, whose recovery from the effects of his war service, to the

---

[23] Mary Greaves contracted polio at the age of three, resulting in severe paralysis. She ran a business school from her own home for 14 years and later joined the Civil Service. She ended her working life in the National Economic Development Office and, after retirement, directed the Disablement Income Group. She also served as chair of the Legal and Parliamentary Committee of the Central Council for the Disabled.

extent that it was possible at all, would otherwise have been a much longer process. Alf's mother always said of him that he saved her husband's life. He had twice been President of the Royal College of Surgeons and was a founder member, in December 1919, of the Central Council for the Disabled. And now, half a century later, here he was working with Alf to help him legislate on behalf of all disabled people. Phyllis Foreman provided indispensable secretarial backing, not only in the many tasks associated with the passage of the Bill, but later when, after its enactment, a further tidal wave of correspondence threatened to engulf Alf.

On 14 January Mary Greaves had the good fortune to be able to discuss the Bill with the Prime Minister on a visit to Downing Street arranged by DIG. She found Harold Wilson sympathetic and constructive and he gave her an assurance that the Government's approach to the Bill would not be obstructive.

Securing essential Treasury support

This reassurance was encouraging, but it was no guarantee of the Bill's success and the support of the Treasury would be crucially important. The chairman of the Standing Committee, Sir Myer Galpern, was soon to make it clear that proceedings on the Bill could go no further without a Money Resolution and this would have to be tabled on the Floor of the House by the Chancellor of the Exchequer. Securing one was no simple matter. To win the agreement of the Chancellor to a Money Resolution making financial resources available for the purposes of a Private Member's Bill made getting blood out of a stone look easy. Alf believes that it was made possible only because Bob Mellish and Fred Peart argued his case, persuading a majority of the Cabinet that no Labour government worthy of the name could fail to rise to this area of social need and survive. Said Mellish, the Government Chief Whip, "If we can't support a Bill like this, we might as well all pack up and go home".

And so it transpired that a Money Resolution was tabled on behalf of Roy Jenkins, then Chancellor of the Exchequer, in the name of Dick Taverne, his Financial Secretary to the Treasury. It read: "That, for the purposes of any Act of the present session to make further provision with respect to the welfare of chronically sick and disabled people, it is expedient to authorise the payment out of moneys provided by Parliament of any increase in the sums payable out of moneys so provided under any other enactment which is attributable to any provision of that Act imposing a duty on a local authority having functions under section 29 of the National Assistance Act 1948 to make arrangements in the exercise of their functions under that section if they are satisfied in the case of any person ordinarily resident in the authority's area who is a person to whom that section applies that it is necessary to make those arrangements in order to meet the needs of that person".[24]

The Government's decision to sanction financial backing for the Bill was announced on 3 February 1970 and warmly welcomed by everyone, both inside and outside Parliament, who had supported Alf's campaign. Jack Ashley was quoted in *The Times* the following morning as hailing "a major breakthrough for the disabled people of Britain" which would "place this country in advance of every other nation in its provisions for the long-term sick and the disabled". What had begun merely as an attempt to put the needs of disabled people onto the parliamentary agenda was now transformed into a realistic bid for legislation.

Twin committees

For some time, the two committees, official and informal, ran side by side, with Alf chairing the informal committee. Bryan Gould, who described the passage of the Bill through Parliament in considerable detail in *A Charter for the Disabled*,[25] records that the Standing Committee's meetings were open to the public and that "representatives of the voluntary organisations were in constant attendance to monitor the progress of the Bill and provide Alf Morris with on-the-spot advice and help as specific points came up".

This was to prove a most effective process of consultation. Gould comments that Alf had also "struck up a good working relationship with the Ministers who were primarily responsible for the Bill". The

---

[24] The implications of the Money Resolution have been the subject of some dispute; but what is clear is that it did not allow for the steps toward a non-contributory cash benefit for severely disabled people envisaged in the original drafting of his Bill. That breakthrough, due clearly to Crossman's influence, had to await Alf's appointment as the first Minister for Disabled People in 1974.

[25] *A Charter for the Disabled* (Eda Topliss and Bryan Gould, Basil Blackwell Ltd, 1981).

work of the committee thus became "notable for the number of clauses and amendments which were proposed formally by the Government (which thereby implicitly undertook some responsibility for the passage of the Bill) or by Alf Morris himself with an acknowledgement that he had had the benefit of Government advice". For their part the sponsors of the Bill were willing to bend here and there in order to make progress and ensure that the Bill succeeded, while at the same time strengthening other parts of the Bill. Progress was increasingly being achieved in a spirit of compromise and consensus. Alf introduced many changes to the original Bill, among them those to strengthen the key clauses introduced by Alf which were to become sections 1 and 2 of the Act, requiring local authorities to identify the numbers and needs of disabled people in their areas and mandatorily provide specified services.

Report Stage and Third Reading

The amended Bill reached its Report Stage on the Floor of the House on 20 March 1970, with nearly four hours given over to new clauses and amendments, including the important provisions moved for Alf by Jack Ashley on special educational provision for children disabled by autism and acute dyslexia. They also supplemented the original clause in favour of deaf-blind children and became sections 25 to 27 of the Act,

These changes having been approved, Alf had the pleasure of moving his Bill's Third Reading. It had, he said, been much improved by close scrutiny in Standing Committee and the detailed debate that had taken place. After thanking everyone who had helped, Alf turned his mind to those who would benefit, reminding the House that everyone is potentially disabled "if only by the ageing process". Thus, prospectively, we could all become "beneficiaries of any measure which sets out to assist those who are disadvantaged by ill-health and are in special need". Shortly before 4 p.m., the Third Reading, which Fred Evans, the Labour MP for Caerphilly, perceptively referred to as "a springboard for further action", was agreed, thereby successfully concluding its passage through the Commons.

Deliberation in the Lords: a race against time

The Bill then passed to the Lords and there was now a need for urgency. Alf had warned in moving the Bill's Third Reading in the Commons that time might prove to be "our keenest adversary" in striving to complete the final stages of the legislative process. These were to be played out against a background of speculation about the possibility of an early General Election. The passage through the Lords, of course, would follow the normal procedures for all legislation, but perhaps no one had reckoned with the unprecedented enthusiasm with which the Bill was to be embraced in the Upper House. Typically, Alf had inspected the course and prepared the way. He had agreed with Lord Longford, the erstwhile leader of the House of Lords, who was to move the Bill there, that it should not go forward on the basis of pleas for 'compassion'. It had won the support of all peers who were themselves disabled or involved in voluntary organisations working in the field of disability, as well as that of the voluntary sector as a whole. When the Bill came up for its Second Reading in the Lords on 9 April 1970, the occasion was marked by a very unusual rearrangement of furniture in the ornate red and gold chamber. The first row of the cross benches was removed to make way for what became known as the 'mobile bench' of peers in wheelchairs, four of whom, including Lady Masham, were to make their maiden speeches.[26]

The Second Reading debate lasted almost four hours and featured 21 speeches, many of them those of peers who had never before attended the Lords. One of these was Lord Cullen, who had previously been silent for 38 years. Alf had met Lady Cullen – herself a disabled person – on a night train from Manchester on the previous Sunday. She told him that she had "instructed" her husband to speak. Having done so, Alf recalls, he became a compulsive speaker.

As in the Commons, Alf's Bill was welcomed on all sides, and was notable for what were then novel assertions of the right of disabled people to take their proper place in society. Lord Longford said that he wanted a Bill that embodied practical provisions, not "pious platitudes". He expressed his determination that henceforward, so

---

[26] *No Feet to Drag* (Arthur Butler and Alfred Morris, Sidgwick & Jackson, 1972).

far as it lay in human power, disabled people should no longer feel themselves to be second-class citizens in their own country. Not only should they acquire "a new sense of independence" but "integration within the community, a feeling of belonging to it". He saw the Bill as "a fundamental Bill of Rights for disabled people".

The Lord Bishop of Bath and Wells, in a maiden speech, praised "this forward-looking, forward-thinking, humanitarian Bill", and Baroness Darcy de Knayth, herself a wheelchair user, also speaking for the first time, said that she supported the Bill with all her heart.

In her maiden speech, Baroness Masham, who as a paraplegic had used a wheelchair for 12 years, stressed how very much more expensive life was for severely disabled people, and emphasised the importance of meeting mobility needs appropriately. Like Lady Darcy, she thought the odds were stacked against people too disabled to drive themselves. Disabled people, she said, echoing Alf's Second Reading speech in the Commons, did not need pity, but rather "the opportunity to lead as normal a life as possible". Disabled children were another priority. Was it right, she asked, to segregate them in special schools? Would they not become more isolated and different from other children? Might it not be preferable to meet special needs in special units in mainstream schools? Above all, disabled people needed "the opportunity to help themselves, so that they might gain the independence which they cherish above all else".

Another first-time speaker, Viscount Ingleby, also a wheelchair user, welcomed the access provisions of the Bill, while Lord Wells-Pestell, who had personal experience of disability, saw the Bill as one of the most important that had come before the Lords for years and thought it might be as important to chronically sick and disabled people as the Charter of Human Rights was to mankind as a whole.

Alf pays particular tribute to Field-Marshal Lord Harding of Petherton, a distinguished solder who led the 'Desert Rats' in the Second World War, directed operations under Montgomery at El Alamein, and after the war chaired the National Fund for Research into Crippling Diseases[27] from 1960 to 1973: "I don't think

---

[27] Of whose Executive Committee Alf was a member.

you would have called John Harding an active parliamentarian. Nevertheless he was very influential in helping to identify and bring together those who could help if and when my Bill reached the Lords. We were all acutely aware that time was the most important commodity in securing the passage of the Bill, and John was very influential in what might be called the 'staff work'."

The press was now reporting every step of the process, aware that great improvements in the lives of disabled people were in the offing. Whether they could be brought to fruition was in the balance. When the Bill reached its Lords' committee stage on 30 April, such was the interest of Members that their well-intentioned suggestions threatened its very survival. Alf and his friends were becoming increasingly uneasy. The prospect of a General Election as early as June was ever more likely and time, as one MP put it, was "seeping away". Such was the zeal of peers that fifteen pages of amendments were tabled for the committee stage, and Lord Longford was insisting that the House must do its duty properly and not rush. There were also last-minute reservations from the Government. Despite the fact that Alf had made it clear that the registration of disabled people would be both confidential and voluntary, Baroness Serota, Minister of State for Health and Social Security, expressed concern about the financial and resource implications that would arise from a 100 per cent registration.

Harold Evans sounds the alarm

At its next committee meeting on 15 May, however, even Lord Longford had realised that the Bill was in mortal danger, and suggested "some adjustment in our attitude". Two days later, in the 17 May issue of the *Sunday Times*, Harold Evans, Alf's school friend from Newton Heath, stoked the fire with a remarkable leading article. He argued for a June election, "because the country is in limbo, with the Government reduced to tactical manoeuvring. There would be few regrettable legislative casualties. Mrs Castle's Industrial Relations Bill is entirely dispensable; indeed the Bill most worth pushing through is not a Government Bill at all but Mr Alfred Morris's Private Member's Bill for the disabled".

Harold Wilson to the rescue

In fact, more than a month earlier, Harold Wilson had "virtually decided" on a June election, and on 12 May his Inner Cabinet colleagues had unanimously endorsed his proposal to recommend a dissolution. He took this formally to the Queen on 18 May, and her agreement was confirmed in a short statement from Downing Street on the same evening.[28] But true to his promise to Mary Greaves, he made it known that "whatever else might have to be abandoned, the Morris Bill would be given enough priority to ensure that it reached the statute book".[29] Remarkably it was given precedence over Richard Crossman's National Superannuation and Social Insurance Bill.

To ensure the Bill's passage through the Lords it was now necessary for the Government to set aside time there for the Report Stage and Third Reading on 20 May and to cut short committee stage debate. While some amendments were lost in the last-minute rush, the Lords had nevertheless introduced a number of valuable changes that considerably enhanced the provisions of the Bill.

Tributes made at the Third Reading fittingly illustrated the unity of purpose behind the Bill. Baroness Serota felt that it would be judged as a remarkable Private Member's Bill; remarkable in its length and scope and also – perhaps most remarkable of all – for the enthusiasm with which it had been received both inside and outside Parliament.

The passage of the Bill was now assured. The penultimate stage of its parliamentary consideration, before Royal Assent, was for the Commons to debate the Lords' amendments, and this was successfully accomplished on 27 May.

The last word went to Dr John Dunwoody, with the memorable statement that it was the Government's intention that the Bill would be "an effective weapon to achieve the aims which have been shared by all supporters on both sides of the House". The Bill, he said, "represented a significant step forward". It was "a compassionate and civilised Charter for the chronically sick and disabled in our community", who in the past perhaps had "not always been treated

---

[28] *The Labour Government 1964-1970* (Harold Wilson, Weidenfeld and Nicolson and Michael Joseph, 1971).
[29] *No Feet to Drag* (Arthur Butler and Alfred Morris, Sidgwick & Jackson, 1972).

as well as they should have been by the House". He thought that this Parliament had "done its best" and that the legislation was "a base on which a great deal more can be built in the future".

The Bill finally received Royal Assent on 29 May 1970, the final day of that Parliament and immediately before it was dissolved for the 1970 General Election – "the last measure to become law before Parliament dispersed to the hustings"[30] – and was promptly greeted by Duncan Guthrie as the *"Magna Carta* of disabled people". Tam Dalyell, then PPS to Richard Crossman, wrote to congratulate Alf on his achievement: "Had it not been for your own dogged determination, the Bill would never have got off the ground, since I well remember how Dick Crossman tried to bully you into either changing drastically or dropping the Bill at more than one point – in vain. (I used to tell him that Alf is not one of our malleable colleagues, and you ought to understand that fact, Dick!). Nor in my judgement would the DHSS – whatever they now say – have produced any similar legislation. Anyhow, well done indeed!".

An Act of historic wide-ranging and lasting value

Notwithstanding many changes, the substance and spirit of Alf's original Bill had survived its seemingly unending passage through Parliament. It finally had 29 sections, amending 39 other Acts of Parliament, as well as legislating in areas where previously there was no legislation of any kind to amend. The Act's scope was extensive. Of its wide diversity of provisions, most were entirely new, imposing duties to identify and help disabled people in localities all over England and Wales. It provided as of right new and wide-ranging practical assistance in the home and for help in the fields of education, employment, housing, outdoor mobility and personal social services. It set out statutory requirements for ensuring access for disabled people to public and social buildings of every kind. It called for the separation of younger from older long-term patients in hospital, provided for the use of powered wheelchairs on pavements up to four miles an hour and a scheme conferring special parking rights on disabled drivers and the drivers of disabled passengers. For the first time anywhere in the world, the

---

[30] *Ibid.*

legislation had special educational provisions for deaf-blind, autistic and dyslexic children. It set down what statistics both central and local government should collect in planning the development of services. Among many other provisions, it sought direct representation for disabled people on councils and committees advising Ministers and others on all policy issues in which disabled people had an interest. Taken together, the Act's 29 sections touched on practically every aspect of the lives of disabled people and the services they need and that should be available to them to achieve their full potential. They comprised a comprehensive statement of Parliament's commitment to transforming not only the quality of life but also the *status* of disabled people in British society. They proclaimed, loud and clear, that disabled people had as much right as everyone else to take part in all the activities of life, gave cohesion to their aspirations, and challenged authority, public and private alike, to meet their needs.

Over the years, many tributes have been paid to Alf's groundbreaking legislation, but none so telling as that of Mary Greaves. Severely disabled herself and a prominent campaigner in raising the profile of disabled people, she contributed a chapter to Duncan Guthrie's *Disability, Legislation and Practice* in 1981 offering a disabled person's perspective on disability legislation with the following assessment: "The awareness that disabled people are *people*, and have the same needs, aspirations and problems as non-disabled has become world-wide... Why did this happen? What brought it about? The single factor which influenced many others was the introduction of the Chronically Sick and Disabled Persons Bill".[31]

The Act was extended to Scotland in 1972 and to Northern Ireland in 1978, and served as a model for legislation in many other countries, not least Australia and New Zealand which had legislative processes very similar to our own. In Britain, the Act remains on the Statute Book, strengthened, as opportunities have occurred, by amendments in all of which Alf was involved. It has stood the test of time, and remains both a living force and a testament to its creator.

---

[31] *Disability, Legislation and Practice*, (Ed. Duncan Guthrie, Macmillan, 1981).

The Hon. Dorothy Wedgwood OBE.

Chapter 9

FRUSTRATION AND FIGHTBACK

1970— 1974

"I know some of the frustrations that the Rt. Hon. Member for Wythenshawe must have suffered when some parts of his Chronically Sick and Disabled Persons Act 1970 were not implemented as he had hoped during the passage of that measure".

John Major, Minister for Disabled People, 17 February 1987.

– The destiny of a new Act in a new administration
– Attendance Allowance introduced – Publication of 'No Feet to Drag'
– A census of disabled people – The Government begins to give way
– Local councils begin to respond – Alf's wider concerns
– Alf sceptical about accession to the EEC
– Founder Chairman of the ANZAC Group

The destiny of a new Act in a new administration

The historic passing of the Chronically Sick and Disabled Persons Bill through both Houses of Parliament awakened a wide new public understanding of the problems and needs of disabled people. The concept of 'community care' had united Members in all parts of both Houses and goodwill from a new Government in a new parliamentary session could surely be guaranteed? Arguing for better provision for disabled people would not just be a matter of pushing at an open door – the door was clearly off its hinges! Who now could stop life becoming better for disabled people?

Any such thinking betrays a very mistaken view of the realities of government, says Alf. Neither sympathy nor legislation can guarantee progress. The popular notion is that once the legislative battle has been won for a just cause that alone will draw down all the resources that could be wished for. Not so. "*Attend the Legislation Committee of the Cabinet, any Tuesday morning and you sit with Ministers from departments of state all across Whitehall, who are there to argue their own corner. They all compete for the same finite resources. Now, as ever before and for always, the battle is one, waged by all Ministers, between infinite demand and finite resources".*

Recalling his studies at Oxford, Alf compares the experience of the wide fellowship of people who worked with him to enact his Bill to that of Sir Edwin Chadwick in achieving the first ever Public Health Act in 1848. Chadwick had made an apparently irresistible case for reducing, if not eliminating, the industrial contaminants that caused so much ill health and gravely diminished life expectancy. He too found that he was pushing at a seemingly open door. But legislating on public health costs money and would make inroads into the profits of manufacturers. Thus they opposed it with furtive subtlety and remarkable skill. The reality of life in Whitehall, now as then, is a dogfight for parliamentary time and limited resources. Even when legislation is in place, there will be new struggles to face with dedicated competitors – *"briefed up to their eyebrows"* – if it is to be fully implemented and legislative precept translated into social provision. *"Otherwise failure to advance will be to retreat, just as surely as if the legislation had not been enacted".*

In 1970, Alf had been convinced that it would be possible to move forward only by consensus. Just as his Chronically Sick and Disabled Persons Bill had needed a supportive body of parliamentary opinion to see it through its parliamentary journey, so now it was necessary to engender a similar sense of common purpose to secure its implementation.

A further persuasion came when Alan Beaney, MP for the mining constituency of Hemsworth, elected with a huge majority, was suddenly afflicted with throat cancer. An operation to contain the malignant tumour tragically led to loss of speech. Like Jack Ashley, who had lost his hearing a few years earlier, Alan had very suddenly become heavily disabled as a parliamentarian: indeed arguably stricken with the ultimate parliamentary disability. Unable to communicate in the House of Commons, a place to which he had been elected to voice the concerns of a needful electorate, he now found himself unable to speak ever again. Alf had been deeply troubled about Jack, whom he held in the highest regard, and was no less concerned about Alan who had so much to contribute and was always well worth listening to. No carpet-bagger he. Like Alf, Alan was elected to Parliament by people he was proud to have lived and worked with, and among whom he had brought up his children.

"He was a very kindly and cultured man of wisdom and vast experience, as widely read as anyone I ever knew, but seldom if ever – and then only with condescension of the most distastefully pompous kind – ever noticed by the chattering classes. He was not seen as a man of great account or worth. That is an habitual failing in Parliament. Many people value only the natural parliamentarians who appear to do everything effortlessly. Alan Beaney was seen as 'ordinary'. To my mind, it's a form of greatness to be ordinary in Parliament. Too many people are extraordinary, cast in a different mould from most of their constituents, who are themselves mostly ordinary people".

Alf discussed with the Speaker, speculatively, how it might still be possible for Alan to make some contribution to parliamentary proceedings. It has been, since time immemorial, the tradition that Members can contribute to parliamentary debates only by the spoken word. But Alan had been left with nothing more than a sort of whisper, which could barely be understood even among lifelong friends. Alf asked the Speaker if he could sit with Alan to help to convey his words to the House and it was agreed that Alan would speak with his residual ability to do so and that Alf would have a copy of the speech and, as far as possible, speak in time with Alan's delivery. Thus, together, on 3 December 1970 they attacked the Coal Industry Bill. It was, Alan and Alf said in concert, "a sinister Bill devised to cloak the avarice and greed of those who would exploit the resources of the National Coal Board and give them to the private investor...I warn the Government that they will rend the mining industry in two. They will create such a situation that there will be no men to man the bridge". It was a swan song, uniquely eloquent in its way, and remarkably prophetic, for it was to be the miners' strike in February 1974 that would cost Edward Heath his premiership. It also served to remind Members of Parliament that their own well-being was precarious and that disability can strike anyone at any time. Again it also served notice – most beneficially for such future MPs as David Blunkett and Ann Begg – that Parliament should never again accept easy excuses for excluding disabled people.

In the following year, Alf's achievement in enacting the Chronically Sick and Disabled Persons Bill was recognised with a special award. Acting in partnership, the Central Council for the Disabled and the National Fund for Research into Crippling Diseases, both directed by Duncan Guthrie, decided to inaugurate an annual award for work of outstanding value to disabled people. This was made, and continues to be made annually, in the name of Field-Marshal Lord Harding who, restored to civilian life after World War II, became Chairman of the National Fund and had been one of those who prepared the way for the passage of the Bill through the House of Lords. Alf's award, as the first recipient, was quite different from today's version: a work by an award-winning sculptor produced with aid from Manchester steelworkers, some of whom were Alf's constituents. It weighed approaching half a hundredweight.

"Selwyn Lloyd, the Speaker of the House of Commons, who could barely move the Harding Award, said that he was a most appropriate person to have been chosen to make the presentation, because, he reminded me, I had paid high tribute to him, five years before, in my maiden speech in the House of Commons. He then proceeded to read the part about me thanking the national figures who came to speak for my opponent – 'they also helped to elect me who merely spoke for my opponent, not least Alec Douglas Home and Selwyn Lloyd, then Prime Minister and Chancellor of the Exchequer respectively' – and brought the house down, no one laughing more uncontrollably than Lord Harding".

Attendance Allowance introduced

In the new Parliament, things began promisingly for disabled people. Richard Crossman, pressed by Megan du Boisson and the Disablement Income Group, had included a clause in the Labour Government's National Superannuation and Social Insurance Bill in 1970 to introduce an Attendance Allowance, but, as we have seen, this was lost with the dissolution of Parliament in that year. The provision, however, clearly enjoyed all-party support and was quickly reintroduced by Edward Heath's Government as Clause 4 of the National Insurance (Old Persons' and Widows' Pensions and Attendance Allowance) Act 1970. This provided for the introduction, in December 1971, of an Attendance Allowance of £4 per week, without means test, for disabled people needing attendance both by day and night.[1]

Implementation of the Chronically Sick and Disabled Persons Act was quite another matter: sidelined by the new Government, despite great public impatience to see it given full effect. Shamefully, within a few months of its enactment, Mrs Sally Oppenheim, the Conservative MP for Gloucester, was calling for the Act to be repealed. This proposal found an echo in the Devon County Council, whose Director of Social Services recommended the council to press for the repeal of Section 2 and a consequent scaling down of the provisions for disabled people.[2] Alf had always accepted that full implementation of some parts of the Act could not be achieved overnight. Realistically, local authorities could not spend money they did not yet have nor immediately match staff numbers with their new statutory responsibilities. *"The Good Samaritan himself would have winced, having given succour to one person in need, if he had then been tasked to find and help other needful persons all across the land"*. But this did not mean that the provisions of sections 1 and 2 were, or should be, made optional. Alf's guns were trained on those officials with a duty to act who were saying that they didn't have to do anything, more especially those who never voiced their opposition, but frustrated the purposes of the Act by doing nothing. What the mandatory requirements of the Act meant was that the necessary funding just had to be found by public authorities for a grossly neglected area of social policy. Given that the financing of the Act had necessarily been the subject of a Money Resolution, the issue was crucially one not of resources but of political will and priorities.

Some inertia would, no doubt, have hindered progress under any Government. But, as we have seen, the Chronically Sick and Disabled Persons Act had received the Royal Assent on the very day that Parliament was dissolved for the 1970 General Election. That election brought in a government of a very different colour and the

---

[1] This was extended in October 1973, at a new lower rate, to people needing attendance by day or night.
[2] *Disability: Legislation and Practice* (ed. Duncan Guthrie, Macmillan, 1981), p.225.

impetus that might have been maintained if the party of the Act's architect had been victorious was lost. Alf, who had again won the Wythenshawe seat, now in a straight fight with his Conservative opponent, was elevated to Labour's front bench as spokesman on social policy, but it was as a shadow minister not the real thing. Even so, progress was expected. The Act had won all-party support and disabled people looked for action to match the high sounding rhetoric about it from those now in power.

They were, at least initially, to be disappointed. There were two sticking points: one resources, the other sheer ignorance around the country both of the Act and its provisions, which the new Government did nothing to address. Much of Alf's time was taken up speaking up and down the country, encouraging local authorities to expedite implementation. One town clerk actually said that because it was a "Private Member's Act" it lacked the force of law. Of course, there is no such thing. Once a Private Member's Bill is enacted it is as much a part of the law as any Government statute. *"The Chief Officers of local authorities were not dullards, but all too often they presented a tin ear, a cold heart and a closed mind. Their focus was on resources rather than need, to which they customarily displayed an arrogant incuriosity"*.

This was a difficult period, when the going was unremittingly uphill. Alf pays special tribute to the late Peter Mitchell, who worked as his research assistant from 1970 to 1974 and also served as research officer and administrator of the All-Party Disablement Group. There was no allowance for assistants in those days but, with the help of Duncan Guthrie, Alf succeeded in attracting funds from a charitable trust. Peter was chosen from a number of candidates and amply fulfilled his obvious promise, assisting in the drafting of parliamentary questions and speeches and keeping Alf's work programme on track. Subsequently, when Alf was the Minister, Peter joined the staff of RADAR, but continued to help Alf in a personal capacity. His unseen hand contributed importantly to a number of Bills in the struggle for civil rights legislation.

Publication of 'No Feet to Drag'

In 1971 Alf, faced with a new Tory Government reluctant to deal with the lack of resources needed to implement his Act and dismayed by widespread ignorance in the country of the Act's provisions, decided to win some much-needed publicity with a book recounting the parliamentary battle and describing how the new Act could assist disabled people. He asked Arthur Butler, who had left Fleet Street to become a leading public affairs consultant, if he would write such a book. Butler was pleased to accept the offer but, knowing how popular and respected Alf was throughout the country, proposed that he should write a chapter or two and so have his name on the cover as co-author. Alf agreed and Lord Longford, who had helped to pilot the bill through Parliament, offered his company Sidgwick and Jackson as the publisher.

When the book was completed the suggested title was *No Feet to Drag*, inspired by a meeting between Alf and one of his constituents. Asked how the new Act was faring, Alf had told her that some local authorities were dragging their feet in implementing it. Looking down she had responded, "Tell them they're lucky to have any feet to drag". Not knowing the reason for this choice, a journalist on the *Evening Standard* wrote that the book should receive an award for having "the sickest title of the year". That did not deter Labour Party Leader Harold Wilson from joining many others who attended the book's launch party in 1972 – and within a few weeks it had received widespread and extremely positive coverage in the press. Butler observed: "Alf's popularity had done the trick again!"

They used the book to inveigh against those in local government who tried to delay and obstruct the implementation of the Act. He described them as people who "disliked being thought of as opponents in principle of the new legislation... at first not only unwilling to identify disabled people, but often reluctant even to identify themselves. They were not silver-tongued orators, but tight-lipped saboteurs. They eschewed public debate in favour of snag-finding and the procedural ploy in committee. They liked to see themselves as shrewd local businessmen and dragged their feet as quietly as possible".[3]

Whitehall departments were similarly slow even to begin the process of implementation. Although there had been a Money Resolution to

[3] *No Feet to Drag* (Arthur Butler and Alfred Morris, Sidgwick & Jackson, 1972).

support the Bill, without which it would certainly have failed, the circumstances of its last-minute enactment meant that its effect was widely misunderstood. The new administration itself was reluctant to commit resources to provisions that seemed to them open-ended. Particularly against their grain were Sections 1 and 2 of the Act. Section 1 required local authorities to take steps to inform themselves of the numbers and needs of disabled people in their areas and then to inform them of the services to which they were entitled under the new Act. Section 2 required the provision of a wide range of practical help to meet the individual needs of each disabled resident. As Ursula Keeble has pointed out, authoritatively, Section 2 absorbed and extended Section 29 of the National Assistance Act 1948. But whereas the earlier legislation had been built on the *hope* that, once the needs of disabled people were pointed out, councils would wish to contribute to meeting them, Section 2 of the 1970 Act, with the bitter lessons of the 22 years in between, *insisted* on local authority help and made all the provisions mandatory. The inclusion of a date – 31 August 1970 – on which Section 2 was to come into mandatory effect was an intended further insurance against procrastination.[4]

The full implementation of Section 2 depended, however, on the effectiveness of action taken under Section 1. The only mandatory requirement in the 1948 Act was that local authorities should keep a register of disabled people who had applied to them for assistance.[5] By contrast, the 1970 Act required positive action. Unless local authorities knew who was in need, they could not effectively meet that need. However, although Section 1 was on the Statute Book, it required the laying of an order by the Secretary of State to bring it into effect. The Conservative Government baulked at doing so. Indeed, the Department of Health and Social Security issued a circular to local authorities which, among other things, advised that it was not a requirement that they should attempt 100 per cent identification and registration of disabled people. Throwing dust in the eyes of its readers, the circular said that "complete registration of the handicapped would be so great a diversion of resources of

---

[4] *Disability: Legislation and Practice* (Ed. Duncan Guthrie, The Macmillan Press Ltd, 1981), page 180.
[5] *Ibid.*

manpower and money that there would be nothing left over to meet the needs of those registered".[6] In 1970, only around 250 thousand disabled people were listed on local authority registers[7] and it was estimated that there were at least another million disabled people who might be registered: those dubbed by the media as "the missing million".

What the Government had not reckoned with was the huge groundswell of demand, from press and public alike, for the Act's full implementation. Disabled people and their families wanted quick action and "letters of complaint and disappointment began to flow in to MPs and voluntary organisations"[8] In November 1970, the Disablement Income Group sent a deputation to see Sir Keith Joseph, the Secretary of State responsible for implementing Sections 1 and 2, who promised to reveal a strategy of his own by the following summer. Then, in a Commons debate initiated by David Weitzman, Labour MP for Stoke Newington and Hackney North, on 18 December 1970, MPs sympathetic to the purposes of the Act stepped up the pressure, complaining about "the remarkable ignorance of its provisions".[9] The main bone of contention was Whitehall's reluctance to encourage registration. Michael Alison, Under Secretary of State for Health and Social Security, repeated the argument that "total discovery to identify disabled people would need such a massive diversion of resources, simply for that operation, that those left over to meet the needs of people so discovered would correspondingly be reduced".[10] His preference was for local authorities to rely on sampling and survey techniques. Closing the debate, Alf drew attention to the increasing pressure from disability organisations for the "quick and effective implementation" of Section 1. He pointed out that it was about "the crucially important problems of finding out where disabled people are and of ensuring that they receive information about the services now available to them".

---

[6] DHSS Circular 12/70.
[7] Clifford Hilditch, *Disability, Legislation and Practice* (Ed. Duncan Guthrie, The Macmillan Press Ltd, 1981), page 32.
[8] *No Feet to Drag* (Arthur Butler and Alfred Morris, Sidgwick & Jackson, 1972)
[9] *Ibid*, page 129.
[10] *Hansard*, Commons, 18.12.1970.

In a biting article in *The Guardian* on 3 February 1971, he castigated those responsible for the delay. Anticipating the future concept of 'community care' – a term created by the Act – he pointed out that by trying to save relatively small amounts of ratepayers' money, the "less progressive" local authorities had been wasting far greater sums, because "the severely handicapped person who is not helped to live in his own home often has to be hospitalised at much higher cost to public funds". The misery of people with learning disabilities was particularly regrettable. In *No Feet to Drag* Alf had said that nowhere was the cost of inadequate Exchequer support for local services seen more clearly than in the "moribund and barrack-like buildings" in which large numbers of people with learning disabilities were detained. They were not so much hospitals as "anti-hospitals...perfect examples of human warehouses". Many of their inmates, not in need of continuous medical or nursing care, or of assistance to feed, wash or dress, could be set free by improving local authority services. The need for change was well recognised, but action to achieve it was painfully lacking.

A census of disabled people

The demand for action was given fresh impetus by the publication in May 1971 of an Office of Population Censuses and Surveys report, *Handicapped and Impaired in Great Britain*, researched and compiled by Amelia Harris, Elizabeth Cox, Christopher Smith and Judith Buckle. This official report, commissioned in 1969 by the Labour administration, took account only of people over 16 years of age living in private households, but nevertheless found that there were 1,129,000 disabled people who needed support or special care, the majority of them over the age of 65. Another 1,942,000 had an impairment, but needed little or no support. It found that about 200,000 households that included disabled people needed rehousing or improvements to accommodation because of the lack of an inside toilet. Another 150,000 "very severely, severely or appreciably handicapped people" were found to be living in inadequate accommodation with inaccessible rooms, or where the disabled person had to sleep in the living room because of their disability. Two-thirds of all disabled people were women. A large number of them were found to be living alone without the help of welfare services, and the report said: "One in five handicapped persons is living alone and even one in 20 of those who need special care has no one living with her, having to bang on walls to attract the attention of neighbours, provided they are at home. Very few of these people had a telephone to call for help. One in five impaired people living alone has a telephone, but only one in eight housebound people living by themselves has a telephone".

This revelation of the scale of need, which had previously been underestimated even by the advocates of reform, turned up pressure on the Government still further. On 21 May 1971, taking advantage of another fortunate success in the Private Member's Ballot, Lewis Carter-Jones, Labour MP for Eccles and one of Alf's staunchest supporters, called upon the "Government and local and other authorities to ensure full implementation of the Chronically Sick and Disabled Persons Act 1970 at the earliest possible date, particularly in view of the report on impaired and handicapped people in Great Britain".[11] This was a lengthy debate drawing explicit attention to the then unmet needs of disabled people and particularly for housing adaptations and conversions, the installation of telephones, the provision of four-wheeled vehicles instead of the one-person 'trike' and – a desperate need – a disability pension and allowance. It would be indulgent now to dwell upon the detailed submissions made by MPs. Most of what were then burning issues have since been addressed. Nor would it be correct to represent the debate as split along party lines. There was now at least a profession of concern to improve provision for disabled people all across both Houses of Parliament. This did not have to be an issue for party animosity, and Alf himself, speaking before the concluding response of the Secretary of State for Social Services, Sir Keith Joseph, acknowledged the "informed and constructive speeches expressing deep concern and understanding" from both sides of the House. What was in contention, rather, was the need for a greater sense of urgency and the commitment of resources, both from the Government and from many local authorities.

Noting that it was about 12 months since the "Alf Morris Bill" went through the House of Commons, Carter-Jones said that it would not

[11] *Hansard*, Commons, 21.5.1971.

be an exaggeration to say that progress in implementing its provisions had been grudging and painfully slow. The report *Handicapped and Impaired in Great Britain* had shown that previous estimates of numbers had been grossly understated. It followed that the action that was needed as a result of the Act would be "extremely costly". It was "a time bomb which is ticking away in our town halls". But the trouble with Government Departments, he argued, is that they always talk in terms of cost. "They never look at the other side of the balance sheet". Some local authorities had done well and should be praised; "but the bad local authorities really are abysmally bad".

Speaker after speaker reinforced the message, drawing attention to what needed to be done. But, as Jack Ashley pointed out, it was also important to recognise the individuality of the problems. There was a danger of regarding disabled people as a group, whereas what the House was discussing was a number of disabled individuals, "each one with a disability of his [or her] own". While action was required on a broad general front, the vital consideration was that it should help individual disabled people. The effect of the provisions of the 1970 Act was to ensure that individual disabled people, every one of them, should "be given their dignity and self-respect and helped to help themselves", a message of abiding relevance and validity.

David Weitzman pointed out that apart from the issue of the 1970 Departmental Circular, no money had been spent on publicising the provisions of the Chronically Sick and Disabled Persons Act. There was no excuse whatever for this dilatory approach on the part of Government. It was "one thing to have a charter for the chronically sick and disabled enacted, and another thing to see that its provisions were carried into effect... The Government," in his view, "had done too little and taken too long to do that little".

John Hannam, the Conservative MP for Exeter, was even more explicit. He believed, as Jack Ashley had intimated, that the drawing-up of a detailed 100 per cent register of sick and disabled people should be initiated in each locality. For a start, he argued, notices should be issued by the Ministry for display in all public places to draw attention to the provisions of the Act and explain how to register for them.

Alf provided a constructive overview. By this time, the number of disabled people on local authority registers had risen to around 600,000: more than double the number known to local authorities when the Act became law less than twelve months earlier. This was a dramatic rise but still well short of the numbers revealed by the OPCS survey and with huge disparities around the country. The demonstrable fact was that some authorities had been "dragging their feet". Nevertheless, Alf felt the purpose of a united House at that stage should be "to praise the good, not to castigate those who could have done very much better". It was too much to hope that full implementation would be achieved in every locality simultaneously, but some local authorities in widely differing parts of Britain, not least in his own native city, had shown that the new provisions could be applied in exactly the way that had been intended. None of the very wide fellowship that made and secured Royal Assent for the new Act, Alf concluded, doubted the size and gravity of the task ahead. Yet he trusted that by working together they had changed the *status quo* for Britain's disabled people and irrevocably removed "the serene satisfaction and complacency by which they were oppressed".

The Government begins to give way

In this climate of expectation, it was difficult to be seen as unsympathetic to the affliction and wanton neglect that was the common experience of disabled people. Indeed, the Government, on the eve of the debate initiated by Lewis Carter-Jones, had made the important pronouncement that 100 per cent registers were as much their aim as that of the Opposition.[12] And in his response to the debate Sir Keith Joseph struck a conciliatory note, even to the extent of expressing the hope that the motion would be accepted. He did not think politicians as a whole could be very proud of their earlier reactions to the needs of disabled people.

Alf, earlier in the debate, had described Section 1 of the Chronically Sick and Disabled Persons Act as "the master key to the main problem in the whole field of social provision for Britain's disabled

---

[12] *Ibid*, col. 1680.

people". Through his legislation he had explicitly oiled the wards of the lock. But the new Government was still reluctant to turn the key. Tardily, and with a final procrastination, the Secretary of State announced that there would be a survey of needs starting in October 1971. It was common ground that there should be no compulsion to register; but short of that and, as Alf had already insisted, subject to confidentiality, Sir Keith confirmed that the Government's aim was "a comprehensive and up-dated register", with the final reservation that Members had to accept that they could not "leap straight to a comprehensive up-dated register". None the less, it was now the Government's stated aim that they should reach it. "Impatience, but realistic impatience," said Sir Keith, was the Government's and his own attitude. He commended the motion, which was finally put and agreed.

On 1 October 1971, some sixteen months after the Royal Assent, Section 1 of the Chronically Sick and Disabled Persons Act was finally brought into effect.

Even so, progress in implementing many of the Act's provisions continued to be slower than MPs were demanding. On 21 February 1972, Dr Shirley Summerskill, daughter of the redoubtable Edith, led a debate on a motion "That this House deplores the long delay in implementing important provisions of the Chronically Sick and Disabled Persons Act 1970 ... and the continuing lack of provision for the chronically sick and disabled". It was not enough, she argued, that there should be general agreement about what should be done for disabled people. A sense of purpose and positive action was needed, something that "we had not had during the nineteen long months that the Government has been in power". Sir Keith Joseph, however, turned her motion on its head by putting an amendment that welcomed his Government's introduction of Attendance Allowance and invalidity benefits, and the "rising provision for buildings and for facilities and aids for the disabled". Ignoring the mandatory effect of Sections 1 and 2 alike, the amendment commended the Government's realism in encouraging local authorities to implement the provisions of the Chronically Sick and Disabled Persons Act "as fast as increasing staff and increasing resources allow". Given the Government's majority and the three-line whip imposed on Conservative MPs, it was the amendment that succeeded (309 for, 271 against). Alf told Sir Keith during the debate that if he went on patting himself on the back so vigorously he would suffer spinal injury and become registrable!

Local councils begin to respond

By now, however, the picture on the ground was far from one of unrelieved gloom. Alf spent much of his time encouraging local action and urging disabled people to seize their rights under the Act. Disability, argued Alf, is something that can affect anyone at any time and the person forever in rude health is the exception.

Some local authorities responded and were enthusiastic about improving provision for their disabled residents and their example shamed those who were not. In Manchester, Cliff Hilditch, the city's first Director of Social Services in April 1971 – with Jill (now Lady) Pitkeathley and Gordon Brown's elder brother John on his staff as social workers – was especially supportive. As he later made clear in *Disability, Legislation and Practice*,[13] the conspicuous priority given to the Chronically Sick and Disabled Persons Act was testimony to the ambitious nature of the Act itself, the energy of its promoters and the continuing debate about its implementation and significance which a vigilant lobby had sustained. Hilditch thought that the message of the Act was "as much evangelical as technical and demanded far-reaching changes of public attitude and professional practice".[14] Another enthusiastic advocate and pioneer of change was Brian Roycroft, the Director of Social Services in Newcastle on Tyne. He saw clearly that an essential preliminary to the delivery of services to disabled people was their identification, and embarked on a massive survey of his area that produced 'shock' findings and set the standard to be aimed at by local authorities elsewhere. When he brought his findings to Alf, he congratulated him before saying, "Now this is what I want you to do next Brian..."

Other progressive authorities pressed ahead with the task of identification without waiting for Sir Keith to act, recognising that help could not be given unless they knew as individuals who

---

[13] *Disability: Legislation and Practice* (Ed. Duncan Guthrie, The Macmillan Press Ltd, 1981), chapter 3.
[14] *Ibid.*

needed help and where they lived. Against these examples of good practice, any authority dragging its feet, as Arthur Butler commented, was likely to be publicly exposed by the mass media. Indeed the most laggardly authorities had already been spotlighted and attacked in the press.

An extraordinary initiative, which must not be passed over, was that of the membership of the Post Office Engineering Union, one of the first organisations to ask itself how it could help speed the full implementation of the new Act. Inevitably its members took a special interest in Section 2(1)(h), providing for certain disabled people to be helped by their local authorities through the installation of a telephone and any special equipment needed for its use. The problem was that local authorities argued a lack of resources. Post Office engineers, first in Liverpool but soon joined by colleagues throughout the country, volunteered to work without pay, at weekends, to install telephones under the Act. When Sir Keith Joseph got to hear of it, his response was that the Government had made provision for such installations within the rate support grant. Whilst he thought it an admirable idea, he rejected it as unlawful, pointing out with conspicuous regret that if the men were not paid for their work they would not be covered by the industrial injuries scheme. Though this obstacle led to a considerable delay, the problem was eventually overcome by the stratagem of paying the men a token amount of two pence for each installation, which was then donated to charity. Over 70,000 telephones were installed in this way, an initiative that Alf still regards as one of the finest examples of co-operation by working people unwilling to stand by with folded arms, in the face of pressing need among disabled people.

To give the Heath Government some credit, it made provision for two annual funding increases to local authorities of twelve per cent, albeit wrapped up in the total rate support grant from central to local government. This went some way to help co-operative local authorities to begin to provide the services required for implementing Section 2 of the Act. An extra £3 million was granted for the purposes of Section 17 of the Act – the building of special hospital units, away from geriatric wards, for young people who were chronically sick, something for which Alf had campaigned vigorously ever since he entered Parliament. Importantly, whereas disabled people had hitherto lived in the shadows, they were now very much in the limelight and their rights had become a major political issue, commanding the attention of party conferences. This pressure was vital. Although it still came slowly, recognition of the need for change had begun to be accepted.

Alf's wider concerns

But despite Alf's major involvement in disability problems, it would be a mistake to suppose that he had become a single-issue politician. Duncan Guthrie once remarked that it was not that he was capable of doing more than one thing at a time, but more a case of his being incapable of doing only one thing at a time. In Parliament Alf continued to be a serial questioner. While his questions were weighted towards disability issues, there was a wide variety of other concerns that he raised or to which he contributed. These ranged across such subjects as agriculture, European policy, trade with Third World countries, overseas development aid, international emergency relief for disasters, the fishing industry, cigarette advertising, corporal punishment in an approved school,[15] the purchasing power of Civil Service pensions, teachers' pay, indirect taxation, school milk and meals, the growth of Manchester Airport, fare increases on British Rail, training with firearms in penal institutions, commercial radio, homeless families, hospitals, hypothermia and prescription charges.

Alf also began to take a surprising interest in police affairs, putting a series of questions about pay, uniforms and the effect on force boundary changes. The explanation for this is as simple as it is remarkable. Shortly after the 1970 General Election, Alf was invited to afternoon tea with Selwyn Lloyd in the Speaker's house. The purpose of the invitation, it transpired, was to sound him out about a request from the Police Federation for England and Wales that he might consider becoming their parliamentary adviser as a successor to Jim Callaghan. "Why me?" Alf asked in astonishment, conscious that Callaghan had been much more obviously qualified and suited

---

[15] A quite fascinating exchange. See *Hansard*, Commons, 22.6.1971.

to the role. "Probably," the Speaker rejoined, "because you're the only one they know nothing about!" But he went on to say that he really thought it was because Alf had shown that he could legislate and was a proven expert in procedure, well liked and respected in both Houses of Parliament. The upshot was that Alf met with the Federation and agreed to give it a try. He attended all the meetings of its Joint Central Committee and was consulted on *"almost everything"* that was going on. Entirely unrepresented in either House, they were keenly interested to have Alf's thoughts about which particular lines of parliamentary action would help their members. One important objective soon emerged where his help would be most welcome. Since the Police Act 1919, the police had been forbidden affiliation with any kind of organisation outside the service, a prohibition that extended even to the Public Services Pensioners' Council. The 1919 Act had been Whitehall's response to the police strike of that year, which started in Liverpool and spread rapidly across the country. Police from London and elsewhere marched on Downing Street and their leaders negotiated with Lloyd-George, then Prime Minister, through an open window at Number 10. This led to the setting up of the Desborough Committee of Inquiry and subsequent legislation provided for increases in pay, defined terms of service, set up the Police Federation (for ranks up to and including Chief Inspector), but banned external associations. The fear was that the police might become unionised and join the Trades Union Congress. When Alf became their link with Parliament, half a century on, the Federation was restive and upset about pay and conditions of employment and subject to public criticism for being too remote and too exclusive, when the fact was that the law specifically required them to be exclusive. They wanted a persuasive advocate to liaise with the Home Secretary for them and the provisions of the 1919 Act to be softened. This was perhaps where Alf might be of immediate help?

On 8 December 1971 Alf presented a Private Member's Bill to relax the prohibition on external associations, which was read a second time without debate on 21 January 1972 and, after a good deal of haggling with the Home Office, a third time on 12 May. It then passed without amendment to become the Police Act 1972 – Alf's third Private Member's Bill to reach the Statute Book in under two years. It was presented as a measure to amend Section 44 of the Police Act 1964 "to allow the Secretary of State from time to time to authorise a Police Federation or branch thereof to be associated with a person or body outside the police service in such cases and manner, and subject to such conditions and restrictions, as he may specify and may vary or withdraw an authorisation previously given": a supreme example of how to secure legislation through astute timing and well-devised drafting, presented in terms such as virtually to preclude opposition.

The Police Federation was deeply appreciative, presenting Alf with the very rarely awarded Police Bowl, a marvellous black Wedgwood bowl that stands on a bookcase and remains one of Alf's most treasured possessions. Some years later his home was burgled. This was treated as serious crime because some confidential parliamentary papers were missing. The investigating officers said that the burglar had clearly entered from the back of the house and had moved systematically through, picking what seemed worth taking on the way, but had stopped at the bookcase. When it became apparent that the bowl bore an inscription linking Alf to the police, this appeared to have deterred the thief from going any further and he left the house where he had broken in. "In that case," said Alf, "in future let's put it on the back doorstep!"

The fact that he was parliamentary adviser to the Police Federation at the time of the industrial unrest that was to unseat Edward Heath's government did no harm to Labour's cause. There was a solid fear among Opposition leaders that Heath might seek to gain electoral advantage if there were to be angry clashes between striking miners and the police. Conflict of that kind, fomented by images in tabloid newspapers, could lend substance to the question posed by the Conservatives, "Who governs the nation?". Alf's very high standing with the Police Federation ensured that this did not happen. Dick Pamplin, the Secretary of the Federation, could see that it was to the mutual interest of the police and the miners to keep the peace, and he readily agreed to do all in his power to ensure that the police did not become the enemy or act in a way that would damage their relationship with the mining community. Alf also had talks with Joe Gormley, a fellow Lancastrian whom he knew quite well. *"He was from Wigan, not Manchester, but near enough to be among my ain folk"*. He understood perfectly that there was a need to avoid conflict between the miners and the police and followed up an arrangement Alf had made for talks with Dick Pamplin. The political link might not have been obvious to everyone, but it was certainly obvious to Harold Wilson. And no doubt to Margaret Thatcher who, when faced with a similar situation in 1984/85, famously handled it very differently.

Alf sceptical about accession to the EEC

But above all – above even the oil crisis, industrial unrest and the three-day-working week – the ill-fated Heath Government was notable for the negotiation of Britain's entry into the EEC and the Bill that led to our accession on 1 January 1973. Labour members were widely divided on the issue. Harold Wilson's autobiography tells us that most Labour MPs were against entry, many of them regardless of the terms, with a smaller number opposed simply to the terms, and roughly a third "dedicated pro-marketeers".[16] Alf belonged to the sceptics, relentlessly putting questions and speaking in debates throughout the period of negotiation and on the European Communities Bill itself, drawing attention to the likely effects of entry on Britain's traditional food suppliers, particularly upon sugar producers in the developing countries, if their interests were not explicitly protected. He was not satisfied that we had or were at all likely to get binding safeguards for the Commonwealth cane growers in the poorest parts of the Commonwealth: very poor countries indeed, that were wholly dependent on the production of a single crop as the only commodity they could produce. *"They didn't choose sugar; sugar chose them"*. At their sub-tropical latitudes, Fiji, Mauritius and the Caribbean countries among others, had relied since time immemorial on growing sugar cane. It was just about the only crop that could survive the ever-present menace of destructive cyclones to which they were exposed. But the world price of sugar now quite often fell below their costs of production. It had fallen because European countries in the temperate zone, when countless alternatives were readily available, chose to grow heavily subsidised beet sugar for £90 a ton and more. This led, notoriously so in the EEC countries, to over production of sugar beet and dumping the surplus

---

[16] *Final Term, The Labour Government 1974-1976* (Harold Wilson, Weidenfeld and Nicolson and Michael Joseph, 1979).

on the world market, thus driving the world price for sugar down to £23 a ton, which was below the costs of growing cane sugar.

Another perceived disadvantage that went with adherence to the Treaty of Rome was an EEC-wide Value Added Tax (VAT) system. As early as March 1970, Alf wrote a best-selling Fabian essay on the subject.[17] It is a publication – in the Fabian Society's research series – to delight taxation aficionados and was years ahead of the reservations of those officials eventually charged with its administration and verification. VAT, of course, has come to be accepted as a fact of life, but back in 1970, as Alf pointed out in closely reasoned argument, its many defects were apparent in comparison with the purchase tax system that it was to replace. Not the least of them was that of significantly increasing retail prices and a hugely increased volume of paperwork confronting a much wider range of businesses. The essay was written while the Chronically Sick and Disabled Persons Bill was under consideration in the House of Lords.

But Alf's main concern about EEC membership was the effect that our accession would have on trade with our traditional suppliers. In 1971, he argued in the House that if rumours were true and, in the event of Britain's entry to the EEC, Australia would be phased out of the Commonwealth Sugar Agreement, then that agreement would be wrecked. If the collapse was sudden it could mean economic disaster for some of the world's poorest countries, which were interested in trade as much as they were in aid. They wanted trade on fair terms with the developed countries and the main political challenge of the future was to ensure that the rich and developed and the poor and developing countries could live in fruitful partnership. The whole matter of British entry to the EEC, he contended, was one that must be decided by the British people, who so far had not been adequately consulted. The debate on entry, he predicted, would be long, detailed and historic; but, whatever the outcome, it behoved the House as a whole at least to make certain it did not disown or dishonour the traditional friends of this country.[18]

---

[17] No.284: *Value Added Tax: a tax on the consumer.*
[18] *Hansard*, Commons, 21.1.1971.

Founder Chairman of the ANZAC Group

To that end, in 1972, a number of MPs and Peers from all sides of the political divide formed the parliamentary ANZAC Group. Alf was its founder Chairman, and Neil (later Sir Neil), Marten, Conservative MP for Banbury, its first secretary. Until then such a grouping would have been thought odd, since relationships between Britain and Australasia were traditionally both close and cordial. An ANZAC Group to liaise between Westminster and parliamentarians in Canberra and Wellington would have been viewed as an indulgence. Most would have understood an Anglo-Bulgarian Group, an Anglo-Sudanese Group or an Anglo-Mexican Group, but they would hardly have seen the case for an Anglo-Australia/New Zealand Group. But by 1972, when there was ever growing concern about impending British membership of the EEC, the prospect was one of a tightly protectionist Common Market with a consequential loosening of ties with the Australasian countries. It was in this context that Alf said at the founding meeting of the Group that it was dedicated, in Jonathan Swift's memorable phrase, to "keeping friendship in good repair".

The Group soon attracted a strong all-party membership of MPs and peers and is still going strong, with Alf serving as its chairman all the way through his remaining twenty-five years' service in the House of Commons and more recently, from the House of Lords, as its Life President. Over the years much work has been done to strengthen links between those countries and some remarkable safeguards for continued access to British markets achieved. The ANZAC Group has provided a forum for visiting leaders from Australia and New Zealand to address and has hosted a great many parliamentarians from both countries in the interests of repairing, where necessary, and strengthening bilateral relationships. Every Australian and New Zealand Prime Minister since it was founded has addressed the Group at least once, as too have scores of other Australian and New Zealand Ministers. It has also kept in regular touch with both High Commissions and is available to their High Commissioners whenever they wish to address the Group's meetings.

For Alf personally, the Group built on the close links he developed with Australia and New Zealand while he was PPS to Fred Peart and at the Ministry of Agriculture, Fisheries and Food in the 1960s; and it paved the way for his *tour de force* in persuading the British

Government to support legislation to give Australia what in *The Times* its then Prime Minister called its 'birth certificate', an achievement to be recounted in a later chapter.

Nothing, in the event, could stop our union with the EEC, favoured as it was by the Government of the day. Approval of the European Communities Bill was nevertheless a close run thing. The second reading went through on 17 February 1972 by only eight votes, 309 to 301, and the third reading on 13 July by 301 to 284, with Alf among the noes on both occasions. The Royal Assent finally came on 17 October. Opposition to the terms of accession had been largely unavailing. Originally all that was offered were vague assurances to 'take to heart' – aura à coeur – the special needs of Commonwealth countries, none of which, as Alf put it, were "bankable". But qualified continuing access for Commonwealth cane sugar and New Zealand butter was achieved; and Alf and others of like mind had made an impact and put down a marker for further negotiation, for which, as we now know, new opportunities for progress would soon open up.

Chapter 10

THE TRAGEDY OF THALIDOMIDE

1958–1978

"DISTAVAL can be given with complete safety to pregnant women and nursing mothers, without adverse effect on mother or child".

From a Distillers leaflet.

– A "tried and tested product" – Medical misgivings
– Legal action puts the issue under wraps – The power of the press
– Harold Evans: publish and be damned – Parliament has its say
– Capitulation – An imaginative settlement of outstanding claims

A "tried and tested product"

There was one distressing issue that does not fit neatly into any one period of Alf's parliamentary life; indeed which began before he was elected and continued – scandalously – through successive Labour and Conservative governments. The aftermath of the Second World War was a difficult time, when many things that needed to be done for disabled people were simply not addressed. But few things could compare for shock to public opinion with the unexpected scourge that was visited upon the 'thalidomide children' and their families.

The drug thalidomide, discovered in 1954, was first marketed by a small German company, Chemie Grünenthal, and sold in many countries. In the United Kingdom[1] it was made available from April 1958 under a variety of brand names of which the best known was Distaval, manufactured by Distillers (Biochemicals) Ltd, who, like other companies, had taken the drug under licence from Grünenthal as a "tried and tested product".[2] Among doctors and other medical professionals it was widely promoted throughout the United Kingdom and extensively prescribed as a sedative or remedy for sleeplessness. It was also used to ease difficulties such as morning

[1] As well as in the USA, Germany, Japan, Ireland, Sweden, Australia, Canada, Brazil, Italy and Spain.
[2] *The history of thalidomide* (The Thalidomide Society website, 1.6.2004).

sickness in the early stages of pregnancy and was at first regarded as entirely safe. So much so that, although it was normally supplied on prescription, it could be purchased quite legally 'over the counter'.

Medical misgivings

Perhaps the first warning that thalidomide might not be wholly benign was signalled in a letter to the *British Medical Journal* from Dr A. Leslie Florence, a practitioner in Turriff, Aberdeenshire, published on 31 December 1960. He drew attention to problems experienced by four of his patients, all of whom had been receiving Distaval over a period varying from eighteen months to two years. Three of them had stopped taking the drug for two or three months and "there had been a marked improvement in their symptoms".

The first link with birth defects followed late in 1961, when in a letter to *The Lancet* Dr William McBride, an Australian gynaecologist, raised the possibility that severe congenital malformations he had observed in three children might have been caused by thalidomide. Almost simultaneously, Professor Widukind Lenz, the Head of Hamburg's University Clinic for Children, expressed similar misgivings. "Both had observed a significant and apparently inexplicable increase in the number of babies born in their countries with a certain pattern of deformities indicating exposure to a teratogenic agent in the second month following the first day of the mother's last menstrual period".[3] Soon afterwards, in Britain and many other countries, reports of a dramatic rise in the numbers of babies affected in this way – many of whom did not survive – confirmed the connection. The drug was withdrawn from sale in Germany on 27 November 1961 and in Britain soon afterwards.

Legal action puts the issue under wraps

In the following year, in the absence of a public inquiry and lacking any other recourse, some of the parents of thalidomide children took Distillers to court. The plaintiffs formed a Society of Thalidomide Parents (now The Thalidomide Society) and an appeal was launched by Lady Hoare, who had established a Trust for Physically Disabled Children to help them. During Alf's first years as an MP, parliamentary questions about the thalidomide problem were muted

---

[3] *Thalidomide – 'Y' List Inquiry* (Sir Alan Marre KCB, DHSS, 1978).

and few and far between. Despite indications that the drug had not been properly tested in Germany and that it had been made available, without UK testing, through the National Health Service, the Labour Government's line from the outset was to distance itself from any responsibility and therefore from providing any compensation. Its duty was seen as providing the support normally available to disabled people. Such help, said Kenneth Robinson, Labour's Minister of Health, in November 1964, was felt to be "more appropriate than a financial contribution" to the Lady Hoare Thalidomide Appeal.[4]

By February 1968, actions alleging negligence had been started in respect of 62 children, almost all of which were settled out of court, but on terms later described as "immorally low".[5] From 1969 onwards, claims by a significantly greater number of families were brought. The effect of these actions, both in Parliament and in the media, was that discussion of the issues around thalidomide, particularly in relation to compensation, was effectively constrained by the *sub judice* principle, "sealed by the laws of contempt".[6]

When a Conservative government was returned to power in 1970, Alf joined with other MPs, notably Jack Ashley and Dr Gerard Vaughan, the Conservative MP for Reading,[7] who were appalled by the procrastination of Distillers, to press for greater help for the families affected by this medical disaster. In October 1972, a flurry of questions was put by Alf, now an Opposition Front Bench spokesman on social policy, Dame Irene Ward, Conservative MP for Tynemouth, Jack Ashley and Lewis Carter-Jones, Labour MP for Eccles. In their replies, Conservative Ministers, like their predecessors, consistently stonewalled. Parents, it was pointed out, received the help from the Government for which they had applied and to which they were entitled.[8] Compensation was a matter for private litigation and the Government's responsibility in that regard was for the proper administration of the courts.[9]

---

[4] Written answer, Kenneth Robinson, *Hansard*, Commons, 24.11.1964.
[5] *A Hack's Progress* (Phillip Knightley, Random House, 1997), extract reproduced in *Tell Me No Lies (Ed. John Pilger*, Jonathan Cape, 2004).
[6] *The Thalidomide Scandal in Tell Me No Lies* (ed. John Pilger, Jonathan Cape, 2004).
[7] Who had been in charge of the Children's Unit at Guy's Hospital, London.
[8] Written answer, Sir Keith Joseph, *Hansard*, Commons, 24.10.1972.
[9] Written answer, Attorney General, *Hansard*, Commons, 25.10.72

Alf's close personal involvement in the thalidomide issue had first arisen from a constituency meeting in 1968 with the mother of David Jones, a little boy who had been born without arms or legs, who lived in Church Road in the Northenden area of his constituency. Alf had a long correspondence with Labour Ministers about the case and later sent full details of it to his friend from boyhood, Harold Evans, then editor of *The Sunday Times*. But the media, like successive Governments, was hesitant to bring the full story of thalidomide before the public, fearful of prejudicing legal action and invoking action for contempt. Phillip Knightley, a journalist closely in touch with the scandal, later described it as "a terrible failure of journalism".[10]

The power of the press

The media dam was breached only when a West End art dealer, David Mason, father of a thalidomide daughter, took his story to David English, editor of the *Daily Mail*. Mason was incensed by the level of compensation offered by Distillers and by their condition that if even only one parent objected the offer would be withdrawn from all. In December 1971, the *Mail* published three articles focusing on the difficulties faced by the parents of thalidomide children, highlighting Mason's view that he was being "legally blackmailed" by Distillers to accept inadequate compensation.

Harold Evans: publish and be damned

The *Mail* was quickly silenced, but the articles sharpened the long-standing interest of Harold Evans, whose Insight team – Phillip Knightley, Elaine Potter and Marjorie Wallace, led by Bruce Page – had been working on the story for some years. Harold Evans was no stranger to controversy. In 1965, Alf had stood bail for him when Sir Frank Soskice, Labour's Attorney General, had issued a writ against him for a leader in the Northern Echo about the case of the wrongly executed Derek Bentley. Now he was equally prepared to 'publish and be damned', even to go to jail in pursuit of natural justice, but on this occasion, according to Knightley,[11] he was

---

[10] In his autobiography, *A Hack's Progress* (Random House, 1997), extract reproduced in *Tell Me No Lies* (ed. John Pilger, Jonathan Cape, 2004).

[11] *A Hack's Progress* (Phillip Knightley, Random House, 1997), extract reproduced in *Tell Me No Lies* (ed. John Pilger, Jonathan Cape, 2004), which has a detailed account of the role of *The Sunday Times* in 'the thalidomide scandal'

overruled by his chairman, Denis Hamilton. Frustrated, Evans asked *The Sunday Times'* legal adviser, James Evans, if some way could be found to circumvent the legal barriers. Evans recalled some trenchant comments made by Lady Hoare. She had referred to the tragic and deplorable situation of parents of thalidomide children. Many of them, she had said, felt ground down by prolonged litigation, degraded by the detailed form-filling they had to undergo and deeply resentful at being made to feel they were going cap in hand for charity, rather than moral justice, from the wealthy Distillers. The concept of 'moral justice', as distinct from legal justice, appealed to James Evans. It prompted him to advise that *The Sunday Times* could legitimately campaign on the idea that the children so appallingly disabled by thalidomide deserved a better deal, irrespective of the question of whether Distillers had been legally negligent.

This was the green light for Harold Evans, who persuaded Hamilton that the risk had to be run. On 24 September 1972, just as it looked as though litigation might go on for another ten years, *The Sunday Times* devoted three pages to arguing that the law was failing to produce justice for the thalidomide children. A front-page lead appeared under the headline 'Our Thalidomide Children: A Cause for National Shame' along with an editorial 'Children on our Conscience'. This proclaimed that the plight of the thalidomide children shamed society, shamed the law and shamed Distillers.[12] It promised, moreover, that in a future article *The Sunday Times* would trace how the tragedy occurred. This was more than enough to trigger Distillers to complain to the Attorney General, the Rt. Hon. Sir Peter Rawlinson QC. Distillers sought and secured an injunction against the planned publication of a second article. But the 'cat was out of the bag'; the way was now open for parliamentary action, again relying on the principle that the issue was one that called for 'moral justice' and that moral concern could legitimately be aired in the House.

---

[12] Part of the text of the editorial is quoted in *Suffer the Children* (The Sunday Times Insight Team, Andre Deutsch, 1979), p.181. Indeed, this source has a detailed account of the whole thalidomide scandal.

Parliament has its say

Initially, Government officials continued to take refuge in the *sub judice* rule, but on 16 November 1972 Jack Ashley secured a brief back-bench adjournment debate.[13] He pointed out that some 430 children were casualties of thalidomide, suffering injuries as appalling as those of "any soldier on the battlefield" – and all of them innocent children. They had been injured because their mothers believed the categorical claim of Distillers only weeks before thalidomide was withdrawn that Distaval could be given "with complete safety, without adverse effect on mother or child". Distillers, he said, had tried to gag the media, but inescapably the unanswered question was what steps had the Government taken to check the veracity of its claim? Did Ministers know that the United States Government was demanding evidence of the drug's safety at that time? The Prime Minister (Edward Heath) had categorically rejected shared responsibility, but the fact remained that the Government had distributed thalidomide under the NHS; and indeed it appeared to have been granted exemption from purchase tax on grounds of exceptional efficacy. The Prime Minister's sympathy and sincerity were quite unquestioned, said Ashley, but he must think again. He must change his mind and establish a fund for thalidomide children immediately.

In his response, Paul Dean, Under-Secretary of State for Health and Social Security, confirmed a statement by the Prime Minister on 14 November 1972 that the Government "should await the outcome of legal arrangements before coming to a firm conclusion about the needs of these children which still require to be met". At this point, Alf rose from the Opposition Front Bench to press what another Shadow Minister sitting beside him called the '64,000 dollar question'. "My hon. Friend the Member for Stoke on Trent," Alf began, "has said that central Government are deeply involved in the tragedy of the thalidomide children. Is there any responsibility on central Government for permitting thalidomide to be prescribed under the National Health Service?" Paul Dean, wriggling of course, sought to deny any such responsibility. Up to 1963, when the Committee on Safety of Drugs was appointed, and the passing of

---

[13] *Hansard*, Commons, 16.11.1972.

the Medicines Act in 1968, he said, new drugs were always marketed on the responsibility of the manufacturer. This had happened under governments of both parties. Doctors exercised their clinical judgment in deciding to use them to treat patients and reported in professional journals their experience of them in use, building up "a climate of professional opinion about the value and risks of a drug". When thalidomide was introduced there were no powers under which the Government or its agencies could check a drug before it was marketed. As to its exemption from purchase tax in 1958, he could only emphasise that at that time no one knew that it was a dangerous drug.

Alf had the last word. The House, he said, had heard an extremely unsatisfactory answer to a compelling case. Both the Government, which had acquired and facilitated the use of thalidomide under the NHS, and the Distillers Company must now face up to their responsibilities.

What was needed to make that happen was a full-scale debate, initiated by either the Government or the Opposition. But that required the scarcest of all commodities for any Opposition, parliamentary time, which the Government was eminently unlikely to provide from its own schedules. Alf, as Labour's front bench spokesman on social policy, requested a meeting with Harold Wilson, then Leader of the Opposition, to ask him to consider allocating Opposition time for a parliamentary debate on the thalidomide issue. He now admits that he did so with little hope of success. The Opposition of the day was allocated no more than four parliamentary days a year for debates on issues of its choosing and competition between Opposition frontbencher for any part of that allocation was always intense, not to say fierce.

But Alf was not entirely without hope. He knew that Wilson, with whom he had been close since his candidature in Garston in 1951 – and with whom he had spoken from the same platform at a mass meeting at The Stadium in Liverpool in the General Election of that year – was a man of deep social concern. Alf's brother Charles was now Harold's Parliamentary Private Secretary as Leader of the Opposition. And Wilson had, of course, already acted courageously in 1970, when he jettisoned Government legislation in favour of the Chronically Sick and Disabled Persons Bill. Amazingly in the circumstances, he was now equally receptive. Alf, whose bid for Opposition time was supported by Sir Elwyn Jones, a former Attorney General soon to become Lord Chancellor, believes that it was greatly to the credit of both men that parliamentary time for the debate was secured. Harold Wilson, Alf believes, has not been properly identified as a very considerable force in resolving the thalidomide issue and in the battle for full civil rights for disabled people. Crucially, on this occasion, it was Harold Wilson who, in addition to providing time for a parliamentary debate, persuaded Selwyn Lloyd, the Speaker (and a fellow Merseyside MP), to accept the proposition that irrespective of the law in respect of the press, "Parliament could not be muzzled and... should be free to debate the thalidomide issue".[14] It meant that thalidomide had now become not just a campaigning issue for an all-party group of back-benchers, but a principal issue of concern to the alternative Government.

The next task was to decide the arrangements for presenting the motion. Harold Wilson invited Elwyn and Alf to a meeting in his room at the Commons, where they were joined by Charles Morris, as Wilson's PPS and, with the Leader's consent, by Alf's boyhood friend Harold Evans and his closest parliamentary friend Jack Ashley. Having agreed the broad strategy, Alf was left as the frontbencher principally involved to decide with Sir Elwyn Jones the precise terms of the Opposition motion.

On 29 November the motion was put to the House in the names of Harold Wilson, Elwyn Jones, Alf and three other Opposition frontbenchers. It called upon Distillers to face up to their moral responsibilities and for immediate legislation to deal with the problems of thalidomide children, including the establishment of a trust fund.[15] On the day, Jack Ashley opened with a withering attack on Distillers. "We are witnessing," he said, "not only a shabby spectacle but a grave national scandal, a display of moral irresponsibility which has seldom if ever been surpassed".

---

[14] *Final Term, The Labour Government 1974-1976* (Harold Wilson, Weidenfeld and Nicolson and Michael Joseph, 1979), p. 226.
[15] *Hansard*, Commons, 29.11.1972.

As the Shadow Minister, speaking from the Opposition Front Bench, Alf wound up the debate. He spoke for twenty minutes. The motion, he said, made two propositions: that Distillers must face up to its undoubted moral responsibilities and that society – not just the government of the day – must do the same. The House as a whole, he urged, "must now lend its weight in the uneven struggle between the authors and the victims of this tragedy". And if Whitehall was prepared to allow thalidomide to be distributed under the NHS and was prepared also to exempt it from purchase tax, then Whitehall had a direct involvement in this tragedy in the eyes of most of the British people. For right to be done urgent action was now required from both Distillers and the Government.

He was at pains to stress that this was not an occasion for party animus. Yet it is difficult in reading the record of the debate to avoid the conclusion that a sharp division existed between the campaigners for action and the Government of the day. All sides might have sympathy in common, but there was an obvious reticence on the part of Government to make a special case in favour of thalidomide children, to see them as different from other severely disabled children or to concede that responsibility for compensation extended beyond the manufacturers of the drug. For the Government to accept any commitment to compensate, argued Sir Keith Joseph – whom Alf recalls, not without some affection, as the "casuist's casuist" – would be likely to relax the pressure to reach a satisfactory settlement. Moreover, this disaster had to be set against the massive benefits that innovation by drug firms and in the laboratories of universities and research institutes had achieved. To which Alf replied that this did not excuse failure to help the victims when things went grievously wrong.

The most telling division of all, however, was the tabling of a shabbily partisan Government amendment to the terms of the motion. The amended version read: "That this House, disturbed about the plight of thalidomide children and the delay in reaching a settlement between Distillers (Biochemicals) Ltd and most of the children and their families; recognises the initiatives taken by Her Majesty's Government to improve services for the handicapped and disabled; welcomes the undertakings of Her Majesty's Government to investigate any case where the needs of a thalidomide child are thought not to be met by the services available, and to consider, as soon as the cases are no longer *sub judice*, whether a trust fund needs to be established for thalidomide children". This form of words, of course, emasculated the original purpose of the motion and used the wide-ranging new help provided by Alf's own legislation to shelter the Government. But given the Government's majority in the House it was the amended version of the motion that was carried.

Capitulation

Nonetheless, pressure on Distillers was now intense and in 1973 the company finally caved in. A settlement was agreed and approved in the High Court on 30 June to meet the claims accepted by the company, on the evidence produced, as being well-founded. Compensation was agreed for 338 children on a so-called 'X' list, where Distillers had accepted that their malformations had resulted because their mothers had taken a thalidomide preparation of their manufacture. In addition, a charitable trust was set up into which Distillers would pay £2 million every year for seven years (with adjustments for changes in the retail price index) for the benefit of all thalidomide-damaged children. The trustees were to be independent in deciding how the funds could best be used for the children's benefit. Moral justice had triumphed.

An imaginative settlement of outstanding claims

Notwithstanding this resounding victory, a list of unsettled cases – the Y list – remained in respect of children with birth defects where it was still unclear as to whether thalidomide had been the cause. The settlement had made provision for them to receive the same compensation as children on the 'X' list, but only if Distillers subsequently accepted that they were thalidomide children or if a judge so decided. It fell to Alf, during his tenure as Minister for Disabled People to clear up their entitlement. By the beginning of 1978, some 75 children remained on the 'Y' list and criticism had built up, particularly in the media. Distillers was accused of acting unreasonably and without compassion and even humanity. Although the company protested that the necessary evidence was lacking, criticism, including parliamentary criticism, continued. Alf decided to try to break the logjam. Although no direct responsibility fell on the Department of Health and Social Security, he intervened as Minister for Disabled People by inviting Sir Alan Marre KCB, the second permanent secretary at the DHSS, to conduct an inquiry to "consider what further steps it may be equitable and reasonable for the Distillers Company to take in relation to any of the outstanding 'Y' list cases, and to make recommendations". Those, at least, were the terms of the formal announcement in the House of Commons on 7 March 1978. Privately, Alf told Marre if necessary to "somersault backwards" to clear every case he possibly could, making exceptions only where he could show that the mother could not possibly have taken the drug. Distillers, for its part, gave wholehearted assent to the inquiry.

Alan Marre's report, published on 3 August 1978 was a model of scrupulous investigation and lucid prose, invaluable for anyone who wishes to learn more about the thalidomide disaster. But the really interesting conclusion – a compelling precedent that even Michael Foot might want to accept – was contained in the closing summary. Marre found that for the most part, after considering all the evidence, he had <u>not</u> been able to conclude that thalidomide could be said to have been shown as the probable cause of damage. But he had taken the view that this was too strict a test to apply in the circumstances. His approach had been whether, after a review of the available evidence, he was persuaded that thalidomide could reasonably be exonerated altogether as the cause of damage. If not, his judgment was that it would be equitable and reasonable for Distillers to compensate the families in the same way as those who had already been compensated. Indeed, in those cases where, even though his personal judgment was that it was clear beyond reasonable doubt that thalidomide had <u>not</u> caused the injuries, he had concluded that the special problems created by the establishment of the 'Y' list – the fact that expectations had been raised and added stresses and strains had arisen – justified the award of an *ex gratia* payment.

Thus Sir Alan had indeed somersaulted backwards, but only to reach a decision that felt morally right. Certainly Distillers were not disposed to contest it. They agreed to increase the Thalidomide Trust Fund by some £3 million, augmented by £5 million from the Government to offset the effects of taxation.

Chapter 11

MINISTER FOR DISABLED PEOPLE

1974–1979

"In 1974 a further new appointment was made. Alf Morris, who as a back-bencher had been dedicated to the welfare of the disabled, became under-secretary of State in the Department of Health and Social Services, to work full time on problems of disablement. Although necessarily constrained by public expenditure allocations, it is no exaggeration to say that he has changed the lives of millions of people".

Harold Wilson, 'Final Term:
The Labour Government 1974–1976' (1979)

– Facing a new challenge – The opportunity of a lifetime – Guiding principles
– First initiatives – Changing the social and economic balance
– Help for war pensioners
– Alf masterminds the formation of RADAR: a merger with a royal accolade
– A surprising discovery – Through the benefits maze
– Expanding provision under the 1970 Act – The drive for improved mobility
– Jim Callaghan – Support for the voluntary sector – Find and inform
– Spreading the message – Development of access provision – CORAD
– A Charter for the 80s: at home and abroad – Links with China
– Appointed to the Privy Council

Facing a new challenge

When the result of the General Election of February 1974 was finally declared, Labour held 301 seats, four more than the Conservatives but not enough to give them an overall majority. It was a minority Government, with the Liberals' 14 seats holding the balance of power. The Labour and Co-operative candidate for Wythenshawe, by contrast, won a comfortable majority of 5,533 over the combined votes of his Conservative and Liberal rivals. For Alf, who had been on the Opposition front bench since 1970, this success marked the beginning of a new chapter in his parliamentary life. With ministerial authority for the problems and needs of disabled people, he now had the opportunity to advance reforms that had proved so hopelessly elusive in the previous three years and was fortunate enough to have the strong personal backing of Harold Wilson as Prime Minister. He was invited to Downing Street and told that Wilson had in mind an entirely new ministerial appointment for him, as the first-ever Minister for Disabled People, a role and title then unknown.

Alf's initial response was that he really couldn't do what needed to be done within the remit of the Department of Health and Social Security, recalling that his Chronically Sick and Disabled Persons Act ranged over the responsibilities of more than a dozen departments of state: involving housing, education, the built environment, employment, local authority services and much more, as well as health and social security. Even the Ministry of Defence was involved, as he had shown in the debates on that legislation. The Minister's job, if he were to become a Minister for Disabled People properly so-called, would involve not merely looking at the priority of the claims of disabled people *within* any single department of state but at priorities *between* departments. It would be a very bold person who claimed that personal social services were more important than cash benefits, or that special housing provision or improved outdoor mobility help for disabled people was less important than either. Agonising choices had to be made, but to be defensible they must be made across as well as within departments, simply because responsibilities for addressing the problems and needs of disabled people were scattered all over Whitehall.

Wilson then appointed a ministerial committee, a Cabinet body known in inner-Whitehall as SS(D), under Alf's chairmanship, to look at the totality of the needs of disabled people and priorities in meeting them, and reporting directly to the PM.

It was a role for which Alf was ideally suited, passionately committed and equipped to fill with flying colours: an example of joined-up thinking before anyone else had thought of the term. Indeed, it is worth noting that in 1975, well ahead of New Labour's current mantra, Alf specifically argued that "only effective co-ordination (indeed co-operation) within and between departments of state, and between central and local government and the voluntary agencies, can ensure that there is a minimum of duplication and waste. We fully accept that a coherent strategy requires cross-departmental thinking in Whitehall and that we must act in the closest possible rapport with the statutory sector locally and the countless voluntary bodies working in the field"[1]

The opportunity of a lifetime

Alf set about his task with vigour. His five years as Minister for Disabled People stand as a testament to his single-minded commitment and boundless energy. His achievement was correspondingly prodigious. A remarkable checklist of the measures taken during Alf's first four years as Minister to bring new help for disabled people and their families comprises more than 150 improvements in provision.[2]

Always an adroit tactician, part of his strategy as Minister, as he now freely admits, was to prompt MPs as well as organisations outside Parliament to bring pressure on him in the policy areas in which he was most keen to make progress. In his short period as a Minister spending on centrally provided services for disabled people almost trebled. Four new cash benefits for disabled people – all of them brand new in global terms – were introduced. Spending on all disability benefits went up from £474 million in 1974 to £1,574 million in 1979 and the Government legislated to link rises in benefit rates to increases in average industrial earnings. Industrial injuries benefits and war disablement pensions also rose substantially. Each of these improvements had been difficult to achieve. He was not just driving the train, but laying the track in what had previously been the most neglected area of social policy.

He was doing so, moreover, against a background of daunting economic difficulties and Treasury constraints. The credit squeeze at times was not only tight but punishingly so. Most departments of

---

[1] From a speech to the Royal National Orthopaedic Hospital and the Institute of Orthopaedics, 24 September 1975.
[2] First published in *Hansard* on 24 January 1977 as a written answer to a question from Sir Harold Wilson to his successor, Jim Callaghan, and later updated to cover the period up to December 1978 as the first appendix of Harold Wilson's *Final Term*.

state were taking cuts in their programmes. Alf, on the contrary, was committed to the delivery of a range of new disability benefits. Even before the General Election of 1974, as 'shadow' DHSS Minister, he had long and frequent meetings with Peter Large, Dr Stewart Lyon and Mary Greaves of DIG to prepare for new benefits needing to be introduced if he got the opportunity. He now faced the challenge of advocating new spending to ministerial colleagues in a context of retrenchment. Outside government one rarely sees the signs of tensions between Ministers, but they are very real. Fellow Ministers told Alf again and again that he had already had more than his fair share. There were things they wanted to do; they too needed more expenditure, yet were being cut back, whereas Alf was seeking entirely new benefits. But he was able to counter that Harold Wilson had said that in this harsh economic climate "the broadest backs must bear the biggest burdens". And unless words had lost their meaning, he argued, this must mean that people with broken backs were the highest priority.

Alf nevertheless always had to watch his own back, and was very lucky that so many other people were on his side, and not just all across Parliament. Outside Westminster, DIG and other disability organisations were doing all they possibly could to make it clear that, when Alf said that he was under relentless pressure to do more, they could document his case with evidence galore of the vitally urgent need for disabled people to receive higher priority.

Guiding principles

We are fortunate to have a contemporary insight into Alf's thinking as Minister for Disabled People from an interview he gave to the *Health and Social Service Journal* in 1977. The anonymous interviewer found his obvious compassion and commitment "positively overwhelming". After speaking to him, confessed the writer, "you feel a certain sentimental numbness paralysing your critical faculties"! If a poll were taken tomorrow on the most respected person in Parliament, he (or she) commented, then Alf Morris would be the likely winner. Being universally loved may not guarantee success in politics, but it is helpful when you are the Minister for Disabled People.

The question and answer session that drew such appreciation is quite revealing: it confirms the innate sense of balance that Alf has retained throughout his parliamentary career. But given the scale of disadvantage then experienced by disabled people (not least disabled children) he was forthright in arguing for positive discrimination in their favour. To enable the disabled child to do as well at school as a non-disabled contemporary of the same ability he was, he said, recalling his speech at Manchester University, more concerned to achieve a 'photo-finish' than to insist on a level start. He also wanted to see more disabled people, even if severely disabled, in open employment and in jobs commensurate with their abilities. So the more publicity that could be given to the abilities of disabled people the better. Most disabilities could be seen but it was often only when abilities were recognised that job opportunities improved. Society needed to be opened up to disabled people. In regard to the built environment, he said, "what we are trying to do is phase out one kind of architecture and phase in another. That's not very easy. You can't right the wrongs of centuries in a moment of time, but you can accentuate the positive and eliminate the negative".

The questioner turned to the issue of integration in education. Alf said that there was an "anxious debate" between those who advocated special educational facilities for disabled children and those who believed, with equal sincerity, that integration was of vital importance. His own view was that more and more integration was needed, but there had to be caution in proceeding to that goal, particularly with the most severely disabled children. He acknowledged that this and other issues – such as the urgency of the need to extend outdoor mobility help to people who did not drive – were sensitive, but one of the things he had done was to increase funds available to organisations of and for disabled people to make their views more widely known. His view had been that it did Ministers no harm to arm their critics so as to ensure that their viewpoints could be fairly considered. But crucial to progress was that disabled people should be aware of their rights and statutory entitlements. He was not satisfied that they were and wanted to encourage the 'single door' concept [what is now called the 'one-stop-shop' approach]. One of the big problems, said Alf, was coping with "the big organisation which seems and often is soulless and impersonal". To help the individual to deal with these Goliaths would itself be an important step forward.[3]

First initiatives

Putting philosophy into practice was, of course, more difficult. But Alf's appointment as Minister gave him an opportunity to think and act creatively for a better future for disabled people and to begin to turn ideas into reality. He could also remedy some glaring omissions of the past, sanctioning improvements in the aids and equipment available to disabled people, not least the standard wheelchairs that left so much to be desired and leg calipers that were supposed to be for the relief of disability but which in practice often compounded the disabilities of those obliged to wear them.

Another item on his unfulfilled agenda of particular concern was the need to bring the victims of byssinosis into the industrial disablement benefit scheme. This disease of the lungs, caused by the inhalation of dust from cotton, flax or hemp, had an emotive history. Firstly it was close to home. Much of Alf's reforming legislation related directly to his own experience, and byssinosis was a classic example. In Ancoats as more generally in Manchester – widely known as 'Cottonopolis' by the mid-nineteenth century – he had lived among its victims. Byssinsosis was the scourge of mill workers who, even before it was given a name, suffered grievously from the effects of cotton dust on their lungs. Nothing explains more conclusively why, in Manchester in 1841, the average span of life was only 17 years.

But there was a second spur to action. One Friday afternoon in the summer of 1969, as Alf was walking to the Chamber of the House, he encountered Leslie Hale, then the MP for Oldham West, leaving in the opposite direction and obviously distraught. Hale was a man of high standing in Parliament – having been there for 25 years – and it was quite clear that he had suffered a very traumatic experience. When Alf asked him what was wrong, Hale replied bitterly, "That's the end of it for me. I'm finished. I'm not coming back here again". Alf knew that he was a veteran of many excoriating parliamentary conflicts. A barrister, he was referred to

---

[3] *Health and Social Service Journal*, 22 July 1977, pp.1072-5.

by parliamentary sketch writers as the fastest orator in the House, often achieving in excess of 250 words a minute. But he was much more than that: a seasoned parliamentarian and fearless campaigner, with a brilliant mind and an abiding passion for social justice. Alf asked him to explain, and with deep emotion Hale replied, "My poor little Bill to have byssinosis recognised as an industrial disease, just as much as pneumoconiosis, has been strangled by Peggy Herbison [then Minister for Pensions and National Insurance]. As a Mancunian you know better than me how important it is to my cotton workers in Oldham. It's a condition that affects far more people in this country than other conditions that qualify as industrial diseases. So who can forgive a Labour government that denies them justice?"

Alf learned that Hale's Private Member's Bill to achieve statutory recognition of the disease had just been talked out, Herbison having made it clear that there was no way that the Government could accept Hale's Bill. Alf had then been a Member for less than five years, but nevertheless tried to take the heat out of the situation, urging Hale not to judge the Minister too harshly. She had, he suggested, been constrained by the "termites of the Treasury" – only the messenger, not the culprit – and there would always be another day. "Not for me there won't – that's it," replied Hale, and he resigned, prompting a by-election.[4]

That chance meeting made a deep impression on Alf, not only because of his respect for Hale but also because he had relatives as well as friends and many constituents affected by the disease. When he introduced his Chronically Sick and Disabled Persons Act later that year, Alf's original text included provision for the recognition of byssinosis. But this was lost along the way due to time constraints. Thus when Alf became Minister for Disabled People in 1974, one of his priorities was to have the clause lost in 1970 inserted in his department's Bill that became the Social Security Act 1975, finally to achieve statutory recognition of and compensation for byssinosis: an historic breakthrough for cotton workers. Leslie Hale, then in retirement, rejoiced. His purpose had been achieved after all.

---

[4] A by-election that first brought Michael Meacher to the House.

Changing the social and economic balance

Throughout his time as a Minister, Alf worked ceaselessly to improve public attitudes towards disabled people and to enhance their educational, employment and other opportunities in society, eventually setting in motion the movement to give disabled people rights in law. Internationally, he also somehow found time to assist other countries in legislating for the benefit of disabled people and, with Rehabilitation International, charted the principles that would inform the United Nations disability strategy for future decades. The huge range of his initiatives, many of which were to resonate across the world, laid the foundations for a completely new structure of provision for disabled people in Britain, from which they still benefit, and for their advance towards a full and equal place in society.

The first priority was to help disabled people financially by securing for them entitlement to cash benefits as of right. Apart from the introduction of the Attendance Allowance in 1971 no progress had been made in this area. In particular, the previous Government had resisted all attempts to bring in a national disability income. Instituting a review of social security provision for chronically sick and disabled people was as far as they had been prepared to go. The Secretary of State was required to report on this by 31 October 1974, the task which, as things turned out, now fell to the new Labour administration. The Disablement Income Group (DIG) seized the opportunity to renew its pressure for a national disability income. On 9 June 1974, they organised a third demonstration in Trafalgar Square. Alf could not be there, but he sent a message of emphatic support reaffirming his determination to do all he could to ensure that the needs of disabled people were adequately met. "DIG," he wrote, "has won the respect of Westminster and Whitehall alike for its aim of promoting the economic and social welfare of all disabled people".[5]

Meanwhile, in Whitehall the wheels were already turning. The report on the review required by section 36 of the Social Security Act 1973 duly appeared as a White Paper on 13 September 1974. The proposals

---

[5] *Morning Star*, 10 June 1974.

were greeted as timid and inadequate, not least by many members of DIG. But viewed historically the reality is very different, for the main provisions were, as a first instalment of the new Government's intended reforms, in principle if not in amount, an historic breakthrough for disabled people in providing benefits as of right. They shattered the longstanding, indeed revered, insurance principle in favour of relating benefits to need. The new proposals envisaged a non-contributory Invalidity Pension (NCIP) for people of working age who had been incapable of work for 28 weeks and whose national insurance contributions were insufficient to qualify them for invalidity or sickness benefit; and secondly an Invalid Care Allowance (ICA) for people forced to forego employment to care for a severely disabled person at home. Married women living with or maintained by their husbands were initially excluded from NCIP, but there was the promise of a new benefit, specifically for disabled housewives, that would first be discussed with disabled people and their organisations and thus inevitably with DIG. Bernard Donoughue's *Downing Street Diary* now reveals that Harold Wilson, having met Alf in Liverpool, was very quick to spot the political significance of the White Paper and to support any action required.[6]

Little more than six months into what has become known as the twentieth century's 'short Parliament' Harold Wilson and his Cabinet colleagues decided that a second General Election was needed, hopefully to shore up Labour's precarious hold on government. On 10 October 1974, the nation returned Labour to power with an overall majority of four seats. Slender though this lead was, it allowed for the continuity of a socialist agenda and, with an increased majority of 8,108, Alf was able to continue with his radical programme of improving the quality of life for disabled people.

The proposals for both the NCIP and ICA were rapidly put forward in a Social Security Benefits Bill. They were, Barbara Castle told the House on 21 November 1974 (leaving no doubt about who wrote the text) "an important breakthrough... the first steps towards a new policy for disabled people" that would "bring a new non-means-tested security to nearly 250,000 people whose needs we

[6] Page 179.

have neglected for far too long". Royal Assent was granted on 13 March 1975 and NCIP was introduced in the same year, along with a concession that allowed disabled people to derive limited earnings from approved work without affecting their entitlement to sick pay and invalidity benefit. ICA followed in 1976. NCIP was replaced by Severe Disablement Allowance (SDA) in 1984 (with new rules), and subsequently, under Margaret Thatcher, withdrawn to new claimants. Nevertheless, at the time of writing SDA remains in payment to over 300,000 beneficiaries. The Invalid Care Allowance has been renamed the Carer's Allowance of which today there are over 400,000 beneficiaries.

With Labour in the driving seat, calls for a better deal for disabled people now resounded from the Conservative side. Forgetful of their recent past, the priority they said was for Labour to keep its other promise to bring disabled housewives into the scope of the new non-contributory invalidity pension. To this end, early in 1976, and little more than a year after the General Election, a DIG delegation met with Alf and Barbara Castle. They argued that implementation in late 1977 or early 1978 was just not good enough. Letters from all parts of the country conveyed the same appeal for urgency.

When the so-called Housewives Non-contributory Invalidity Pension (HNCIP) finally arrived in 1977 financial constraints – tighter now than before – meant that like most new benefits it was hedged about by a straitjacket of rules, notably in this case a 'household duties test'. Married women would have to answer questions denounced by Dr Margaret Agerholm as "intrusive, impossible, illegal, unacceptable and cruel". Whereas the test for NCIP was continuous incapacity for work for at least 28 weeks, the rule for HNCIP required that a woman within the qualifying categories must also be continuously incapable of normal household duties. This was a test, it was estimated, that would exclude 240,000 disabled married women from the new benefit. Yet seen in a more positive light, the introduction of HNCIP was a major breakthrough, for no such benefit was available in any other country and it had finally established the principle of including disabled married women in the social security system. Reflecting to me on Dr Agerholm's epithets, one parliamentary activist on disability issues – who knew all about Alf's battles in innermost Whitehall to secure funding for HNCIP – described the outcome as "amazing, totally innovatory, groundbreaking, uncanny and *incroyable*".

Set against the practicality that benefits could be introduced only with tight restrictions was the far more worrying fact that many disabled people simply did not know that, for the first time ever, financial help was now available to them. Moreover, in many poorer communities there remained a culture of low expectations and a reluctance to claim benefits at all – an ingrained disposition towards self-reliance, however painful the consequences. Elsie Murphy, back in Alf's constituency, typified this determination. Afflicted with severe rheumatoid arthritis, she relied upon a wheelchair and lived with constant pain. At one of his Wythenshawe 'surgeries', Alf told her that he was absolutely certain that she would qualify for Attendance Allowance and explained what it was about. He persuaded her to make an application and she was soon awarded the allowance. Meeting her again, a little time later, Alf suggested that she also qualified for the new Mobility Allowance. "Oh," she replied, "I don't want them to think I'm being greedy".

Help for war pensioners
Alongside his work for disabled people, and complementary to it, Alf was also Minister for War Pensions, a role for which he was also well qualified, given his father's early death from war-related injuries and the suffering his family had faced when he died. In a recent autobiography, Philip Dixon, who chaired both the British Limbless Ex-Service Men's Association (BLESMA) and the World Veterans Federation (WVF), recalls the importance of Alf's personal involvement in addressing the problems faced by war veterans, both in this country and abroad: in particular at the WVF's second Congress held in France in 1976 where, accompanied by Madame Veil, the French Minister for War Pensions, Alf met leading representatives of veterans from countries on both sides in the Second World War. Another of WVF's concerns was the plight of veterans in Zimbabwe following the war of liberation. As Philip Dixon remarks, facilities for disabled people in Zimbabwe were virtually non-existent, and he went to Alf for advice. There was no

money available from the Government of Zimbabwe and neither equipment nor components for even the most basic needs. It took a few years, writes Dixon, to sort out the problems, but BLESMA, the WVF and Alf combined to provide the essentials.[7]

Lt. Col. Ray Holland, BLESMA's General Secretary during Alf's ministerial years and for more than a decade subsequently, recalls the benefit of Alf's help and advice. This continued long after Labour's defeat in the General Election of 1979 when, shorn of the restraints of ministerial office, Alf was elected to chair the BLESMA All-Party Parliamentary Committee. Ray Holland adds a personal tribute, recalling that Alf "was always on the end of a telephone and never failed to return a call or respond to a letter irrespective of how busy he was. His personal support and, on countless occasions, parliamentary action in and out of office, played a significant part in improving the war pensions scheme. Disabled people generally and BLESMA members in particular owe a very great deal to Alf Morris".[8]

Alf secures the formation of RADAR: a merger with a royal accolade

Two other famous campaigners were compulsive visitors to his office and became good friends: Douglas Bader, constantly seeking improvement in the care, aids and equipment provided at Roehampton for amputees, and Sir Ludwig Guttman, as head of the Stoke Mandeville Spinal Injuries Hospital, crusading for better opportunities for disabled people to take part in sports.

Another early visitor, who prompted a remarkable development in the voluntary sector, was The Rt. Hon. Richard Wood, a former Conservative Minister for Employment and younger son of the Earl of Halifax, who in 1940 was, with Winston Churchill, on a short list of two to become Neville Chamberlain's successor as Prime Minister. Richard Wood was a double amputee, having as a young officer lost both his legs in the savagely contested Rhine crossing towards the end of the Second World War. His purpose was to say that Alf now had a splendid opportunity as the first Minister for Disabled People to end the tension, bordering on open conflict, between the British Council for the Rehabilitation of Disabled People and the Central Council for the Disabled. They were major organisations in the

---

[7] *That Affable Familiar Ghost* (Philip Dixon, The Memoir Club, 2005), pp.130-1.
[8] Personal letter, 23 September 2005.

disability field and Richard felt strongly that the task of enhancing the status and well-being of disabled people – to which he knew Alf was totally committed – would be daunting enough without friction, strife and duplication of effort in a voluntary sector with strictly limited resources.

Alf agreed and determined to do all he could to bring the two organisations together. He had at the Department an able Assistant Secretary, Gerard Bebb, whom he asked to look into the possibility of merging the two organisations into a new federal body of which disability organisations more generally would become affiliates. Bebb duly reported that it was feasible if some funding could be found for pump priming. Keen to proceed, Alf was glad to make that help available and, to make doubly sure that the new body would have every chance of doing so, he decided to attempt what was widely seen in Whitehall as unthinkable, namely to give it the Royal prefix from its inception. There were reproving reminders that normally an organisation would need to be in existence for upwards of a hundred years for such a bestowal to be even considered. Nevertheless, and always ready to contest established norms, Alf thought it would be worth attempting. The man who could recommend to the Queen that what he proposed should be done was the Leader of the House of Commons and Lord President of the Council, none other than Michael Foot, who had deep respect for Alf and was always totally supportive of his endeavours. While he lacked the power to dispose the bestowal of the Royal accolade, he certainly had the power to propose it and anyone who knows anything about Michael, recalls Alf, knows that he too ranked among the lowest of the low as a respecter of precedents. Indeed, for Michael the *status quo* was there to be shot at and there were few better marksmen than him. Thus it was that the <u>Royal</u> Association for Disability and Rehabilitation, generally known as RADAR, came into being.

Alf was able also not only to support the new organisation with Government grants but to facilitate its affiliation to Rehabilitation International (RI) forthwith. The distinguished Australian champion of disabled people, Kenneth Jenkins, then President of RI, was brought to Westminster by Alf's close friend and parliamentary colleague Lewis Carter-Jones and, at a meeting with him, Alf readily agreed that RADAR would be helped by the Government to play an international role.

A surprising discovery

It would be a mistake to represent the business of Ministerial office – even for someone as proactive as Alf – as being a process of constant achievement and dizzy heights. Some of Alf's work was essentially routine; none more so than the chore of initialling his ministerial approval, file by file, of war pension upgradings, all of which had already been accepted by two doctors and carefully scrutinised for him by his principal private secretary. This fell to Alf in his office at Alexander Fleming House, where he worked with his friend of many years David Ennals, the Secretary of State. One Friday morning he was going through a formidable pile of green folders, each relating to the case of an individual war pensioner, which the procedures required him to initial as the Minister to give them legal force. This somewhat mindless duty was interrupted by a telephone call from Jack Ashley drawing Alf's attention away from the task in hand to an article in that week's *New Statesman and Nation* about the report of Sir Alan Marre's widely praised inquiry into outstanding issues in the thalidomide affair. When Alf finally went back to initialling the files he noticed that the folder open before him was that of an ex-service man of the same name as the Secretary of State. His interest quickened, he examined its contents more closely and, seeing details of the applicant's wartime injuries, it dawned upon him that this *was* indeed the Secretary of State. The recommendation was that David's war injuries – of which he subsequently died – entitled him to the maximum rate of war pension, *plus* the Unemployability Allowance. When Alf met up with David at lunchtime, he told him he had just approved a legal document testifying that he was now 100 per cent war disabled and unemployable. "So," joked Alf with a big smile, "I think you'd better clear your desk, David"!

Through the benefits maze

Wearing his more familiar – disability – hat and having now brought in the Housewives Non Contributory Invalidity Pension, it was time for Alf to take stock. The benefit system, which had grown up like Topsy, was in danger of being seen as a tangle of different provisions and full of seeming anomalies. The grant of one benefit would sometimes result in the loss of another. DIG focused on the benefit maze in a brilliant study commissioned from The Economist Intelligence Unit and published in October 1977 under the title *Whose Benefit?* The authors examined the structure of the benefits system in detail and concluded that with all the new disability benefits it had become so complex that it baffled many potential clients and did not reach many intended beneficiaries.

A few days after publication, Alf met representatives of DIG and The Economist Intelligence Unit. This was followed by further discussion at the DHSS, in which DIG made it clear that what was really needed was a national disability income with, in particular, an allowance for the costs occasioned by disability, payable to all disabled people including children and pensioners. In the House, Lewis Carter-Jones and Robert Kilroy-Silk pressed home the case for such a scheme, fully aware of Alf's commitment and that he was actively considering the way forward. We now know that, in fact, work had already been put in hand to prepare a consultative document on a national disability income scheme, frustrated only by Labour's fall in the 1979 election.

Another of Alf's priorities in 1974 was to address the inertia of the previous administration in failing to bring into effect some parts of the Chronically Sick and Disabled Persons Act: provisions that had received the Royal Assent four years earlier. Sir Keith Joseph had done absolutely nothing to carry out the clear statutory instruction to the Secretary of State in section 24 of the Act to collate and present evidence to the Medical Research Council on the need, identified by the Act, for an Institute of Hearing Research. This may have seemed small beer compared with the previous Government's gross dilatoriness in regard to the full implementation of the centrally important Sections 1 and 2 of the Act. It was, however, important to Alf himself as it was also to his very close friend Jack Ashley, as well as to Laurie Pavitt and David Weitzman, both of whom, while not being totally without hearing, were substantially hearing-impaired.

What was required to get the Institute into existence was initial spending of between half and three-quarters of a million pounds, at that time not an insignificant sum. One of the representatives on the ministerial committee Alf chaired, however, was Denzil Davies MP, the Financial Secretary to the Treasury, and the spending was approved. The next job was to meet the MRC. Alf called a meeting of leaders of the Council in his ministerial room at the House of Commons to which he also invited Jack Ashley and they began by talking about how impractical it would be to implement this part of the Act. They said they were simply being realistic. Alf told them: "We're not here to talk about whether it can be done. I'm informing you as the Minister for Disabled People that it <u>will</u> be done. This isn't negotiable. The decision was taken in 1970 and I'm very concerned that nothing has been done for four years notwithstanding the clear statutory instruction in Section 24. With Treasury approval we're going ahead".

The person appointed to take matters forward was Professor Mark Haggard. He headed the first such institute anywhere in the world, regarded by common consent among people with any interest at all in hearing impairment, not least Jack Ashley, as a huge step forward for hearing impaired people everywhere.

Expanding provision under the 1970 Act

The implementation of Section 1 of the Act had also been slow and, in particular, it was clear that unless disabled people were identified their needs were likely to remain unmet. Very few disabled people knew the extent to which local authorities could now help them or how to go about being assessed. With Alf in the ministerial lead the pace of change quickened, but the demand from disabled people nevertheless outstripped supply. Ursula Keeble has meticulously documented the progress made in the years of Alf's term as Minister for Disabled People in providing help under the Chronically Sick and Disabled Persons Act.[9] Sections 1 and 2 had the effect of vastly increasing the demand for aids and appliances for and adaptations to the homes of long-term sick and disabled people. There was also pressure for better quality and innovation, stimulated by the dynamic growth in technical development and

---

[9] *Disability: Legislation and Practice* (ed. Duncan Guthrie, Macmillan, 1981), chapter 8.

commercial opportunities that the Act's provisions had created. But not even Alf could overcome the financial constraints under which councils operated, nor dictate the manner in which they disposed their resources. Keeble tells us that the cost of aids and adaptations was met from a finite social services budget, rarely above two per cent of the total amount allocated to social services and a "minuscule fraction of local authority spending as a whole". Given these limitations, many local authorities, according to Keeble, took the "easy way out" by imposing charges, usually means-tested, as was (and remains) their statutory right. Some councils would exhaust their budget before the end of the financial year and delay further expenditure until the next financial year. Occasionally, where inadequate budget levels had been set, a supplementary grant might be voted, but elsewhere disabled people were placed on a waiting list. As financial stringency increased so did the waiting lists. Towards the end of the Wilson/Callaghan years, despite the fact that Government spending on disabled people had increased dramatically, some social services departments began to ration their services. Others confined provision to disabled people deemed to be 'at risk', a curtailment which ran counter to the central purpose of Section 2 of the Act. The problem was a failure to 'ring fence' central government funding intended for the improvement of services for disabled people, which otherwise was often diverted to other purposes.

It also became apparent that there was a wide gap in provision between the best and the worst local authorities. In 1978–79, for example, the London Borough of Newham supplied aids to 19.6 households in every 1,000, while in Newcastle upon Tyne the figure was only 0.9. "Where you live," Keeble noticed, "may have a disproportionate effect on your chance of being helped with an aid or an adaptation", a malaise that we now call the 'postcode lottery'.

Alf saw the parsimony, whether in central or local government, as a failure of political will and a lack of proper sense of priorities. Many councils, by contrast, saw the demands being made upon them as being 'new money' that they were reluctant to spend. One official in Manchester told Charles Morris: "Your brother's Act has cost us a fortune". The anomaly remained that what Parliament had enacted as a clear duty was, in some areas, being side-stepped on the pretext that it was a duty that could not be afforded.

Notwithstanding these difficulties and discrepancies, however, the overall picture was one of massive improvement. From 1972–73 (the first year for which detailed statistics are available) there was a steady and consistent rise in provision. In March 1979 the DHSS reported a 278 per cent increase in the number of disabled people registered with their local social services departments and thus receiving help under Section 2 of the Chronically Sick and Disabled Persons Act.[10] In a similar period the number of households in England receiving one or more 'personal' aids increased by over 200 per cent.[11]

The drive for improved mobility

There were many other pressing issues of importance arising from what Alf saw as the 'four lost years' of the previous administration. One was that of greater personal mobility for disabled people, to which the Chronically Sick and Disabled Persons Act had devoted more than one section. The provision for outdoor mobility that Alf had inherited was the Ministry-supplied three-wheeled vehicle popularly known as the 'trike'. Disabled drivers – there were around 18,000 of them who satisfied very tightly drawn eligibility criteria – were often fiercely fond of a vehicle that provided them with cheap and easy mobility. But, with its single seat, it was an anti-family vehicle which, moreover, was widely held to be dangerous. The great majority of disabled people able to drive did not qualify for a trike and there was no outdoor mobility provision at all for those who could not drive.[12]

From the late 1960s there was a gathering momentum for a completely new system. The Hon. John Astor, Conservative MP for Newbury (as secretary of the All Party Disablement Group), Jack Ashley, Lewis Carter-Jones and Sir Neil Marten, Conservative MP for Banbury, and others on both sides of the House, along with the

---

[10] From 304,188 to 846,790.

[11] From 118,784 to 237,372.

[12] Baroness Masham, as we have seen, drew attention to the mobility needs of those too disabled to drive during the passage of the Chronically Sick and Disabled Persons Bill through the Lords. But Alf was then unable to legislate beyond provision for a scheme of special parking concessions for cars used by disabled people (which today helps 2.3 million disabled drivers and passengers) and a relaxation of the conditions for using "invalid carriages" on highways (Section 20).

Disabled Drivers' Association and BLESMA were all campaigning for better outdoor mobility for disabled people. They were able to work together, regardless of party attachments and without adversarial politics, to achieve improvements for disabled people. Alf himself, during a debate on 21 March 1971 calling for the full implementation of the Chronically Sick and Disabled Persons Act, had drawn attention to the disadvantages of the trike and had asked, rhetorically, why there was so much official reluctance to provide four-wheeled vehicles. John Hannam, the Conservative MP for Exeter, also supported a call for "four-wheeled vehicles instead of the standard three-wheeled, one-person vehicle which condemns many families to be split, with children separated from their mothers and husbands from their wives whenever they wish to travel anywhere".[13]

But such replacement was likely to be fraught with difficulties in failing to address the wider mobility needs of disabled people, most of whom would never be able to drive. In April 1972, Sir Keith Joseph asked Dame Evelyn Sharp to examine the issues.[14] By the time her report was published, the Government had changed and it fell to Alf, as the Minister for Disabled People, to consider her recommendations.

Lady Sharp's main recommendation was that the trike ought to be replaced by small four-wheeled cars. The three-wheeled vehicles had been criticised as being "dangerous, noisy, uncomfortable, liable to break-down". Above all they were criticised because they could not carry a passenger and had to be driven by a disabled person, a condition that applied equally to the alternative private car allowance. Lady Sharp argued that once the car replaced the trike, "disabled drivers and non-drivers must be treated alike". But if eligibility otherwise remained the same, she thought the cost of the service would treble. Her remit was to come up with proposals that were cost neutral: reform within the limits of available resources. She therefore proposed that entitlement should no longer be based on severe physical disablement alone, but also on the individual's *need* for a car, basically to maintain him or herself and the family or to

---

[13] *Hansard*, Commons, 21.5.1971, col. 1696.

[14] For the terms of reference, see Adrian Stokes, *Disability Legislation and Practice* (ed. Duncan Guthrie, Macmillan, 1981), p.145.

contribute to their support. Therefore the test should be a practical one: would the car enable the disabled person to live independently whereas without it, given the particular circumstances, he or she could not – or could do so only with great difficulty.[15] There could hardly have been a sterner test, since it meant that only a disabled person who could show that, without a car, she or he would be dependent on institutional care would qualify for outdoor mobility help.

Lady Sharp's proposals were not acceptable to Alf. He was much more attracted to the views of Peter Large, who was pressing alternative proposals for reform. Peter was a physically frail colossus, a man of towering intellect, incisive judgement and passionate commitment to social justice who, but for becoming very severely polio-disabled in 1962, was destined to become the youngest ever Chief Executive of a major oil company. He joined the Civil Service in 1966 – confined to a wheelchair – but soon became better known as one of the most astute campaigners for disabled people, channelling his gifts into securing a fairer deal for people disadvantaged by their disabilities. Denny Denly, the Access Officer of the Central Council for the Disabled, invited him onto the Joint Committee on Mobility for the Disabled in 1968, which is why he later worked closely with Alf when he was legislating to introduce the Orange Badge (now Blue Badge) parking scheme in Section 21 of the Chronically Sick and Disabled Persons Act. As chairman of the Association of Disabled Professionals and parliamentary spokesman for the Disablement Income Group from 1973, his influence behind the scenes was increased. His personal experience of disability at its severest, coupled with his business acumen, qualified him to help in the drafting of speeches and amendments to Bills and to place and draft parliamentary questions for members of the All Party Parliamentary Disability Group in both Houses.

Within a month of Alf's appointment as Minister, he and Peter began to discuss the compellingly urgent need for fundamental change in provision for outdoor mobility help for disabled people; and Peter's undeviating advice was to base outdoor mobility help on the severity of disability, not on the disabled person's ability to drive. He argued

---

[15] *Mobility of Physically Disabled People* (Lady Sharp GBE, Department of Health and Social Security, 1974)

the case for both a cash allowance and the means to convert it into a vehicle suited to individual need.

At this stage there were no specific proposals; they talked about the essential principles of any defensible future scheme. Once convinced of the merits of Peter's view of the way forward, Alf pursued its implications with his customary unrelenting determination. In her autobiography, Barbara Castle, Secretary of State for Social Services during Alf's time as Minister for Disabled People, refers to his single-minded persistence. He was, she recalled, "a mild but dogged man, who gave me hell as he fought for a new charter for the disabled".[16]

Alf's view of their relationship, not unnaturally, is somewhat more prosaic: *"Barbara's pressures and priorities were sometimes different from mine and her understanding of disability issues, as her autobiography makes clear, was not all that finely tuned. I recall an occasion when, during a meeting of Ministers, Barbara reminded us that the credit squeeze and the concern expressed by the International Monetary Fund meant that we were all in the same boat. On occasion she was not best pleased with my insistence on the rights of disabled people, but we were very good friends to the end of her life, both fighters if sometimes with a different agenda. Mutual respect always governed our relationship in and out of government"*.

Inevitably, after a long wrangle, Alf was delighted by the outcome. Outdoor mobility help would henceforth be based not on whether a disabled person could drive but on individual need.

Alf had first met Barbara Castle when he was studying at Ruskin College. He was one of a number of students who took time off during a vacation to help in Labour campaigning in marginal seats. In the 1950 General Election his chosen campaign was to re-elect Barbara as the Member of Parliament for Blackburn. The campaign there was masterminded by the fearsome Scot, George Eddie, in a political situation demanding maximum support for Labour candidates in marginal seats if the Attlee Government was to survive. With Eddie's indefatigable help, Barbara narrowly won Blackburn. Twenty years later, during the 1970–4 Parliament,

---

[16] *Fighting All the Way* (Barbara Castle, Macmillan, 1993), p.468.

Barbara and Alf were together on Labour's front bench. A contemporary recalls a particular occasion at Prime Minister's Question Time when Alf rose to ask Edward Heath about the Government's failure to do anything to relieve the anxieties of families affected by the thalidomide tragedy. When Alf sat down, Barbara Castle shouted to Heath across the table "Beat that for sincerity!" Alf enjoyed Barbara's trust right through to the sickness that finally brought her combative life to an end.

"In the final year of her life, unable to keep a commitment to move some amendments for the Rev. Paul Nicolson of the Zacchaeus 2000 Trust in the Lords, she told them 'You must get Alf Morris to do it – no one else".

The foundation stone of the radically new scheme for outdoor mobility help that Alf announced to the organisations of and for disabled people was a weekly 'mobility allowance'. This was to be payable to disabled drivers and passengers alike, but with an eligibility test based on the severity of the applicant's disability: either that their physical condition as a whole was such that they were unable or virtually unable to walk, or that the exertion required to do so would put them in danger or would be likely to lead to a serious deterioration in their health.[17] The allowance would be paid irrespective of circumstances peculiar to them, such as where they lived or the place or nature of their employment.

The financial backing for the new allowance was hard-won. It would obviously bring in tens of thousands of new beneficiaries and Treasury officials were predictably sceptical and severely critical. Alf was, however, entitled to what was called a 'bilateral' with Denis Healey, Chancellor of the Exchequer: a half-hour meeting arranged for a Minister proposing a major new spending commitment. On a momentous day in August 1974, Alf and his officials arrived at the Treasury early enough to have a last discussion about how he might best present the case to the Chancellor. They were still doing this at 11 a.m. – 15 minutes prior to the scheduled bilateral – when Denis Healey put his head round the door and said, "You can come in now Alf". The Chancellor's first question was to ask how many

---

[17] This qualification was modified in 1979 by defining "virtually unable to walk" as being where "ability to walk is so limited, as regards the distance over which or the speed at which or the length of time for which or the manner in which [the disabled person] can make progress on foot without severe discomfort, that [he or she] is virtually unable to walk".

people would benefit. To which Alf replied that he was proposing a phased introduction of the allowance: he was aiming, first, to get the allowance to severely disabled young people in the age-range 15–24, needing outdoor mobility help to start out on life. Later on the allowance would be extended to those aged 25–50, then to children aged 5–15 (payable to their parents) and finally to disabled people over 50. Once in receipt of the allowance – given no lessening of their disability – beneficiaries would be able to keep it after their retirement and hopefully, if more resources became available, it could be extended to new claimants over retirement age. What he was now proposing would benefit an estimated 30,000 claimants. It would be for Ministers in future annual spending rounds to decide if and when the allowance could be extended. At this point one of the Chancellor's senior advisers eased into the discussion and said, "Chancellor, I think the Minister is perhaps understating the cost implications of his proposal". Healey immediately cut him short: "I'm talking," he said, "to my ministerial colleague, and do not want him to be interrupted".

Alf had succeeded. The Government announced the scheme in September 1974. Outdoor mobility help would now be available to a hugely increased number of disabled people, while beneficiaries of the existing scheme who wanted to keep their trikes – as many did – would be able to do so as an alternative to receiving the new allowance. Ultimately, up to 100,000 disabled non-drivers would benefit, heralding a significant innovation and a new era. Alf told an audience in Liverpool: "Although they cannot drive, they have as much right as anyone else to look beyond their own four walls".

To those on the Opposition benches who thought the new benefits were less than adequate, Lewis Carter-Jones drew attention to a saying of Confucius that when a man takes his first step on a journey of 1,000 miles, he is on his way.

Even so, the idea was not universally welcomed. Alf recalls: "I had never felt as unpopular as when the Mobility Allowance was announced. From the tens of thousands who were to benefit I heard very little, but from people who, because of the need for a cut-off point, were excluded, there were loud protests". Again there were trike drivers who did not believe that they would be able to retain and replace their vehicles, notwithstanding a firm undertaking not only of retention and replacement but to continue to provide trikes into the next century for those who wanted to stay with them. This promise was honoured in full and there are still some trikes on the road. The Mobility Allowance was introduced on 1 January 1976, initially at the rate of £5.00 a week, and is now paid to over 1.9 million disabled people at a cost of £4 billion-plus a year.

But in 1976 Alf knew that the job was only half done. What was needed now was a scheme to help disabled people who were unable to meet the capital cost of purchasing a car to convert the mobility allowance into a vehicle: to turn cash into cars. The political climate could not have been less promising. It was still a time of relentless credit squeeze, with Treasury control of public spending at its most stringent. When Alf first mooted the idea of a commutation scheme it must have seemed that he was barking not just up the wrong tree but in the wrong forest.

Nevertheless in 1977, through the good offices of David Ennals, Secretary of State at the DHSS, and Sir Patrick Nairne, Permanent Secretary at the DHSS, he sought the help of the redoubtable Lord Goodman. What was needed, Goodman was told, was to find a practical way to provide disabled people with cars in return for the assignment of their mobility allowance.[18] Jeffrey Sterling (later Lord Sterling) was especially supportive. He "threw himself into the task with total dedication",[19] winning the co-operation of the clearing banks and four motor manufacturers, insurance companies and motoring associations, with all of whom Alf had discussed his proposals. But it was not all plain sailing, more particularly for the clearing banks. If they were to be able to help there would have to be some relaxation of the credit squeeze. John (now Sir John) Quinton, of Barclays Bank, told Alf that it would need a special provision to release a further £100 million, since it would be quite wrong for the banks to refuse credit to the generality of their customers while lending this huge sum to a new and unproven scheme to finance the purchase of a car fleet for disabled people.

---

[18] *Tell Them I'm On My Way* (Arnold Goodman, Chapmans, 1993), page 241.
[19] *Ibid*, page 242.

Fortunately, when Alf explained his problem to them, there were those in Whitehall who were prepared to bend the rules to help. Simply stated, it was about resolving to substitute hope for despair in the lives of disabled people, empowerment to replace segregation with independence and social inclusion. The Treasury conceded a special dispensation, treating disabled people as a special case, and Goodman's task force was able to come up with a scheme dubbed 'Motability', staffed initially by civil servants seconded by Alf.

The result was announced by David Ennals on 6 December 1977 in the House of Commons. The four clearing banks had joined forces to set up Motability Finance Ltd to fund the purchase of cars on special terms, with a separate independent charitable organisation, Motability, offering all disabled people in receipt of the mobility allowance a package deal. This allowed them to lease a private car on preferential terms, either as a driver or a passenger, adapted where necessary to their needs, against an initial down payment and transfer of their mobility allowance for the period of the lease, usually three or four years. The car would then be surrendered, but could be replaced by a new one and a new agreement. The scheme had the advantage of negotiated discounts from manufacturers for bulk purchasing, as well as built-in insurance and maintenance charges. Additionally a charitable fund was set up to help customers unable to afford the initial down payment or the cost of necessary conversions to accommodate their disability. This was quickly followed in 1978 by exemption of mobility allowance beneficiaries from vehicle excise duty and, in 1979, by remission of value added tax on the purchase price of cars leased to disabled people. All of these improvements to the original scheme had been secured by Alf. In 1981, car adaptations were zero rated for VAT and in the following year mobility allowance itself was exempted from income tax.

There were initially two potential disadvantages: a narrow range of choice and the necessity to change cars every three or four years. But even these limitations were overcome in 1979 with the introduction of an alternative hire purchase scheme. Gradually, over the years, demand to retain the cherished but tottering trike has ebbed away, so that now there are said to be only nine left on the roads of England and Wales. Yet before Alf became Minister for Disabled People in 1974 that had been the one and only provision for the outdoor mobility of people unable or virtually unable to walk. In this case at least – although Alf never talks of revolutionary change from any of his enactments – that is precisely what he had achieved within five years in this field alone and at a time of grave economic crises and remorseless credit restraint. It would be difficult to overestimate the scale of his achievement in giving severely disabled people a pathway to independent mobility – the emancipation of wheels. Since Motability was launched in 1978, it has provided over 2 million vehicles for more than 700,000 disabled people. Chaired by Lord Sterling of Plaistow, Motability runs the largest car fleet in Europe offering a choice of 200 models from 14 manufacturers and providing more than 140,000 new cars every year: a vehicle fleet, Alf reminded Lord Sterling, when he phoned to inform him that the millionth car had been handed over, "but still surpassed by that of the Chinese army, Jeffrey!"[20]

Jim Callaghan

Lord Goodman, in his autobiography, was to describe his association with the Motability project as his greatest achievement.[21] But Alf believes that even greater credit belongs to the late Jim Callaghan who, at a time when cuts in public spending were having to be made, was prepared, exceptionally, to relax the Government's fiscal straitjacket to make the scheme possible. Eventually, he and Alf were together in Parliament, first in the Commons and then in the Lords, for over 40 years. What is not widely known is that from the outset Callaghan had a strong personal commitment to people with disabilities and long-term illness. If one looks at his family context this is not surprising. Like Alf, his father was wounded in the first world war, resulting in his untimely death when Jim was just nine, further blighting a childhood lived on the brink of destitution. Jim's wife Audrey, whom he married in 1938, became a very considerable figure in the field of child health. She chaired the board of governors of Great Ormond Street Hospital from 1968 until 1982 and later proved to be a remarkably successful fund-raiser for the hospital.

---

[20] For a detailed history of Motability see *Motability, the road to freedom* (Allan Beard, The Book Guild Ltd, 1998).

[21] *Tell Them I'm On My Way* (Arnold Goodman, Chapmans, 1993), page 243.

Based there she was also very much linked with the Institute of Child Health. She also became a member of the Committee on Restrictions Against Disabled People which Alf set up in 1979. In later years, of course, her increasing frailty meant that Jim again came to have a very close personal experience of disability.

Over time, Jim heard quite a lot about the work that Alf was doing and was strongly supportive. Never more so than in April 1976 when he became Prime Minister, in succession to Harold Wilson, during Alf's term as Minister for Disabled People. Many of the achievements set out in the checklist in the appendix to Harold Wilson's autobiography *Final Term* were actually introduced during Jim Callaghan's premiership. And later, in 1986, when Tom Clarke's Disabled Persons (Services, Consultation and Representation) Bill received its third reading, Jim travelled from Cardiff and stood at the Bar of the Commons to ensure a quorum to allow the measure to proceed.[22]

Support for the voluntary sector

One of the conspicuous hallmarks of Alf's years as Minister for Disabled People – indeed of his entire parliamentary career – was the constancy of his support for voluntary organisations. Within two days of his appointment as Minister, he met two people, Pat Osborne and Leslie Matthews,[23] who wanted Government funding to get the Crossroads Care Attendants scheme off the ground. In very quick time Alf told them he accepted the bid and awarded them a grant of £90,000 payable over three years. A very senior official then said, "But Minister, I think you may have acted a little precipitately. We haven't really discussed it". Alf told him that as far as he was concerned there wasn't anything to discuss. He was convinced before the meeting that it was the right thing to do and was prepared to defend his decision at the highest level of government. Almost as quickly another grant, of £60,000 over three years, was made to the then fledgling National Bureau for Handicapped Students (now Skill).

---

[22] *Hansard*, Commons, 5 April 2005, col.1316, recalled by Tom Clarke during the second reading of the Equality Bill.
[23] Leslie Matthews was a senior figure in Central TV. It supported the scheme and its flagship programme *Crossroads* gave the organisation its name.

Dame Flora Robson was another early visitor. As well as being a theatrical legend she chaired the National Council for the Single Woman and her Dependants. She urged upon Alf – again pushing an open door – the need for financial help for carers of elderly parents unable to live alone, which happily Alf was able to gratify in the following year when he legislated for the world's first-ever carer's allowance. While he was Minister for Disabled People many other voluntary organisations were to benefit from this sense of common purpose. He knew well enough, and accepted, that he would come to be seen in Whitehall as a serial violator of convention and ministerial tradition.

One organisation particularly close to Alf's heart – of which he later became the Honorary Patron – was Manchester's Royal School for Deaf Children. He had, of course, legislated for children who were both deaf and blind, as well as those with dyslexia and autism, in Sections 25–27 of the Chronically Sick and Disabled Persons Act. It was therefore natural that soon after the provisions became law he began a close association with the work of this famous charity. The school was founded in 1823, when Queen Victoria was four years old, the battle of Waterloo was only eight years past and it would be nine years before Manchester had its first Member of Parliament under the Reform Act of 1832. Deaf people were not only isolated, ridiculed, treated with contempt and marginalised: they were non-people. So the founding of the School for the Deaf (only later to be given its prefix 'Royal') was a revolutionary development in the climate of neglect that was then the lot of disabled people. Times have changed, but even now the challenge to the school's teachers is huge. They are providing education and 52–week residential care for children and young adults with exceptionally complex social and learning needs and a range of additional disabilities including multi-sensory impairment, epilepsy, low cognitive ability and communication difficulties. Many of its young people require 24–hour one-to-one care and even two-to-one care.

Alf soon learned that to understand their daunting problems you needed to have been to the school and have seen the children. They provided a reminder that disability is not an homogeneous condition and that a well-intentioned but single strategy towards independence and choice appropriate for fit, bright wheelchair users cannot meet the needs of all disabled people.

Find and inform

Also high on Alf's agenda was the provision of information to disabled people. It had been his starting point in Section 1 of the Chronically Sick and Disabled Persons Act and in his subsequent years in opposition he had campaigned relentlessly for local authorities to fulfil the primary duty it imposed on them to "find and inform" disabled people. A significant development towards the fulfilment of this provision arrived, albeit by coincidence, from the voluntary sector in 1977. Three years earlier, Ann Darnbrough, from the Multiple Sclerosis Society, had introduced a monthly information bulletin for people with MS and their families. But it was not about MS. Each month she focused on a particular area of the services and opportunities available to disabled people – holidays, arts, sport and leisure, education, financial benefits, employment, sex, social services, aids and equipment, mobility and motoring, friendship, audio books and magazines and, not least, helpful voluntary organisations – signposting the resources that were already in place.

In 1975, a publisher, Martin Woodhead, who happened to be visiting the Society, spotted the two-years worth of bulletins and said to Ann, "I think there's a book in this". The result was the *Directory for Disabled People*, enthusiastically welcomed by Alf, who called it the 'encyclopaedia disibilitatis'. The Directory ran through eight editions until 1999, when finally overtaken by electronic media. Nearly thirty years on, some of Alf's remarks in the original foreword can now be seen as a measure of his own achievement:

"The need for a *Directory for Disabled People* has never been greater. Happily the reason for this is that the range of help for disabled people has never been wider... As Minister for Disabled People, I feel that both the statutory and voluntary sectors can take some pride in the range of new benefits and services now available to help disabled people to increase their independence and lead fuller lives. There are cash benefits, aids and equipment to assist in daily living, help with housing adaptations, holidays and many other benefits and services including special sports and recreational facilities...The list is extensive and continually growing. At the same time, the number of agencies providing benefits and services is also growing...The complex network of providers sometimes leaves the disabled person confused, or simply unaware of who to approach to obtain the help or information that is needed, yet not knowing just what help is available and where to get it can be a major barrier to the full integration of disabled people into society...Yet it is not only disabled people who will benefit from the publication of the Directory. Many professionals in direct contact with disabled people often tell me how difficult it is to keep fully abreast of a changing situation. An important part of my own job, as a Minister, is to ensure better co-ordination between all those involved in providing services to disabled people; but this can only be achieved if the professionals in the field are familiar with all the avenues of help. I am sure that this Directory will be an invaluable companion to them. Its ultimate effect will be to provide better services to disabled people and that is the end to which we are all aiming".

Spreading the message abroad

Alf was also in demand internationally. He was invited, in January 1978, to address an International Conference in Manila on 'Legislation Concerning Disabled Persons' organised by Rehabilitation International. This gave him the opportunity to review, on a major international occasion, what had been achieved in Britain. More than a quarter of a century later, his Manila speech now provides not only a perspective on progress that had been made but also an insight into the tension then existing between the need to provide for those dependent on support while meeting the aspirations of those questing for greater independence. Looking back at our history of state provision for disabled people it was apparent, he said, that much of what now existed ought to have existed sooner. In 1978 no one imagined that the existing edifice was perfect; nor that it would not be added to in the future. Optimistically, he felt certain that Britain's legislation would be the base for much further progress in the years ahead. Already there had been a dramatic change of direction. Financial help given to disabled people in the immediate post-war years had been confined almost entirely to those injured or made ill by service in either the armed forces or industry. By contrast, in the seventies, vastly more people had been helped, since the assistance given was related more to the nature and degree of their disabilities, not to their cause. There remained, nevertheless, a problem in deciding whether – and to what extent – provision should be mainly in the form of cash or of direct services. On one side, it was argued that cash gave disabled beneficiaries freedom of choice; on the other side, that only help in the form of direct services could ensure that scarce resources were deployed where they were most needed and that the disabled person received the right package of help at the right time. Both sides of the argument, Alf recognised, had merit, but it was important then, as it is now, to recognise that the two policies were complementary, not competing. The main skill was to get the mix right.

Development of access provision

A most important initiative during Alf's tenure as Minister for Disabled People, in terms of its ultimate dividend, was to establish a committee to campaign for improved access for disabled people. It seems incredible now, but in the seventies even the Palace of Westminster was inaccessible. Nor could a guide dog be brought into its precincts. Had David Blunkett been a Member of Parliament at the time he would have had to leave his dog with the police at the St Stephen's entrance and be escorted into the building. Similarly, the headquarters of the Royal Institute of British Architects was barrier intensive for disabled people.[24] Access, or rather the lack of it, was a major issue on Alf's agenda. Increasingly he received complaints from all over the UK about the physical obstacles that prevented disabled people from taking their rightful part in social life and public indifference to them.

On 24 May 1977, mindful of and in response the impending 25th anniversary of the Coronation of Queen Elizabeth II, Alf announced the creation of the Silver Jubilee Access Committee. His original intention was simply to address and overcome the day-to-

---

[24] Alf was able to persuade them to remedy this and as a result RIBA took a leading role in advising architects how to provide access for disabled people. He was made a Fellow in Building Engineering, but warns against anyone commissioning him to design a building!

day restrictions faced by disabled people. In that limited aim, however, Alf was to lay the foundations for full civil rights for disabled people, the first fruits of which came in the legislation so laboriously and painfully extracted from a Conservative administration eighteen years later by the enactment of the Disability Discrimination Act 1995.

In drawing up the membership of the Silver Jubilee committee, Alf was determined that the majority should have direct and practical experience of the problems of disability. Although serviced and financed by the Department of Health and Social Security, Alf ensured that the committee was an independent body free to act as it wished and to make such recommendations as it saw fit. In this respect, the choice of chair was crucial, and for this vital role he approached Peter Large. Other members of the Silver Jubilee Committee included such famous names in the disability world as Norman Croucher, Claudia Flanders, Duncan Guthrie, Joe Hennessey, Colin Low, Dr Adrian Stokes, Claire Tomalin and George Wilson, all of whom gathered to hear Alf address their first meeting on the 15 June 1977. He said that he hoped that they would be able to do three things: find out about the present position on access; take action aimed at improving it; and consider longer term ways in which to make further progress.

The Committee welcomed these tasks and agreed the following terms of reference: "To consider ways of ensuring that disabled people can use and move about within the environment, inside and outside; to recommend changes to those responsible; and to consider ways of altering public attitudes in favour of the Committee's aims".

It was decided that in order to gather evidence of the access difficulties encountered by disabled people it would first be necessary to wage a campaign to increase public awareness of the problems of access and to secure from disabled people first-hand information on their access problems. Unsurprisingly (we would now say), the committee found innumerable worrying instances of discrimination against disabled people, not only in respect of being unable to enter or use public buildings, but also of other blatant restrictions.

In January 1979, the committee published its report under the title *Can Disabled People Go Where You Go?* – a message clearly aimed at non-disabled people generally. The report noted that disabled people were becoming increasingly firm in demanding the rights of full citizenship and that access was crucial to success in pursuing that goal. While an ideal situation in which every public and social amenity became totally accessible to all disabled people was recognised as being a long-term aim, much of what was suggested could be achieved with only minimal expenditure of resources. The committee believed further that there was sufficient public support to maintain a programme of improvement.

Although the committee was a large one, its report was unanimous save in one respect. The only issue on which its members could not agree was the possibility of legislation to end discrimination against disabled people, something not strictly within its terms of reference but one that was raised for further discussion. One of the committee's key recommendations, therefore, was for continuing action by a successor group with similar but wider terms of reference.

CORAD

Alf accepted this recommendation immediately – leaving those who knew him best suspecting that he may have had no small part in inspiring it – and announced the formation of a successor body in the same month. It was to be called the Committee on Restrictions Against Disabled People (CORAD) – again chaired by Peter Large, with whom he always worked in the closest harmony – and included several other members of the Silver Jubilee Committee.

To strengthen the team, Alf invited the participation of a new member, Larry Walters. Born with cerebral palsy into a working class family, Larry was no stranger to the barriers faced by disabled people. His recent autobiography, *To the Mountain Top*,[25] gives a graphic account of the reality of disabled living in the mid-20th century and the deep-rooted obstacles, both physical and attitudinal, over which he had to triumph. On 13 May 1978, *The Guardian* published a letter from Larry arguing that the Equal Opportunities Commission could be extended to cover discrimination against

---

[25] Hayloft Publishing Ltd, 2005.

disabled people. Such legislation would be in line, he wrote, with the UN Declaration on the Rights of Disabled People, which held that they should be "protected against all exploitation...and all treatment of a discriminatory, abusive or degrading nature".[26] In the same year he took the issue to his local Constituency Labour Party (Solihull) who appointed him as their delegate to the Labour Party Conference in Blackpool, armed with a resolution that began: "This Conference calls for effective legislation to be introduced so as to prevent any unfair discrimination against disabled people. This shall apply to all forms of employment, leisure and recreational activities. It shall also prohibit any kind of unfair discrimination in any public place...". To his dismay, however, the conference organisers were either unable or unwilling to make room for the resolution on the agenda, and it was cast into oblivion. Near the end of conference just one delegate from the floor was allowed a brief mention of disability. "To say that I was gob-smacked," records Larry in his autobiography, "was an understatement". The only person to offer him hope was Alf, who had assured him that, even if the Solihull resolution was not heard, it would not be the end of the matter.[27] True to his word, an invitation to join CORAD followed, only three months later, early in 1979.

CORAD's task, set by Alf, was to "consider the architectural and social barriers which may result in discrimination against disabled people and prevent them from making full use of facilities available to the general public; and to make recommendations". At the outset of the committee's work, Alf explained that consideration of architectural barriers should be loosely interpreted to imply the continuation of the Silver Jubilee Access Committee's campaign to improve access and that this should be an important part of CORAD's work.

"Access" was to be interpreted widely to include not only the problems of people in wheelchairs, but also the much greater number who could walk only with difficulty or who could not see or hear clearly. In addition, the committee should consider the difficulties encountered by people whose physical appearance

[26] Article 10.
[27] *To the Mountain Top: Meeting the Challenge of Disability* (Larry Walters, Hayloft Publishing Ltd, 2005), pp.150-158.

caused them to be refused admission to various places. Alf pointed out that, looked at from this even broader perspective, access was far more than an architectural question. The committee would need to look at social barriers and the whole area of discrimination that could manifest itself as a limitation on access. These two aspects of CORAD's remit, as outlined both by Alf and the predecessor committee, were complementary and, as the committee soon found, often overlapped.

Peter Large charted the way ahead at CORAD's first meeting on 5 April 1979 in suggesting that one of the gravest threats to disabled people arose not from malevolent, direct discrimination but from indirect and often inadvertent "discrimination by default, ignorance or apathy". Nobody was really to blame because nobody had any responsibility to safeguard the rights of disabled people or any need to take account of their rights in deciding what to do or not do. The task of CORAD, said Peter, was therefore to help correct past practical mistakes and to devise means of avoiding similar mistakes in the future so that "nobody has any excuse for discriminating against disabled people". Somehow the committee must find ways to prevent society riding roughshod over the rights of disabled people. Whether this required the "club or the carrot, education, exhortation or legislation" remained to be seen.

A Charter for the 80s: at home and abroad

Two further initiatives enhanced Alf's astonishing record as Minister for Disabled People, both with an international dimension and both to bear fruit in the next Parliament. The first was his role as the architect of Rehabilitation International's (RI's) *Charter for the 80s*, a statement of consensus on international priorities for action to improve the lives of disabled people world-wide in the decade 1980–1990 in order to promote the goals of full participation and equality for disabled people everywhere. Work was begun on the Charter in 1978 and its core values were developed through the most extensive international consultation ever undertaken in the fields of disability prevention and rehabilitation. Throughout this process, Alf chaired the World Planning Group appointed by RI to draft the Charter. There were meetings in countries across the world to co-ordinate the content of a document that had been contributed to by leading representatives of disability groups in RI's well over one hundred member countries in preparation for its approval by its next World Congress in Winnipeg in 1980.

This work was to prove harmonious with the work of another international committee. For some time the United Nations, no doubt influenced by the new emphasis placed on disability issues in member states since 1970, had been considering the creation of an International Year of Disabled Persons. Who better than Alfred Morris, the only Minister for Disabled People in the world, to crystallise their thinking? The Silver Jubilee Committee had seen the need to keep its message before the general public. The publicity initiatives that it had established had attracted interest from New Zealand, Australia, Sweden, the United States, Canada and France.[28] Now Alf saw the opportunity to widen the debate and open it to the whole world. In March 1979, he was invited to New York to open a discussion in the UN building on a proposition for an International Year of Disabled Persons as one of a special group of national representatives to a United Nations Advisory Committee. He commended to the meeting a number of key objectives and drew attention to the importance of ensuring the fullest possible involvement of non-governmental organisations in the UN's plan of action. After that, there was a continuing and close rapport between the UN Advisory Committee and the World Planning Group of RI.

Links with China

One of the countries with which Alf established particularly close and cordial relations on disability issues was the People's Republic of China. But he had first needed to overcome a perception of that great nation still resonating from the days of his youth. His mother Jessie, who from time to time attended mothers' meetings at a nonconformist church in Newton Heath, had returned one afternoon after hearing an address from a missionary who had recently worked in China. For whatever reason, Jessie Morris came home extremely worried about the moral standards of the Chinese people. " Cruel"

---

[28] *Can Disabled People Go Where You Go?* (Report by the Silver Jubilee Committee, DHSS, January 1979), paragraph 9.17.

and "treacherous" were the aphoristic descriptions she felt compelled to impress upon her son.

Alf was first invited to visit China in 1973 to advise Ministers on the principles to follow in legislating on disability. Shortly afterwards, when he became Minister for Disabled People, his friend Jack Ashley suggested that one practical way to help China would be to offer them some of the huge quantities of body-worn hearing aids that had been phased-out in Britain, where they had been superseded by the new NHS behind-the-ear aids Alf had quickly introduced. Cosmetically, the old body-worn Madresco aids were nothing if not unlovely and widely disliked in Britain, most of all by hearing-impaired women and young people. But, as Jack had discovered in Sri Lanka, they would be warmly welcomed by hearing-impaired people in developing countries where no provision whatever was made for them. With his cross-departmental role, Alf had arranged through the Ministry for Overseas Development for discarded aids to be despatched to a number of countries, one of which was China, where he also arranged for therapists to go to show how the earpieces should be moulded to the individual user's ear. This kind of overseas aid, Alf reflected, was much better targeted than financial aid which, although given to help the poorest of the poor, tended often to end up with the richest of the rich. Alf was also instrumental in arranging for the supply of vaccines to the remote mountainous rural areas of China.

Five years on, Alf's involvement at the United Nations inevitably further increased his standing with representatives of disability organisations across the world, not least in China. In the run-up to the International Year of Disabled People, he was again invited to Beijing to discuss further with Ministers and leading members of the National People's Congress the principles of legislating on disability. Interest there was heightened by the fact that Deng Pufang, the first son of Deng Xiaoping, the Chinese Head of State, was a paraplegic. In 1968, during the 'Cultural Revolution', marauding Red Guards had targeted Deng Xiaoping and his family. They located and attacked the young Deng Pufang, throwing him out of the window of a third-floor university dormitory, where he lay until a gardener rescued him, lifting him onto an old door on top of his wheelbarrow and taking him to hospital. He was left with a high lesion spinal cord injury. Now, in 1979, he met Alf as the respected Chairman of the China Handicapped Persons' Federation.

Alf had travelled to Beijing with Irene, Jack and Pauline Ashley and, among others, Duncan Guthrie and Leonard Cheshire, who was keen to explore the possibility of opening a Cheshire Home in China (then one of the few major states without one). Their flight arrived late; not grievously so, but enough to result in them being whisked away from the airport on arrival by Deng Pufang and Wang Luguang, secretary of the Federation, among other welcoming officials, straight to the Great Hall of the People in Tianamen Square. It had been suggested to Alf before he left Britain that the Great Hall was something they should try to see during their stay in Beijing. Now they found themselves escorted to this magnificent building as guests at a banquet in their honour, hosted by Deng Xiaoping. It was a prodigious meal stretching well into the night that Alf still recalls with mixed feelings. His luggage and that of those travelling with him was still at the airport.

He subsequently addressed members of the Chinese People's Congress in Beijing, making it clear that his guidance could only be about precepts and principles and not provision. Chinese common law was quite different from ours, notably in laying a clear legal duty on families to take due care of close relatives in pressing need of help. Income could be reduced at source if an individual failed to meet that basic responsibility.

"It would have been impractical for me to suggest the provision they should make, but entirely appropriate to spell out from my experience as a legislator on disability, both as a backbench MP and a Minister, the principles it might be helpful to have in mind in legislating on the problems and needs of disabled people in China. Such basics as understanding that, without knowing the size and scope of the problem, policy-making itself is blind – and that meant not just national population figures, but the numbers of disabled people in all of the various categories of impairment. Clearly you had first to know who you were going to provide for and what needs could be met, in terms of available resources, if it was decided to legislate; and secondly to spell out the areas that should be addressed – access to the

built environment and to educational and employment opportunities, adequate outdoor mobility help, special housing provision and so on."

Alf's message was accepted and is reflected at length in what is now China's basic law on provision for its estimated 120 million-plus disabled people.

Away from the great urban centres Alf was later able also to see at first hand something of the needs of the millions of people living in poverty in rural China. But from Beijing they moved first on to the historic city of Xi'an, formerly the capital city of China for two thousand years. There they were shown the famous terra cotta warriors and horses found near the tomb of Emperor Qin Shi Huange in 1974 and first opened to the public on China's National Day in 1979. Then on to Chungking, where Alf was scheduled to address a meeting of four hundred 'rehabilitation experts' at the headquarters of the Chinese Army's Medical Corps. When they mounted the staircase to enter the huge hall, Alf and his companions were taken aback by the sight not only of the expected 400 specialists but of thousands of army personnel primed for their arrival and clearly under instructions to provide a tumultuous welcome, stamping their feet in unison and applauding as they entered. Alf began with what he had thought would be a fitting introductory statement but – facing this hugely inflated 'audience' – quickly became aware that the periodic deafening applause was unrelated to the detail of his speech: *"I might as well have been reading from the Hong Kong telephone directory, as my first syllable was greeted with thunderous stamping and clapping, which broke out anew whenever I paused to take breath. The point eventually came when an unseen conductor gave the signal for them to stamp and applaud as never before and troop out, leaving us with the 400 experts!"*

Alf's contacts with Deng Pufang led to him setting up of the Sino-British Group on Disability – of which Duncan Guthrie became the secretary and Leonard Cheshire an active member – and culminated in a formal agreement pledging to work together in the service of disabled people, a concord renewed in 1988 when Deng led a Chinese delegation on a reciprocal visit to Britain.

Appointed to the Privy Council

In 1979, Alf could look back on five years of solid achievement – an unparalleled record in addressing the needs of disabled people. This was clearly recognised by his appointment to the Privy Council in that year, an honour normally reserved for members of the Cabinet and other senior political and public figures. As we have seen, his appointment as Minister for Disabled People had come at a time of serious economic difficulties but, even when public expenditure in almost every other field was being cut back, there had been rapidly increasing spending on new help for disabled people that evidenced an entirely new emphasis on their rightful claims to higher priority in the allocation of resources. He had set three hugely important projects on course: CORAD, the Charter for the 80s and IYDP.

Sadly, however, none of them could be fulfilled during his period as a Minister. For some time during the so-called 'winter of discontent' the Labour Government's grip on power had hung by a thread and on 28 March 1979 Margaret Thatcher led on a motion "That this House has no confidence in Her Majesty's Government", which momentously was carried by 311 votes to 310. Prime Minister Callaghan said that, now the House had declared itself, the Government would take its case to the country and that Parliament would be dissolved as soon as possible. All of Alf's initiatives would thus be at the mercy of a new administration with a new agenda. His valedictory message as Minister for Disabled People was that he was leaving a long unfinished agenda of unmet need. Sadly, his words fell largely on deaf ears.

1978: Arrival in Beijing. Jack Ashley, Alf and Dr Duncan Guthrie.

c.1979: Visit to China. Irene, Sir Harry Fang, Pauline Ashley, Alf, Duncan Guthrie (photo by Jack Ashley).

China c.1979: Alf, Duncan Guthrie, Jack and Pauline Ashley visit a school for deaf children.

5 April 1979: First meeting of CORAD. Alf is seated between Audrey Callaghan and Peter Large. Colin (now Lord) Low and George Wilson are in the right foreground. Other members include Dr Adrian Stokes and Joe Hennessey with their backs to the window.

1978: Alf appearing on TV in Roy Hudd's popular show.

c.1978: Brooklands Trade and Labour Club, Wythenshawe. Alf with supporters.

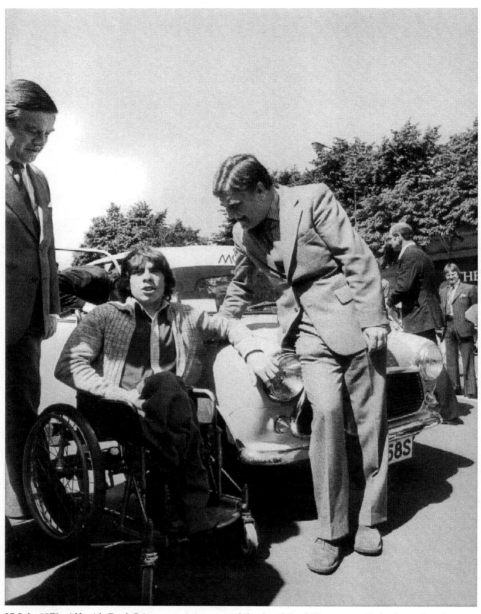

25 July 1978: Alf with Paul Cripps, receiving one of the first Motability cars at Earls Court, London.

1978: National Rehabilitation Centre, Dun Laoghaire, Irish Republic. Alf with disabled children, having opened a new facility, following the signing of an accord with the Irish Minister for Health.

1976: Ditchley Towers. Mary Greaves and Michael Flanders in wheelchairs. David Ennals, then recently appointed Secretary of State for Social Services, third from left on second row; James Loring left on third row; Duncan Guthrie above Alf on back row.

Riding for the Disabled. Young horseman Karl – a thalidomide child – at Buckingham Palace stables.

Chapter 12

THE TORY YEARS:

1979–1990

"Conservatism discards Prescription, shrinks from Principle, disavows Progress"

Benjamin Disraeli

"Those were the cold days indeed, and they continued year after year. Let us not have any Tory romantic mythology about their wonderful association with disabled people. They kicked them into the gutter".

Dennis Skinner, 10 June 2004

– An ill-wind for disabled people – Alf's new agenda – International acclaim
– The International Year of Disabled Persons – Publication of the CORAD report
– The long struggle for legal rights begins
– The opponents of disability rights reinforced – A question of priorities
– The Brighton bomb – A new call for rights
– Yet another Conservative victory
– The Tory view of anti-discrimination legislation spelt out
– Alf puts science to a dramatic test – Alf's ties with New Zealand cemented
– Child care in Montserrat – Repatriating the Australian Constitution.

An ill-wind for disabled people

In the 1979 General Election Alf again triumphed in Wythenshawe, bucking the trend with a – for Wythenshawe – thumping overall majority of 8,260. And he remained on Labour's front bench, but now as 'shadow' Minister for Disabled People. To that extent it was 'business as usual'. But there could be no disguising the change of political climate, bringing an ill wind for disabled people. It was out with the pro-active drive to improve their lot, in with an era of fiscal retrenchment and a return to the economic principles of a strictly market economy. Alf's brief parliamentary experience of Conservative rule at the beginning of the 70s had been uncomfortable enough, but there had then been a good measure of broad cross-party support for what he was trying to achieve. The party that he now faced across the floor of the House, with a majority over Labour of 71 and an overall majority of 43, had new priorities and a new confidence that focused not just on the survival of the fittest, but their elevation. A new Minister for Disabled People (Reg Prentice, a former Labour Minister of Education) was appointed, who said his task could be simply stated: it was to go on with the work that Alf Morris had begun and relentlessly pushed forward. But in Alf's opinion he served an administration that was not merely at odds with the philosophy of social justice and co-operation but repudiated it entirely.

It stopped Alf in his tracks, and set back the campaign to win equality for disabled people by more than a decade. Maria Eagle, herself a former Labour Minister for Disabled People, is emphatic in her view of the historical impact of the ideological change:

"It was very unfortunate for disabled people in this country that Labour lost power when it did, because Alf was on the cusp, with Peter Large's committee, of persuading the Government – which Ministers have to do, by the way – that civil rights legislation was needed. If Labour had not lost power in 1979 we would have been the world's first country to have such legislation. But typically of Alf, that didn't stop him. He moved from being a Minister who had the power to initiate reform, back to being a campaigner again".[1]

Alf's new agenda

In October 1980, Jim Callaghan stood down as party leader. He was succeeded by Michael Foot, who promptly confirmed Alf in his role as leading on disability issues. "His work in promoting the claims of Britain's disabled people and their families," wrote Foot, "at a time when the Government has downgraded their importance, will involve Alf Morris not only in the fields of services and cash benefits, but in the social, educational, employment, environmental and all other problems of disabled people. As a principal front bench spokesman, he will co-ordinate and promote our whole approach to the problems of disability. Reflecting their own new

[1] Interview, 14 October 2004.

aspirations, his work will put an increasing emphasis on the rights of disabled people to full social equality".[2]

Initially, Alf's energies were mainly directed at trying to sustain the momentum for improving services within the gift of local authorities and defending the four new cash allowances – and all the other benefits – he had legislated for from 1974–79. Karen Buck, now MP for Regent's Park and Kensington North and a Parliamentary Secretary at the Department of Transport, remembers those days in the early 80s when, alongside her work as research officer with the charity Outset, part of her time was devoted to helping Alf:

"Outset organised head counts all over the UK. One of the places we visited was Northern Ireland. When I look back on it now, it was an extraordinarily ambitious thing to do, but we took it in our stride and got on with it at the height of the 'troubles' by knocking on every door to find out the scale and extent of disability. We did the same thing in Milton Keynes, Barnet, Hackney, Haringey, North Tyneside: all sorts of places. That kind of assessment was very dear to Alf's heart. He recognised that if you wanted to reach the most marginalised people you had to go to them; and he was a guiding spirit, very interested and very much wanting to be involved in knowing about what was being done. His sincerity always shone through; he was never just a professional politician. One small detail says a lot about him: I was only 21 at the time but when he introduced me to anyone he would never say 'Karen works for me', but always 'Karen works with me'. I have never forgotten it. He was unlike other politicians in the way he was personally nice to people and would appreciate everybody from the big stars to the most junior people, and be equally gracious to all of them. But he was nonetheless a tough campaigner and in those cold years of public spending cuts, the activities in which he involved me ran counter to the prevailing ethos. It was Alf's form of retaliation. Going out and pro-actively assessing need was a very powerful way of striking back against cuts in social services by increasing public demand for them. The prevailing orthodoxy of the Thatcher Government was very much about individualism and standing on your own two feet,

---

[2] Contemporary statement.

whereas Alf knew that, metaphorically and sometimes in reality, many people had no feet on which to stand".[3]

At least one of those survey reports has survived. It was carried out in the London Borough of Barnet,[4] having been commissioned by Alf in 1978 and published in 1981. The researchers aimed at identifying disabled people in private households, recording their difficulties, the help they received and the further help they needed. It focused on people with long-term disabilities and disorders that interfered with their performance in activities essential to their independence and which, therefore, created preventable difficulties for which they needed special or extra help. Responses to a brief questionnaire were sought from all households, since negative replies (no disabled resident) were seen as just as important as positive responses if an accurate picture of disability in the community was to be drawn. The overall response rate was a remarkable 80.2 per cent and led to visits to 6,141 households. At this stage, interviewees expressed their own perception of their disability and the problems they faced because of it. Altogether, including those who could not or did not want to be interviewed, 7,807 disabled people were identified, representing 2.7 per cent of the population, mostly over the age of 64.

Alf's other retaliatory tactic was one of strenuous opposition both inside and outside Parliament. He attacked a Government "whose policies favour the strong and fortunate against the weak and vulnerable".[5] He knew, however, that the road to any immediate further progress was blocked by an administration that he regarded as caring more about profit than social priorities.[6]

This was not just rhetoric: it was harsh reality. Once in office, the first priority of the new Conservative Government was made clear in former 'social reformer' Chancellor Geoffrey Howe's first Budget Statement. It was to "make savings in public spending and roll back the boundaries of the public sector". Economies of some £4 billion were buttressed by a new, simplified, easier-to-understand and higher VAT rate of 15 per cent and Alf Morris had given his view of

---

[3] Interview, 4 October 2004.
[4] 'A Survey of the Handicapped in the London Borough of Barnet' (Alan Whitehead and Karen Buck, 1981).
[5] *New Horizons for the Disabled* (Co-operative Party, May 1980).
[6] Speech to the Co-operative Conference 1981.

that in his Fabian Essay nine years before. Income tax rates were reduced, but whereas the top rate was cut from 83 per cent to 60 per cent, the basic rate fell only from 33 to 30 per cent. Notwithstanding the disparity, both reductions heralded the beginning of a marked shift from direct to indirect taxation. This was good news for higher earners, but not for those with no taxable income – people, for example, whose disabilities prevented them from working or ever finding work. The ingenious explanation of his successor, Reg Prentice, was that he would not insult disabled people by suggesting that they could contract out of Britain's problems.

One of the first signs that disabled people would indeed be expected to bear 'their share' of the burdens imposed by recession was evidenced by the new Government's Social Security (No.1) Bill. This legislation, proclaimed among other things as "simplifying" the supplementary benefits scheme, had the effect of restricting payments for exceptional needs to people entitled to supplementary benefits. It left many disabled people – those who did not qualify for Supplementary Benefit at all – even worse off. At the Report Stage on 19 March 1980, many amendments were tabled by the Labour Opposition, including a number from Alf, aimed at building into the Bill modest provisions to meet the extra costs of living occasioned by chronic sickness or disability in the family. This would be a stopgap. The overriding need was for a comprehensive new benefit for disabled people which Alf and his officials had been working on and prioritising before the fall of the Callaghan Government, when they had in preparation a consultative Green Paper on the subject. Alf's successor quickly made it clear that work on that document had ceased. He told the All Party Parliamentary Disability Group in July 1979 that, because of the cuts in public expenditure, the implementation of a general disablement costs allowance must be "a long-term aim". Alf refused to accept that there was no money available to help disabled people. "One of the Government's first acts," he said, "was to give £1,500 million in tax relief to the richest five per cent of taxpayers". His amendments were about easing the problems of the most needful people in society.

None of this dented the armour of the Government's overall majority. The amendments were lost by 294 to 254. Moreover, as Mr Prentice was at pains to confirm, "holding out the expectation of meaningful progress towards a disability income in the next year or two would be to raise expectations that could not be fulfilled. That would be no service to the disabled". And Green Papers, said Mr Prentice, although fully aware that customarily they are the precursor of legislation, "butter no parsnips".[7]

Alf believed that the time would never be right for a Government of this persuasion. The idea of a national disability income had now become a pot of gold at the end of an illusory rainbow. In contemporary politics, Peter Large remarked, there were now some MPs "to the right of Genghis Khan but who lack his compassionate urge to put people out of their misery".

In March 1980, Sir Geoffrey Howe announced that in order "to restore a fairer balance between incomes in work and out of work" a number of social security benefits, including invalidity pension, would at the next uprating be increased by five percentage points *less* than forecast price movements. This abatement of Invalidity Pension, described by Alf at the time as "one of the unkindest cuts of all", formed part of a package of measures, the primary purpose of which was unashamedly admitted to be the saving for the Treasury of £270 million in 1981/2 and £480 million in 1982/3. The cuts, said the now somewhat questionably named Minister *for* Disabled People, were unpalatable to everyone, but were a necessary part of reducing social security in the Government's economic strategy. Alf lamented that Britain, having led the way internationally in new provision for disabled people, was now sadly in retreat. By the end of 1981 most disabled people in Britain would be poorer than they were at the beginning. Some 650,000 of the most needful of disabled people and their families would lose out.[8]

To add to their personal sacrifice, disabled people in many parts of the country found that they were paying more and more for, and getting less and less from, local authority services. Mr Prentice, their

---

[7] *Hansard*, Commons, 19 March 1980, cols. 490 to 512.
[8] Speech at the Usher Hall, Edinburgh, 31 May 1981.

'representative in the Government', argued that it had been necessary for local authorities to make some difficult decisions in determining their priorities within available resources. Few services for disabled people had remained unscathed. In some cases, even where the services had remained intact, local authorities had introduced charges to the limit they were entitled to do.

Alf took a different view. "Relentless pressure from Government," he told an audience in Woodford Green, "is now forcing many local authorities to break the law"..[8] In a scathing press release, he pointed out that some authorities were refusing even to assess need on the grounds that they had decided to abandon spending on one or more of the services provided for in Section 2 of the Chronically Sick and Disabled Persons Act. Some were continuing to assess but failing to make any arrangements to meet need, while others had simply withdrawn services in default of their statutory duty, without a word of criticism from the Minister for Disabled People. In the London Borough of Redbridge, notwithstanding advice from their own MP, Patrick Jenkin, the Secretary of State for Social Services, that no charge could be made to people on Supplementary Benefit, the council's Conservative majority had decided to charge some of the poorest and most needful of its disabled citizens £1.50 a week minimum for its home help service. As a result, over 300 elderly and disabled people had to cancel their home helps as unaffordable. "Let no one be in doubt," said Alf, "we are facing the most serious attack on social services for many decades".

Writing in 1981, two years into the Thatcher administration, Ursula Keeble pessimistically concluded that there was unlikely to be enough money available ever to meet all the requests for aids and adaptations. Most social services departments had discontinued their efforts under Section 1 of the Act to seek out and discover new needs, while still being unable to keep up with identified demand. She saw a danger that disabled people might now be "pushed to the wall". What had to be resisted at all costs, she felt, was a growing tendency to restrict the provision of aids and adaptations to certain classes of disabled people. It was more important than ever before

---

[9] Speech at a public meeting at Ray Lodge School, Woodford Green, 20 October 1980.

that disabled people, and those who worked for them, insisted that local authorities had a clear duty to provide aids and adaptations to those who needed them, if necessary without cost, and to a high standard.[10]

International acclaim

Fortunately for Alf, the Westminster scene was not the whole story. While faced there with systematic and well-organised Conservative resistance to his aims, Alf's stock internationally had never been higher. The Chronically Sick and Disabled Persons Act had awakened interest around the world, not least in Australia and New Zealand. Alf liaised with representatives of the governments and disability organisations in both counties about the growing pressure for similar legislation there. The legislative processes of all three countries were broadly similar, making it practicable for Alf's legislation to be used as a model. Eventually many important parts of the Chronically Sick and Disabled Persons Act found their way onto the statute books of both Australia and New Zealand.

A special honour for Alf was to be invited to give the first Kenneth T. Jenkins Oration at the National Convention of the Australian Council for Rehabilitation of Disabled People in Canberra on 16 November 1979.[11] Jenkins, who had chaired the World Commission on Rehabilitation from 1972–76 and became President of Rehabilitation International in 1976, was held in the highest esteem not only in Australia but by disability campaigners the world over. He had visited over sixty-three countries at the invitation of governments and non-governmental organisations alike, to consult, advise, confer and speak on the problems of disabled people. His advice was sought by countries of widely differing ideologies in both the developed and the developing world.

Jenkins' astonishing outreach included official invitations by the heads of government in twenty-nine countries, including Britain, and honorary life membership of the national associations of and for disabled people in fifteen countries around the world. It was therefore a signal honour that Britain's leading pioneer in the field of disability – whose work was reflected now on the statute book of Jenkins' own country – should be invited to give the inaugural

[10] *Disability: Legislation and Practice* (Ed. Duncan Guthrie, MacMillan, 1981), p.219.
[11] The oration was published in full in *Rehabilitation in Australia*, vol.17, no.1, January 1980.

oration in the name of a man who so closely shared his vision of the inclusive society that needed to be forged. Jenkins knew well that Alf's special contribution was his experience of the practical measures needed to achieve this goal. The groundbreaking progress in Britain stemming from the Chronically Sick and Disabled Persons Act and supplemented during his more than five years as Minister for Disabled People could inform legislation in any country, but particularly one with such close historical ties with Britain.

Alf's international status was given further enhancement with the launch of the *Charter for the 80s* at the 14th World Congress of Rehabilitation International (RI) in Winnipeg, Canada on 26 June 1980. Alf was there – having chaired the expert group that drafted the Charter – to explain its origins and philosophy, not least that disabled people "shared the rights of all humanity to grow and learn, to work and create, to love and be loved". The Charter went on, "yet they live in societies that have not yet learned to protect their rights, and all too often are denied the opportunities and responsibilities that should be theirs".

Here was a document that for the first time put disability issues firmly onto an international agenda: "a blueprint," said the UN Secretary General Boutros Boutros-Ghali, "that sets out with unequivocal clarity what needs to be done", even though individual states might not be able to meet its objectives immediately. The members of the World Planning Group that had worked under Alf's guidance and chairmanship were drawn from all corners of the world. They reflected widely differing ideologies and cultures and came from rich and poor countries alike, but they agreed on four main aims, each put forward as being of equal importance, broadly as follows:

- to save as many people as possible from becoming disabled by maximising the prevention of disability,

- to reduce the handicapping effects of disability by the provision of adequate rehabilitation services,

- to ensure that disabled people are a part of and not apart from society and that they can participate fully in the life of their communities, and

- to promote full public awareness of the problems and needs of disabled people and their right to full social equality.

Every country was urged by the Charter to prepare a comprehensive plan for the achievement of these aims, in the light both of the detailed targets for action set out in the document and of its own circumstances. To ensure the success of the plan, the Charter called for all governments to include a co-ordinator, of senior rank and directly responsible to the head of government, to direct both the preparation of the plan and its implementation.

Alf and his team had been particularly concerned to prioritise effective international action to address the plight of disabled people in the poorest countries still at the early stages of economic and social development. Here nearly three-quarters of the world's 500 million disabled people lacked the basic help they needed to live a full life. Fifteen out of every 100 children born in the developing world could be expected to die before their first birthday. One quarter of the rest would suffer from deficiency diseases, and three-quarters would lack any kind of modern medical care. Millions of people would become preventably blind, some both deaf and blind. In a rousing speech, delivered in the Usher Hall, Edinburgh on 31 May 1981, Alf recalled that Robert Burns saw a future "where man to man shall brothers be the world over". He told his audience that in these countries "poverty joins with impairment to poison the hopes and diminish the lives of disabled people and their families". "We live," he said, "in a world of obscene disparities of wealth, literacy, health, opportunity, life expectancy and hope. And we shall never have a really safe and stable world while we have the gross and glaring inequalities which so divide and disfigure the world today".

This mirrored the philosphy of the Co-operative Movement to which he had given life-long allegiance. Co-operation, he said, was a social philosophy about caring for each other as well as about the making and marketing of goods. The Charter, similarly, insisted on a redistribution of resources in favour of disabled people, not only within individual countries, but also between them. "Let no one say," he declared, "that the resources are not available to achieve a better life for the world's disabled people. The truth is that too much is spent on the munitions of war and too little on the munitions of peace. If only one per cent of what is now spent on armaments were to be spent instead on the prevention of disability and the rehabilitation of disabled people, the lot of disabled people in the Third World could quickly be transformed. That is why we must insist that the problem is not one of resources but of political will and priorities".

The *Charter for the 80s* excited interest around the world, particularly in countries already well disposed to improving the lot of their disabled people. As Rehabilitation International's ambassador, Alf was in demand to present the Charter to Heads of State in scores of countries around the world, but his commitments at Westminster and in Wythenshawe made it possible for him to do so in only a few.[12] These included Austria, Hong Kong, Kuwait, the Republic of Ireland and India – where supported by Mother Theresa he had been invited to present the Charter to Indira Gandhi, at a state ceremony in New Delhi, in the presence also of the President of India. Within days of his return he presented the document to Margaret Thatcher at a ceremony in 10 Downing Street. Rehabilitation International had also asked him to present the Charter to the UN Secretary-General who described it as the most definitive world policy statement on disability ever written. Thus it came as no surprise when the he later announced that it would become the basis for the World Programme of Action Concerning Disabled Persons and the UN Decade of Disabled Persons 1983–1992. The World Programme of Action, adopted by the UN General Assembly in 1982, signified the world community's ongoing commitment to taking forward initiatives started during IYDP: a global strategy aimed at preventing disability, enhancing rehabilitation and ensuring the full participation of disabled persons in the social life and economic development of their communities. Boutros Boutros-Ghali later described the Charter as the cornerstone of the United Nations disability programme.[13]

---

[12] Nevertheless, including his visits to China and the United States, Alf went to countries in which approaching half of the world's disabled people live.

[13] General Assembly, October 1992.

The International Year of Disabled Persons

The message of the Charter dovetailed perfectly with the aspirations for 1981's International Year of Disabled Persons (IYDP). This had been in the planning stage since 1978, with Alf heavily involved from the outset. Indeed, as we have seen, the United Nations Secretary-General had chosen him in 1978 – as the world's first Minister for Disabled People – to open the debate at the UN that led to the decision to launch an International Year. IYDP was by no means just a symbolic occasion for the UN and the capital cities of the world. It was a year in which everyone could make his or her contribution, and which at grass-roots level stimulated new programmes for action in a spirit of goodwill. It was, Alf remarked, the best ever opportunity to break down the barriers of public indifference and ignorance.

From the perspective of the United Nations, IYDP was part of a continuum of declarations asserting human rights without distinction. The Year would endorse principles in its Universal Declaration of Human Rights that by implication applied as much to disabled people as to everyone else. Already the UN had published a *Declaration on the Rights of Mentally Retarded Persons (1971)* and a *Declaration on the Rights of Disabled Persons (1975)* that specifically applied the principles of the Universal Declaration to disabled people. Now it recognised that more needed to be done to bring disabled people out of the shadows and into mainstream society. It declared that IYDP's theme would be "full participation and equality", a concept embodied in a logo representing two people holding hands in mutual support.

As one of the countries that had led the way in sponsoring the UN resolution proclaiming IYDP, the United Kingdom Government was committed to pursuing its aims. Its main response was to invite national voluntary bodies to set up IYDP committees in each of the UK countries. These were funded and supported by Government, but were all independent of it and "free to plan the Year as they think best"[14] within the UK's overall aims of increasing awareness of the needs, abilities and aspirations of disabled people;

---

[14] *IYDP and After - the UK Response* (DHSS, July 1982), paragraph 2.6.

encouraging their participation, equality and integration; seeking new ways to prevent disability; and advocating more positive attitudes towards disabled people. "The main thrust of the Year", the House of Commons was told on 3 February 1981, "must be borne by the voluntary organisations".[15]

It soon became clear, however, that these aims would not be backed by any significant expenditure. In a debate on the IYDP in the House of Lords on 14 January 1981, Baroness Young, in speaking for the Government, said bluntly: "I have no doubt that in the course of the debate the Government...will be asked to find more resources for a great many good causes, and I am equally certain that I shall have to resist"[16]

IYDP fell within the remit of a new Minister for Disabled People, Hugh Rossi. The Year began badly for him (and for disabled people) with a further 1 per cent cut in the value of the Invalidity Pension. There had also been a swingeing 500 per cent increase in prescription charges and spiralling electricity costs. Unemployment was very high, with disabled job seekers worst affected. The Government's reluctance to commit extra resources to celebrate the Year was underlined in a debate on poverty on 3 February 1981. Norman Buchan (Labour, Renfrewshire, West) reminded the Commons that earlier in the month Alf Morris had tabled a wide-ranging series of questions to find out what new initiatives the Government had in mind to mark IYDP and at what cost. He had, he said, looked through the answers from nearly a score of Ministers. Everyone had made clear that there would be virtually no new expenditure. Perhaps alone in the world, he said, Britain had not responded and had not brought forward any new provision. Mr Rossi was turning the IYDP into a kind of sick joke which was beginning to fray the nerves and try the patience of activists in the voluntary sector.

In the same debate there were contributions from Paul Dean (Conservative, Somerset North) and Tom Benyon (Conservative, Abingdon) arguing that 1981 would be a good time to respond to the Disablement Income Group's proposals for a Green Paper on a

---

[15] *Hansard*, Commons, 3 February 1981 col. 229.
[16] *Hansard*, Lords, 14 January 1981, col.53.

disablement costs allowance, about which, said Mr Benyon, expectations had been raised in the Conservative manifesto. However, it was again made clear that this was not among the Government's plans for the foreseeable future. It would, said Mr Rossi, "raise expectations unnecessarily if we went as far as to publish a Green Paper, even on the basis of a long-term consultation".[17] The Conservative view of things, as Jack Ashley pointed out, had been spelled out by the Prime Minister, who had marked the beginning of the Year by expressing the hope that it would "call forth a lot more voluntary effort on the part of the disabled". "Most of us," Mrs Thatcher had ventured, "think that it is more laudable to do something for oneself than to get up and take a public stance on an issue to try to persuade the Government to do it".[18]

As the Year progressed, it appeared that far from strengthening legislative provisions for Britain's disabled people, the Government was intent on diluting them. Thus when the Education Bill was introduced to codify the recommendations of the 1978 report of the Warnock Committee, appointed by Alf, – *Special Educational Needs* – its commitment to educate children with 'special educational needs' in mainstream schools was hedged by a proviso that the arrangements should be compatible with "the efficient use of resources". This was not merely a last-resort safeguard. As Alf pointed out at the Second Reading on 2 February 1981, Baroness Young, the Minister of State for Education and Science, had already told the Advisory Centre for Education that it was "not possible to pretend that the availability of resources is not also a factor in the rate of desirable integration...[Thus] in the present economic situation no rapid acceleration in the trend towards integration can be expected".[19] The Government's policy, Alf said later, was "Warnock on the cheap".[20]

Again, when Dafydd Wigley, then leader of Plaid Cymru, in close consultation with Alf and supported by the All-Party Disablement Group, introduced the Disabled Persons (No.2) Bill – a measure

[17] *Ibid*, col. 230.
[18] *Hansard*, Commons, 13 January 1981, col. 1239.
[19] *Hansard, Commons*, 2 February 1981, col. 46.
[20] *Hansard*, Commons, 3 July 1981, col. 1144.

intended further to strengthen the access provisions of the Chronically Sick and Disabled Persons Act – the Government was initially extremely reluctant to help or even sit on the fence. Eventually, they let the Bill through to Royal Assent as the Disabled Persons Act 1981, but only after insisting on draconian amendments. At the Third Reading on 1 May 1981, Mr Rossi welcomed the Bill "in its present form" and was glad that the Government had been able to assist Mr Wigley in putting it "into a correct form". *The Sunday Times*, however, offered a contrary view, commenting that it had been "emasculated beyond recognition" ... "Not only have the teeth been removed: they have removed its gums as well".[21]

As the prime mover since its outset in promoting IYDP, Alf was dismayed by the lack of any meaningful progress in Britain. On 3 July 1981 he brought a motion to the House welcoming and endorsing the aims of IYDP, calling on the Government henceforth to pursue policies consistent with its aims and urging Ministers to initiate discussions with all relevant organisations, before the end of 1981, on a programme of action to maintain the impetus of IYDP in the years ahead. It was an opportunity both to look forward and take stock. Alf began by reminding Members of the aims of the Year, both national and international. They could not all be achieved at once; IYDP had to be seen rather as "the start of a new era". In Britain there had been major progress in the previous decade, but much remained to be done if the aims of the Year were to be achieved in the foreseeable future. Yet now, he said, notwithstanding the Government's clear electoral undertakings to disabled people, all the emphasis of their policies was on cuts in provision and every call for further advance was drowned in the reality of retreat. "For the poor and disabled, they cut benefits. For the rich and fortunate, they cut taxes. How can that possibly be consistent with the aims of IYDP?" Alf drew attention to a statement by Peter Large, published by the Disablement Income Group, the very title of which, *Disastrous Years for Disabled People*, was a damning criticism of the policies the Government had pursued in the previous two years. Nor was DIG alone in its criticism. Professor Peter Townsend, then chairman of the Disability Alliance, had written in a similar critique: "the

---

[21] *The Sunday Times*, 10 May 1981.

prospects in the early 1980s for the disabled population are gloomier than at any time in the last two decades".

Faced with this blistering attack, Mr Rossi was short on ammunition. He had put himself about at events, competitions and meetings with voluntary organisations up and down the country and he readily accepted the motion, but his "one regret" was that he had come to the task at a time of grave economic difficulty and against a background of world recession. It was "impossible to contemplate the enormity of what is required to be [done] without a deep sense of frustration at the current lack of resources to do it". Nevertheless, he said, the Government had been able to make additional provision, albeit modest, for disabled people. For example, it had been possible to zero rate VAT on adaptations to disabled drivers' cars, to double the tax allowance for blind people and to increase the mobility allowance well above the level of inflation. Spending on personal social services and support for local authority social services had increased in real terms. The pace was not as fast as he would wish, but was as fast as the economy permitted.

The question that Mr Rossi could not answer, however, was put by David Ennals: "Will the Minister say how much has been saved by cuts in benefits that affect disabled people, compared with the additional expenditure on the various projects to which he referred in his speech". "I shall write to the right hon. Gentleman," Mr Rossi replied, in total embarrassment, "I have to deal with a number of other matters".[22]

The same debate also brought a further cross-party opportunity for Paul Dean, David Ennals and David Trippier to raise what was becoming the perennial question of the need for a Green Paper on a disablement costs allowance. "Everyone knows," said Mr Ennals, "that introducing a new benefit, which will be complicated because it will relate to a range of other benefits, requires a great deal of thought and consideration", a process that "should be taking place now". Mr Rossi's reply was typically inscrutable: it was, and would continue to be, the Government's long-term objective to remove the anomalies over multiplicity of benefit provision, and eventually to

[22] *Hansard*, Commons, 3 July 1981, cols. 1139-1202.

arrive at a general disablement benefit. Work on this matter was going on all the time, but it would be cruel at this stage to raise expectations by publishing a scheme for a general benefit when there was not the remotest chance of the enormous amount of additional resources that would be required being available for such a scheme. So, commented Peter Large in DIG's magazine, if disabled people didn't like being cold, unemployed and housebound, they could comfort themselves by remembering that 1981 was their international year and that Ministers now had the right attitude towards them: they were very sorry they were cold, unemployed and housebound.

But despite the distinct lack of enthusiasm at Westminster, IYDP was making a significant impact in the voluntary sector, where there was genuine commitment to seeking improvement. The Rt. Hon. The Earl of Snowdon, who was charged with the Presidency of IYDP in England, had in 1976 chaired the working party that produced the seminal report *Integrating the Disabled*.[23] The dominant theme of that report, very much in tune with Alf's vision as the then Minister for Disabled People, was a "demand, in the name of humanity, for the better and wider understanding at all levels in our society of the emotional and material needs of disabled people".

Lord Snowdon had begun IYDP with the earnest hope that the aims of the Year would long outlast 1981 and that the initiatives taken and insights gained during the Year would provide the opportunity to begin a new era of "understanding and action when social barriers of fear, prejudice and ignorance will be broken down".[24] A major theme of the Year was to encourage integration for disabled people within local communities. And to a significant extent this was a message still needing to be understood. Even in some parts of the voluntary sector the entrenched traditions of paternalism, with control entirely in the hands of non-disabled people, all too often remained the order of the day. Here, as well as among social care and health professionals, a pervasive view prevailed of 'we know what is best for disabled people'. Reflecting Rehabilitation

---

[23] *Integrating the Disabled* (Ed. Rosemary Thorpe-Tracey, National Fund for Research into Crippling Diseases, 1976).

[24] Foreword to the third edition of *Directory for Disabled People* (Ann Darnbrough & Derek Kinrade, Woodhead-Faulkner Ltd, 1981).

International's *Charter for the 80s*, IYDP challenged such perceptions head on, insisting that disabled people should lead and accept responsibility for the governance of matters affecting their rights and the goals to which they aspired.

It is, in retrospect, much to the credit of those who steered IYDP that the core principles of the *Charter for the 80s* began to sink in. They reinforced Alf's crusade in chairing its drafting committee and generated genuine change in a constructive spirit. Local authorities started to look at what more they could do to make things better for disabled people; national disability organisations sought to become more representative of the people they served; and many new ventures were launched in response to needs revealed. Bankable rights for disabled people were still some way off, but IYDP was another important milestone on the way.

Publication of the CORAD Report

In February 1982, the Committee on Restrictions Against Disabled People (CORAD) – commissioned by Alf in his final year as Minister for Disabled People – published its historic report. As a matter of record, it did so as a majority, with three minority reports. One member dissented and would not sign, another wanted the legislation to cover all citizens and a third expressed an individual view on the committee's conclusions about employment. Nevertheless, the majority of members believed that the recommendations of the main report constituted a package of essential measures. They had consciously sought out the views of disabled people and their close companions and had concluded that "the frustrating experience of almost all disabled people is that not only are they often restricted by their own physical limitations, but they have imposed on them additional restrictions by the structure of the society in which they live".

At the beginning of their deliberations, most members of CORAD had been opposed to confronting these "additional restrictions" by making it unlawful to discriminate against disabled people. But by the end of its thoroughgoing study all but the one dissenting member of the committee decided that legislation was both necessary and urgent. They had become "convinced that education and persuasion alone will not bring about the changes that are needed" and that "an attempt to change behaviour merely by changing attitudes is not a cost-effective option".[25] They did so on the basis of examples of discrimination from a host of individuals, from national bodies of and for disabled people and their branches, from local societies of disabled people and from many other organisations and groups. And CORAD knew that the totality of discrimination in Britain was far wider and more pervasive than that of which they had direct evidence. The committee recognised that IYDP had pointed to a wealth of benevolence, albeit unfocused, towards 'the disabled' but argued that benevolence was not invariably beneficial in that people could become entrapped in a state of dependence, lacking the opportunities and choices that non-disabled people expect as of right.[26] More constructively, IYDP had encouraged disabled people to expect more than they had hitherto been offered and emboldened them to voice their complaints rather than suffer indignities in silence.[27]

Having provided evidence of the restrictions and prejudice experienced by disabled people in their daily lives, the CORAD report's "fundamental and most controversial" recommendation was its unequivocal call for anti-discrimination legislation and positive moves to implement such legislation in the near future.[28] The committee did not believe educational campaigns could succeed in its absence. It recommended further that anti-discrimination legislation should cover employment, education, the provision of goods, facilities and services, insurance, transport, property rights, occupational pension schemes, membership of associations and clubs, and civic duties and functions. CORAD also advocated a regulatory body or Commission with powers to investigate, conciliate and, if necessary, take legal action on individual complaints.

The report concluded with the hope that its recommendations would be given the weight of consideration they merited by virtue of the

---

[25] Peter Large's covering letter when submitting the report.
[26] *Report by the Committee on Restrictions Against Disabled People* (chaired by Peter Large MBE, Her Majesty's Stationery Office, 1982), paragraph 7.3.
[27] *Ibid*, paragraph 7.7.
[28] *Ibid*, paragraph 7.4.

seriousness of the problems they were directed toward solving. The committee hoped too that those to whom they now looked for action would eschew sympathetic gestures and kind words and concentrate on strong and durable solutions.

Put that way, of course, the report implied an expectation of disappointment, and not without reason. There had already been indications that the Thatcher administration was less than enthusiastic about the work of the committee. In the latter stages of its deliberations its secretarial support had been cut back from the level approved by Alf in 1979 – with no intervention from Hugh Rossi – to one part-timer and sometimes not even that.[29] When Peter Large finally submitted CORAD's majority report, Mr Rossi, as Minister for Disabled People, chose simply to respond by issuing a curt press release thanking the committee for its work, but rejecting its principal recommendation. He took a quite contrary view. While recognising that "some" disabled people suffered unnecessary restrictions, he held that much had been done to improve the position. Mindless of the precedents in the Equal Opportunities Commission (EOC) for women and the Commission for Racial Equality (CRE), he thought it better to build on the present position than to legislate for what he called "positive discrimination" as a right. He felt that "the loss of goodwill might outweigh any advantage gained".[30]

In a letter to Peter Large on 25 May 1982, Mr Rossi was even more explicit: "The Government would need to be convinced that there were significant breaches of human rights and I do not think that your report substantiates this". As far as the CORAD report was concerned this was equivalent to a four-line obituary notice. The idea of anti-discrimination legislation was anathema to the Conservative Government and was to remain so for the next 13 years. But although the CORAD Report was left 'on the shelf' by Rossi and his successors in the long Thatcher regime, it was welcomed in the United States which had earlier become the first country after the enactment of the Chronically Sick and Disabled Persons Act to legislate on access to the built environment. And

---

[29] *Hansard*, Commons, 11 February 1983, col. 1260.
[30] *Ibid*, col. 1263.

while the initial reception of the CORAD report in Whitehall was predictably unenthusiastic, it can now clearly be seen as the foundation stone in the (painfully slow) movement towards constructing statutory civil rights for Britain's disabled citizens.

The long struggle for legal rights begins

The first attempt to give legal force to CORAD's call for anti-discrimination legislation was made by Jack Ashley. On 6 July 1982 he introduced the Disablement (Prohibition of Unjustifiable Discrimination) Bill under the ten-minute rule. This was a one-paragraph statement calling for the prohibition of "unjustifiable or unreasonable discrimination, whether intended or not, in the provision of a service, facility or opportunity on the grounds of disability" and for the establishment of a regulatory Commission with powers to "investigate, conciliate and if necessary take legal action on individual complaints of discrimination; and to promote the integration of disabled people into society".[31] In moving the First Reading – which was as far as it could possibly go – Jack Ashley emphasised the word "unjustifiable". He was not, he said, asking for something unreasonable. He believed that a sense of proportion was necessary. He went on to make it clear that it would not be an offence to discriminate where the costs would be disproportionate to the benefits, if it was absolutely impractical to make changes or if the changes created definite safety hazards. Nevertheless, unjustifiable discrimination undoubtedly existed. Legislation to outlaw it would confer "rights rather than hopeful expectations". So far, he concluded, disabled people had suffered discrimination in silence, but since 1970 there had been "a new awakening among them and a growing demand that they should have the same rights as everyone else".[32]

Jack Ashley's Bill was no more than a parliamentary gesture, a toe in the water; and to nobody's surprise that water was stone cold. The Bill was ordered to be read a second time on the following Friday, but on the appointed day the Second Reading was summarily removed from the Order Paper by the inevitable Whip's call of

---

[31] Brought in by Jack Ashley, Lewis Carter-Jones, Jack Dormand, Alfred Morris, Dennis Skinner and Dafydd Wigley.
[32] *Hansard*, Commons, 6 July 1982, cols. 151-152.

"object", and the gesture ended then and there, with the Bill dead in the water.

Next to enter the list was Donald Stewart (Western Isles), then Leader of the Scottish National Party, who had won a high place in the ballot for Private Member's Bills and was persuaded by Alf to use his good fortune to press forward CORAD's call for legislation on disability discrimination. His Bill had the same title as that introduced by Jack Ashley, but a much more elaborate text. The main variation of substance was a provision that the legislation should be regulated by the Equal Opportunities Commission rather than by setting up a new body, a change said to have been prompted by Hugh Rossi in prior discussions but which he opposed in the debate. The Second Reading on 11 February 1983 went on for over four hours and shed more light on the nature of the determined Conservative resistance to anti-discrimination legislation. It was not, the House was asked to accept, that the opponents of the Bill were any less caring than others in their attitudes to disabled people: simply that they did not see legislation as the route to progress. Long contributions to the debate (so long as to prompt allegations that the Bill was being talked out) were made by Jill Knight (Conservative, Birmingham Edgbaston), the Minister, Hugh Rossi, and Ivan Lawrence (Conservative, Burton), who between them adduced every conceivable reason for rejecting the Bill, which they regarded as uncalled for and unworkable. While they were not opposed to care and improved benefits (so far as resources permitted), they repudiated the introduction of enforceable rights, not least because the proposed legislation would inevitably impose further legislative procedures and burdens on industry at a time when firms were struggling to survive. The House had to consider whether education, enlightenment and example would be preferable to punitive legislation, imposing the risk of court proceedings against those whose failure was not yet to have understood the needs of disabled people.

Ivan Lawrence was still speaking when Alf rose at 2 p.m. and moved "That the Question be now put". Although 77 Members voted in favour and none against, this was short of the majority for closure (100 votes) prescribed by Commons Standing Order 31. The debate was adjourned, to be resumed on 18 February, when it was killed off by Conservative Whips with the age-old cry of "Object".

Such overt obstruction, of course, further exasperated disabled people for whom, beyond any doubt, discrimination was a daily reality, prevalent throughout society in countless areas of daily living. They and their supporters knew that the intention of Donald Stewart's Bill had been to accord disabled people enforceable rights so that they could enjoy the "full and equal participation" prioritised by IYDP; and who were convinced that this would never be achieved simply through education and persuasion. None more so than Alf who had lent his name and given his total backing to the Bill.

The opponents of disability rights reinforced

In June 1983, despite an indifferent record, the Conservatives were returned to power with fewer votes but a hugely increased majority of 144 seats. It was a result that owed much to the formidable – some would say abrasive – personality of Margaret Thatcher, crucially reinforced by the British victory in the Falklands, and further assisted by disarray in the Labour ranks under Michael Foot. The severance from the party of the so-called 'Gang of Four' – Roy Jenkins, David Owen, William Rodgers and Shirley Williams, to form the Social Democratic Party – was a death blow to Labour's chances. Although the SDP/Liberal Alliance won only 23 seats it took 25.4 per cent of the vote and fatally split the opposition to the Conservatives.

Charles Morris, first elected in December 1963,[33] was one of the victims of the 1983 contest, though not through electoral defeat. His seat disappeared in boundary changes and, having no prior claim to stand in another constituency, he left Parliament to work for the Union of Post Office Workers to whose Executive Council he had first been elected when he was 22. Alf was more fortunate. Remarkably, against the national trend, his vote in Wythenshawe suffered only a modest fall and he retained the seat with a substantial overall majority. He remained on the Opposition front bench as a principal spokesman, but now faced a Government able

---

[33] As MP for Manchester Openshaw in a by-election.

to set its own agenda without any fear of defeat – at least to the extent that they could remain united behind their leader.

It was a strange paradox that Alf now enjoyed international esteem while embattled in his own country. Not that he was without honour – everyone gave him that – but his determination to bring the key recommendation of CORAD into effect continued to find no favour with the government of the day. The next opportunity to challenge its resistance came when Robert Wareing (Labour, Liverpool West Derby), whom Alf had first met when he contested Garston at the 1951 General Election, came second in the private members' ballot of November 1983. At Alf's request he chose to introduce a Bill "to accord human rights to disabled people rather than the lip service paid by so many people".[34] The Chronically Sick and Disabled Persons (Amendment) Bill – which Alf and Peter Large helped him to draft – combined measures further to strengthen Alf's 1970 Act with provisions to outlaw discrimination against disabled people as envisaged by CORAD. Again it was apparent from the outset that the Government did not intend to allow it to succeed. Robert Wareing revealed, during the course of the debate, that some months earlier he had been approached by Mr Garel-Jones, an assistant Government Whip, and asked what subject he intended to raise in his Bill. When told its title, Garel-Jones's immediate reaction was said to have been that he would give instructions to kill it.[35] As though to confirm this, the new Minister for Disabled People, Tony Newton, went on the radio on the morning of the debate to say that the Government was not persuaded that the Bill would be effective or practical.[36] The Government did not impose a formal Whip, but was accused of working on a negative basis to ensure a sufficient majority of Conservative Members to vote down a Closure motion; tactics described by one new Member, Tony Blair (Labour, Sedgefield), as "a cynical attempt to whip up opposition to the Bill". Did this not show, he asked, the Government's appalling attitude to those in need in our society?

The debate on the Second Reading went on to and fro for nearly five hours with little new in the arguments on either side of the House.

---

[34] *Hansard*, Commons, 18 November 1983, col. 1097.
[35] *Ibid*, col. 1120.
[36] *Ibid*, col. 1093.

Donald Stewart remarked at one point that he felt he was seeing the same film over again. Mr Newton professed himself against discrimination, but was obdurate in resisting measures to combat it by law. The problem, said Michael Meadowcroft (Liberal-Democrat, Leeds West), was that the Government was prepared to do everything for disabled people except give them the power to fight for themselves. The Minister and the Government, he observed, had approached the Bill with a predisposition to oppose it.

What had changed, however, was the climate *outside* the Chamber. And it was to this significant change that Alf turned when he came to speak from the Opposition front bench. He pointed out that the Bill had the support of a host of important organisations of and for disabled people. John Hannam (Exeter) revealed that in the Spastics Society feelings ran high in support of the Bill and the Society's executive council had voted unanimously in favour of it. Members of Parliament, said Terry Lewis (Labour, Worsley), had been deluged with correspondence asking for their support. Westminster Hall was laid open for a lobby of disabled citizens and there was a crowded meeting there of disabled people unable to enter the public gallery and see the debate. According to Roland Boyes (Labour, Houghton and Washington) the British Association of the Hard of Hearing alone had 500 of its members involved in the lobby. The Disablement Income Group also threw its weight behind the Bill. Members were exhorted to do everything possible to press their case in support of the Bill, and in a major article in *Therapy Weekly*, Peter Large, DIG's spokesman to Parliament, spelled out the hard facts: "Contrary to the popular view, raw discrimination does take place. And it is lawful... The election has changed nothing. In an increasingly abrasive economic environment, and with the threat of a return to Victorian attitudes and morality, the need for legislative protection increases".

On the eve of the second reading, DIG with a number of other disability organisations commissioned a Gallup poll, finding that a substantial majority (61 per cent) thought that it should be illegal to discriminate against disabled people.

Alf pointed out that the Bill was wholly consistent with the *Charter for the 80s* which the Prime Minister herself had "warmly welcomed" on behalf of her Government during IYDP. The case for legislation had been eloquently made by Peter Large and his colleagues in the CORAD report. There was no more felicitous text for any debate on this subject than the one that was quoted by the Chairman of CORAD in his first public comment on his committee's report. The words were those of Martin Luther King, who said: "Morality cannot be legislated, but behaviour can be regulated. Judicial decrees may not change the heart, but they can restrain the heartless". The Minister should now explain why a Government committee's recommendations had been treated so scurvily.

In retrospect, it is clear that there was an intractable philosophical divide between a model based on giving people care and one that reinforced care with rights. The Bill, as Donald Stewart pointed out, was concerned with human dignity. Even if the Government was to feather-bed disabled people it would not meet the Bill's objectives. The Rev. Martin Smyth (Ulster Unionist, Belfast South) perceptively compared the impasse with William Wilberforce's 20–year campaign to secure the abolition of the slave trade. Many would say that Wilberforce's vision was narrow. Nevertheless, he achieved his objective. This Bill, he remarked, again the work of a back-bencher, was another shot in the long battle to get proper treatment for disabled people. But he hoped that "we do not have to wait 20 years to achieve the liberation of the disabled".

Alf finally rose at 2.22 p.m. in an attempt to secure closure by moving that the "Question be now put", but this brought only disheartening confirmation that liberation was still some way off: the Ayes for closure 164; the Noes 210. "What we have witnessed today," said Alf, "is a total abuse of power. What has happened means that the Conservative Party is uniting against disabled people even without a Whip". In reality, he believes, the Whips had done their handiwork well in advance of the debate, making the result entirely predictable. There had, however, been no decisive vote to close the Second Reading and it was brought back a week later, only to be stopped in its tracks by the intervention of an anonymous Member, "in a strangled voice",[37] saying "Object". Despite a barrage of points of order led by Alf, nothing further could be done to

---

[37] *Hansard*, Commons, 25 November 1983, col.623.

progress the Bill. Thereafter, and into April 1984, the Second Reading was repeatedly brought back, but eventually killed off after a long series of deferrals and objections. The supporters of the Bill had been extraordinarily persistent in keeping the issue before the House, but the Government remained no less obdurate in its hostility to the legislation it sought to achieve.

While all this was going on in the Commons, Lord Longford announced that he would take over the Bill and introduce it in the House of Lords, where, as the Chronically Sick and Disabled Persons (Amendment) no.2 Bill, it was given an unopposed Second Reading on 16 December 1983. Nevertheless, after amendments had been made to the Bill in Committee, when it came back to the floor of the Lords on 3 April 1984 Lord Glenarthur, speaking from the Government Front Bench, made it clear that there would be no change of heart: "However worthy and sincere the motives behind the Bill," he said, "we do not believe that it would be right to adopt the legislative framework which the Bill proposes". Conservative peer Baroness Lane-Fox went further, arguing that, despite its name, the Bill went against the interests of disabled people. Lord Renton too felt that the Bill was well intentioned but misguided. When the question was put "That the Bill do now pass?" the 'not-contents' prevailed by 68 votes to 49.

Following the defeat of Robert Wareing's Bill in both Houses, Lord Campbell of Croy, a Conservative peer, who was quite severely war disabled, introduced a new Disabled Persons Bill in the Lords, seeking to achieve similar ends by making simple arrangements to investigate cases of alleged discrimination and for the setting up of a small commission to report to Parliament on these matters. What was different in his measure was that it would not operate through the law courts and would involve minimal public expenditure. The Bill was given an unopposed Second Reading on 16 December 1983. It went through all its stages with minor amendments, was given an unopposed third reading, passed and sent to the Commons on 12 April 1984, whereupon Lord Campbell surprisingly decided he did not propose to promote his Bill any further and it simply lapsed at the end of the parliamentary session having, as one hawk-eyed observer noted, "served its purpose in distracting attention from the vastly more important Wareing Bill".

A question of priorities

Disabled people in Britain were still without rights. Discrimination against them remained rampant and remorseless. And Alf was given to wonder if spending to save people from preventable disabilities would ever be seen as more important than disabling them. The priority given to the nuclear arms race over the relief of human suffering was such that he was moved to air his views on being invited to speak in ITN's Comment slot on 11 July 1984. Much the most compelling case against nuclear rearmament, he said, was that the resources it required were so desperately needed to save lives and prevent suffering. The £400 million it would take to eradicate malaria in the Third World was said to be more than governments could afford. Yet twice as much was being spent every day on arms. In Southern and South East Asia over 10 million people were blind for want of a simple operation costing little more than one bullet. Five million children were disabled every year by six infectious diseases which, at a cost of £3 per child, could be eradicated within the decade. Polio caused half of the crippling impairments of Africa, yet at modest cost the disease could already have been conquered. Enduring peace and stability, said Alf, could never be achieved while the gross and glaring inequalities that so divided and disfigured the world continued. Governments needed to be constantly reminded that disabled people had not only a special interest but a moral claim to be heard in every debate about priorities. For they and their families knew the true cost of spending too much on the munitions of war and too little on the munitions of peace.

The Brighton bomb

Alf also recognised, as he did when moving the Third Reading of his Chronically Sick and Disabled Persons Bill in 1970, that everyone of us is potentially disabled: a truth that most people who are not yet disabled tend to shun. Eventually, most of us can expect to become disabled if only by the ageing process, and some of us, unexpectedly, in the prime of life. On the night of 11/12 October

1984 a stark reminder of just how tenuous and fragile is the hold on personal well-being was brought home to politicians at the very epicentre of the Conservative Government. An IRA bomb, intended for the Prime Minister, exploded at Brighton's Grand Hotel, where the Conservative leaders were staying for their party's annual conference. Five people were killed and many seriously injured, including Norman Tebbit, then Secretary of State for Trade and Industry and President of the Board of Trade, and his wife Margaret. Both survived, but Margaret was paralysed from the neck down and had to come to terms with life confined to a wheelchair. Years later she movingly described the adjustments that have to be made when disability strikes. How, quite apart from the physical effects, it is remarkable how one's circle of friends changes; how very good friends of yore fade into the middle distance, some disappearing entirely. That is the common lot of disabled people: they must not only adjust to their impairments but also to disturbances in the pattern of their social life: what Jack Ashley described as "subtly changed relationships".[38] And while politicians are ostensibly sympathetic, the course of government policy grinds remorselessly on, apparently unimpressed by personal tragedy.

A new call for rights

In the following year Alf, with Michael Meacher and Margaret Beckett, responded to the Tory Government's disability policy in a booklet under the title *As of Right*, which called emphatically for full citizenship for all disabled people. The Government's record, they claimed, was "a story of constant attacks on the living standards of the poorest and most vulnerable people in Britain for the purpose of giving tax cuts to the very rich". The fact of life was that being disabled in the Britain of 1985 meant the probability of poverty, unemployment, bad housing and inadequate or even non-existent services. "We may no longer be sending thousands of people into remote institutions to shut them away from public view, but the effect of this Government's policies, which is isolation within the community, is hardly less cruel". The booklet ended with the message that there was a responsibility upon everyone who wanted disabled people to live more fulfilling lives as full and equal citizens.

---

[38] *Journey into Silence* (Jack Ashley, The Bodley Head, 1973), p.157.

It was to explain the truth of contemporary society, with its preventable poverty, ill-health, bad housing and unemployment for the most needful. The authors aimed to start the process of exposing what life had been like for disabled people during the Thatcher years and to set the agenda for radical change. It was "a call not to reflection but to action".

Even though advocates of radical change in disability policy were whistling in the political wind in the 1980s, there was increasing recognition of the needs of disabled people and their right to social fairness. Despite the Government's negative approach, real progress was being made by many local authorities, not least in improving access to the built environment. And as the fourth edition of *Directory for Disabled People* noticed in 1985, the most significant trend was the growth in organisations run by disabled people themselves. Increasing numbers of disabled people were being enabled to live in the community in lifestyles of their own choice, helped by new centres for independent living. Similarly, the section of the *Directory* on further education reflected a move away from specialised institutions to integrated further and higher education in mainstream colleges and universities, where many severely disabled students were pursuing studies of their choice with their non-disabled peers. This edition of the *Directory* was twice the size of the 1975 edition, reflecting a major advance in the scope and range of facilities and information available on living with a disability.[39]

There was also a significant legislative development. On 4 December 1985, Tom Clarke (Labour, Monklands West) introduced a Bill, sponsored by Alf and ten others of all parties, to improve the provision of services for people with mental or physical disabilities or mental illness, to make further provision for the assessment of their needs and to establish new consultative processes and representational rights for them. This was the Disabled Persons (Services, Consultation and Representation) Bill, which was to be contested and amended, clause by clause, well into 1986, with Alf, leading for the Opposition, conspicuously involved in the skirmishing. The Conservative Government accepted in principle

---

[39] *Directory for Disabled People* (Ann Darnbrough and Derek Kinrade, Woodhead-Faulkner Ltd, 1985), p. vi.

much that Tom Clarke had proposed but trimmed on the detail with some radical and substantial amendments. It was, Alf remarked in one debate, rather like demolishing what was thought to be a very desirable residence and replacing it with something much less attractive.[40] Nevertheless, "this humane and important Bill," he said, "would take disabled people much further along the road to full attainment of the objective spelled out in the World Charter: to have the same rights as all mankind to grow and to learn, to work and to create, to love and to be loved".[41]

The main sticking point was the proposed right to representation – what we would now call advocacy – which was seen by the Conservative Minister as having unsupportable resource implications. Alf was unconvinced. He noticed that the Government of which the Minister was a member had given over £4.4 billion in tax relief to those earning over £30,000 a year. In that context, implementing Tom Clarke's Bill, with its modest price tag, was eminently supportable and, surely, a "priority of priorities".[42] During the passage of the Bill, he took the unusual course of writing to the Prime Minister Margaret Thatcher. She simply confirmed that while some provisions of the Bill might be enacted, it would not be possible to make commencement orders to bring them into effect "until such time as the necessary funds could be made available".[43] Alf thought and said that to use the word 'resources' in Committee had been made to seem like swearing in church, but there was no dodging the fact that unless, in partnership with the local authority associations, the additional resources required by the Bill were made available, it could not achieve its purpose.[44]

The Bill, weakened by the Minister's amendments, received the Royal Assent on 8 July 1986. It provided for the assessment of needs of disabled people and of children on leaving special education, with an important new duty on local authorities to have regard to the ability of carers to provide personal care on a regular basis. In addition, Section 1 of the Chronically Sick and Disabled Persons Act

[40] *Hansard*, Commons, 11 April 1986, col. 522.
[41] *Ibid*, col.546.
[42] *Hansard*, Commons, 4 July 1986, col.1346.
[43] *Ibid*, col.1317.
[44] *Hansard*, Commons, 11 April 1986, col.546.

was strengthened to ensure that anyone receiving social services was given information about all other services provided by the local authority and any other agency that might be considered relevant to individual needs.

Even now, however, the Conservative administration delayed implementation of the Act because of its funding implications; and from the Opposition front bench Alf introduced a debate on 17 February 1987 in which he launched a devastating critique of the Government's record on assessing and addressing the needs of disabled people.[45] Other governments across the world, he said, had responded with vigour and urgency to the United Nations programme of action based on Rehabilitation International's *Charter for the 80s*. Whereas Britain was once a world leader in provision for disabled people, we now lagged behind other developed countries. Many of our leading organisations of and for disabled people, he continued, were protesting that Britain had not only stood still while other countries had advanced, but gone backwards since the present Government came to power, due to priorities that helped not those in special need, but the fit and fortunate.

A tetchy debate, emphasising party political differences on disability issues, focused sharply upon the Government's hostility toward and tardiness in implementing Tom Clarke's Act. Seven days earlier, at Question Time, Margaret Thatcher had unequivocally repeated that the provisions of the Act could be brought into effect only as and when resources could be provided.[46] Jack Ashley was unimpressed. The Act, he said, had been passed for two reasons: firstly, the skill and determination of Tom Clarke; and, secondly, the consent to its enactment by the Government. It now emerged, said Ashley, that this support had been bogus, given for purely public relations reasons. They had sought credit for endorsing the Bill, but refused to provide the cash to implement vital sections of it.

To all such attacks, the Government, with its unassailable majority, remained deadpan and unmoved; indeed even indulged in self-congratulation. The new Minister for Disabled People, John Major, successfully moved an amendment to Alf's motion, the effect of

[45] *Hansard*, Commons, 17 February 1987, cols.788-828.
[46] *Hansard*, Commons, 10 February 1987, col.156.

which was to pretend that everything in the disability garden was rosy. It reaffirmed the Government's commitment to the provisions of the Disabled Persons (Services, Consultation and Representation) Act 1986 "with implementation as resources become available and [belt and braces] as priorities allow". Some very low-cost sections were given effect on 1 April 1987, but those relating to children with special educational needs were further delayed until 1 February 1988.[47]

The Conservatives, notwithstanding the role of the "kindly" John Major as Minister for Disabled People, also continued to be obdurate on the issue of rights. On 4 March 1987, Robert Wareing introduced a new measure, the Disabled Persons Rights Bill, under the ten-minute rule, supported by Alf from the front bench and by other campaigners. It is now notable largely because, for the first time, its title (though not its content), alluded to rights. In commending the Bill to the Commons, Wareing said that it would "give basic human rights to all those who are disabled, whether physically, mentally or sensorily". Since his previous attempt to address this issue, there had been "more irrefutable evidence of widespread discrimination against disabled people". Equally, it was clear that "bringing about an increased understanding of disabled people's needs and promoting a spirit of positive co-operation in dealing with them", as advocated by the Minister for Health three years ago, "had not paid off". The country was looking to see who was and who was not prepared to support this important measure on human rights. The First Reading was not opposed, but a month later, "the country" saw all too clearly where the Government stood, when a Second Reading for the Bill was blocked by the all too familiar cry of "Object" from the Conservative Whips.

Yet another Conservative victory

In the General Election of 1987, on 11 June, Alf held Wythenshawe with an increased majority of 11,855 over his nearest Conservative rival. But across the country as a whole the Alliance again split the opposition and the Conservatives gained a comfortable majority of 102 seats. It was Margaret Thatcher's third consecutive victory,

---

[47] The Act's provisions on advocacy for disabled people have still to be brought into effect ten years after the election of the new Labour Government in 1997.

effectively extinguishing any hope of progress to secure disability rights. It was to be another two years before the issue was again brought to the House of Commons. On 6 June 1989, with extraordinary persistence, Robert Wareing made a further attempt to achieve at least part of his goal when he moved an amendment to the Employment Bill that would have the effect of prohibiting discrimination against disabled people seeking work. The amendment, he said, would enable the House of Commons to vote on the issue of discrimination against disabled people for the first time. By pushing forward the boundaries of equal opportunities, the House would be doing what would have been done had a Labour Government been in office after 1979, when "my right hon. Friend the Member for Wythenshawe appointed the Committee on Restrictions Against Disabled People". Alf was there to speak in support of the amendment. The figures for unemployment among disabled job seekers, he said, shouted of discrimination against them. They suffered both from low pay and lack of opportunity. But again the efforts of Labour campaigners were to no avail. Conservative MPs flocked into the 'No' Lobby like the cavalry at Balaklava. The amendment was rejected by 259 votes to 169.

The Tory view of anti-discrimination legislation spelt out

In June 1990, the Tory Government published a consultation document under the title *Employment and Training for People with Disabilities*, in the name of the then Secretary of State for Employment, Michael Howard. It provides us now with a clear statement of the Tories' position at that time: "An anti-discrimination law would be too complex to draft and uncertain in its application. There is a danger that faced with a law uncertain in its application, employers would become more reluctant to hire people with disabilities. The relationship of people with disabilities with employers may be damaged and the task of persuasion made harder. Some kind of enforcement agency (perhaps like the Commission for Racial Equality) would probably be needed, involving substantial cost. Anti-discrimination legislation, therefore, is unlikely to be effective in achieving policy objectives and might be counter productive by making a constructive approach by employers less likely".

Alf puts science to a dramatic test

From 1988–92, Alf chaired the Parliamentary and Scientific Committee, one of the most important forums for the discussion of scientific and technological issues, not least the growing environmental problems facing the world, in particular the threat of global warming. In the opinion of Arthur Butler, then secretary of the 'P&S', Alf's period of office coincided with the most important years in the history of the committee. Perhaps above all there was an imperative need for Parliament to be provided with competent, unbiased information concerning the physical, biological, economic, social and political effects of advances in technology, on the lines of an American model. Butler believes that Alf played a centrally important role in successfully pressing for the setting up of the Parliamentary Office of Science and Technology, now a highly important parliamentary institution. "Without his diplomatic skills as chairman," he says, "it would never have happened".

Alf's involvement in things scientific, however, was not merely theoretical and bureaucratic. He had close links with the University of Manchester Institute of Science and Technology and his constituency included Manchester International Airport where, in 1985, fifty-five people had lost their lives in a fire on board flight KT328. Most of them had died not from the flames but from thick, black toxic fumes that had engulfed the plane, choking them before they could escape. Horrified by the tragedy, Alf initiated a campaign to persuade airlines to provide their passengers with more protection against deadly smoke. The Government promised urgent action, but nothing was achieved until 1989 when the television company Granada decided to screen a programme on the issue. It had been said that 45 of those who died in 1985 would have survived if smoke hoods had been available to them. Granada now wanted to demonstrate that lives could be saved in future by the introduction of such hoods for passengers on all aircraft. To do so they planned a simulated experiment, duplicating as far as possible the conditions that had obtained in the disaster of 1985 with a live volunteer to test the effectiveness of a smoke hood. Alf was the obvious candidate and he agreed without hesitation. In a broadcast in the series 'Out of Order', shown on 9 March 1989, Alf dramatically proved the point by his own survival.

Viewers watched as a smoke hood, made of thin plastic and with a built-in oxygen supply, was placed over Alf's head and sealed at the neck. Clad in red overalls and 'Wellington' boots, he ascended a metal staircase, walked through a pool of aviation fuel, and took a seat in a mock aeroplane. Perilously, the fuel was then ignited beneath the test cabin, bursting into a wall of flames and engulfing the 'aircraft' in dense, poisonous black fumes. Within seconds the test cabin became a 'pressure cooker', the temperature rising to a level that threatened human endurance. Firemen looked on anxiously, accompanied by a doctor ready with emergency resuscitation equipment. Just short of a minute into the test it was decided that the heat inside the cabin was too great and the fire was quickly extinguished. Alf, appearing somewhat shaken but none the worse, slowly emerged. Divested of the smoke hood, he coolly remarked that it had been "a very singular experience". The central and crucial fact, he said, was that without the smoke hood he would now be dead. "Inside it was like hell on earth – which is what the passengers on the 737 faced without breathing help". Now he would do all he could to have the hoods introduced very quickly.

British Airways, aware that the programme was about to be seen by thousands of viewers across the nation, had already written to Alf to agree in principle that they would be taking steps to provide smoke hoods for their passengers – the first airline in the world to do so.

Alf's ties with New Zealand cemented

In the same year Alf was honoured in a way most unusual for a non-Kiwi when he was awarded the Queen's Service Order of New Zealand, bestowed, as he puts it, by the Queen of New Zealand. The honour was given in recognition of Alf's distinguished work in strengthening the bilateral relationship between United Kingdom and New Zealand. It acknowledged, in particular, his role as founder chairman of the all-party Anzac Group of MPs and peers, in which he remains active as its first President. The Group was formed in 1972 when, in both New Zealand and Australia, there had been anxious concern that Britain's increasing progress towards signing the Treaty of Rome and joining the European Common Market would adversely affect the relationship with the 'mother country', as we were still very widely described then. The very name Anzac – Australia and New Zealand Army Corps – was and remains a deeply emotive one both for Australia and New Zealand, recalling the grievous toll of upwards of a quarter of their manhood killed at the awesome battle at Gallipoli in 1915. The honour recognised also that Alf's legislation on disability since 1970, very closely watched by New Zealanders, had strongly influenced New Zealand's subsequent legislation on disability and, by example, made life better for all disabled people there.

Child care in Montserrat

In October 1989, Alf travelled to Montserrat, accompanied by Dr Gordon Piller, the father of a thalidomide daughter, who was much involved in child health policies internationally and with organisations promoting improved child care, and Dr Chris Rolls, a distinguished paediatrician based at Southampton General Hospital. Their visit was made at the request of Dr Lowell Lewis, then the island's Chief Medical Officer, whose duties included running the island's only hospital in the capital, Plymouth. Lewis was deeply concerned that children there with life-threatening conditions were dying through lack of appropriate medical facilities. One child who was seriously at risk was four-year-old Marquita O'Garro, a 'blue baby' suffering from congenital malformation of the heart. But there was nothing that Lewis or the island's Governor could do about it. After examining Marquita, Dr Rolls said that she would be dead within three months unless she was taken off the island and treated in a modern hospital. But there was no scheme to fund such a move. Alf's reaction was that it was manifestly unacceptable in a British 'dependency' to neglect the well-being of its people for which, by definition, Britain had a direct responsibility. He was determined to make Marquita's plight known to Westminster and Whitehall and get something done about it. His concern attracted extensive publicity, particularly in the *Sunday Times*, whose coverage led to a charitable donor financing her referral to Southampton General Hospital, where Dr Rolls performed the life-saving operation. The wider question, of course, was the plight of children similarly at risk in all nine of the British dependencies. Margaret Thatcher at first argued that we would be flooded with thousands of children. Alf pointed out that this was gross exaggeration; referrals to UK hospitals would not be on anything like that scale. His plea, he emphasised again, was for children with life-threatening conditions for whom appropriate medical facilities were not available in the dependency; and happily she relented. The policy of denying access to British hospitals was reversed. Time has validated Alf's perspective: over the years children referred were to be counted in hundreds not thousands, but for each one of them, of course, the scheme was literally and demonstrably life-saving. He credits the scheme to Dr Hugh Greenwood, founder both of the Children's Research Fund and Children's Research International, without whose help – as with so many other initiatives to help children in urgent medical need in countries across the world, over and above his support for child health research projects in most parts of Britain – the scheme could never have come about. Hugh Greenwood – the most modest of men – ranks high among Alf's gallery of unsung heroes.

Repatriating the Australian Constitution

In that same year, other international matters claimed Alf's attention. He had been to New Zealand in connection with the conferment of his Queen's Service Order, and on the way back he called on Mike Codd, the Australian Cabinet Secretary in Canberra. From his private contacts Alf knew that, for many years, Australia had been striving to secure the original of its Constitution from London.[48] Year-in, year-out there had been a total failure to agree in talks between the bureaucracies of Whitehall and Canberra about the issue. Alf asked whether any progress had been made in recent talks. None, replied Codd, if anything things were going backwards. Then, said Alf, since you're still getting nowhere 'behind the scenes' perhaps we should bring it on to the scenes by introducing a Private Member's Bill for the purpose at Westminster. This would at least let people know what had been happening, he said, and would surely help because most people in Britain would see it as unjust that Australians were denied possession of their own Constitution.

---

[48] The original was kept in the House of Lords and a copy in the Public Records Office.

The idea was well received and was put as a positive request when Bob Hawke, the Australian Prime Minister,[49] visited Westminster to address the Anzac Group and said he would welcome anything that could be done to resolve the impasse between the Australian and British governments. The story of what followed is worth telling in some detail as an example of the procedural expertise Alf could deploy to achieve his goals.

Precisely, Hawke was intent on persuading the British Government to release a vellum original of the Commonwealth of Australia Constitution Act 1900. He had personally raised the issue with Margaret Thatcher yet again during his visit, only to be told that while the Act's importance to Australia was widely recognised in Britain and she and other Ministers were strongly in sympathy with the Australian position, no way of meeting it could be found.

Alf was unconvinced. His first shot, on 25 July 1989, was to write to Sir Robin Butler, Mike Codd's opposite number as the Secretary of the Cabinet and Head of the Home Civil Service – once labelled by Alf as "the real Sir Humphrey".[50] Sir Robin replied on 3 August to the effect that there was no provision for the Public Record Office to lend or give a public record that would remain outside the United Kingdom and not necessarily be well preserved. Moreover, he wrote, any such moves "would undoubtedly be interpreted by other countries as a precedent for making claims of their own". The other original formed part of an archive going back to the 15th century. Its release "would be likely to arouse spirited resistance in Parliament". Alf's reaction was that he must, therefore, mobilise spirited support.

He decided that the situation could only be resolved through legislation. Since the Government would not do anything on its own initiative, a Private Member's Bill was the only way forward. On 12 February 1990,[51] with typical ingenuity, he introduced a Bill under the rarely used Standing Order 58. This allowed a private member to secure a First Reading of a Bill without any speech whatever. In the normal course, it was eminently unlikely that such

---

[49] Prime Minister of Australia, 1983-1991.
[50] Referring to the character epitomising public-service bureaucracy in the popular television series *Yes Minister*.
[51] Coinciding with the centenary of an Australasian Federation conference that resolved to bring together the six Australian colonies.

a Bill would get an inch nearer to the Statute Book. Rather it was a procedure to put an issue on the parliamentary agenda and, on the day of the First Reading, to explain its purpose to the media. In order to emphasise that there was strong and wide-ranging support in the House, Alf carefully secured a number of high profile, cross-party MPs to add their names as supporters. These included Jack Ashley, Sir Richard Body, Sir Bernard Braine, Robin Corbett, Margaret Ewing, Denis Healey, Merlyn Rees, the Rev. Martin Smyth, Sir David Steel and Dafydd Wigley. Others, including Edward Heath and Winston Churchill, would readily have added their names had more been permitted. The Bill was designed to amend the Public Records Act 1958 to permit the making of a permanent loan or a gift of a public record. But, to assuage likely concerns, this would be subject to the discretion of the Lord Chancellor, who would first consult the Speaker of the House of Commons and satisfy himself concerning the arrangements for the preservation of the document.

The Bill was formally presented to the Speaker who, according to normal procedure, asked "Second Reading, what day?" Alf knew that an early date would be an open invitation for someone on the Government side quickly to dispose of it by standing up and calling "Object", which would consign his Bill to the scrap heap. Thus he pitched the date some weeks forward to allow time for the Bill to be talked about publicly, in Australia as well as Britain, and to give him time to probe all possibilities of finding a supporter within the Cabinet to give the Bill a fair wind.

Putting his weight behind Alf's strategy, Bob Hawke, most unusually for the Prime Minister of another country – though with some help from Alf behind the scenes – contributed an article to *The Times* of 22 February. Headed by a plea to "give us our birth certificate", it made the case for the repatriation of the Act to Australia. "For Australians," he wrote, "our written Constitution is not a dry and dusty piece of paper, but a living document which continues to have a direct and immediate impact on a vast range of our country's affairs".

The issue having thus been brought into the public arena, the British Government now found it harder than ever to refuse the courteous request of a Commonwealth country with which it shared such history, heritage and traditions. Alf's next step was to arrange a visit to the Lords, accompanied by Conservative MP Sir Richard Body, to meet The Rt. Hon. The Lord Mackay of Clashfern, the Lord Chancellor, to explain the purpose of the Bill. He well knew that Lord Mackay was well disposed to both Australia and New Zealand. He also had ministerial responsibility for the Public Records Office and was, therefore, a pivotal figure. Alf asked him to look at the Bill and, knowing that the Lord Chancellor could not act outside the Government in which he served, to consult colleagues. To make all this possible, Alf agreed to defer the date scheduled for the Second Reading by two weeks, which he later extended by another two weeks, a sign that progress was being made. Behind the scenes, Margaret Thatcher was persuaded to give way, and the Bill was taken over by the Government to make sure it got through and onto the Statute Book. The lady who had declared herself "not for turning" had somersaulted through 180 degrees, but Alf naughtily suggests that she wreaked her revenge on Bob Hawke by phoning at 3.30 a.m. Canberra-time to tell him that what had previously been regarded as unthinkable could no longer be resisted. Hawke immediately phoned Alf with the message: "Your Prime Minister's been on to say you've won!"

On 23 August 1990, ninety years after its enactment and to the delight of all Australians, their 'birth certificate' came home to a place of honour in the new Parliament House in Canberra. In a ceremony that included drum-rolls and a toast to the Queen, Sir Geoffrey Howe, the Foreign Secretary, and Alf – as the architect of its homecoming – presented the precious document to Bob Hawke. Alf's stock 'down under' rose to new heights as the Australian Prime Minister thanked him for campaigning long and hard to garner cross-party support for the Bill, which had yielded "a gift of inestimable value". The success of Alf's initiative was also celebrated in London at a joyous party at the Australian High Commission. The Hon. Doug McClelland, the High Commissioner, said his guests were there to mark "an historic moment of enormous significance for all Australians" and there was a sense of enormous indebtedness to Alf and those who had striven with him at Westminster. Of course, all Alf's co-signatories of the Bill were there. So was Lord Mackay, the Lord Chancellor, so well chosen by Alf as the Minister most likely to lend his support from within the Government. But who else was there? Why Sir Humphrey himself – Robin Butler – who, it appeared, "had always thought an inventive Private Member's initiative was the best way forward"!

Soon afterwards Alf received the coveted Order of Australia from the High Commissioner, acting on behalf of Australia's Governor General. This made him the only British national outside the Royal Household to have received both the Queen's Service Order of New Zealand and the Order of Australia. It was a fitting tribute, since the ties and friendship that had inspired the former applied no less strongly to the latter.

By contrast, Margaret Thatcher's popularity was now in steep decline, both on the back benches and in Cabinet, and events were soon to conspire to bring about her tearful resignation on 22 November 1990. Might this be the beginning of the end of Tory rule?

c.1991: Nelson. South Island, New Zealand. Alf with the President of the Federated Farmers of New Zealand.

1992: Estelle Morris flanked by Alf and Charles after her election to Parliament.

23 August 1990: Sir Geoffrey Howe and Alf; presenting to Bob Hawke the original of the Australian Constitution.

1989: Buckingham Palace. Alf with Cathy, Irene and Gill, having received the Queen's Service Order of New Zealand from Her Majesty.

1988: Palace Yard, House of Commons. Visit of Deng Pufang with other visitors from China and representatives of the Chinese community in London with Alf and Jack Ashley.

c.1982: Alf meets a constituent serving in the Far East.

1981: In Kuwait to present and explain the Charter for the 80s to leaders of the 22 Arab countries.

13 May 1988: Alf and Anna Ford receive doctorates at the University of Manchester. Anna is now Chancellor of the University.

Alf, wearing a smoke hood, appears in Granada TV's 'Out of Order' in March 1989.

Chapter 13

THE TORY YEARS:

1991–1997

"Government, even in its best state, is but a necessary evil; in its worst state, an intolerable one".

Thomas Paine, Common Sense.

– New attempts to put disability rights on the Statute Book
– The tide begins to turn – Two new Bills run side by side
– The Tory Disability Discrimination Bill becomes law
– Alf elected to presidency of the Co-operative Congress
– The 1970 Act honoured – Alf contemplates retirement
– Constraints on community care: the Gloucestershire judgement
– An historical perspective

New attempts to put disability rights on the Statute Book

Despite the Conservative Government's previous hostility to disability rights, another attempt to put anti-discrimination legislation onto the parliamentary agenda was made on 6 February 1991, when John Hughes (Labour, Coventry North-East) sought leave to bring in a Bill to render unlawful "certain kinds of discrimination [relating to employment, transport and access] on grounds of disability". This was a fierce blast against the prevailing "indifference to the needs of disabled people", which Hughes regarded as "nothing short of a national scandal". Both the process of education and attempts to create public and establishment awareness, he argued, had failed miserably. In particular, the Government chose to ignore unjustifiable discrimination that frustrated employment opportunities.

If campaigners had hoped for a softening of attitude under John Major, the new Prime Minister, they were quickly disappointed. John Hughes's flag-waving Bill did not survive beyond its First Reading. Hope was rekindled, however, when, in November 1991, Alf came ninth in that year's private members' ballot. It came as no surprise that he chose to introduce another Bill to outlaw discrimination against disabled people. What was new this time, however, was its emphasis, reflected in the title, the Civil Rights (Disabled Persons) Bill. Alf felt that it was better to be seen as positively for rights and social equality and not only totally against discrimination. He reasoned that legislating *for* civil rights would underpin the drive for equality and that the provision of services necessary to enhance independence would then follow much more sensibly, fully and successfully.

Alf also knew, however, that he was working against unrelenting hostility – not from all Tory MPs but a great many of them. "It was characteristic of him," Maria Eagle recalls, "that he wasn't going to let that stop him. He knew from previous campaigning that it would be difficult to get any improvements, but there was now so much more momentum and a much more modern approach, and he had wide support on the Labour side of the House as from other enlightened back-benchers".[1] Alf too had unprecedented support from disability organisations. At a London conference organised by RADAR and MENCAP, Employment Secretary Michael Howard was lobbied for a change in policy, while the British Council of Organisations of Disabled People launched an anti-discrimination campaign backed by a report detailing widespread "institutional discrimination against disabled people".[2] At the same time the Institute for Public Policy Research published a report, *Equal Rights for Disabled People*, that called on the Government to bring in legislation against discrimination, including a special commission to enforce the law and promote equal opportunities for disabled people.[3]

Alf realised from the outset that no progress would be possible unless and until a viable, wide-ranging measure was brought forward. A great deal of expertise went into the drafting of the new Bill. In opening the Second Reading debate, Alf acknowledged the assistance he had received from Peter Mitchell, Ian Bynoe, Pat Healy,[4] who was then helping him with research, and "others who

---

[1] Interview, 14 October 2004.
[2] *Disability Now*, October 1991.
[3] *Ibid.*
[4] formerly social services correspondent of *The Times*.

could not be named".[5] As ever pragmatic, he had also done his homework to anticipate Government objections. Thus a person would be "qualified" for employment only when able to perform the essential functions of the job, taking account of any adaptations or alterations to the employer's workplace or organisation that it would be "reasonable" to introduce. To help determine what changes it would be reasonable to require an employer to make so as to accommodate a person's disability, the Bill provided for five factors to be considered, relating to the cost of the adaptations and the nature, scale and financial resources of the employer's business. The Bill had been drafted to ensure that the extra costs needed to ensure compliance with its provisions should not be such as would jeopardise the financial viability of the businesses affected. Moreover, the Bill recognised that deciding to treat a disabled person differently could sometimes be justified. A similar approach was taken in relation to the provision of goods and services. The proposed obligations would not require any change that was "technically impracticable or unsafe" and, again, the test of what was reasonable would be determined by what was achievable without "undue hardship" being caused to the person or body needing to effect changes.

The Bill ran to thirteen expertly drafted clauses, including proper definitions and provisions for enforcement and a final schedule dealing with a Commission to be set up within six months of the enactment of the legislation. Although, as events were to prove, the Government remained determined to continue its delaying and blocking tactics, Ministers now knew that things were getting serious.

Alf heralded the Second Reading with a press release on 3 December 1991. He could now make the case for treating the issue as one of civil rights because the United States Congress had already accepted as much with the passing of the Americans with Disabilities Act 1990. Yet in Britain disabled people continued to face "outrageous discrimination in every aspect of their lives". And the Government's stance was contradictory. In its *Citizen's Charter* it was said "that services should be available regardless of race, sex or disability". But with no civil rights legislation there was no weapon that

---

[5] *Hansard*, Commons,, 31 January 1992, col. 1241

disabled people could use when they were denied the same quality, choice and standards as other citizens.

Alf moved the Second Reading on 31 January 1992. He posed two basic questions: one was moral and other practical. What sort of a society did we want to create? And what must we do to create that society? This time there was strong support from both sides of the House, with a particularly powerful contribution from the Plaid Cymru leader, Dafydd Wigley, who referred to a recent publication *Disabled People in Britain and Discrimination – a case for anti-discrimination legislation*, a study funded and supported by the Joseph Rowntree Foundation. This had established beyond doubt that discrimination was far from being eradicated.[6]

The response of Nicholas Scott, the Minister for Disabled People, however, was muted. He acknowledged that there had been all-party support for the Bill and all Members knew that there was still too much unjustified discrimination against disabled people. They knew that it was wrong and that it often had a cruel impact on the quality of life of disabled people. He claimed that he remained "benevolently neutral" in his attitude to the arguments for and against anti-discrimination legislation, but it was soon clear that his neutrality veered against such a course. There was not by any means, he argued, unanimity in the 'disabled community', let alone among others in society, that legislation was necessarily the right way "at this time" to carry that work forward. In particular, he emphasised, the Employers Forum on Disability seemed to feel that legislating was not the best way in which to encourage the employment of disabled people. The Minister did not wish to rule out legislation, but felt that "for the time being" it was best simply to continue to encourage, educate and increase awareness. The House must decide whether to opt for the legislative route straight away or, at least for a while longer, continue with the other approach, without ruling out legislation if the alternative was shown to be inadequate. For the time being, he was anxious not to create a bean feast for lawyers.[7]

[6] *Hansard*, Commons, 31 January 1992, col.1247.
[7] *Hansard*, Commons, 31 January 1992, cols. 1251/6.

The "benevolent neutrality" of the Government, ventured Paul Boateng (Labour, Brent South), amounted to the "kiss of death". The Minister's speech had been "the kiss of Caiaphas".[8] At 2.16 pm, Robert Hayward (Conservative, Kingswood) rose to speak. Despite having given assurances both beforehand to the Speaker and during his speech that he was not going to talk the Bill out and despite numerous calls to sit down, he was still on his feet at 2.30 p.m. when time ran out, ensuring the procedural death of the Bill.[9] Alf is by no means alone in believing to this day that the Government engineered the demise of the Bill. Orders to resume the second reading were successively frustrated by objections, and on 10 March 1992 Robert Jackson, Under Secretary of State for Employment, confirmed that neither he nor the Government believed that a legislative approach was the right way to deal with the problem. Citing the failure of the quota system introduced under the Disabled Persons (Employment) Act 1944, he said that "rather than adopting an inappropriate legislative approach, we must persuade people and affect attitudes".

Alf did not, however, simply wait while this inevitable process was played out. Following the frustrating proceedings at the end of January he passed his Bill to Baroness Lockwood – who had chaired the Equal Opportunities Commission in its early years – and she reintroduced it in the Lords on 6 February. On 21 February, the Bill was duly read and sent to a committee of the whole House.[10] Lord Henley, Under Secretary of State at the Department of Social Security, said that he was unconvinced that legislation could abolish prejudice and ignorance, but had no intention of opposing "Alf Morris's brainchild".

Once again, however, the Bill was stopped in its tracks, this time by the dissolution of Parliament before the General Election of May 1992. Margaret Thatcher had now famously departed the scene and the contest nationally was one led by John Major for the Conservatives and Neil Kinnock for Labour. Conservative support was diluted, but still sufficient to gain a majority over all other parties of 21 seats.

---

[8] *Ibid*, col.1256.
[9] The Speaker, Jack Wetherill, later required Hayward to apologise to the House for misleading it.
[10] *Hansard*, Commons, 21 February 1992, col. 1473 et seq.

In Wythenshawe, by now a Labour stronghold, Alf secured an overall majority of 7,868, and in the new session he quickly ensured that his Bill was reintroduced in the Lords, again by Baroness Lockwood. While the Government did not support the measure, neither, by convention in the Lords, did they oppose it at Second Reading.

The stage was now set for a breakthrough, and Peter Large, who had been so influential in working with Alf in the past, took an unforeseen public opportunity, on 30 September 1992, to throw his weight behind the aims of the Bill. As the 21st successor as recipient of the Harding Award, Peter chose to speak on the subject closest to his heart: 'Education and Persuasion? The need for anti-discrimination legislation'. Back in February 1982, he said, the Committee on Restrictions Against Disabled People had, among other things, recommended legislation to make discrimination on grounds of disability illegal. After ten years they still awaited that legislation, despite the fact that nobody now denied the widespread existence of discriminatory practices. Opponents of such legislation stressed the need to change attitudes, citing the widespread existence of goodwill towards disabled people. They pointed to the potentially miraculous effects of education and persuasion. Peter, however, was far less troubled by attitudes than by behaviour. While it was true that legislation could not make people love each other, it could prevent improper behaviour.

One undeniable and highly important practical advantage of legislation, said Peter, was that it would vouchsafe the right of an individual disabled person to access the law to secure equal treatment. Legislation, moreover, was a means of gaining the attention of apathetic people and providing a foundation on which good practice could be built. It could be cited as evidence of a national commitment to improving the lot of disabled people and thereby to strengthen local campaigning. Anti-discrimination legislation would not, Peter realistically pointed out, solve all the woes of disabled people: it would not end the grave financial distress that so often accompanied disability; it would not immediately make the environment accessible nor, he suggested, end unemployment amongst disabled people. It would not provide homes for disabled people, or reasonable education, or "so-called care in the community". Additional action would be required in all these areas. But if it were correctly devised, Peter firmly believed that legislation could provide the foundation to promote the help and positive discrimination that disabled people needed and inhibit those things that injured their interests. In his opinion, legislation to make it illegal to discriminate against disabled people on grounds of disability was long overdue. And that was what the Civil Rights (Disabled Persons) Bill – which Peter had helped to draft – was all about.

By 12 November 1992, the Bill had completed all its stages in the Lords. It was then passed and sent by the Lords to the Commons, where Alf neatly timed its Second Reading for 26 February 1993, to coincide with a debate on a motion with all-party backing there calling for its enactment. The motion was approved, but a Conservative Whip then used a procedural device to block the Bill. So for a second time and after seven hours of debate overwhelmingly supportive of the Bill the Commons, itself now humiliated having minutes earlier carried a motion for its enactment, was again prevented even from giving the Bill a Second Reading.

Alf, accompanied by Lord (David) Renton, Brian Rix and others, now took his concerns direct to the Prime Minister, John Major, who had succeeded Lord Renton as Conservative MP for Huntingdon. *"We urged him to relent to allow the Bill to go forward. It was quite clear that the only people who were now speaking against the Bill in the whole of Parliament were members of his administration and certain of their backbench supporters who were totally committed to voting whenever and for whatever they were asked to vote by his Whips. I said that he had the power to allow it through and I asked him as a former successor of mine as Minister for Disabled People to do so. John gave me the first honest response. He pointed out that his was a deregulating government, whereas my Bill would increase regulation. I suggested that this was an illogical position unless he wanted also to repeal the legislation on gender and race and get rid of the Equal Opportunities Commission and the Commission for Racial Equality. In effect his reply was 'I would if I could, but I can't!' His stance was bitterly resented and comprehensively unacceptable to disabled people but, unlike his parliamentary colleagues blocking the Bill, at least he was straightforward and frank about the reasons for his Government's opposition"*.

On 7 May 1993, when the Bill was brought back from the House of Lords to the Commons, yet again it was met with the familiar call of 'Object' from the Conservative benches. The same thing happened on the 14 May and again, finally, on 2 July, when it was unceremoniously killed off.

The tide begins to turn

Nonetheless, the introduction of the Civil Rights (Disabled Persons) Bill had begun what, in the words of Maria Eagle, "can only be described as a four-year battle for civil rights which redoubled the ferocity of previous fights and during which hand-to-hand fighting on Private Members' Bill Fridays led to heavy Tory casualties".[11] "By 1992," she recalls, "the Government was gradually losing its majority, having absolutely refused to allow the Bill to proceed. It wasn't 'benign neutrality', it was hostility, an ideologically driven view that this wasn't the way to go. And so, when Britain should have been in the vanguard of reform, we were standing still on the issue of disabled people's rights and being overtaken by others. Still, you couldn't stop Alf. He was always pragmatic; he wouldn't make unreasonable demands, but used the parliamentary process and systems that were there until it became impossible to stop him, and that was the way in which he proceeded".[12]

Alf's next move was to secure the agreement of Robert Hayward's successor, Roger Berry (Labour, Kingswood) – who came high in the private members' ballot of 1993 – to republish and promote his Civil Rights (Disabled Persons) Bill, promising him total support. This began with a blistering article in *The Sunday Times* of 23 January 1994 under the headline 'Britain's Shameful Wall That Must Come Down'. Alf pointed out that the Government could afford civil rights for everyone except disabled people. As a result we lagged behind the United States, Australia, Canada, France and Sweden, which had long since legislated to give disabled people legal

---

[11] Maria Eagle, Minister for Disabled People, *Hansard*, Commons, 10 June 2004, col. 427.
[12] Interview, 14 October 2004.

protection against unfair discrimination. Without full civil rights, he pointed out, disabled people were doubly disabled. The handicapping effects of their impairments were made even harder to bear by gratuitous social handicaps for which there was no moral justification. And why on earth should what was morally indefensible any longer be legally permissible in Britain?

Roger Berry moved the Second Reading of the Bill on 11 March 1994. It now enjoyed substantial support on all sides of the House, and was cleared to go into committee by 231 for and none against. But it was another false dawn. The Government's opposition to anti-discrimination legislation had not gone away. When the Bill was next considered, on 6 May 1994, having gone through its committee stage in the Commons, Alf immediately began by putting a "deeply serious" point of order to the Deputy Speaker, Michael Morris. He had been informed by a highly authoritative source that no fewer than eighty amendments for the Report Stage of the Bill had been drafted by the Government for tabling by five Conservative Members. The House should surely know whose amendments these really were. Not to clear this up could only increase the now widespread suspicion that the Government had decided to wreck the Bill by proxy.

Frustration intensified as the long series of amendments slowly proceeded, until Dale Campbell-Savours (Labour, Workington) asked the Minister, Nicholas Scott, straight out, whether he or his Department had been in any way involved in the drafting of any of the amendments or a new clause that had been tabled. Scott replied, "No part whatever in the drafting of any of the amendments and, to the best of my knowledge, nobody in my Department has been involved in the drafting of any amendments in this area". Alf pressed the point, "Were they in any way contributed to or drafted in Whitehall?" – in other words by any Minister or Government official. Mr Scott said that he had responded as best he could from the knowledge that he had of the situation.

Further consideration of the Bill then stood adjourned, to be resumed on 20 May. But Alf meanwhile was able to confirm that all eighty amendments tabled on the Report Stage of the Bill in the names of five Conservative members had indeed been drafted in Whitehall, in fact by the Office of Parliamentary Counsel, which drafts legislation only on the instruction of Ministers. When, on 9 May, this revelation was confirmed in a parliamentary reply from the Leader of the House to Alf, and raised by him with the Speaker as a point of order, Betty Boothroyd immediately grasped its implications.

Unwisely, however, Ms Lady Olga Maitland (Conservative, Sutton and Cheam) rose to say: "I would like to make it abundantly clear that I raise my own amendments. I sought consultation, but it would be totally unfair to suggest that they came from any other source. It seems," she went on – with what Alf describes as 'unbelievable hardihood' – "that disabled people are being used as a political football for political purposes by the Labour party".

But on the following day a chastened Nicholas Scott made a personal statement to the House. To the effect that while his previous statement that his Department had not drafted any amendments had been true, his officials, authorised by him, had been "involved in their preparation". He very much regretted that by not giving a fuller explanation at the time, the effect of his reply was misleading and he offered unreserved apologies to the House. Alasdair Palmer, the home affairs editor of *The Spectator*, writing in the next edition of *The Sunday Times*, was unimpressed. Under a banner headline 'Shame – Shocking Behaviour Of Government That Shied Away From A Matter Of Principle', he commented that Nicholas Scott had misled Parliament and got away with it. He had confessed to what he had done but did not consider his offence serious enough to cause him to resign. To avoid the embarrassment of having to admit that he had opposed a Bill that would benefit the very people whose interests his job existed to promote, he had been "economical with the truth".

Late on 11 May, a BBC journalist approached John Smith, then Leader of the Opposition, as he emerged from a fund raising occasion in Park Lane. Having answered the journalist's question, John told him that he would also like to say something else – about the appallingly shabby tactics of Conservative MPs in blocking the Civil Rights (Disabled Persons) Bill, a measure so urgently required for disabled people. Not only blocking the Bill, he said, but misleading Parliament about it so as to be brought to book by the Speaker. He thought the House of Commons had been brought to a very low ebb. It was to be John's last comment to the media and the country, for he died suddenly early the next day.

Some MPs wanted Nicholas Scott's resignation. Alf was more concerned with the progress of the Bill. On 16 May, he took the unusual step of writing to John Major asking for his personal intervention. Following John Smith's death, the Prime Minister, from the floor of the House, had paid tribute to his memory and had called for "less confrontation, more decency" in British political life. Would not then the most fitting tribute to John Smith's memory and the most practical way of embracing political decency be for the Prime Minister to respond to John's condemnation – only hours before he died – of the shocking behaviour used to obstruct progress on the Civil Rights (Disabled Persons) Bill? This could most effectively be done by advising the five MPs who had tabled wrecking amendments to withdraw them so that the Bill could proceed to the House of Lords when its Report Stage resumed on 20 May. "You know how strongly John felt about the Bill," he wrote, "and that, much to their honour, scores of Conservative MPs have given the Bill strong backing. It has a clear parliamentary majority in its favour and an even more emphatic majority of the British people. For it to be blocked again... would be a shocking further affront to political decency".

But when the Bill came back on 20 May, the amendments trundled on, and on, and on, and this despite the fact that Roger Berry and others tried to take a short cut by accepting them. Nicholas Scott, at length, set out the Government's position, which in essence was that they now wanted legislation in this area, *but not this legislation*. He underlined the Government's opposition to seeing the present Bill reach the Statute Book, but nevertheless stressed his personal commitment to ensuring that there was " a proper, new legal framework, in particular to protect disabled people in employment". The Government would consult on this over the following six months.

With discussion uncompleted, and with the bulk of the Bill's supporters attending John Smith's funeral in Scotland, the House divided – Ayes 28, Noes 1. As the Deputy Speaker immediately pointed out, this was short of the 40 Members who needed to be present for the Bill to proceed. Among a fusillade of points of order, Alf took the opportunity to make it clear that the campaign for a Bill that had been with Parliament for two and a half years since he first published it in December 1991 would go on for as long as it took to win full citizenship for Britain's disabled people.

The last rites on the Bill, belatedly, involved Ms Lady Olga Maitland. On 25 May, Madam Speaker announced that the hon. Member had written to her to say she was "anxious to accept personal responsibility for the amendments in her name, and that she did not intend to imply that they had not been drafted by others in the first instance". I cannot accept, Madam Speaker went on, that the words "it would be totally unfair to suggest that they came from any other source" did not amount to a denial that the amendments had been drafted by others. At the time the hon. Member volunteered her disclaimer, the House had already been told that the amendments had been drafted by the Government's own parliamentary counsel. Her statement did not so much mislead the House as exasperate it. In this respect, said Madam Speaker, I believe that the statement fell below the standards that the House is entitled to expect from its Members. I strongly rebuke her for her conduct on that occasion. Ms Maitland rose to respond: "In the light of your statement, Madam Speaker, may I make an unreserved apology to you and the House?"[13]

Sadly and most unjustly, however, the Government's strategy had succeeded. It was a shameful episode, so much so that in an article in *The Sunday Times*, Alf commented that in thirty years at Westminster, he had witnessed only four personal statements of unreserved apology for misleading the House of Commons, three of them concerning his Civil Rights (Disabled Persons) Bill.[14] Nevertheless, it was clear that due to manifest foul play the Bill could not now proceed.

[13] This episode is recounted in Betty Boothroyd's autobiography (Century, 2001)., p.202.
[14] *The Sunday Times*, 12 June 1994.

Two new Bills run side by side

The final lap of this epic marathon need not detain us overlong, remarkable though it was. Harry Barnes (Labour, Derbyshire North East), successful in the 1994 private members' ballot, reintroduced Alf's Bill yet again on 14 December 1994, only to find its Second Reading overtaken by the Government's own Disability Discrimination Bill. Limping from a series of self-inflicted wounds in its efforts to stop such legislation reaching the Statute Book, John Major's Government had finally capitulated, unable to bear the continued embarrassment of resisting disabled people's clamour for civil rights and the political damage that it was doing to them. It represented, said Tony Newton, then Leader of the House, "the Government's view of the best way to make sensible, practical and realistic progress towards an aim that we all share".[15] William Hague, the latest and – in Maria Eagle's view – by far the most humane in a long line of Conservative Ministers for Disabled People, moved the Second Reading of the Disability Discrimination Bill on 24 January 1995. Described by Harry Barnes as "wholly inadequate" and "seriously flawed",[16] it was nevertheless obvious that it would prevail over a private member's bill.

Notwithstanding this, it was ruled that the two Bills were sufficiently incompatible for both to proceed, so that for some months both ran a parallel parliamentary course. But Hague had made it clear from the outset that the Government intended to ensure that their Bill became law. They believed it would be more effective in ending discrimination against disabled people and Hague was emphatic that they would not provide any additional parliamentary time for the revived Civil Rights (Disabled Persons) Bill beyond that which would arise in the normal course of events. Thus the writing was on the wall for its demise.

At its Second Reading, the Government's Disability Discrimination Bill survived (by 307 votes to 280) an amendment by Tom Clarke (Labour, Monklands West). This set out a depressing catalogue of the Bill's inadequacies and, had it succeeded, would have denied a Second Reading on the grounds that it was not an acceptable or

---

[15] *Hansard*, Commons, 12 January 1995.
[16] *Hansard*, Commons, 24 January 1995.

enforceable measure to ensure civil rights for all disabled people. Clarke pointed out that the Bill's employment provisions would extend to less than five per cent of firms; failed to provide for a comprehensive definition of disability or for a Disability Rights Commission to work towards the elimination of discrimination; specifically excluded access to the means of public transport; and failed to make discrimination in the sale and letting of premises unlawful.

The Civil Rights (Disabled Persons) Bill, however, also secured a Second Reading (175/0), and continued to progress in tandem with the Government's Bill. It was given the support of a money resolution and successfully completed its committee stage against Government opposition. But when it eventually came back to the House on 14 July, Alistair Burt, by then the new Minister for Disabled People, reaffirmed the Government's opposition. Consideration was adjourned at 2.30 p.m. and no further time was allowed. It had been a lingering but inevitable death.

Yet it marked an epic achievement, one the story of which should be required reading for anyone parroting the tale that parliamentarians in opposition can achieve nothing.

The Tory Disability Discrimination Bill becomes law

By contrast, the much-criticised Disability Discrimination Bill went on to cross the line of Royal Assent on 8 November. The embattled Conservative Government, as Maria Eagle was to comment nine years later, "had been dragged kicking and screaming to put partial and inadequate legislation on the Statute Book...at a time when their majority was crumbling and the demand for action was growing".[17] "For 16 of their last 18 years in office they did regrettably little when they had the power to change disabled people's lives". They had repeatedly squandered the opportunity to build on Alf's work in the 1970s to enable Britain to go on leading the world on disability civil rights.[18] "The Act was a landmark but a minimalist one with lots of omissions and sections they had no intention of bringing into effect: a start, not an end. Present day

---

[17] Maria Eagle, Minister for Disabled People, *Hansard*, Commons, 10 June 2004, cols.423 and 425.
[18] Maria Eagle, *Hansard*, Commons, 23 March 2005.

Tories would like to forget all this and take credit for having introduced anti-discrimination legislation, whereas what they handed down when they left office was really a disgrace".[19] The most serious omission was the failure to create a Disability Rights Commission. It was, as Alf remarked later, "like a car without an engine".

Nonetheless, despite its imperfections, the Disability Discrimination Act 1995 could be, and was, built upon.[20] Thirteen long years after Jack Ashley's short Bill of 1982, Alf's parliamentary skill and legendary persistence had paid off, bringing embryonic rights for disabled people onto the Statute Book. Looking back on those long, cold years, Karen Buck (Labour, Regent's Park and Kensington North) saw Alf's survival at the forefront of disability politics – despite a hostile administration and the militant agitation of some sections of the disability movement – as a tribute to his steadfast sense of purpose: "If you're not faith-driven in your politics I think you will get blown off course. And this is back to the fact that Alf and his family are quite remarkable in where they have come from and what they've achieved. He has always been a gritty, down-to-earth socialist – which doesn't apply to all members of the Labour party then or now. He is a very rooted man in his own sense of person, but his guiding light has always been socialism: *delivered socialism*, not philosophical socialism, but socialism none the less".[21]

Alf's elected to presidency of the Co-operative Congress

Alf does not dispute this verdict, but adds that indivisible from his socialism has been his lifetime commitment as a Co-operator. In 1969 he had commended his Chronically Sick and Disabled Persons Bill to the House of Commons as "a practical expression of the social philosophy of the Co-operative Movement". And in 1995 that commitment was recognised by an honour especially dear to his heart: his election as President of the Co-operative Congress, the movement's highest elective office. Speaking in that role at the

---

[19] Interview, 14 October 2004.
[20] Notably, in the Labour years, the Disability Rights Commission Act 1999, the Special Educational Needs and Disabilities Act 2001, the regulations that became operative on 1 October 2004, and the Disability Discrimination Act 2005 which, like Alf's Chronically Sick and Disabled Persons Act 1970, received the Royal Assent on the last day of Parliament before a General Election.
[21] Interview, 4 October 2004.

Co-operative Congress of that year, under the title 'Daring to Care', he asked how many people outside the Co-operative Movement knew that it had 140,000 employees; that its turnover in 1994 in retail trade alone was £7.5 billion; that in the same year 40 per cent of households visited its stores; that it retained 18 per cent of the milk market; that it was the market leader in travel and funerals and Britain's biggest farmer; and that the Co-operative Insurance Society insured four million families? How many people knew of the striking successes of The Co-operative Bank or the Movement's highly successful involvement in the motor trade? Business, however, was invariably linked with practical social concern: improvements in environmental protection, help for homeless people and for the world's poor, achievements in legislating for consumer care, the example set in ethical trading standards, and the social responsibility that local co-operative societies showed in caring for the most needful people in their communities, demonstrating, day by day, that theirs was a movement with a heart.

Alf used this important occasion to face his audience with a new challenge, one that remains with us today. What role, he asked, could the Co-operative Movement play in tackling the undoubted scandal of over-priced provision, often of dubious quality, of respite and longer-term care for elderly and other vulnerable people in pressing need of such care? Could co-operators help to end the scandal and find a co-operative way between rapidly declining public provision and the vast growth of the private sector in a policy area where human values and social concern should come first? Medicine and science had enabled many people to live much longer than their parents and grandparents. But sadly, for many, there was a price to pay for longevity: that of frailty, chronic illness or disability. Thus here we were not looking at the problems of other people, but our own future prospects. While no Government could provide total funding to cope with this demographic explosion, current policies offered only "an inexorable march toward total privatisation". Even the cherished concept of care in the community was failing through cuts, capping and "the triumph of ideology over humanity". Many people, said Alf, were better off in the community, but care in the community was now too often seen by policy-makers as a way to save money and evade responsibility. It was now left largely to charities and self-help groups to provide services for them, but there was a strict limit on what they could provide and increasingly the cost burden fell upon the individual. Not least those needing to move into residential care who, having paid national insurance and taxes, local and national, all their working lives, now found themselves forced to sign away their homes to pay for their care. It was hardly surprising, said Alf, that they felt grossly betrayed. There was a crying need for not-for-profit care (best of all co-operative care) providing care at an affordable price and delivered from a sense of service, moral purpose and humane commitment.

Alf closed by reflecting on the fact that, although the beginning of the co-operative movement could hardly have been smaller, it had inspired a world following reflecting man's humanity to man. He urged present members to take a renewed pride in their history, firm and steadfast in support of their ideals, confident in their future and ever more strongly committed to a Co-operative Movement vision of enduring and inestimable value to humankind.

It fell to Tom Philbin to move a vote of thanks and present Alf with a Lowry. Tom was very much a contemporary of Alf's, and both came from Newton Heath. When Alf was at Brookdale Park School, Tom was at St Bede's Catholic High School. It was natural, therefore, for him to reminisce about their school years. Alf, he recalled, had then been the bane of his life. He had made his life hell. Why? Because Tom's mother was always saying, "Why can't you be like Alf Morris? He brings our papers round at six o'clock in the morning while you're still in bed; then goes off to do another round. And when I get to the market, just when you're getting ready for school, who is at the front of the queue but Alf Morris? And then, when school is over, he is round here delivering our *Manchester Evening News*, while at weekends you will find him stacking the shelves of the Co-op store in Ten Acres Lane. And what do you do?" Apparently neither Tom nor his mother had attempted an answer to that one.

The 1970 Act honoured

The year 1995 was also the 25th anniversary of the passing of the Chronically Sick and Disabled Persons Act, an occasion marked by a RADAR publication, *Be It Enacted*. The anniversary prompted an adjournment debate in the Commons, led by Tom Clarke. Describing Alf as "a giant among pygmies when we discuss disability", he praised the 1970 Act as the foundation stone of everything achieved for disabled people in the subsequent 25 years: "If we now argue about disabled people's rights and how to outlaw discrimination rather than debating whether disability discrimination exists, that is largely because of the achievements of the Act that we are debating today". Of all the effects of that Act, he said, none was more important than the change in status of disabled people in society, in their own eyes and those of the community as a whole. In the past 25 years, more than in any other period of human history, disabled people had become able to advance their own interests and aspirations to the point where the pressure for full civil rights was unstoppable. There had been delays and obstacles along the way, but a single continuous thread joined the 1970 Act to the now successful civil rights campaigns of the past three years. On that basis, Tom Clarke concluded, "I ask the House to join in celebrating 25 years of growing recognition of the rights of disabled people. I ask hon. Members to join me in applauding the Act of Parliament that made that possible" They must now, he said, make the celebration of the 'Alf Morris Act' the launching pad for a further new chapter in the story of the emancipation of disabled people in this country, "to stand for ever as a beacon to the rest of the world".

The new Minister for Disabled People, Alistair Burt, while insisting that the Conservative Government also deserved credit for the achievements of the past 25 years, added his "genuine" tribute to the first holder of the office, the right hon. Member for Manchester, Wythenshawe.

Alf at this point looked back not only on 25 years since the enactment of his seminal Private Member's Bill but on over 30 years as a Member of Parliament. He began in conciliatory mood. Many of those most honoured in his gallery of old and trusted friends had laboured with him to enact his Bill in 1970. They were not all of one party. They were of all parties, but of one mind. What had united them, he said, was the shared determination that Parliament must no longer ignore the rightful claims of long-term sick and disabled people, who must be free to live their own lives as normally as possible, to have the same opportunities to contribute to industry and society as everyone else, and live under laws based on rights and not charity. Twenty-five years on, the task was not just to assess the Act's impact and take stock, but also to address the issues still facing Parliament on a long, unfinished agenda of unmet need among disabled people. The best way of marking this anniversary would be to vouchsafe full and enforceable rights to disabled people. "In continued fellowship with them," he concluded, "let that remain our urgent goal".[22]

Alf contemplates retirement

By the mid-1990s the government of John Major was deeply unpopular. Like Micawber, but more so, he was carrying on in the hope that something would turn up. None the less, although Alf could look forward to a higher than ever majority in his Wythenshawe seat, he decided in 1995 not to contest another General Election. He had by then been an MP for 31 years and was 67 years old. He was beginning to feel the wear and tear of being probably the most travelled person ever between London and Manchester. Quite often he was travelling the route in both directions not once but twice and even, sometimes, three times a week. Wythenshawe was a very challenging constituency to serve and he had also been on Labour's front bench for 23 of his years in Parliament, in and out of government. Since 1991, when he published his Civil Rights (Disabled Persons) Bill, he had been involved in what amounted to trench warfare in attempting to end years of inaction by Conservative Ministers on the recommendations of the CORAD Report. Although that particular tide was turning, he felt that already he was not doing things as effectively as before for the people he represented. A slipped disc had left him with spinal damage requiring surgical treatment and the certainty of life-long dependence on pain killers; and he knew too that his problems

---

[22] *Hansard*, Commons, 19 October 1995, cols. 552-92.

could get worse. Throughout his time in the Commons, Alf had always made it a rule to be available at any time rather than taking defensive measures to preserve a private life: *"People don't hesitate to contact you at any hour of the day and on any day of the year if they have what they regard as an urgent problem. If you are prepared to accept their entitlement to do so as part of the job it does you no harm electorally. Whereas if people say 'I was in deep trouble and just didn't know where to find him' it doesn't do your reputation any good at all".*

But to be constantly at everyone's beck and call can be very wearing. Alf realised that success at the next election, then two years ahead, would mean being 74 by the end of the parliamentary term. He was, in short, minded to ease up and retire to Manchester where his family roots remained and which he and Irene have always regarded as their home place. It had not been by choice that he had maintained a presence in London as well as Manchester; they were places of work as well as of housing accommodation and a necessity if he was both to represent the constituency properly and have a base from which to perform effectively in Parliament.

In keeping with a then quite new parliamentary trend, some colleagues who were 'in the know' did not want him to announce his intention to stand down until near to the date of the next election: *"I acted, however, in fairness to the constituency I had been representing for over 30 years and, more especially, to give those who had chosen me time and again as their parliamentary candidate, the opportunity to select my successor without being rushed and pressurised. Some people leave it very late, with the result that control over the re-selection process passes into the hands of the party's National Executive. Therein lies the increasing tendency for candidates to be 'parachuted' into safe seats, without much of a say for local people".*

Alf would have none of this, and made it clear well in advance of the next General Election that he would not be standing again. It was announced first in *The Manchester Evening News* in June 1996 and soon after, in the city's *Metro News*, he wrote:

> "I now know that it can be harder to cease being an MP than to become one. Certainly you can find yourself being pressed by many more people to stay than you were at first to start ... Better to leave the fast lane five minutes too

soon, I felt, than the slow lane five years too late...While I look forward to spending more time with my family (not least my six grandchildren), I'll go on doing all I can and for as long as I can for Wythenshawe; to hasten the return of a new Labour government; and for the causes to which I have devoted my parliamentary life".

In 1997, one unforgettable morning in darkest January seemed to confirm the soundness of Alf's decision. As he was dressing, stooping to buckle a shoe, he suddenly collapsed on the bedroom floor and lay there in excruciating pain, unable to move. Irene found him there and phoned the local health centre, only to find that at that time of the year, in deep midwinter, the practice was under intense pressure. Alf lay in agony for over two hours before medical help arrived. The doctor gave him valium tablets and injected cortisone and, with Irene's help, managed to get him onto the bed. He fell asleep almost immediately and was still lost to the world when the phone rang three hours or so later. It was the Opposition Whips' Office checking that Alf would be in the House at 10 o'clock that evening for a three-line whip on a "crucial vote"!

Irene said that she was afraid that this would be impossible and recounted the events of the day. What she was saying, the Whip responded, was that they needed to send a long vehicle so that Alf could be brought to the House lying down? "No," said Irene, "what I'm saying is that he can't make it at all. It would be refined cruelty to expect it". But the upshot was that an estate car came and Alf was taken, still in pain and barely conscious, to Palace Yard for his vote to be registered. The rules of the House were that, in order to be "nodded through" by his Chief Whip and counted, the Member had to be within the precincts of Parliament at the time of the vote. The late Donald Dewar, then the Opposition Chief Whip, and his Conservative counterpart, came down to identify him and confirm his presence in the precincts. Alf remembers that on seeing the Conservative Whip, as the car window came down, he inquired "What do you want? Is it to ask me about your pension?" his customary response when Members buttonholed him in his capacity as Chairman of the Managing Trustees of the Parliamentary Contributory Pension Fund. Alf recalls little else about that astonishing evening but Irene was told later that, with a General Election in the offing, his vote had made a vital difference.

If these were cold years in a political sense, they were also notoriously cold for older people in real terms. There were nights as bitterly cold as any in living memory during the winter of 1996–97. Under the Government's strict rules, however, special 'cold weather payments' to Britain's elderly poor people (£8.50 a week) could be triggered only if the temperature had been or was forecast to be at freezing point or below for at least seven days together. This exact formula, rigorously applied, took no account of the wind chill factor or that pneumonia might result from exposure to extreme cold on a single day, although experts were clearly saying that ignoring it involved many elderly people in the added risk of hypothermia. In *The Manchester Evening News*, Alf inveighed against the inhumanity of Government policy. The Ministerial response to the urgent plea for more help to heat the homes of Britain's old people had simply been to say that the system was being reviewed. But, wrote Alf, the old and cold were dying there and then. The compelling need was for action, not leisurely reviews. While the Minister stalled, more and more older people were striving to cope with preventable suffering, and this was something that deserved to be remembered by everyone who cared about social decency.[23]

If this was an ill-wind for old folk, it shook a Government already on the ropes and facing the prospect of defeat when they went to the country. It was a time for Labour optimism and high hopes for an end to eighteen years of Conservative rule. But for Alf personally it was a difficult period. Through the run up to the General Election, he was increasingly afflicted by severe lumbar spasms. His spinal damage now involved 'referred pain' in both of his legs. Nothing much could be done about the spinal damage itself, but he had two surgical operations to cut and burn away nerve fibres that were causing the pain referral. To make matters worse, one of the painkillers he had been prescribed led to intestinal damage, revealing two duodenal ulcers. It was quick-acting and powerful enough as a painkiller to allow him to get through a parliamentary speech, but seriously damaging in its side effects. Alf became visibly

---

[23] *Manchester Evening News*, 24 January 1997.

ill, tired and weak. The disturbing results of a blood test, followed by other tests, revealed that there had been insidious internal bleeding. All but one of the painkillers he had been using had to be dropped. He had to rely – and continues to rely – on what the doctors call 'minimal pain management'.

Constraints on community care: the Gloucestershire judgement

Alf now had time to reflect. His Mobility Allowance, Severe Disablement Allowances and the Carer's Allowance were going to more people than ever before; a beginning had been made towards giving disabled people legal rights to social equality, and the Chronically Sick and Disabled Persons Act remained on the Statute Book as a blue-print for further progress. Indeed Section 2 of the Act, one of the pillars of his parliamentary achievement (of which there had been more than twenty million beneficiaries since 1970) had been reinforced. It now required local authorities to assess the needs of disabled people who appeared in need of community care services and to decide whether they called for the provision of services under that section. Moreover, since 1986, disabled people or their carers were able to *require* a local authority to undertake such an assessment and decision. In theory, disabled people were now in a much stronger position, both in securing an assessment of their needs for aids and adaptations and having those identified needs met. Indeed, with official endorsement of the concept that disabled people should be helped to live in the community, the outlook – at least 'on paper' – seemed far more hopeful.

Alf knew, however, that the reality was somewhat different. Community care in all its aspects was then tightly constrained within inadequate budgets. Back on 19 October 1995, in the debate to mark the 25th anniversary of the Chronically Sick and Disabled Persons Act, he had drawn attention to the pressing need to defend the services it had introduced. Powerful voices were already asking for more "flexibility" in applying the Act, by which they meant the right to dilute its provisions. Council leaders of all parties said that the Government's rationing of resources was turning them into lawbreakers by forcing them to choose which of their legal duties to fulfil. Studies suggested that cash-strapped councils were finding it more and more difficult to meet their statutory duties to disabled people. The Act's benefits, Alf had said, were clearly not reaching many disabled people in the way intended by Parliament; and there was intense concern among them about the absence of any clear commitment from the Government to honour the statutory responsibilities on them imposed by the Act. Why should disabled people so often have to resort to court action, and why did Ministers allow some councils to play cat and mouse with them by deferring assessments of need, thus delaying the provision of services even where urgent help was demonstrably necessary? Disabled people and their organisations were complaining bitterly that the provisions of Section 2 were being trampled on in many parts of the country.[24]

In March 1997, with a General Election and Alf's retirement as an MP only weeks away, these matters came to a head with a legal set-back that threatened to undermine the very foundations of community care provision. The problem began with an individual complaint. Michael Barry, an elderly, disabled man living in Gloucestershire, had been assessed in 1992 as needing a number of basic services, which his county council then duly provided. But two years later the council wrote to Mr Barry regretting that they would no longer be able to meet his full needs as assessed because the financial support provided by central government had been reduced and the council's resources were "nowhere near enough" to meet demand. Dissatisfied, Mr Barry and others similarly affected in Gloucestershire began proceedings for a judicial review, and were successful in securing a declaration that the council had acted unlawfully in withdrawing services provided under Section 2 of the Chronically Sick and Disabled Persons Act solely on the basis that it had exhausted available resources. But the court also held that *when assessing* the needs of a particular individual a council must balance that person's needs against the needs of others and its available resources. The effect of this was to prompt the council to reassess some 1,500 disabled people receiving services under Section 2, of whom 440 lost their provision. The potential repercussions for the rest of the country were truly alarming.

[24] *Hansard*, Commons, 19 October 1995, col.588.

Michael Barry appealed against the court's ruling on the balancing of needs and resources in the making of assessments and in 1996 the Court of Appeal, by a majority, found not only that the council had breached its duty in withdrawing services from Mr Barry but also that, in assessing or reassessing whether it was necessary to make arrangements to meet a disabled person's needs, a local authority was *not* entitled to take account of the availability of resources.

It was a verdict that those wanting a fair deal for disabled people thought right and just. But Gloucestershire County Council, jointly with the Conservative Secretary of State for Health, appealed to the House of Lords, where the Law Lords, by a narrow majority of three to two, reversed the Appeal Court's decision. They held that when assessing and reassessing a chronically sick or disabled person's needs, a local authority was entitled to take into account the impact the costs of providing the necessary services would have on its resources.

It was a great blow. Leading authorities on social policy legislation could not come to terms with the judgement. They saw it as totally in conflict with Parliament's original intention in approving the Act. In this they were most eloquently supported by the opinion of Lord Lloyd of Berwick, one of the minority two. His reasoning was impeccable. He observed that the failure of central government to provide funds necessary to enable the council to carry out its statutory duty departed from "the fine words" contained in its White Paper *Caring for People: Community Care in the Next Decade and Beyond* (1989). Without such funds the council was in an impossible position. Even if it wanted to raise the necessary money it could not do so because the government had imposed rate-capping. Need, he pointed out, is not the same as want. Need is the lack of what is essential for the ordinary business of living. Resources can [and did] operate to impose a cash limit on what was provided. But the idea that resources could help to measure need, he contended, was a fallacy. It could not have been Parliament's intention that a local authority should be able to say, "because we do not have enough resources, we are going to reduce your needs". Every child, he said, needs a new pair of shoes from time to time. The need is not the less because his parents cannot afford them. Simply looking at the legislation was enough to show that Parliament did not intend that provision for the needs of disabled people should depend on the availability of resources. The intention, Lord Lloyd concluded, was to treat disability as a special case.

Nor, he said, should needs be assessed differently in different parts of the country; still less because some local authorities had suffered more than others on account of variations in central government funding. Parliament could not have intended that the standards and expectations for measuring the needs of disabled people in Bermondsey should differ from those in Belgrave Square. The passing of the Act of 1970 had been a noble aspiration. Having willed the end, Parliament must be asked to provide the means.

Fortunately, in the longer term and with a change of Government, the Law Lords majority ruling did not generally play well among those committed to the advancement of community care and the social well being of disabled people. Lack of resources had always restricted provision, but it was quite another thing to argue that such limitations should also impact upon the assessment of need. Lord Lloyd's opinion was in tune with those who wanted to press ahead with a positive agenda that looked to find the necessary funding and give disabled people maximum independence. Many local authorities simply ignored the Law Lords' ruling and, as we shall see, a Government statement eventually restored the *status quo*.

An historical perspective

Now, 37 years on from the enactment of the Chronically Sick and Disabled Persons Act, it is possible to view progress in implementing Section 2 in a clearer historical perspective. The reality is that through successive governments provision has dramatically improved. It has included practical help in the home of the disabled person, the supply of personal aids and equipment, help with telephones and other communications equipment, television and radio, holidays, adaptations to property and the provision of purpose-built housing. Statistics are incomplete, but a reasonable estimate would suggest that the provisions of Section 2 have so far helped more than 20 million long-term sick and disabled people in Britain. Although the question of financial resources and who can or should foot the bill has never been free from controversy, the

Chronically Sick and Disabled Persons Act has come to be accepted philosophically and its objectives perceived – here and across the world – as the mark of a civilised society on which all subsequent disability legislation has been built. A distinguished French legislator, himself disabled, described its enactment as "un moment critique" for disabled people everywhere, setting an agenda for the most neglected social policy area world-wide. It was by common consent an example to the world and quickly became a model for the legislation of many other countries. Because of it, Alf became recognised, throughout this and other countries, as the champion of disabled people.

In the Commons he had come to be acknowledged as its leader on disability issues, and he left, as Lewis Carter-Jones once put it, as the undisputed captain of our disability team. The forthcoming General Election would bring to power his own party, with new blood committed to taking his enduring mission forward. And although he did not know it, Alf himself stood on the threshold of yet another fresh challenge.

1995: Alf, as President of the Co-operative Congress, with Irene.

2000: Speaker's House, Palace of Westminster. Celebration of Irene and Alf's Golden Wedding.

2001: Canberra. Presentation of the Charter for the Third Millennium to John Howard, Prime Minister of Australia, in his room in the Parliament building.

1995: Speech as President of the Co-operative Congress (with Lloyd Wilkinson, long-serving General Secretary of the Co-operative Union).

Chapter 14

THE OTHER PLACE

1997–2006

"...with a House of Peers composed exclusively of people of intellect, what's to become of the House of Commons?"

W.S.Gilbert, Iolanthe (Act II, Lord Mountararat)

– The phoenix – Playing by the rules – The dead hand of tradition – Settling in
– The role of the Lords – A new Charter – Saudi-Arabia – Friends and allies
– The 30th anniversary of the 1970 Act: a time to take stock – Golden wedding
– A gap in provision: the right to read – Food labelling – War pensions
– Informal carers – A timely reminder of the need to be ready for natural disasters
– New anti-discrimination legislation – Audrey and Jim Callaghan leave the scene
– Alf welcomes moves towards a wider concept of equality – Estelle Morris
– Lifetime achievement – Alf's values confirmed.

The phoenix

At the beginning of 1997, Alf's decision to retire from public life seemed well taken and irrevocable. In the General Election of that year (which initially brought such hope that the long, cold years were over), he was succeeded as Wythenshawe's[1] Labour MP by Paul Goggins, who, in his maiden speech on 20 May, set the seal on Alf's long and distinguished career in the Commons. He told the House that, although then 20 years older than the youngest Member, he had still been at primary school when Alf Morris was first elected to Parliament. Recalling some of Alf's achievements in the subsequent 33 years, he characterised him as having "always been a tireless campaigner for disability rights and equality and, indeed, for all his constituents". *The Times*, in October 1996, had contrasted Alf's "Quiet altruism and dogged persistence" with the "sharp young blades at the Labour Party Conference". Members on both sides of the House, he said, would agree that Alf Morris was in every sense a gentle man, but he was also "a considerable blade in his own right". In Wythenshawe, he concluded, Alf was respected

---

[1] By then Wythenshawe and Sale, East.

for his political contribution. But, above all, people there loved him as their friend and champion.[2]

To say that a politician was "loved" was a rare and remarkable tribute. One to which Sir George Young added: "If the hon. Gentleman [Goggins] does as well as Alf Morris did in representing his constituents, he will have done very well indeed".[3] On another occasion, near to the same date, Sir George said of Alf: "Half the people of this country think he's still the Minister for Disabled People – and the other half wish he was!"

Apparently the curtain had now fallen on Alf's parliamentary career. He did not expect, or think, that he would be offered a life peerage: there are always more candidates – not to mention the volunteers – than places and Alf had never behaved as a candidate. And when, in the summer of 1997, he was invited to serve in the House of Lords, he was faced with both a surprise and a dilemma. By then he was coping somewhat better with his health problems, more his old self after a rest and tempted by the opportunity to watch over, at close quarters, what was happening to all the legislation he had introduced and prompted in his 33 years in the Commons. He felt that he still had a great deal to contribute, but hesitated, talking it over with Irene and family members, reflecting on the implications of accepting a peerage on the planned farewell to London. All of his family, while mindful also of his daily experience of pain, realised that accepting would enable Alf to 'keep his hand in' parliamentarily, yet have freedom in future to choose the level of his involvement. There are, according to Alf, five types of peer: the peer, the allegedly working peer, the working peer, the workaholic peer and the dead peer. So he knew the score. Eventually he decided to accept the singular opportunity that was being presented by a New Labour Prime Minister to an Old Labour parliamentarian.

Playing by the rules

There is, of course, a paradox in the process of entering either House of Parliament: the requirement to conform to the ancient orthodoxy of the Establishment. None more so, perhaps, than The Speaker

---

[2] *Hansard*, Commons, 20 May 1997, col.586.
[3] *Hansard*, Commons, 20 May 1997, col.595.

who, having been elected to that position by the Commons, must present himself to the Royal Commissioners in the Lords and submit himself "with all humility to Her Majesty's gracious Approbation" and "with all humility and gratitude to Her Majesty's gracious Commands".[4] Alf, likewise, on 27 October 1997, was perforce expected to accept the traditional flummery of a formal introduction to the House as a condition of membership. Wearing a borrowed robe, he entered the Chamber of the House of Lords – as all new peers do – from the Moses Room, flanked by his good friends Lord Ashley and Lord Rix. From whence they processed past the Opposition benches to the Table to hear the Queen's statement of conferral read by a senior clerk of the House and to affirm allegiance. Then on, past the Government front bench, to the Woolsack to shake hands with Lord Irvine, the Lord Chancellor, and out past the Throne to the Prince's Gallery.[5]

There was also the question of title. Alf's preference was to be known as Lord Morris of Wythenshawe, but contrary to popular belief the choice is not ultimately a matter for the new peer. They may request, but the decision rests with Garter King of Arms, Head of the College of Heraldry, who, it is believed, felt that Alf's name should be linked to his native city. The decision to make him Lord Morris of Manchester was, perhaps, an unwitting honour, but most unexpected since on a previous occasion another peer who wanted to be 'of Sheffield' had been told by the then Garter King of Arms that only a duke could be assigned in his title the name of a major city!

As part of a time-honoured but largely irrelevant process, Alf, like all other peers, receives before each session of Parliament a Writ of Summons from the Queen, couched in the most grandiloquent language:

> "To Our right trusty and well beloved Counsellor Alfred Morris of Manchester in Our County of Greater Manchester Chevalier Greeting. WHEREAS by the advice and assent of Our Council for certain arduous and urgent affairs concerning Us the state and defence of Our United

---

[4] *Hansard*, Lords, 12 May 2005, cols. 3-4.
[5] Since Alf's introduction to the Lords, over 500 hereditary peers have been excluded from the House and the ceremony for introducing new peers has been shortened and modified.

Kingdom and the Church We have ordered a certain Parliament to be holden at Our City of Westminster.... and there to treat and have conference with the Prelates Great Men Great Women and Peers of Our Realm We strictly enjoining COMMAND you upon the faith and allegiance by which you are bound to Us that the weightiness of the said affairs and imminent perils considered (waiving all excuses) you be at the said day and place personally present with Us and with the said Prelates Great Men Great Women and Peers to treat and give your counsel upon the affairs aforesaid And this as you regard Us and Our honour and the safety and defence of the said Kingdom and Church and dispatch of the said affairs in nowise do you omit".

The dead hand of tradition

Alf is very much of the view that the ceremonial in the Lords – in which the Commons remains inextricably involved – impedes progress in the name of tradition. Back in the 60s, as we have noticed, he questioned whether the Government would introduce legislation to extinguish, over time, hereditary peerages and/or deny hereditary peers the right to sit in the legislature. He had made no secret of the fact that for him the ultimate absurdity was the State Opening of Parliament, a ceremony that, as even one former monarch admitted, "celebrates an authority long extinct",[6] indelibly associated in many minds with the noisome odour of mothballs and perfume. For over three decades he had trooped into the Lords with Mr Speaker and other MPs, standing to hear Elizabeth II having to call the Prime Minister's prose the 'Queen's Speech' – a ludicrous charade completely at odds with government of, by and for the people and the aspiration some years ago to 'modernise the monarchy'.

Settling in

None of the cherished rituals, pomp and pageantry of the House of Lords has changed Alf. He and Irene remain unpretentious. His

[6] *A King's Story* (G.P.Putnam's Sons, New York, 1947), p.323. In the same chapter HRH Edward, Duke of Windsor has described how, when as King Edward VIII he opened Parliament on 3 November 1936, he found his senses suddenly assailed by an almost suffocating odor of mothballs...The smell was nauseating...!.

title, of course, goes with the job and there are conventions within the House of Lords that confer an automatic deference to peers. But none of this finds much favour with him. He comes and goes, mostly by train and bus, with his simple canvas bag, and recognises that while there is a place for respect it needs to be born of merit and commitment rather than rank.

Alf, who was to become very much a working – not to say workaholic – peer was soon allotted room 31 on the second floor, west front of the House of Lords, formerly used by Cledwyn Hughes and now shared with Baroness (Elizabeth) Smith of Gilmorehill, widow of the late John Smith, Labour's revered former Leader. Working in this room, within close range of the periodic chiming of Big Ben and facing vast arched windows of stained glass, gives a sense of being encased in antiquity (though in reality that part of the building dates only from 1845). It was to become the unlikely nerve centre for the continuity of Alf's guerrilla campaigns to seek redress for the unfortunate victims of unnatural disasters. His maiden speech on 15 December 1997 came during a debate on dyslexia, an appropriate contribution in that his Chronically Sick and Disabled Persons Act 1970 had been the first-ever statute to legislate on dyslexia in Britain or any other country. At that time, he said, one education Minister – known to be concerned about the cost of his proposal – had told Alf of his department's finding, based on extensive research in Britain and abroad, that dyslexia simply did not exist. He had thus been found guilty in quick succession not only of "thinking the unthinkable and speaking the unspeakable" (by Richard Crossman) but also of "discovering the undiscoverable" by the Minister of State for Education. He revealed to the Lords that he had simply told the Minister that, if he was right to say dyslexia did not exist, then *ipso facto* at least his intention to legislate would not cost the Government anything! Since then, Alf recalled, dyslexia had become very much more widely understood and accepted. The condition that did not exist, he said, was now known to afflict 10 per cent of us to some extent, and for over 2 million children and adults it was still a serious barrier to learning and, sadly, often because assessments came too late. Ending a forthright speech, Alf hoped that, in seeking to make life better for disabled people, not least those with dyslexia, Parliament as a whole could act as one, concerned not only with costs but also human values.

After 33 years in the Commons, it took Alf very little time to get the hang of things in the Lords and to slip easily into his accustomed ways. He continued to play a leading role in two major campaigns in which he had been deeply immersed in the Commons: first to win compensation for people with haemophilia infected with life-threatening viruses by contaminated blood supplied by the NHS; and second, redress for veterans of the first Gulf War who had subsequently developed medically unexplained illnesses. His involvement in these struggles demanded the utmost commitment. Yet he found time for other issues too. On 21 July 1998 he raised the question of the wrought-iron gates that separated Downing Street, and therefore the Prime Minister's London home, from the hurly-burly of Whitehall. Did the Government see any early prospect of the removal of this "temporary" barrier? Lord McIntosh responded that at present, given the range of possible threats to Downing Street, the gates provided the most efficient and cost-effective means of controlling access. Whereupon Alf rose again to remark that this reply was one "up with which at least one former celebrated occupant of no. 10 would not have put". There had been no gates during the Second World War, nor even in 1919 when the police went on strike and marched to the door of the Prime Minister's residence. Moreover, if security gates were so crucially important at one end of the street, why was comparable provision not equally important at the other end? Lord McIntosh, while agreeing with the sentiment of Alf's wish to see the gates come down, said that there was a difference between the front and back of the building: the back was "protected by a considerable flight of steps, which could make access for bombers difficult". Lord McCarthy was astonished. "Is my noble friend saying seriously that assassins cannot run upstairs?" "Not when they are carrying heavy bombs," replied the now beleaguered Lord McIntosh![7]

In November of the same year, the Royal British Legion, of which Alf had been Honorary Parliamentary Adviser since 1989, was dismayed when H. M. Customs & Excise moved to make the Remembrance

---

[7] *Hansard*, Lords, 21 July 1998, col.708.

Day poppy appeal subject to value added tax. The plans threatened to cost the Legion £500,000 and put 150 employees at its poppy factory – mostly disabled ex-servicemen – out of work. Alf promptly approached Gordon Brown, Chancellor of the Exchequer, explaining the devastating effect of the decision. To his eternal credit, Brown was persuaded and on the eve of Remembrance Sunday made it known that Customs & Excise would have to change its decision and, in revising the VAT exemption rules, ensure that charities such as the Legion were not penalised.

The role of the Lords

Being close to Alf over a period of time in the House of Lords brings home not only his own dynamic energy as he attempts to fit a quart of work into an eggcup of time, but also the crucially important role of the House as a whole. There is, undoubtedly, a popular myth that the Lords is a place akin to the sidings in the railway system, where peers in their dotage play out a largely irrelevant role by way of a pastime. The truth, in large degree, is now precisely to the contrary. For it is in the Lords that accumulated expertise and experience can be brought quickly to bear on the issues of the day, where distinguished figures from the law, medicine, the armed services and other professions or, like Alf, parliamentarians seasoned in the Commons, can contribute long parliamentary experience and from it their accrued wisdom and insight. By that measure, the Lower House, even including many with ministerial office, may be regarded as the resort of novices, not least by people who observe both Houses at work at close quarters. As one correspondent observed in a letter to *The Guardian*:

> "In watching the Lords, I have never before witnessed such consistent quality of thought and reasoned debate over such a long period... Then I saw the Commons debate, with its infantile name-calling, puerile attempts to score political points and the barefaced mendacity of the Home Secretary. Our so-called representatives spat on the efforts that some of our foremost lawyers, scholars and parliamentarians had made to try to prevent the destruction of our most basic rights to justice".[8]

---

[8] Simon Lyon, referring to the debates on the Terrorism Bill, *The Guardian*, 14 March 2005.

Nor are wisdom and insight the only advantage of the Upper House over the Lower. For whereas democracy is being rapidly eroded in the Commons by the hugely increased time-tabling or 'guillotining' of debates on Bills – now almost as much the order of the day as the Order Paper itself – there is no such constraint in the Lords. Indeed the only way left to bring issues that go undebated in the Commons, due to severe time-tabling, is for amendments about them to be passed in the Lords that will then have to be debated in the Commons.[9] So that much apart from frustrating democracy, amending Government legislation in the Lords is now the only way of unshackling MPs stopped from debating it in the Commons. Alf believes fervently in robust checks and balances on executive power; and antagonistic therefore to the appointment as peers – by any administration – of men and women simply because they who can be relied upon unquestioningly to support Government legislation. *"Rushing measures through the Commons without proper scrutiny and debate to a largely quiescent Lords would certainly expedite business, but it is a perilous parliamentary strategy"*.

A new Charter

But there were matters outside the House to occupy Alf. With the approach of a new century, the beginning of the Third Millennium, the thoughts of Rehabilitation International turned to the desirability of updating its *Charter for the 80s*. A World Planning Group was set up to draft a new charter, and Alf responded to an invitation to chair a distinguished team that included HE Chief Emeka Anyaoku, then Commonwealth Secretary-General; Justin Dart, who formerly chaired the US President's Committee on Employment of People with Disabilities; Deng Pufang, chairman of the China Disabled Persons' Federation; Archbishop Desmond Tutu of South Africa; Ms Jameela Al-Qasimi of the United Arab Emirates; Shri D K Manavalan of India; Anatole Ossadchikh, a Minister of the Russian Federation; Prince Ra'ad bin Zeid of Jordan; Professor Stephen Hawking; and Sir Harry Fang of Hong Kong, a former President of Rehabilitation International.

---

[9] *Hansard*, Lords, 10 February 2005, col.940 (Railways Bill).

The *Charter for the Third Millennium* was approved by the Assembly of Rehabilitation International in London on 9 September 1999, proclaiming the need for action by all humankind in the conviction that every government and all relevant non-governmental and international organisations had a primary responsibility to implement its aims. The previous charter had impacted on the statute books of many countries around the world and, as we have noticed, became the basis for the UN World Programme of Action for the Decade of Disabled Persons. But much remained to be done. The *Charter for the 80s* had been about the importance of providing basic rehabilitation services of the right kind, at the right time and in the right place; full representation for disabled people on all public bodies making decisions affecting their lives; equal opportunities in education and the workplace; a basic income and access to the built environment in a world where most countries still had no disability legislation of any kind. By contrast the new charter concentrated on two compelling priorities: recognition and protection of the basic human and civil rights of the world's over 600 million people with physical, intellectual and sensory disabilities; and the prevention of disability by global immunisation programmes and other strategies. The new charter's central purpose was to translate the vision of human rights for all into a universal reality. It looked to a world where equalisation of opportunity for disabled people would become a natural consequence of enlightened legislation and policies supporting full inclusion in and access to all aspects of society.

On 5 July 2000, the charter, already presented in many countries around the world, was received and welcomed in a ceremony at 10 Downing Street by Britain's Prime Minister, who said that he believed that it would form the basis of a global consensus on priorities for at least the next decade. He later confirmed that this absolutely remained the Government's view; a massive tribute to Alf's achievement in forging the global consensus and to his world standing, indeed pre-eminence now in a policy area – of crucial importance to more than 600 million of the world's most needful people – he had made his own. Prime Minister Tony Blair said his Government would continue to focus on action to take forward their commitment to comprehensive and enforceable civil rights for disabled people in the United Kingdom. This policy, he concluded, presently ensured that the UK was ahead of many other countries in legislating for and promoting civil rights for disabled people.[10] At the charter presentation ceremony on 5 July, the Prime Minister went even further than his parliamentary reply in complimenting Alf, recalling that, 20 years previously, he had chaired the committee that had drafted Rehabilitation International's *Charter for the 80s* that became the basis for the UN World programme of Action for the Decade of Disabled Persons. Thus twice now he had led the world in his chosen field.

What Britain had done in 1995 to counter discrimination against disabled people had been done reluctantly and tardily under intense pressure from Alf's team promoting his Civil Rights (Disabled Persons) Bill, and was far from complete. But the Major Government had at least been brought to acknowledge the need for some legislative steps toward the full inclusion of disabled people in all aspects of society. Of course, some countries still lagged far behind. Neither Rehabilitation International nor Alf were under any illusions on this score. They knew, and made it known world-wide, that disabled children were still routinely excluded from international development programmes. Indeed in a debate on 14 July 2000, Alf and several other peers highlighted disability, more than ever before, as a key development issue. Lord Rix reminded the House that appalling conditions in institutions for disabled people were "sadly commonplace around the world". Mary Robinson, then the UN Human Rights Commissioner, had rightly said in August 1998: "Disabled people frequently live in deplorable conditions owing to the presence of physical and social barriers which prevent their integration into, and full participation in, the community. Millions of children and adults world-wide are segregated and deprived of their rights and are, in effect, living on the margins. This is unacceptable".[11]

---

[10] *Hansard*, Commons, 25 March 2002, cols.618-19w (in response to a question from Gerald Kaufman MP).

[11] *Hansard*, House of Lords, 14 July 2000, cols. 552-74.

This was the context in which the *Charter for the Third Millennium* was presented to the world; not in a spirit of complacency, but in the knowledge that change was desperately needed, and that the first step toward change must be – as it had been in Britain before Alf's Chronically Sick and Disabled Persons Act – a formal recognition of the need both to lift disabled people from poverty and empower them as full citizens.

At the United Nations General Assembly in November 2000 a resolution calling for an international convention on the rights of disabled people, as envisaged in the charter, was adopted. Subsequent action included the establishment of an *ad hoc* committee[12] to consider proposals for an international convention to promote and protect the rights and dignity of disabled people. A convention acceptable to all parties and all countries has been slow to emerge, but as Lord Hunt of Kings Heath acknowledged in January 2006, Alf had provided "inspirational leadership" and had been "pivotal" in helping to make progress.[13]

As well as being the principal author of the new charter, Alf was also one of its most powerful advocates; and it was not to the easiest option available to him that he went to spread its message. Yet he was never so evocative as when, in September 2001, he travelled to West Beirut, only eight days after the terrorist attack on New York's twin towers, to speak at a Rehabilitation International conference of its affiliates, in all 22 of the Arab countries. Shock was in everybody's mind in the wake of an atrocity that traumatised and enraged a complacent America. But there, in Lebanon, he spoke neither of summary revenge nor of fighting a war on terror, but of the need to focus on man's *humanity* to man as expressed in the charter, with its recognition that the knowledge and skills existed to enable all countries to overcome the problems that afflicted their disabled people. Translating the words of the charter into purposeful action, said Alf, could bequeath a precious gift to the new Millennium. His concluding words, cherished all over the Arab world, were *Allah ya'teekum al-airfiyye*! (God is all knowing).

---

[12] Resolution 56/168, December 2001.
[13] *Hansard*, Lords, 12 January 2006, col.296.

Saudi-Arabia

Alf next took the message of the charter to Saudi Arabia, where he was to deliver the keynote speech at a further conference of disabled people from the Arab world held in its capital city Riyadh. The visit was to prove notable as much for Irene Morris as for himself. It was common knowledge that, whatever its record on recognising the rights of disabled people, Saudi Arabia was not noted for progress towards sex equality. Disenfranchised, not allowed to drive, required in public to wear an all-enveloping black dress – the abaya – and segregated from men, Saudi women still lived their lives as second-class citizens. Even serving in shops for the sale of women's clothes was confined to men. Irene knew something of this but was unaware that the strict code of male dominance would apply equally to her as a visitor from England and indeed within the conference itself at which her husband was the keynote speaker.

Their Gulf Air flight was late getting into Riyadh. They were met by a member of the Saudi royal family and driven from the airport post-haste by stretch limousine to the hotel where the conference was to be held. A journey by magic carpet could not have been more comfortable or swift, but even so they had barely three-quarters of an hour before the official opening of the conference.

Irene's account of what followed was punctuated with acknowledgements of the need for tolerance on her part and her wish not to give offence. She found the Saudi people she met extraordinarily hospitable; but for a down-to-earth Mancunian woman – and that is all she ever wants to be seen as – there was a line that could not be crossed:

> "In the middle of our somewhat frenetic preparations, there was a knock on the door and a tall man in a sheikh's outfit – a thobe gown, ghuttera headscarf and rope – said that he had brought me a gift. I thanked him and he told me that his daughter would be with me in a minute or two to show me how to wear it. With time at such a premium I thought that was not my priority of the moment, but the girl soon arrived and unwrapped the parcel, revealing an abaya. She draped the garment around me, covering me

352

from top to toe save for a see-through slit for my eyes. All the time I was thinking, uncharitably, 'hurry up and go, it will be very rude of us to be late'. When she eventually left, I rolled up the dress, returned it to its box, put it in the wardrobe, thinking it to have been offered as a memento of our visit, and got dressed in my own clothes: a mid-length black skirt and a black blouse which I thought would not cause offence.

"With very little time to spare, Alf and I went down the hotel's circular staircase to meet our host, Prince Salman bin Salman, a brother of the Crown Prince at the time, who had worked with Alf when drafting Rehabilitation International's new charter and was presiding over the opening of the international conference. We found a line of sheikhs on one side and abaya-clad women on the other, standing as though on parade. When we got to the bottom of the staircase, they moved in. Alf was escorted away in one direction with the men, and I was shepherded off in another with the women. I was at a loss to understand what was going on, and I could see Alf looking towards me with considerable concern as he was led away. At the same time I sensed discomfort among the women I was left among, and it was explained that the ladies did not sit in the same place in the conference as the men. Then one of them said, "you're not wearing your abaya". I told her that I didn't know I was supposed to wear it; that I thought it was a gift to take home as a souvenir.

"Remarkably – given that the conference was about rights, inclusion and integration – I soon discovered that while the proceedings went on in one hall with hundreds and hundreds of men, most of the females watched the proceedings on closed circuit television in another. Even then they didn't know where to put me. I was placed on a dais at the back of the hall and a screen put round me. I asked if there was a problem, and if so what it was, explaining that I didn't want to sit there having travelled several thousand miles to hear Alf opening the conference. Reluctantly, I was allowed to sit on the back row.

"Next morning, I went downstairs to join a group of European women visitors to the conference who were to visit a museum, and found them all clad in abayas. One of them called to me 'Hello, Irene'. She had sunglasses on in the two inches that showed and I just couldn't recognise her. I thought, I don't know who the heck you are. I'm afraid I still wasn't wearing an abaya. While I didn't want to cause offence, I couldn't see the point. I told them that it wasn't right for me to wear it just because I was from abroad and would consider it disrespectful to their faith and culture for me to do so. Later that day I wanted to have a swim, and went to the reception desk to ask where the pool was. I was told that I must not go there; ladies were not allowed to use the swimming pool. Similarly, meals were taken separately from the men. And when an invitation arrived to visit the home of Prince Salman bin Salman, I was not included.

"I was in Riyadh for four days. Female 'ex-pats' told me that they had to wear the abaya for safety's sake, since you would otherwise be regarded as a loose woman. If you went round the shops without one, you risked being pinched, pestered, spat at and other unpleasant experiences. But I felt safe enough with the people with whom we travelled. I never wore the abaya. Somebody suggested I do so for a laugh. I said I didn't find it funny. I don't now".

Friends and allies

By this time, Alf had established himself in the Lords among colleagues of serious intent and like mind. As in the Commons, he had around him friends and allies brought together by a common interest and shared values; Lords Ashley and Rix, of course, along with the 'mobile bench' of Lady (Davina) Darcy de Knayth and Lady (Sue) Masham from the heady days of the Lords' proceedings on his Chronically Sick and Disabled Persons Bill. Also Lord 'Dickie' Attenborough, with whom Alf had worked closely for the Muscular

Dystrophy Group, to which Dickie gave so much of his time. They had long been special friends. Earl Snowdon, himself disabled by polio, who again had worked with Alf ever since 1969–70, was another close friend. So was the late Lord Holderness, formerly Richard Wood, who, as we have seen, prompted the setting up of RADAR and who spent all his years in the Lords helping other disabled people. When Alf was in hospital in 1997, Richard phoned him every day. Lord Ian McColl, a distinguished doctor and professor of medicine and author of a famous report on the wheelchair service, also shared many of Alf's interests and supported him on a number of issues,[14] as did Lord Walton of Detchant, a former President of the General Medical Council; Lord (Dukie) Hussey, a former officer of the British Limbless Ex-Servicemen's Association; and Lord Clement-Jones, a compensation lawyer very much to the fore in debates on Gulf War illnesses and people with haemophilia infected by contaminated NHS blood products. Colleagues formerly with Alf in the Commons are still very much of his circle – Lord Stanley Clinton-Davis, Lord Barry Jones and Lord Robin Corbett among them – and some still in the Commons – particularly Tom Clarke and Roger Berry. Outside Parliament, Lewis Carter-Jones, who although he retired from the Commons in 1987 continued for some years to chair the British committee of Rehabilitation International and subsequently was a member of the Disablement Services Authority, inevitably kept in close touch with Alf. Lewis had supported him not only by his undeviating backing for the Chronically Sick and Disabled Persons Bill, but also after the Act came into force in working for its full implementation. Alf held him in the highest admiration and his recent death was a grievous loss.

The 30th anniversary of the 1970 Act: a time to take stock

While Alf continued to be involved in a wide range of issues outside disability, the needs and problems of disabled people remained his central focus. Few, if any, parliamentarians could match this undeviating commitment in any policy area. So much so that on one

---

[14] Professor McColl chaired a committee that reviewed the artificial limb and appliance service. Its report in 1986 proposed sweeping changes in the way the service was run. As a result, responsibility for artificial limbs and wheelchairs was transferred to the Disablement Services Authority from 1 July 1987 and was integrated within the National Health Service in April 1991.

occasion when, having been pole-axed over Christmas by influenza, he returned to the Lords having missed a debate on the Disability Discrimination Bill, Lord Addington speaking for the Liberal-Democrats, was moved to say: "I am very glad that the noble Lord, Lord Morris, is present". Delighted by Alf's return to the House, he went on: "Our earlier deliberations had a certain feeling of not being official".[15]

The constancy of his dedication won the respect of friend and foe alike. No better expression of this universal admiration can be found than during a debate held in the afternoon of 19 April 2000, when for a full two and a half hours, disabled people took centre stage in a House of Lords debate that will fascinate any student of the history of the disability movement.[16] Its primary purpose was to mark the 30th anniversary of the Chronically Sick and Disabled Persons Act 1970. But by a happy chance the celebration coincided with the inauguration of the Disability Rights Commission, providing Members with an opportunity both to congratulate Alf on what he had achieved, reflect on current progress and setbacks and look forward to what more needed to be done. Tributes to Alf's pioneering legislation came from all parts of the House: a non-partisan remembrance that was entirely appropriate given that those who had helped to enact Alf's Bill were not of one party. They had come together with one mind, said Alf, determined to create for disabled people what had then seemed an impossible dream: to forge an instrument that would reduce their dependence on others and allow them to live as normally as possible in their own homes, with their own families, and to have the same opportunities as everyone else to contribute to the life and work of their society.

Peer after peer rose to honour and pay tribute to Alf as the man who, through all of those 30 years, had instigated and driven an astonishing realignment of social policy towards the realisation of that dream. Lord Rix (who introduced the debate), Lord Campbell of Croy, Lady Barker, Lady Darcy de Knayth, Lord Ashley of Stoke, Lady Pitkeathley, Earl Snowdon, Lord Astor of Hever and Lord Hunt of Kings Heath were as one in recognising Alf's achievement as an

---

[15] *Hansard*, Lords, 13 January 2005, col.80.
[16] *Hansard*, Lords, 19 April 2000, cols.712-52.

extraordinarily significant milestone in the history of social legislation. But no tribute was more limitless than that of Earl Longford, the doyen of the House and the unsung architect, if not the creator, of Beveridge's Welfare State. He had, as we have seen, introduced Alf's Bill to the House of Lords in 1970, something, he now reflected, that might earn him "a day off purgatory".[17] The Act, he said, was "a tremendous triumph" that constituted "a fundamental human Bill of Rights". He would listen to Alf "for all time – including in the next world". Although backed up by many others, in the last resort it was Alf's achievement.

All of the speakers, however, recognised that more needed to be done if Alf's vision was to be wholly fulfilled. Earl Snowdon recalled that in 1981 he had described the International Year of Disabled People as "a celebration of a beginning not an end". Sadly, he said, that end was still a long way off. Lord Morris would be the first to agree that there was still a long way to go to reach the goals of total integration, equal opportunities, equal rights and a society that applauded the abilities and achievements of disabled people. Lord Lipsey pondered on the paradox that an Act that had appeared to be such a signal advance at the time, nevertheless left a situation where still many people with disabilities were frustrated at the level of provision for them.

There was talk of finite resources and escalating demand, and the debate provided an opportunity to inveigh against the 'Gloucester judgement' of 1997: a shadow, as Lord Rix put it, across the path towards disability rights. It weighed heavily in the background, agreed Lord Addington, leading to help for which Alf had legislated being curtailed in some areas. Lord Ashley was more emphatic. He regarded it as an opportunity for social services departments to plead poverty and to cut or remove vital services for disabled people. If local authorities were short of resources, he said, they should look all across the board and not select disabled people as the first victims.

The decision, in Alf's view, flew in the face of Section 2 of the Chronically Sick and Disabled Persons Act, which quite clearly imposed an unqualified duty on local authorities to make necessary

[17] *Hansard*, Lords, 19 April 2000, col. 738.

arrangements in the exercise of their legal functions. And he took the opportunity in this important debate to comment, as promoter of the Act, on a "perverse – in fact bizarre – judgment", which had led to provisions of Section 2 of the Act being "trampled on in many parts of Britain". The policy intention, said Alf, had been made utterly clear at all stages of the parliamentary proceedings on the Bill: to ensure that help for disabled people would in future depend not on where they lived but strictly on the extent of individual need. Section 2 had opened up the opportunity for a life of dignity for disabled people. Now it had been put partly in abeyance by judge-made law in direct defiance of a statute that was far better drafted than most Government legislation he had seen in his 36 years of parliamentary life.

The comments about the Law Lords' ruling, flushed out by the debate of 19 April 2000, brought to the surface a fundamentally important concern still shared by specialists both inside and outside Parliament. It drew from Lord Hunt, closing the debate, a statement of the Government's view. He understood the concerns expressed on all sides during the debate. The Government did not believe that the Gloucestershire judgment should have led to changes in the provision of social services. It had, he said, confirmed what had long been the Department of Health's understanding of the law. This did not, however, give authorities a licence to take arbitrary decisions on the basis of resources alone. The department had made this clear in guidance issued in November 1997. It strongly emphasised that the judgment did not mean authorities were not under any legal duty towards disabled people. "Once an authority has decided that it is necessary in order to meet the needs of a disabled person for it to arrange a service listed in Section 2 of the [Chronically Sick and Disabled Persons] Act, it is under a duty to do so. Where individuals consider that their authority is not satisfying these requirements, it is open to them to make a complaint through the social services complaints procedure".[18]

Golden wedding

Another anniversary followed in September 2000, a personal and 'golden' one that for Alf and Irene marked 50 years of marriage. But

[18] *Hansard*, Lords, 19 April 2000, col.747.

whereas their wedding reception had been held in Johnny Clynes's committee rooms over the Co-op butchers in Varley Street, Manchester, their Golden Wedding anniversary was celebrated, by courtesy of Betty Boothroyd, in the splendour of the State Rooms of the Speaker's House in the Palace of Westminster. Alf had known Betty for all of those fifty years. When he first chaired the national consultative committee of the Labour League of Youth, Betty had been the representative of West Yorkshire. Both had similar roots – of which they were proud – but both, at least outwardly, had undergone a marked change of status. Betty, now one of the most celebrated tenants of the Speaker's House, was apologetic that all the silver might not be there because it was the parliamentary recess. Alf responded that there hadn't been much silver in Johnny Clynes's committee rooms. All four of Alf and Irene's children were there: Cathy, now a widow living in the Welsh village of Pont Robert; Paul, a secondary school head teacher in South London; Stephen, a regional officer with the GMB Union; and Gill, who lives and works in London. All were born in Manchester and, together with seven grandchildren, stay in very close touch with Alf and Irene. They were now joined in the Speaker's House with distinguished parliamentarians, including the present Speaker, Michael Martin, Jack Ashley with his wife Pauline, Alf's niece Estelle Morris, then Minister for Education, and Rosie Winterton (a friend of Gill's). There too were people from voluntary organisations whom Alf had known for decades: John Nichol and his wife Susy, Colonel English of the Royal British Legion and Ann Darnbrough of the National Information Forum. And many others came together to fête a union as firm as it had been in the outing to Kinderscout, toasted with wine of a vintage – with due respect to the one-and-sixpence a bottle 'British Empire Wine' served at Alf and Irene's wedding – somewhat improved upon the unknown and unknowable 'vintage' of September 1950'.

A gap in provision: the right to read

For over more than three decades Alf and fellow campaigners had striven to advance the cause of disabled people and dismantle the barriers they faced in their daily lives. The Chronically Sick and Disabled Persons Act was the starting point, rightly described,

32 years later, by Ian Bruce, the Director General of the Royal National Institute of the Blind, as having "marked the beginning of a long revolution in the life chances of all disabled people".[19] While not repudiating the value of charity or of charitable organisations like the RNIB, the parliamentary campaigners had sought to reinforce the limited efficacy of benevolence with comprehensive rights. Now, at the dawn of a new century, they could justly claim to have made enormous progress. Yet, as they were always the first to stress, there were still conspicuous gaps in provision.

One of the most glaring of these was the fact that people with visual impairments were still mostly excluded from access to much of the world of information and culture enjoyed by others. Blind and partially sighted people could not simply walk into a bookshop or library and choose a book in large print or braille. While there were a few specialist publishers of large print and audio books, most mainstream publishers did not find it commercially attractive to make copies of works other than in standard print. Only five per cent of the 100,000–plus titles published each year in the UK were available in formats accessible to Britain's two million visually impaired people. And most of these were produced by voluntary organisations or teachers of visually impaired students. Yet even this activity was massively constrained by copyright restrictions. Before accessible copies of a copyright work could be produced, the explicit permission of the right-holder was required. This was usually granted but, typically, there were significant delays of anything from a month to two years and, occasionally, some outright refusals.

To right this wrong a Private Member's Bill was introduced in the Commons by Rachel Squire MP[20] in March 2002, with the support of the RNIB and some help from the Government. It won wholehearted cross-party support and it fell "naturally", said Rachel, to Alf to introduce the Second Reading in the Lords, where he persuasively explained a measure that was skilfully crafted to overcome the need to obtain copyright clearances to access formats of copyright material suitable for the use of visually impaired people, while also protecting the legitimate interests of right-holders in certain exceptional

---

[19] *Hansard*, Lords, 12 July 2002, col.903.
[20] Rachel died 5 January 2006 following a long battle against brain tumours.

circumstances. It was, in the words of Lord Ashley, "yet another laurel to add to the many he has gained in Parliament".[21] Baroness Andrews, for the Government, went further: "After his long record of commitment to and action for people with disabilities, his ability to champion this Bill so eloquently is extraordinary. The Bill matches his personal ideals and the collective values not only of the Government, but of all parties in this House which have given it such a fair wind today. It is another measure to add to his outstanding record".[22] The Bill was read a second time, successfully completed its remaining stages and as the Copyright (Visually Impaired Persons) Act 2002 received Royal Assent.

Food labelling

Another of Alf's concerns at this time was that of misleading food labelling. His lifelong membership of the Co-operative movement and his election in 1995 to its highest elective office as President of the Co-operative Congress had fixed him firmly as an enthusiastic supporter of the tradition of honest and responsible trading it represents. Co-operatives have led the way in developing ethical labelling policies and – thanks to the pioneering work of Terry Hudghton of the Co-operative Group – had achieved a world 'first' by creating the technology to braille the packaging of a range of products for the benefit of blind and visually impaired people, for whom misleading labelling could prove extremely dangerous. But people with 20/20 sight were also in danger. The Co-op had published a report, *Lie of the label*, in 1997, exposing food retailers and manufacturers who marketed their products with no regard for ethical values. This had been followed up in 2002 with *Lie of the label 2*, highlighting a worrying lack of progress in addressing serious health concerns. Thus the prevalence of obesity in England had trebled over the previous 20 years and was continuing to rise. By 2002 over half of all women and two-thirds of men were either overweight or obese.

On 8 January 2003 Alf rose to ask what steps the Government was taking to combat this increasing menace.[23] Citing examples of

---

[21] *Hansard*, Lords, 12 July 2002, col.908.
[22] *Hansard*, Lords, 12 July 2002, col.912.
[23] *Hansard*, Lords, 8 January 2003, cols. 1079 *et seq.*

cunningly deceptive food labelling and advertising, he emphasised the relationship between the heavy marketing of food products – particularly 'quick-fix' convenience foods, high in fat and sugar – and the upward trend of obesity, particularly among children. It was, he said, crucially important for food labelling to be clear, readily understandable and governed by effective legislation. But that was not happening; nor was it even in sight. The provision of nutritional information was merely voluntary and legally required only when a nutrition claim was made. As a result, producers of fatty, sugary and salty foods often chose not to list nutrition on the pack. All too often, said Alf, manufacturers – including many household names among the producers of chocolate, sweets and soft drinks – were beggarly with the truth. Millions of British consumers were involved "in about the biggest stitch-up since the Bayeux tapestry". Even when manufacturers declared nutritional information, people simply did not understand it. Stronger legislation could reduce the advantage that lying so often enjoyed over truth in the retailing of goods, and increasingly so in respect of food labelling.

Lord Hunt of Kings Heath, responding for the Government as a health Minister, shared Alf's concern about obesity. He could scarcely do otherwise. The Department of Health reckoned that 21 percent of adults in England were obese and a further 34 per cent of women and 45 per cent of men were overweight. Taking health, social and financial costs together, the National Audit Office estimated that obesity was costing the economy in excess of £2.5 billion each year. There was no room for complacency; but legislation, he said, had to be harmonised at European Union level where a "comprehensive review" was intended. The Government would give urgent consideration to all that had been said from both sides of the House.

But progress was slow and in May 2004 Alf repeated his call for action in opening a further debate, to which Lord Warner, who had succeeded Lord Hunt at the Department of Health, responded.[24] By then, as if timed almost to coincide with the debate, the Government had just launched a "Keep fit, not fat" campaign to tackle what was

---

[24] *Hansard*, Lords, 5 May 2004, col.1187 *et seq.*

described as "the 'couch potato' culture now consuming the nation". The launch stressed that physical inactivity and obesity were now thought to be costing the country more than £10 billion a year, but, said Alf, some 200 school sports grounds had been sold off since 1998. Ministerial consent had been refused in only six cases. And misleading food labelling persisted in encouraging a "keep fat, not thin" way of life. It had been rightly described as a "public health time bomb"[25] Yet decisions in this policy area seemed unrelated to any coherent plan: a situation for which Alf coined the word *"adhocracy"* – policy made on the hoof. It was an overall strategy to combat unhealthy eating that was urgently needed.

Healthy eating – as Lord Warner agreed – had many more aspects than food labelling. One contributor to the debate[26] had noticed that America, with the strictest food labelling in the world, also had the highest rate of obesity. Alf knew this and indeed, as he had said in his speech opening the debate, effective prevention and management required an integrated, cross-departmental approach in Whitehall. The point was that a start had to be made and the prohibition of misleading labelling and advertising would be an important first step. He conceded that education and persuasion were important, but he believed – as in the case of discrimination against disabled people – that effective legislation was needed.

Characteristically, Alf had sounded a 'wake-up call' that led to innumerable ministerial initiatives and ultimately to Jamie Oliver's appearance on the national stage. Although the European Commission has still to propose amendments to the relevant directive,[27] few people can now be unaware of the relationship between diet and health, not least as it affects the well-being of the nation's children.

War pensions

Not all of Alf's interventions have been as well received. He has always been prepared to stand his ground for what he believes to be right, even when this brings him into conflict with Ministers of his own persuasion. A prime example arose when the Government

---

[25] Chief Medical Officer's annual report for 2002.
[26] Lord Skelmersdale.
[27] Nutrition Labelling Directive 90/46/EC.

moved to change the rules for the award of war pensions. This story had begun in 2001, when, as part of "a more integrated approach", the War Pensions Agency was transferred from the then Department of Social Security to the MoD. This development immediately prompted disquiet among sections of the ex-service community already disaffected by the hostility of that department to their claims. Lord Bach, however, sought to reassure the House (and veterans) that there was no question of the Agency losing its impartiality since it remained bound by the legislation underpinning the War Pensions Scheme. In particular, the Agency's decisions would continue to be based, *inter alia*, on "the standard of proof required by law".[28] This calmed fears at the time, but what was not foreseen was that the merit of such reassurance was entirely dependent on the legal standard not being changed. Yet that is precisely what happened when, in December 2003, the Government introduced a Bill to revise the arrangements for pensions and compensation for service personnel, a move perhaps not unconnected with the MoD's record of sustained unsuccess in disputing claims of Gulf War veterans. The Armed Forces (Pensions & Compensation) Bill offered some improvement to serving personnel and future entrants to the Armed Forces; but it also presaged radical changes in both the burden and standard of proof in deciding whether incapacity was properly attributable to active service.

The standards then used had been established sixty years earlier in 1943 in recognition of the wholly exceptional risks of service with the armed forces, not least the commitment to lay down one's life for the State. That was why the burden of proof in relation to war pensions rested on the Government and why in order to refuse a war pension to an incapacitated ex-service man or woman the Secretary of State had to show beyond reasonable doubt that service had not played any part in causing or worsening the condition for which a claim was made.

Under the new Bill, the burden of proof would in future be transferred from the MoD to the claimant and the standard of proof – previously based on a much easier test of 'reasonable doubt' –

---

[28] *Hansard*, Lords, 17 October 2001, cols.693-700.

would henceforth be assessed using the much sterner 'balance of probabilities' standard, in line, it was said, "with civil law and common practice".[29] The Royal British Legion – basing its prediction on a vast experience of casework – reckoned that the new standards, together with a reduction of the time limit for making a claim to five years, would cut the number of successful war pension claims by some two thirds.

Nevertheless, such was the Government's majority, the Bill passed through all its stages in the Commons by 6 May 2004 and was sent to the Lords. There, however, the Government encountered a formidable adversary. This was a Bill that offended Alf's most cherished principles. At the Report stage on 8 September he introduced an amendment to provide that in any scheme established under the proposed legislation both the burden and standard of proof should remain as in the current War Pensions schemes. With one of the most brilliant speeches of his entire parliamentary career, Alf attracted support from all sides of the House. Lord Bach, friendless in debate and forced onto the defensive, told the House that significant changes to any area affecting either the coherence or the affordability of the schemes would inevitably cause the Government to look again at the overall package and might mean that they would be unable to progress some or all of the features that it then contained. The noble Lords were mostly unimpressed and Alf's amendment was carried by 183 votes to 128.[30]

The New Labour Government, of course, was able to take steps to ensure that this change to the Bill was reversed by its huge majority in the House of Commons. On 2 November 2004, Lord Bach moved that the House of Lords should not insist on Alf's amendment, against which the Commons had produced reasons for disagreement. In particular, he cited two anonymous examples of claims where, he suggested, a cause other than service was far more likely to have been responsible.[31] Alf was (and remains) deeply sceptical about their relevance, which he made plain to the House. In any case, to justify the dismantling, after sixty years, of the whole

[29] *Hansard*, Lords, 16 September 2003, cols.166-68.
[30] *Hansard*, Lords, 8 September 2004, cols. 570-591.
[31] *Hansard*, Lords, 2 November 2004, cols.162-167.

system of burden and standard of proof on the basis of only two extraordinary and previously unknown cases, implying that they were in any way proof of systematic abuse of the war pensions scheme, would be seen as an unpardonable slur on the ex-service community.

Dr Harcourt, President of the Pensions Appeal Tribunals, was at once strongly critical of Lord Bach's use of the two examples. For him to have turned the first of them into what was evidently intended to be a criticism of the appeal process was, he said, "disgraceful".[32] If anything, Concannon declared, the second example was even worse, appearing to ignore the principles of causation in war pensions. The essential principle was that the relevant 'factor of service' need only be an operative cause; it need not be the only cause. Providing that some factor of service plays a role in the causal process, it may not even be the predominant cause providing it is material. Lord Bach had implied a serious criticism of the tribunal that made the decision without giving his reasons or any justification for doing so. His suggestion that a cause other than service was far more likely to have been the cause of the condition or death betrayed the Minister's misunderstanding even of the rules on causation.[33]

But this unquestionably impartial and highly authoritative judgement of Bach came too late. Faced by the Government's huge majority in the Commons it was inevitable that the Lords' amendment could not prevail. The Bill received the Royal Assent 16 days later.

Magnanimity towards war widows too was in particularly short supply. Notwithstanding the huge sums being expended on military action in Iraq and Afghanistan, the Government was meticulously prudent in its approach to those left bereaved by war service. On 13 November 2004, a leader appeared in *The Sun* under the headline 'How Dare We Neglect our War Widows?'. It pointed out that, while the usual ministerial tributes to those who had fallen in combat were being paid that Remembrance week-end at the Cenotaph in Whitehall, many of their widows were struggling to make ends meet on meagre pensions. As vice-president of the War Widows' Association and honorary parliamentary adviser to the Royal British

---

[32] Letter to T.C.House, Head of Pensions, The Royal British Legion, 29 November 2004.
[33] *Ibid.*

Legion, Alf's views were faithfully and sympathetically reported in detail by the newspaper. The fact was that Parliament had allowed war widows' pensions to lose value compared with other state benefits. MPs and peers were then haggling over a change of rule to help the most elderly war widows that would cost very much less than the MoD's entertainment budget. The basic pension for a pre-1973 war widow was £96.50, some £30.75 below the Government's minimum income guarantee of £127.25. What was the worth of being the fourth richest economy in the world, Alf was reported as asking, if it did not enable us even to act justly and generously to the most elderly of our war widows? *The Sun* added its own comment on another page: "A society can be judged," it remarked, "on the way it treats those in need". And, on that basis, it was clear that Britain was failing abjectly.

Informal carers

In the same year Alf played his part in correcting a legislative omission on another subject close to his heart: provision for the great army of 'informal' carers – nearly 10 per cent of the UK population – who devote themselves week in, week out, to looking after other people. Thanks to Alf, while he was Minister for Disabled People, they already enjoyed some rights. As we have seen, he had then introduced the world's first Carer's Allowance. And legislation enacted between 1986 and 2000 gave carers the opportunity to request and have arranged an assessment of their ability to provide care, either in association with an assessment of the needs of the person for whom they cared or independently in their own right. What was still missing, though, was any onus on local authorities to inform carers of their right to an assessment and to ensure it included consideration of the possibility of the carer having opportunities beyond caring: both to work and take part in education, training or leisure activities. In 2004, this shortcoming was addressed by a Private Member's Bill introduced by Dr Hywel Francis. It successfully passed all its stages in the Commons and was sent, in June, to the Lords. On this occasion, Lord Ashley led. Carers, he said, were simply not receiving the help, guidance and assistance they so desperately needed, and the main reason was that they were unaware of what they were entitled to or what was available. This he described as "an astonishing state of affairs". Alf was next up in support of the Bill, once again paying tribute to the co-operation there had been between the leading voluntary organisation in the field, parliamentarians and Ministers and officials across Whitehall, led by the Department of Health, in promoting the Bill. It was, he said, about giving carers more choice and the opportunity – free of drudgery – to lead fuller and more fulfilling lives. It also recognised the crucial importance of making sure that carers were fully informed and, no less important, updated on the help to which they were entitled. Lord Ashley had already pointed out that people who were denied information about rights were effectively denied those rights. Now Alf pressed this message home by citing a disturbing set of figures published by Macmillan Cancer Relief two days earlier. Disability benefits, they had found, went unclaimed by some 83,000 people terminally ill with cancer in the UK and their carers. Their total loss in benefits was £126.5 million.

Lord Warner, for the Government, confirmed its full support for the Bill. It offered "real and tangible benefits for carers, recognising their status as individuals, as well as the prospect of more flexible and responsive services, developed through collaboration [between local health and social services authorities]". The Bill proceeded serenely to the Statute Book. It had been, said Dr Francis in a celebratory speech, "a journey of hope": a journey needed to allow carers to have an ordinary life beyond caring. Now, he said, "we must pledge that the Carers (Equal Opportunities) Act becomes a reality and makes a difference to the lives of carers".[34]

A timely reminder of the need to be ready for natural disasters

Disability continued to feature prominently in Alf's activities, but in October 2004 he found time to renew his longstanding friendship with the people of Australia. As the representative of all members of the UK branch of the Commonwealth Parliamentary Association in both Houses of Parliament he journeyed with Irene to Perth for the Association's 27th Australasian Regional Conference. Delegates were invited to compete for three debates on topics of their own choice,

[34] 19 July 2004, Church House, Westminster.

and Alf gave the first of these on 'Minimising delay and maximising effectiveness in addressing humanitarian disasters in the region'. Time was short, but as he remarked at the time, the highest of parliamentary virtues is an abiding regard for brevity. As a former Prime Minister once irreverently told him, in Parliament brevity comes not next to but *before* Godliness. Alf's subject was none the less of high importance. Its purpose was to focus attention on improving co-operation between Governments in the Region on the pre-commitment of resources and forward planning in anticipating transport, medical and other essential needs for emergencies when they occur. Alf drew attention to the failure of governments to react promptly and effectively to humanitarian disasters. Almost always, he said, they were still taken completely by surprise whenever they occurred. Their reaction was invariably one of 'shock, horror'. Time after time we learned after the event that much more could have been done to reduce loss of life and casualties in communities hit by natural and other disasters for which much more could have been done to prepare. Again and again, too little was done too late.

Alf's call for action envisaged not only the pre-commitment by governments of resources but also a guarantee of anonymity for donor and beneficiary alike. It was not good enough, he said, for countries capable of helping to look first at the warmth of its bilateral relations with other countries rather than the urgency of the need when disaster struck. Regional disaster task forces were needed in the Australasian region as elsewhere in the world. Responsibility could not be left with charitable organisations alone, important though their role could be. Trained personnel, appropriate transport and essential medical and other supplies were needed to prepare for any contingency that could arise. And that required backing from governments and non-governmental organisations alike. Surely we should not be working out the logistics of reacting to and reaching the locations of humanitarian disasters *after* they occur; and determining only then from which potential donor countries vital medical and other help might be obtained. Alf profoundly hoped that the Perth conference's necessarily brief consideration of the problems might be the catalyst for more detailed examination and action soon.

Alas, a definitive decision could not be taken at that stage. The best that could be agreed was to put the paper and proposition on the agenda for the next conference and circulate a report of what had been said in Perth to all CPA branches for their consideration and that of governments in the region 'holding the purse strings'. Unfortunately the Great Tsunami that struck little more than two months later on 26 December 2004 did not wait for that to happen.

New anti-discrimination legislation

At the same time, however, positive action was now in hand to extend the civil rights of our disabled people. On 1 October 2004, the final part of the Disability Discrimination Act 1995 was brought into effect and on 25 November a new Disability Discrimination Bill was introduced. It had been a long road, but the new legislation would widen, deepen and strengthen the way disability discrimination legislation was applied. In looking forward to the enactment of the new provisions, Maria Eagle, the Minister for Disabled People, said that Labour members should take pride in their record on disability rights. She paid tribute to the "tireless work of her predecessor Alf Morris" and also to Jack Ashley, Tom Clarke and others who had "kept the issue of disability rights alive during the long years of the Tory administration". The Government had "transformed disability rights since coming into office. This was the culmination of many years of work, started by Alf Morris, and was a true Labour issue"[35]

Nor was the transformation simply a matter of improvement in law. Writing to *The Daily Telegraph*, Janet O'Sullivan, whose daughter was congenitally disabled, observed:

> "On the day that the final part of the Disability Discrimination Act 1995 comes into force it should not be forgotten that, for a large section of society, life is infinitely better today.
>
> "If my beloved daughter had been born in the Fifties, she would have been shunned, called a mongol, stared at,

[35] Proceedings of a Parliamentary Labour Party meeting, 10 March 2004.

denied education and, in all likelihood, hidden away in an institution.

"Today, she is welcomed and smiled at (by most people), looks forward to mainstream education and inclusion in employment. There is still a long way to go, but it would be wrong to overlook the improvements made in the past 50 years for members of our society who do not fit the 'normal' mode".

First presaged in March 2001, a new Disability Discrimination Bill followed a report, *From Exclusion to Inclusion*, put to Ministers by a specially appointed Disability Rights Taskforce, which had been followed by consideration of a draft Bill by a Joint Committee of both Houses of Parliament. That committee heard powerful evidence from, among others, Sir Peter Large, who was still actively expressing concerns about the detail of the Bill on the day before his death on 23 January.

Highly influential 'behind the scenes', although not a prime mover of the new Bill, Alf was again acknowledged to have "laid its foundations".[36] It was now promoted as completing the Government's programme of disability rights legislation that had its roots in the Chronically Sick and Disabled Persons Act 1970 and had found its first specific, compelling justification in the CORAD report of 1982 that Alf had commissioned in 1979. The new Bill set out to remedy and extend the tightly limited scope of the Disability Discrimination Act 1995. Anne Begg (Labour, Aberdeen South) described it as "the final missing piece in a jigsaw of equality legislation".[37] Though not free from controversy in the detail of its provision, it was, as a Government Bill, guaranteed enactment and needed only goodwill and a fair parliamentary wind to reach the Statute Book quickly. Like the Chronically Sick and Disabled Persons Bill, its passage took place in the run-up to a General Election. Time was disturbingly short, but the will to ensure that it became law was widely shared among MPs and peers alike and was decisive. Royal Assent was secured on 7 April 2005, on the final

---

[36] *Hansard*, Commons, 23 March 2005, col.899.
[37] *Hansard*, Commons, 23 March 2005, col.916.

day of the 2001–05 Parliament. History, as Mark Twain noticed, does not repeat itself, but it sometimes rhymes.

The House of Lords played a considerable part in improving this "deeply important" Bill,[38] forcing no fewer than thirteen concessions on Report. As the Disability Rights Commission commented: "As a result of tough cross-party scrutiny in the Lords, and effective engagement with disabled people and their organisations, the Bill has been strengthened to deliver major gains for disabled people".[39] The Commission's chairman, Bert Massie CBE, expressed his personal thanks to Alf for his "tremendous support" on key issues. Because of the effectiveness of Alf's work and that of other colleagues of the All Party Parliamentary Disability Group in the Lords – notably Lord Ashley, its chairman – a "good Bill had been made even better". Bert Massie's letter to Alf went on: "Your record of fighting for disabled people with such vigour for over 40 years has produced so many benefits for all of us".[40] The Act extended the definition of disability to include at least 175,000 more people – including those with progressive conditions such as HIV, multiple sclerosis and cancer from the point of diagnosis – and removed the onerous requirement that mental illnesses must be "clinically well recognised". Importantly, it extended the coverage of the Disability Discrimination Act 1995 to most activities in the public sector, placing a duty on public authorities to promote equality of opportunity for disabled people, to tackle all forms of harassment and bullying and to promote participation in public life. In the provision or reorganisation of its services, local authorities would in future have to think first of their impact on disabled people. There were also provisions that imposed a duty on landlords to make reasonable adjustments for tenants and prospective tenants with disabilities, short of physical changes to the premises. Where a lease gave tenants a right to carry out alterations to residential premises with their landlord's consent, it would not be lawful for landlords unreasonably to withhold their consent for alterations needed by a disabled person living in the premises. The new Act also, for the first time, protected disabled passengers against discrimination, thus

---

[38] *Hansard*, Lords, 13 January 2005, col.GC79.
[39] *Hansard*, Commons, 23 March 2005, col.909.
[40] Personal letter, 9 March 2005.

"ending the anomaly of transport not counting as a service under the DDA"[41] and allowing the Government to set an end date of 2020 for all rail vehicles to be subject to the accessibility regulations providing access for all disabled people.

Audrey and Jim Callaghan leave the scene

While the new Disability Discrimination Bill was still before Parliament came the sad news of the death on 15 March 2005 of Lady (Audrey) Callaghan, who, as we have seen, was one of the members of the Committee on Restrictions Against Disabled People (CORAD) set up by Alf in 1979. Her husband died only eleven days later, as though his work and that which gave meaning to his life was now complete. As one of Alf's most consistent supporters, disabled people owe a significant debt to a Prime Minister who has not always been accorded the recognition he deserves. He left behind among his papers a note that was a feature in a service of thanksgiving for him and his wife:

"I would like any Memorial Service for me to be cheerful and joyful.

The last hymn could be that splendid American one:
'Mine Eyes Have Seen the Glory Of The Coming Of The Lord. Hallelujah!'

The congregation all singing.
The great organ chords crashing out.
The Marines on trumpets.
That would be a splendid finish!"

Alf welcomes moves towards a wider concept of equality

The Disability Discrimination Act 1995 had lacked the apparatus necessary for its enforcement and had required a change of government to bring the Disability Rights Commission provided for in the Civil Rights (Disabled Persons) Bill into being. Essential to the implementation of the reinforced disability rights legislation was that the Commission's championing of disability issues should remain at the core of any new regulatory body's remit in this policy area, a key principle well recognised by the Government.[42] The Equality Bill, launched by Ministers in the House of Lords on 18 May 2005, set

---

[41] *Hansard*, Commons, 23 March 2005, col.909.
[42] *Hansard*, Commons, 23 March 2005, col.900.

out to dissolve the various existing equality commissions – for gender, race and disability – within a single new body; to make provisions on discrimination on grounds of religion or belief, to impose duties relating to sex discrimination in the performance of public functions and to establish a Commission for Equality and Human Rights, the remit of which would be extended to cover unfair discrimination on grounds of age.

Alf welcomed this measure, among whose strengths would be to allow greater consideration of priorities and provide a wider vision of discrimination. Up to this point the various commissions had, perforce, operated narrowly within their own special remit, but the fact was that many people suffered double, even triple discrimination. Someone who experienced discriminatory exclusion because of disability, for example, might also be unfairly excluded on grounds of age, thus, said Alf, being left "in double hardship and double despair".

The new Disability Discrimination Act and the moves to extend the boundaries of equality and civil rights marked another milestone on the road to the advancement of the status of disabled people that Alf had begun and striven to achieve. Over the thirty-five years from the Chronically Sick and Disabled Persons Act 1970, legislative stone by stone, Alf's vision of an inclusive British society was moving ever closer to reality.[43]

Without any doubt, history will judge Alf kindly. But that would be to underestimate his achievement. As William Wilberforce ended the slave trade and prompted others to secure their freedom, so Alf Morris, over the best part of four decades, has led the emancipation of disabled people, not only in Britain but throughout the world. Even now, the task, like that of Wilberforce, is unfinished. It will be for new crusaders to take forward the mission of transforming the lives of the 600 plus million disabled people on our planet, so that nowhere will they continue to be treated as outcasts on the fringes of society, and to work to bring equality and full citizenship where impairment is met by exclusion.

---

[43] *Hansard*, Lords, 5 June 2004, cols.1471-94.

Reading the day-by-day, week-by-week, parliamentary record of debates, questions and reactions to new legislation on disability can seem mundane, but taken together, along with the great international charters, they represent a testimonial to a famous triumph. When so much else in Britain has moved in the wrong direction during Alf's parliamentary span, disability has been raised from a graveyard of neglect to a prime position in the proceedings of both Houses, not to mention the impact of his legislation on other parliaments worldwide.

Estelle Morris

Alf's work is not yet done. But even now there is the happy knowledge that his family traditions will continue to be carried forward when he has gone. On 21 June 2005, in the Chamber of the House of Lords, Alf, alongside his friend Lord (David) Puttnam, had an unprecedented delight: to introduce his niece Estelle as Baroness Morris of Yardley. Uncle and niece – the first ever to serve together in Commons or Lords – were reunited to begin a new chapter in 'the other place'.

On 3 November, Estelle made her maiden speech in the Lords during an important debate welcoming a report from the Hansard Society, *Members Only? Parliament in the Public Eye*. This concerned how Parliament communicated with the people it served, and the consensus was that it did so very badly. Estelle's message, like that of her familial predecessors, looked boldly to the future. It was a myth to suppose that Parliament was no longer relevant to people's lives and, equally, that people were no longer interested in politics. Nothing, she said, could be further from the truth. But there was an increasing disengagement from the institutions driving political change: the two Houses of Parliament. In her view, the first step of response was to accept that the fault as Parliament's and not the people's. She was "immensely proud of the traditions of the Houses of Parliament...However, that pride in tradition should never ever prevent us changing to face the future...we should respect it but move forward".[44]

---

[44] *Hansard*, Lords, 3 November 2005, cols.323-6.

Lord Jopling's response nevertheless began by looking back. The noble Baroness, he remarked, was the third member of her family with whom he had had the good fortune to serve in the House of Commons. "It was a great pleasure," he said, "to see my old friend, her uncle Alf, standing at the Bar of the House listening to her maiden speech. She comes from a very distinguished parliamentary family, and I hope that she will not be offended if I were to call it one of our most distinguished parliamentary dynasties".[45]

Lifetime achievement

That accolade was reinforced on 1 December 2005 when Alf received the highly prestigious e.Politix Lifetime Achievement Award, the climax of a series of 'Charity Champions' awards honouring the hard work, time and effort given by MPs and peers to a range of voluntary causes and organisations. Ordinarily, these related to outstanding achievement over the year, but Alf's award – the last of its kind – recognised an outstanding contribution to charitable causes over a parliamentary career of 42 years. The citation recognised that his Chronically Sick and Disabled Persons Act had given disabled people "a new place in society, and spawned a host of new organisations and thinking which raised awareness of disability issues well beyond the strict provisions of the Act". But, the tribute continued, he was "not one for resting on his well-deserved laurels". He remained at the forefront of the campaign for improved rights for disabled people, warning against the dangers of 'serene satisfaction' with what had been achieved and urging the need to keep challenging and improving.

Alf's response was brief but pointed. He looked back to his time as a Minister which began with the approval of financial support for a number of voluntary organisations, including the Crossroads Care Attendants Scheme and The National Bureau for Handicapped Students, now Skill. Pound for pound – even allowing for having legislated for a raft of new disability benefits – he now regarded those two grants as being the best spending that he ever authorised. He was reminded of Dick Crossman's view on the charitable sector at that time: "With all his customary pedantry – to which I listened

---

[45] *Ibid*, col.326.

with all my customary fortitude – he had predicted that as the frontiers of statutory provision expanded, the role of the voluntary sector would shrink and wither away. Dick never did things by half measures; if he was wrong, as he was in this case and so many others, he was 180 degrees out: comprehensively wrong". In fact, as we now know, Alf's 1970 Act, as well as massively improving state provision, also spawned in subsequent years a burgeoning of new voluntary organisations of and for disabled people. Both Crossroads and the National Bureau, along with many other voluntary organisations, achieved progress that the state could never attempt, let alone match.

Alf's values confirmed

Now in his later but by no means declining years, Alf continues to deploy a vast parliamentary experience to maximum effect in the Upper House. Always a shrewd tactician, he also remains firmly rooted in and keeps faith with the political principles that have characterised a career at Westminster now in its forty-third year. No better example of this, perhaps, can be found than that of his contribution in June 2006 to the Lords' Second Reading of the International Development (Reporting and Transparency) Bill. This measure, introduced in the Commons as a Private Member's Bill by his close and longstanding friend Tom Clarke (Labour, Coatbridge, Chryston and Bellshill), sought to ensure that promises on aid for Third World countries made by the Government at summit conferences such as the Gleneagles G8 were kept and that there would be accountability in delivering aid effectively to the world's poor. Like the measure to extend provision for disabled people Tom successfully piloted to the Statute Book in 1985/6, this new Bill was very much in keeping with Alf's concern for the poor and powerless. He now rose in the Lords to give unqualified support to a "humane and long overdue measure". Initially he was pragmatic. It was a fact that there would be no further parliamentary time allocation for the Commons to debate amendments to the Bill from the Lords. Thus amending it in the Upper House would end any realistic prospect of it becoming law.

Yet its enactment, Alf pointed out, would "help parliamentarians more effectively to discharge their duty – some would say sovereign duty – to subject policy-making in this deeply sensitive and crucially important field to much more detailed scrutiny than is possible today". Scrutinising the annual report required by the Bill, he went on, could only improve policy-making on issues such as aid, debt and trade and benefit those most in need, provided, of course, that it was "not just about listening and responding to well-heeled lobbyists but hearing the cries of those now unheard".

Alf drew attention to UNICEF's 1994 report on the state of the world's children. This had unequivocally cited "one central, shameful fact": that failure to resolve the problems of the Third World was not because the task was too large or too difficult or too expensive. It was simply that what was needed was not given sufficient priority, because those most severely affected were almost exclusively "the poorest and least politically influential people on earth".

This was now in the territory of Alf's deepest conviction: his commitment from youth to underprivileged people everywhere. He turned to Dr Samuel Johnson who, holding forth in his customary role of oracle supreme, had written:

> "How small of all that human hearts endure,
> That part that laws and Kings can cure".

By hastening Royal Assent of Tom Clarke's Bill, said Alf, the House could refute that cynical assessment of what could be achieved by parliamentarians acting together. It would not be the first such refutation, as demonstrated by Wilberforce's campaign against human slavery, but never was it more necessary than now to wield all the influence at the command of Parliament "to ensure that right was done in transforming endurance into lives worth living for the poor, vulnerable and afflicted people" the Bill could help. The Prime Minister had recently said that too few aid pledges were made for real and too many for show. This Bill, Alf concluded, was about being real.[46]

---

[46] *Hansard*, Lords, 29 June 2006, cols.1425–7. The Bill was subsequently read, unamended.

Tom Clarke was swift to thank Alf for "a wonderful, generous and supportive speech". He had, he said, many reasons to be grateful to Alf and Irene over many years. "This speech was yet another reason for further gratitude and regard to a loyal friend".[47]

Alf's mother Jessie, eking out a precarious existence in Ancoats among the poorest of Manchester's poor, cannot have dreamed that two of her children and a grandchild would become a parliamentary dynasty. That uniquely two of the family, Alf and Estelle, uncle and niece, would serve together in the House of Commons, one having been and the other later to become a Minister, or that her youngest son, Alf, was destined to become Lord Morris of her and his native city. Alf, ever fiercely proud of his mother, knows that in no small measure it all traces back to her.

2000: At the launch of the *Charter for the Third Millennium* in the Church of St Mary Undercroft at the House of Commons. From the left: Alf, The Rt. Hon. Michael Martin MP, Speaker of the House of Commons, The Rt. Hon. The Lord Irvine of Lairg, Lord Chancellor (greeting Bert Massie, chair of the Disability Rights Commission), The Rt. Hon. Sir Edward Heath MP (representing Her Majesty's Opposition) and Dr Arthur O'Reilly, chair of Rehabilitation International.

---

[47] Personal letter, 4 July 2006.

2001: Marlborough House, Presentation of the Charter for the Third Millennium to the Commonwealth. Left to right: Alf, Prince Ra'ad of Jordan; Chief Emeka Anyaoku (then Secretary General of the Commonwealth).

January 2002: Alf (left) sits as a co-opted member of US Congressional Committee of Inquiry into Gulf War illnesses in the House of Representatives, chaired by Christopher Shays.

21 June 2005: Estelle Morris introduced to the House of Lords, flanked by her uncle and Lord (David) Puttnam.

2005: Annual parliamentary pancake throwing contest. Alf as captain of the House of Lords team, with Lords Dubbs and Dholakia.

2000: Presentation of the Charter for the Third Millennium to the Republic of Ireland. Alf, President Mary McAleese and Arthur O'Reilly, then President of Rehabiliation International.

2001: Co-operative store, Stepney. Launch of brailled information on packaged goods. Alf, Colin (now Lord) Low (Chair, RNIB), Peter White (BBC correspondent) and David Blunkett MP.

1999: Opening of a Co-op Care residential home in Staffordshire. Alf with leading representatives of the Midlands Co-operative Society.

2000: People of the Year Awards. Alf's daughter Gill and granddaughter, Katie, with TV's Ground Force presenter, Charlie Dimmock, after receiving a Lifetime Achievement Award on Alf's behalf.

Chapter 15

GULF WAR ILLNESSES

1993–2006

"We all, I think, recognise a remarkable man when we meet him, and all I can say is when I first met Lord Morris of Manchester, and everything I have seen of him since, confirms my view that he is a very remarkable man and we all owe him a great debt of gratitude".

The Rt. Hon. Lord Lloyd of Berwick DL, senior former High Court judge and Lord of Appeal in Ordinary, 12 April 2005.

– Counting the cost – Valiant in war, discarded in peace – MoD disparaged
– Hazards faced in the Gulf War – The watchdog of the Legion
– Investigating the incidence of disease – A new Government, old arguments
– A public inquiry denied – Alf invited to join US Congressional Inquiry
– The case of Nigel Thompson
– First-ever meeting of a US Congressional Committee of Inquiry in the Palace of Westminster
– The case of David Peachell – The politics of delay
– A revolutionary initiative: the Lloyd Inquiry – Veterans' Minister stays away
– A report from the USA – The Lloyd Report – Military chiefs call for action
– Time for a change of direction – The American exemplar – A bid for closure
– Ministers continue to prevaricate – Ecclesiastical interventions
– Breakthrough – Denunciation in the USA
– Surely time for the final curtain – Justice delayed – A supreme achievement

Counting the cost

The longest-running of all Alf's moral crusades – and arguably one of the most testing and inspired – has been his determined struggle to secure just treatment for British troops involved in the 1991 Gulf War who, fit and well when they were deployed, have since developed a wide range of medically unexplained illnesses. The first such cases among the 50,000–plus troops deployed were reported in 1993 and built up gradually to several thousands. They were stricken with a range of conditions which their doctors attributed to service in the Gulf.

That war ended much more quickly than was expected and was hailed as a great military feat. But the cost had still to be counted in terms of its effects on coalition troops involved. While the media have always talked of their varied illnesses as a syndrome, as early as April 1994, a US National Institute of Health Workshop found that "no single disease or syndrome was apparent, but rather multiple illnesses with overlapping symptoms and causes".[1] What could not be doubted was that thousands of personnel who were medically A1 in 1990/1991 were now in broken health, some of them with life-threatening conditions. The UK's Ministry of Defence, however, rejected any inference that this was necessarily connected with deployment to the Gulf. The War Pensions Agency was legally bound to give claimants the benefit of any doubt in the award of war pensions in respect of "symptoms and signs of ill-defined conditions"[2] that the Ministry of Defence could not prove to be unconnected to war service. But the MoD persisted in rejecting claims for additional entitlement, denying liability for conditions that could not, they said, realistically be characterised as a syndrome. And that, more or less, remained its position for the next twelve years.

Valiant in war, discarded in peace

Alf's view, put in simple terms, was that having been hailed as heroes when called upon to evict the invading Iraqi army from Kuwait and, having fought successfully the good fight, they were now being treated unjustly. They were praised when fighting for their country, but held of little account afterwards. Like the old soldier in Rudyard Kipling's *Shillin' a Day*, it was a case of *"Think what 'e's been, Think what 'e's seen, Think of his pension an'...Gawd save the Queen"*.

From that first rebuttal, the MoD's resistance to their claims and its failure properly to acknowledge and respond to the problems and needs of Gulf veterans, has provoked deep resentment and increasing anger among them and the widows and other dependants of those who, year by year, succumbed to their illnesses.

---

[1] Group Captain W.J.Coker OBE: *A Review of Gulf War Illness*, first published in the *Journal of the Royal Naval Medical Service*, vol.82, pp.141-46, referring back to a report by the Presidential Advisory Committee on Gulf War Veterans' Illnesses, February 1996.

[2] *Hansard*, Lords, 2 July 2003, col.873, referring to a diagnostic category of the *WHO International Classification of Diseases*, 10th edition, 1992.

In many ways the situation mirrored the experience of Alf's own father and widowed mother after the First World War.

MoD disparaged

Alf has by no means been alone in his criticism. Successive reports of the Commons Defence Committee commented adversely on the MoD's very poor record in getting to the bottom of the issues. The Committee's 1995 report stated sharply: "In responding to the allegations of a Gulf War syndrome the MoD has been quick to deny but slow to investigate...[their] response has been reactive rather than proactive and characterised throughout by scepticism, defensiveness and general torpor". In 1997, concern about the MoD's conduct was reinforced when the Committee summarised its view in the exquisitely worded understatement: "We do not feel that the Ministry of Defence has been dogged in pursuit of the facts". Three years later, the Committee asserted that veterans and veterans' families had no confidence in the way the MoD was pursuing the matter; nor in a situation where the department with overarching responsibility for British troops in the Gulf War was charged with investigating its own behaviour toward them.[3]

Hazards faced in the Gulf War

There were many factors in the 1991 Gulf War quite different from those met with in any other deployment involving British troops. To begin with, compelling evidence has emerged that the multiple immunisation programme – which for some combatants involved fourteen and more inoculations in the space of two weeks and the first-ever issue of nerve agent pre-treatment sets (NAPS) tablets that included pyridostigmine bromide[4] – damaged the immune systems of many of those they were intended to protect. In a debate in the House of Lords initiated by Alf in 2001, Field Marshal Lord Bramall, a former Chief of the Defence Staff, described the cocktail of tablets

---

[3] Statement of Hon. David Laws MP, *Research into Persian Gulf War Veterans' Illnesses, Congressional record no.107-237*, page 88..

[4] Described by Malcolm Hooper, Emeritus Professor of Medicinal Chemistry at the University of Sunderland and Chief Scientific Advisor to the Gulf War Veterans and Families Association, as a very questionable drug for use by the military (statement to a US Congressional committee meeting at Westminster, 18 June 2002).

and vaccines as "by far the most likely common factor for inducing some subsequent indisposition, or worse".[5]

The 1991 Gulf War was the first conflict since 1918 in which our troops had faced an enemy known to possess and have used chemical weapons. Known, moreover, to have used them, not only against the Kurds in Halabja in 1988 – where over 5,000 of Iraq's own citizens were annihilated – but even more seriously in terms of loss of life in neighbouring Iran in the year preceding Saddam Hussein's brutal invasion of Kuwait. In March 1991, in pursuit of retreating Iraqis evicted from Kuwait, the Americans bombed and destroyed a huge Iraqi arms dump at Al-Khamisiyah in Southern Iraq, totally unaware that this was where Saddam Hussein's stockpile of chemical weapons were stored. The explosions released a huge toxic plume. At first it was thought that the resulting fall-out affected very few of the coalition forces. Indeed in March 1997 Nicholas Soames, then Minister of State at the MoD, told Alf in reply to a Parliamentary Question that only one British soldier could possibly have been exposed and, in effect, that he was in rude health. Yet three years later it was conceded that some 9,000 British troops could have been affected. A United States Congressional Committee of Inquiry was soon working on a well-documented assumption that *all* of the 700,000–plus American troops deployed could have been exposed.[6] It was in a report by the US Government Accountability Office on 1 June 2004, that the sites destroyed by the bombings were revealed to have contained 33 tons of sarin and cyclosarin, two of the most dangerous gases. The report also drew attention to a considerable body of evidence that low-level exposure to nerve agents could produce serious long-term health effects. Statistics released by the US Secretary for Veterans Affairs showed dramatically higher death rates among US veterans exposed to the release of nerve agents by the Al-Khamisiyah explosions. Such deaths are now automatically treated in the US as Gulf War-related. But not by the MoD, which undertook no research whatever into the effects of the explosions on British troops.

---

[5] *Hansard*, Lords, 15 January 2001, col.1014.
[6] Keith Rhodes, Chief Technologist for the US Government Accountability Office (GAO) in evidence to the Lloyd Inquiry, 2 August 2004.

There were other very serious health hazards. Some troops were exposed to the effects of heavy use of organophosphates to protect them from the threat posed by fly-borne diseases. In 1994, Nicholas Soames, responding for the MoD to a question from Paul Tyler, downplayed the extent of their use. Two years later, when the issue of Gulf War illnesses was debated in the House of Commons,[7] he was obliged to apologise and concede that their use had been far more widespread than previously reported. The tented accommodation occupied by British forces in the Gulf was regularly sprayed with organophosphates, some of which – purchased from local suppliers – were even more dangerous than those taken out from the UK. Troops employed in spraying have spoken of being soaked to the skin in organophosphates (OPs) and exposure on that scale was seen as a virtually certain cause of some Gulf War illnesses. There was also the question of the dusting powder used to delouse Iraqi prisoners of war, where an official inquiry found that the number of prisoners involved ran to many hundreds rather than the 50 previously reported to the House of Commons. Even when this was discovered and admitted, however, the MoD is alleged to have "failed to acknowledge and investigate with sufficient urgency and resources the significance of the connection, or the fact that other allied forces, not exposed to OPs, experienced less symptoms of illness".[8]

Other British troops were exposed to toxic dust when cleaning-up after the use of depleted uranium (DU) weapons. In this case, the MoD has argued that not everyone who was near to the theatre of operations where such weapons were used would have been significantly affected by the dust. But undoubtedly those deployed to create the huge tank 'cemetery' on the Basra road out of Kuwait for the hideously mangled Iraqi tanks hit by depleted uranium weapons were very exposed. It remains widely believed, among veterans, some of whom paid for themselves to be tested in Canada for harmful exposure, that the effect of DU dust was the cause of their ill health. Indeed, a report from Professor Hari Sharma, Professor Emeritus in the Department of Chemistry at Canada's

---

[7] *Hansard*, Commons, 10 December 1996, col.121.
[8] Statement of Paul Tyler MP, June 2002, *Research into Persian Gulf War Veterans' Illnesses, Congressional record no.107-237, pp 96/100.*

University of Waterloo in Ontario, showed that as many as 30 British Gulf War veterans had tested positive there to "depleted uranium oxide".[9]

On top of these hazards, the firing by Iraqi troops of oil wells all across Kuwait led to massive atmospheric pollution. It was estimated that the 600 burning oil wells released into the atmosphere 50,000 tons of sulphur-dioxide, 100,000 tons of soot and 85,000 tons of carbon dioxide every 24 hours. Air samples detected the presence of carbon monoxide, nitrogen oxide and polycyclic aromatic hydrocarbons together with benzine, cadmium copper, molybdenum, nickel, lead, vanadium and zinc in above average concentrations. For an entire calendar month there was virtually no distinction between day and night in Kuwait. Philip Congdon, then a squadron leader in the RAF, wrote: "The result was not a fog but rather the pollutants, held by ugly thick smoke, rose into the atmosphere producing a dirty sable black dome that extended from horizon to horizon over Kuwait and often drifted well into Saudi Arabia. Within this dome a mist of oil particles would occasionally precipitate". Congdon described the results as "passive smoking of the most deadly type".[10] It was reasonable to conclude that many people living in that environment would be affected and especially those with breathing ailments. But Nicholas Soames did not think so. In a 1996 debate, speaking for the MoD, he thought it "interesting to note" that there was no sign of any illness among the indigenous populations of Kuwait and Saudi Arabia, "who would have been expected to be the first to suffer".[11] Yet when Alf went to the Gulf in 1998, accompanied by Colonel Terry English of the Royal British Legion, and spoke to Ministers there, including the Kuwaiti Minister for Health, about the effect on the civilian population, he was told there had been a marked increase in cardiothoracic deaths arising from it.

There was also post traumatic stress disorder, a new name for an old consequence of war but, for some Gulf War troops, a jeopardy experienced in previously unimagined circumstances. Although the

[9] *Hansard*, Lords, 24 March 1999, col. 1383. See also *Depleted Uranium - Deadly, Dangerous and Indiscriminate* by Anne Gut and Bruno Vitale (Campaign Against Depleted Uranium, 2003).
[10] *Ibid*, col.1384.
[11] *Hansard*, Commons, 10 December 1996, col.135.

number of fatal British casualties during the conflict was lower than had been expected, many of our troops witnessed events that were psychologically highly disturbing. The horrendous injuries inflicted on Iraqi soldiers by the heavy use of depleted uranium had a marked traumatic effect on personnel who came into close contact with them and particularly those responsible for treating the injuries of Iraqi troops who survived this new and devastating weapon of war. Depleted uranium weapons, which previously had hardly been used at all by the British Army, did not merely destroy a tank but turned it into a grotesquely distorted wreck. And it scattered the remains of those who had been manning it into often irretrievable parts. Not unnaturally the soldiers whose job it was to try to recover and bury the Iraqi dead faced a gruesome task that was to take its toll on many of them in later years.

The watchdog of the Legion

Alf became Honorary Parliamentary Adviser to the Royal British Legion in 1989 and continued in that role after entering the House of Lords. As such he became not just acutely aware of but often closely involved in the cases of afflicted veterans and bereaved families as they were reported to the Legion. He was also a founder member, in 1994, of the Legion's Inter-Parliamentary Gulf War Group. This included parliamentarians of all parties and of none: Lord Burnham, the Countess of Mar, Gisela Stuart MP, Michael Mates MP, Paul Tyler MP; representatives of the ex-service charities; the late Major Ian Hill and Flight Lieutenant John Nichol from the veterans' associations; and leading scientists, senior doctors and nurses.

In the Commons, Alf was also among the small group of MPs – they included Llew Smith, David Clark, Tam Dalyell, Paul Tyler, Edwina Currie and Maria Eagle – who began to probe what they saw as the languor of the MoD in investigating the increasingly disturbing level of illnesses among men and women who served in the conflict. He and others launched a cascade of pointed parliamentary questions. The Government's response to the first indications of medically unexplained illnesses among Gulf veterans had been to set up, in 1993, a "Medical Assessment Programme" (MAP)". Individual veterans with health problems causing them concern were invited to become involved. But in 1995, in response to a question from Tam Dalyell, it emerged that only one "medical expert and consultant" was available to carry out examinations.[12] Of some 500 men and women who had come forward only some 200 had been examined. The numbers grew steadily. A year later, a question from Alf revealed that 937 veterans had come forward of whom only 592 had been seen.[13]

The result of the examinations was always the same: "no convincing scientific or medical evidence" of a Gulf War syndrome had been revealed. The Government's kindlier critics said these findings were entirely predictable. They said it had to be recognised that belated individual examinations by MAP, no matter how scrupulous, as no doubt they were, could not be expected to find direct evidence of cause and effect, especially when relevant medical records were mostly no longer available. It was openly admitted to the Commons that "medical record keeping in the Gulf was not satisfactory...not good enough".[14] As many as 10,000 records were said to have been lost.[15]

"In any event, it had been clear from an early stage that the MoD's objective of seeking to deny the existence of 'Gulf War syndrome' as a discrete pathological entity was misconceived, some veterans would say deliberately misconceived. What was really at issue was the presentation by veterans of a wide range of unexplained illnesses thought to be connected to a wide variety of mostly new wartime hazards. The essential question, therefore, was whether the scale and character of illnesses presented by Gulf veterans differed significantly from those of similar men and women not involved in the war."

Investigating the incidence of disease

The need was for epidemiological studies, a course of action finally conceded by the Government in December 1996 on the advice of the Medical Research Council. These studies would, it was said, take about three years to complete and would be co-ordinated with a

---

[12] *Hansard*, Commons, 2 May 1995, cols.158/9.
[13] *Hansard*, Commons, 18 June 1996, cols.412/3.
[14] *Hansard*, Commons, 10 December 1996, col.125.
[15] *Ibid*, col.124. Later revised to 15,000 (*Hansard*, Lords, 12 February 1998, col.483).

US-funded study being carried out in parallel at Kings College, London.[16]

Nicholas Soames, Minister of State for the Armed Forces, announced this initiative in a formal statement that signalled a belated change of approach and an admission that previous information from the MoD, although given to the House in good faith, had been flawed. Conservative members congratulated the Minister on his "candour" and the Government on its unstinting concern for "our gallant troops": a response to the statement that angered Gulf veterans who had endured years of delay and ministerial vacillation. The Government's critics – not least Alf – castigated the MoD's sluggish reluctance to get anywhere near to resolving the well-founded claims of Gulf veterans. They noted too Soames's narrowly legalistic approach in saying that "any Gulf veteran who can be shown to be suffering from illness caused by the Department's negligence will be entitled to compensation in line with common law principles".

The exchange that followed Soames's statement was one of the last in which Alf was to take part in the House of Commons. But his move to the Lords in 1997 meant that he could continue to be closely involved in developments. If his intention in accepting a life peerage had been to ease up in the new environment, the bitterly contested campaign that ensued, along with his parallel struggle on behalf of people with haemophilia infected with life-threatening viruses by contaminated NHS blood products, was to prove wholly incompatible with a quiet life. On the issue of Gulf War illnesses he was faced by a Ministry of Defence no less intransigent than the Department of Health on the other front. Ministers remained totally unwilling to concede compensation except on the basis of facts that could be proven beyond doubt, notwithstanding the MoD's failure to achieve even the keeping of proper medical records. Nothing could have been more conducive to ensuring that Alf remained tirelessly dedicated once again to opening the floodgates of executive government. Within a month of his introduction to the Lords he was already weighing up what it would take to force an opening in the MoD's mighty barrier.

---

[16] *Hansard*, Commons, 10 December 1996, cols.119/120.

What consideration, he asked, had been given to President Clinton's announcement on the handling of inquiries about the Gulf War illnesses suffered by 60,000 US veterans of the conflict? Was any parallel action being taken in Britain to help service men and women stricken by these illnesses?[17] Lord Gilbert, the first Minister of State at the MoD in the new Labour government, well respected by Alf, responded that the implementation of US policies would be closely monitored and said that the Government was "committed to ensuring that all British Gulf War veterans receive appropriate medical help and financial provision with the minimum delay".

A new Government, old arguments

Through the years Alf, supported by other members of the Legion's Inter-Parliamentary Gulf War Group and faced by a succession of Ministers, maintained his relentless questioning and pressed the claims of sick veterans and bereaved families in debate after debate before leaving the Commons. Their sense of anguish and anger had already led some veterans to threaten to return their campaign medals to the MoD. But with the change of government in 1997 there was renewed optimism and it was anticipated by some that John Reid, another new Armed Forces Minister, might come to be acknowledged as a friend of the veterans. No one, it was said, knew better how important it was to try to understand their sense of anguish and, at times, anger. The publication of a Government paper, *Gulf War Veterans Illnesses: A New Beginning*, also brought hope that a change of ministers would bring a change of heart.

In fact the new beginning proved illusory. There was a growing lack of confidence in the Medical Assessment Programme. Progress was painfully slow, Alf urging that sick veterans must be spared the hurtful indignities involved in the long delays in receiving urgently needed help.[18] But the MoD was unmoved. They required clear proof that the illnesses reported by Gulf War veterans were war-related and insisted that further research was needed on how to approach them. Robust scientific research was a time-consuming but essential process. Should it establish legal liability, the Government would pay common law compensation. It was not enough for the

---

[17] *Hansard*, Lords, 25 November 1997, col. WA 110.
[18] *Hansard*, Lords, 2 February 1998, cols.479-98.

MoD that an interim report in January 1999, from Professor Simon Wesseley of Kings College, had shown that Gulf veterans were presenting up to three times more ill-health than control groups, or that he found a link between multiple vaccinations and poorer health specific to the Gulf cohort.[19] Wessely, Alf reminded the House, had gone on record as saying that his interim findings required "explanation and action not complacency".[20] But neither this nor a later report from Professor Nicola Cherry of Manchester University,[21] another distinguished research specialist, was sufficient to change the mindset of the MoD.

At the beginning of 2000, Baroness Symons conceded for the MoD that the information available from four research projects was consistent in finding that Gulf veterans were reporting between two to three times more ill-health than comparable groups, but that did not constitute a single condition, nor illnesses unique to Gulf war service. The same symptoms were also reported, but less frequently, by service personnel who had never been deployed to the Gulf and in those who were not in the Gulf conflict but who were involved in operations in Bosnia. There was also, she accepted, a hypothesis that "war syndrome" existed, arising from conflict generally. That had some quite strong support among experts. Notwithstanding "significant shortcomings in the MoD's performance", she concluded, answers to questions about the health of Gulf veterans' could only be addressed by scientific and medical research.[22]

This continued insistence upon yet more research, of course, offered a perfect excuse for further procrastination on the issue .of compensation and also ensured continued resentment and rising anger among veterans. "To many of us," Lord Clement-Jones commented in a debate in October 2001, "the strategy of the Ministry of Defence is to play for time. The essence seems to be to commission endless research papers while having no intention of actually compensating the veterans". The wheels of the MoD had

---

[19] *Hansard*, Lords, 24 March 1999, col.1402.

[20] *Ibid*, col.1382.

[21] Who, while not accepting that there was such a condition as Gulf War syndrome, found that Gulf veterans reported more illness than non-Gulf veterans; that the severity of the symptoms was greater in the Gulf than in non-Gulf veterans; and that three factors were consistently related to severity – the number of inoculations, days spent handling pesticides and days exposed to smoke from oil fires (*Occupational and Environmental Medicine*, May 2001).

[22] *Hansard*, Lords, 26 January 2000, cols. 1655-60.

ground exceedingly slow. It seemed almost that they were insisting that there must be a single 'syndrome' before liability could be accepted.[23]

A public inquiry denied

Ministers had also consistently refused to set up a public inquiry. The first such request to do so had been made by the Royal British Legion to the Prime Minister on 11 June 1997 following a motion at the Legion's annual conference. *"Inexplicably, and without any meaningful apology, a reply was not sent until 26 October 1998, more than 16 months later, obliterating any doubt that attention to the concerns of the ex-service community was of scant concern to New Labour. Even then it came from John Spellar, a junior Minister at the MoD, not Tony Blair to whom the Legion's Secretary-General had written. Moreover, it curtly rejected the call for a public inquiry because, in the MoD's view, such an inquiry would 'simply not be able to answer the question of why the Gulf veterans are ill'. This despite the fact that in the United States a Presidential Commission of Inquiry had been established very soon after the war ended. The British Government's negative response – which was to be repeated year on year – turned resentment into bitterness among Gulf War veterans."*

Having consulted with the Legion, Alf made a further effort, writing personally on 16 November 1999 to Tony Blair, to persuade him to reverse the decision, and it was not until over two months later that he had a negative reply.

On 14 March 2001, the Prime Minister announced the appointment of a Minister for Veterans Affairs, a new post to be filled by Dr Lewis Moonie. All veterans, it was said, would now have a single ministerial focal point for any queries or problems arising from their service in the armed forces. An interdepartmental veterans' task force, supported by a veterans' forum, was also established to assist the Minister. According to Lord Bach, newly appointed as a Joint Parliamentary Under-Secretary of State to speak for the MoD in the House of Lords, its first meeting, held on 24 July 2001, had been "a great success". Making his first comment on Gulf War illnesses, Bach agreed that a study by a team led by Dr Nicola Cherry of Manchester

---

[23] *Hansard*, Lords, 17 October 2001, col. 688-690.

University had found that Gulf veterans reported greater severity of symptoms than those who were not deployed to the Gulf; but this overall severity, he said, was "not high" (*calling into question the use of "severity"*). He said also that mortality among Gulf veterans was almost exactly the same as in a comparison group that did not deploy to the Gulf. And, said Lord Bach, a team of Guy's, King's and St Thomas Schools of Medicine had noted that "no evidence has emerged to date of either distinct biomedical abnormalities or premature mortality". Research was ongoing and in the meantime the MoD would keep an open mind about the causes of ill health experienced by Gulf veterans. The Government was committed to dealing with them "openly, honestly and fairly".[24]

Alf invited to join US Congressional Inquiry

Lord Bach's view was strikingly at odds with the mood of the Royal British Legion and that of the 1,890 veterans and family members who had lodged active legal notices of intention to claim. Nor did it square with what was happening on the other side of the Atlantic. In January 2002, in recognition both of his parliamentary work and standing with the ex-service community in Britain, Alf was invited - uniquely for a non-American – to sit on equal terms with Congressmen at hearings of a US Congressional Committee of Inquiry into Gulf War Illnesses. Appointed by the US House of Representatives, the inquiry was important in throwing light on differences in approach of the defence departments of Britain and the US. The US Department of Defense (DoD) was faced with claims from veterans on a far greater scale, the US having deployed over 700,000 troops to our 50,000–plus, suggesting that they would have perhaps fourteen times the number of sick veterans in the UK. While neither the DoD nor the MoD had suggested any cause and effect for commonly presented symptoms, the American approach was significantly more conciliatory and humane than in Britain, where legal costs had risen steeply and looked certain to go on rising.

The case of Nigel Thompson

One event in that same month was of considerable concern to British veterans. On 23 January 2002, Petty Officer Nigel Thompson, a Gulf

---

[24] *Hansard*, Lords, 17 October 2001, cols.693-700.

War veteran, died at the age of 44 of motor neurone disease. Alf was aware that a research study had found this condition to be more than twice as prevalent among US Gulf War veterans than in the general population as a whole and that it was accepted in the US as war-related. Returning from Washington he asked whether this would lead to reconsideration of the claim for Nigel's illness to be accepted as war-related. Not yet, responded Lord Bach for the MoD: research findings in the US had still to be published in peer-reviewed scientific literature. When they were, the Government would consider carefully their implications for UK Gulf veterans.

US Congressional Committee of Inquiry meets in the Palace of Westminster

With all his usual determination, Alf continued to press the issue and pulled off a remarkable coup. He succeeded in arranging a hearing of the US Congressional Committee of Inquiry in the British Parliament, which he himself opened. Among other notable Congressmen, the Hon. Christopher Shays (Connecticut), who chaired the committee, the Hon. Bernie Sanders (Vermont) and the Hon. Adam Putnam (Florida), the youngest member of the United States Congress, were there. The hearing, held on 18–19 June 2002, was a 'first' in the history of the Palace of Westminster as the first-ever Congressional hearing to be held in the British Parliament. In fact it was the first such hearing at Westminster of a parliamentary committee from any other legislature in the world. It was also historic for two other reasons. Firstly, that it gave US congressmen the opportunity to hear UK veterans and bereaved family members speak. With huge coverage by the media in Britain and the United States, they did so, in the words of Christopher Shays, "with the same quiet, aching eloquence" he had heard so often from their US counterparts. He shared with them what he described as "their sense of frustration and betrayal over a decade of official denials from both sides of the Atlantic about the role of wartime exposures in causing their illnesses".[26] Secondly, and no less memorably, they now heard a presentation by a panel of eminent researchers on "subtle but objectively discernible brain cell damage resulting from toxic exposures", at which it was shown that cells thus damaged could

---

[26] *Research into Persian Gulf War Veterans' Illnesses, Congressional record no.107-237.*

send distorted chemical signals throughout the body, offering a tenable explanation of the variety of symptoms suffered by Gulf War veterans.[27]

Alf had set the scene for the congressional hearing with a short, but notable speech, recalling that US and British troops had fought side by side in the war to liberate Kuwait. It was therefore, he said, entirely appropriate for elected representatives in the two countries to work as closely as possible in ensuring a parliamentary involvement in addressing the problem of the still medically unexplained illnesses of Gulf War veterans and to vouchsafe just treatment both for those afflicted and the dependants of those who had died since the conflict.

One of those who gave evidence, and did so most movingly, was Samantha Thompson, the widow of Nigel. Another, and one of the most impressive, was John Nichol, formerly a Flight Lieutenant in the Royal Air Force and then President of the Gulf Veterans' Branch of the Royal British Legion. He had served in the Falklands, Bosnia and Iraq over a period of 15 years. On the first day of the war with Iraq, his aircraft was shot down over Baghdad and he spent seven weeks of brutality as a prisoner of war, exhibited by his captors on television screens all over the world.

John Nichol argued that the circumstances of the Gulf War were markedly different from those of other recent conflicts, leaving in its wake a range of illnesses that spread across the medical spectrum. The MoD's reaction when veterans started to complain of medical problems had, said Nichol, been "far from satisfying". Little had been done to address their problems. They felt neglected and believed the only answer would be for the Prime Minister to set up a public inquiry where all relevant issues could be openly reviewed and any lessons learned acted upon quickly. If there was nothing to hide, asked Nichol, why shy away from an open inquiry to try to establish why our veterans were inexplicably ill and dying? In peace, he concluded, they truly deserved far better treatment from the politicians who were so ready to send them to war.[28] As it was,

[27] *Ibid.*
[28] *Research into Persian Gulf War Veterans' Illnesses, Congressional record no.107-237, pp.63/67.*

this was the only inquiry British veterans had been invited to address.

Another to be heard at the Congressional hearing on 18 June was Patrick Allen, President of the UK Association of Personal Injury Lawyers and a senior partner of Hodge Jones & Allen, Solicitors. Since 1998 his firm had been contracted by the Legal Services Commission to carry out investigations into Gulf War illness compensation claims. They had acted personally for around 600 veterans and co-ordinated the claims of around 2,000 of them involved in a class action. Allen revealed an interesting sub-plot played out beyond the House of Commons. By then many comparative studies carried out in the UK, Canada and US had all come up with roughly the same conclusions: namely, that veterans who served in the Gulf suffered ill health two or three times more than those who did not. In the absence of any other resort, claims for redress had necessarily to be brought through the courts and the burden of proof was in all cases on the claimant. Such were the legal and scientific complexities of claims, however, and the time and expense involved in court proceedings, Hodge Jones & Allen believed that attempts should now be made, with the assistance of mediators, to reach an out-of-court settlement of the claims. This idea was quickly pursued by Alf and on 27 February 2001 the Prime Minister exchanged letters with him, the outcome of which was that a meeting was arranged on 21 March with Dr Moonie. In the event, however, the Veterans' Minister was not prepared to allow a mediation of the claims and the initiative evaporated in a number of *ad hoc* meetings to discuss peripheral areas of dispute.

The case of David Peachell

Through 2002 and into 2003, the pressure was kept up on the MoD. One question Alf asked on 11 December 2002 is of particular interest. It concerned the Rev. David Peachell, a Gulf War veteran who had served as an army chaplain during the conflict, now afflicted with auto-immune and depressive disorders, neurological diseases, diabetes and post-traumatic stress disorder, who had to take early retirement as an Anglican vicar on grounds of ill health. The medical advisers of the Church of England Pensions Board had readily accepted his condition as having been caused by 'Gulf War illness'. Why then, asked Alf, did the MoD persist in going from defeat to defeat in contesting the validity of that term at pension appeal tribunals and the courts alike? Lord Bach yet again repeated the department's stock reply: "A war pension can be paid for any disablement provided that a causal link to service is accepted". Awards were for "service-related disablement, not a list of specific diagnoses".

"Even the most distinguished students of semantics may find this line of reasoning hard to follow, but Lord Bach was radiantly content to rest on the assertion that there was, as yet, no proper basis for recognising Gulf War syndrome as an appropriate diagnostic label".[29]

The Rev. Peachell was himself by no means silent, having been reported in the world edition of BBC News as saying that successive governments had not faced up to the illness: "None of them is good enough to say sorry. They are hoping that we will die [but] I am not prepared to crawl away and die like a poisoned rat. America has come clean about it and pensioned and treated people compassionately. Here no politician or Prime Minister can hack it. They have not got the calibre".[30]

Alf also renewed his questioning on the use of vaccines and their effects and secured and led yet another debate in the House of Lords on 15 July 2003. In blatant breach of all the conventions of the House, one of his most important parliamentary questions, tabled on 22 January 2003, went unanswered until 9 October, involving the MoD in considerable embarrassment all across Parliament and throughout the ex-service community. When it finally came, the reply ran to over 12 columns of *Hansard*, possibly the longest answer in parliamentary history, and brought to light disturbing facts about medical records and the supply and use of vaccines that had never previously been admitted. Of particular concern was the revelation that pertussis (whooping cough) vaccine, then licensed in France but not in the UK and not recommended here for use in adults, had been used in the immunisation programme in combination with anthrax vaccine in the belief that it offered a way

---

[29] *Hansard*, Lords, 11 December 2002, cols.222-225.
[30] News report, 30 October 2002.

of increasing protection. This notwithstanding prior concern expressed by the UK's National Institute for Biological Standards and Control, based on animal testing, that the co-administration of anthrax and pertussis vaccines might be dangerous. Although the Department of Health was alerted to the importance and relevance of this finding on 21 December 1990, which then faxed the information to the MoD and discussed it with two, possibly three, MoD officials, the immunisation programme, which began on 2 January 1991, included the co-administration of the two vaccines. Just how the vaccines were administered was not made clear, but it was admitted that because records were often not properly kept it was impossible to estimate the precise extent to which vaccination schedules were complied with. Nor was it possible to say to what extent issues – such as what other medication individuals were receiving – were discussed with those receiving vaccinations.[31]

The politics of delay

By 2004, over thirteen years had elapsed since the end of the Gulf War and the MoD's patchwork of excuses was now looking woefully threadbare. While they continued to insist that research was the only way forward, their programme of research was woefully inadequate and proceeded at slower than snail's pace. The programme, said Baroness Crawley in response to a question of Alf's on 26 February, was extremely complex and they could not hurry the assessment of its results.[32] By then, over 5,000 veterans had reported a wide range of undiagnosed illnesses since the conflict. Some were already dead; others, now in broken health, still found themselves locked in what the Legion described as "a long hard battle" to have their illnesses accepted as war-related. *"They were entitled to be angry that, having rightly sanctioned public inquiries into the sinking of the Marchioness and the Paddington rail crash, among others over recent years, the Government adamantly refused to commission one into the thousands of still medically unexplained illnesses among its own troops".*

---

[31] *Hansard*, Lords, 9 October 2003, cols. WA67-79. Alf's question prompted a review of the safety of administering the vaccines together, resulting in later guidance from the Committee on Safety of Medicines that, if necessary, anthrax vaccine could be given at the same time as other vaccines, but administered by separate injections into different anatomical sites, ideally into different limbs. There was then, however, no suggestion that anthrax was to be used in combination with pertussis vaccine.

[32] *Hansard*, Lords, 26 February 2004, col.338.

In a public statement on the 14 June 2004, Alf addressed the Government's refusal to act fairly toward them: "The Legion," he said, "acted in keeping with its highest traditions in calling for a public inquiry into all aspects of the handling of Gulf War illnesses; and there are those on both sides of both Houses of Parliament who believe it to be profoundly wrong that an inquiry has so long been resisted. They fully accept that mistakes made in 1990–91 were not deliberate. They know as well as anyone in executive government that decisions about protective measures often have to be made on a 'needs must' basis; but they rightly insist – and believe that any public inquiry worthy of the name would strongly have insisted – that the nation as a whole must play its part in meeting the cost of such decisions.

"None of us at Westminster, least of all Ministers, can want to see the afflicted and bereaved of the Gulf conflict made to suffer the strain and hurtful and demeaning indignities that protracted delay in dealing with their concerns can impose. Yet sadly many veterans feel that such delay has occurred and their public representatives must go on pressing for the truth about their illnesses".

"Of all the duties that fall to parliamentarians to discharge, none is of more compelling priority than to act justly to citizens who are prepared to lay down their lives for their country, and the dependants of those who do so. There was no delay in the response of our troops to the call of duty in 1990–91. Nor should there be any further delay now in discharging in full our debt of honour to them".

Shortly after this statement, researchers at the London School of Hygiene and Tropical Medicine published the results of the widest survey yet of Gulf War veterans. They had compared the self-reported health status of more than 24,000 of them with that of 18,500 who did not go to the Gulf. The survey confirmed that Gulf War veterans reported far more illnesses than those who were not deployed there. The symptoms reported in all groups studied was the same: what differed was the frequency at which they occurred.

A revolutionary initiative: the Lloyd Inquiry

Having no realistic expectation that his appeal to honour alone would achieve a change of policy, Alf had now formulated a strategy unique in the annals of parliamentary history. The catalyst that brought it into the open came in a letter sent to him on 5 February 2004 by Stephen Irwin QC, Chairman of the Bar Council, and other lawyers who had taken a close and continuous interest in the problems and needs of Gulf War veterans. By prior arrangement with Alf, the lawyers asked him if, in his capacity as Honorary Parliamentary Adviser to the Legion, he would make one further approach to the Government drawing their urgent attention to the veterans' worsening plight. The class action then in motion would have had to establish not only the probability of a clear causal link between the veterans' illnesses and their Gulf War service, but also negligence and/or breach of statutory duty; and this was "not currently viable". Thus the legal road to a settlement was now closed. Even so, thousands of Gulf veterans were suffering ill-health that science had not explained and which experts world-wide associated with their service in the Gulf conflict. The lawyers' letter therefore urged that the Prime Minister himself should "consider instituting a full public review of the position of veterans (as has been called for by the Royal British Legion) and to instigate a process of conciliation with the veterans' groups". This, they argued, should be designed "to mark the effects of war service on the veterans who are suffering and to make good by *ex-gratia* payments the deficiencies of the War Pensions Scheme".

Alf's first step was to make the letter the basis of a final approach to the Prime Minister, urging him to yield to the lawyers' pleading. When Tony Blair's reply came – restating the Government's inflexibility on the issue of an inquiry – Alf was ready to proceed to the next stage in his predetermined strategy, which was to set up an independent public inquiry on his own initiative. As Anthony Howard, a veteran and highly distinguished parliamentary correspondent, later pointed out in a feature in *The Times*: "The Government had failed to take into account the sheer resourcefulness of the Gulf War veterans' most formidable parliamentary champion, Lord Morris of Manchester. Honorary adviser to the British Legion at Westminster and, before he became a peer, the most effective Minister for Disabled People this country has ever known, 'Alf' Morris has been around long enough to know how to outwit bureaucratic obduracy. And he has managed to give younger figures at Westminster an object lesson in how to do it".[33]

While awaiting the Prime Minister's response to the lawyers' plea, Alf had pragmatically consulted widely and in confidence on the possibility of finding a retired judge of the highest standing to conduct an independent public inquiry. He found the perfect fit in The Rt. Hon. Lord Lloyd of Berwick, a former senior High Court Judge and Lord of Appeal in Ordinary, the same Lord Lloyd to whom Alf had paid such warm tribute in his maiden speech in the Lords.[34] Lloyd, moreover, was willing to lead the inquiry without payment of any kind, even of personal expenses. Two men who were to be further huge assets to the inquiry responded to Alf's call: a distinguished medical assessor, Dr Norman Jones,[35] and Sir Michael Davies, who until very recently had been Clerk of the Parliaments and thus the administrative head of the House of Lords. Both agreed to sit with Lord Lloyd as his assessors. The inquiry's terms of reference, Alf now announced, would be "to investigate the circumstances that have led to the ill-health and, in some cases death, of over 5,000 British troops following deployment to the Gulf, and to report". It would meet in public.

A more independent and impressive team could scarcely have been conceived; nor a more unquestionably impartial one. None of the inquiry members had previously been involved in either campaigning or debates on the issue of Gulf War illnesses. That they should have been prepared to offer their services for what was to be an arduous inquiry on a voluntary basis was in itself remarkable and reflected the highest credit on Lord Lloyd, Dr Jones and Sir Michael. There would be other expenses, of course, not least those of helping veterans and widows to appear before the inquiry, of meeting the costs of remunerating and setting up an office for Vijay Mehan – a

---

[33] *The Times*, 9 November 2004.

[34] For his advocacy of the view that help for disabled people must in future depend not on where they lived but strictly on the extent of individual need, in the famous case of R. v. Gloucestershire Council, ex parte Michael Barry.

[35] Emeritus Consulting Physician at St Thomas' Hospital and formerly Treasurer of the Royal College of Physicians.

gifted young solicitor who would serve as secretary to the inquiry – and of recording and reporting its proceedings. There were promises of funding from independent charitable trusts made on the assurance of confidentiality and also uninvited small contributions from disabled war pensioners – including one from a Chelsea pensioner – but doubt remained as to whether sufficient funding could be raised. Alf recalls a meeting in the Judges' Room in the House of Lords ten days before his announcement of the inquiry where, in order to maintain the momentum and move on, he undertook to meet any eventual shortfall himself.[36]

It was important that the inquiry should be seen to have no hidden agenda. It had to be made plain also that its task was to establish facts not to apportion blame. In an opening press conference, Lord Lloyd made it clear that "if people can make use of the facts then it is up to them to do so if they want". It was, however, accepted from the start that there was no single underlying cause for all the illnesses, nor were all the illnesses identical.

It was clear also from the outset that although courteously invited by Lord Lloyd to attend, the MoD had no intention of doing so. Having resisted an inquiry since 1997, the prospect of an independent inquiry held in public was anathema to Ministers. But plenty of worthy supporters welcomed Alf's groundbreaking initiative. Typical of many messages of congratulation was a letter from Charles Busby CBE, one of the bravest and most celebrated of our Battle of Britain pilots and subsequently national chairman of the Royal British Legion. "I know," he wrote, "that you have battled for so many years, but you are made of sound timber and do not give in. All power to your elbow, and I am sure that the result of the Inquiry will be of benefit to many now stricken veterans".[37]

Over many weeks in July, August and September, 2004, the inquiry sat taking evidence in the ecclesiastical tranquillity of 1 The Abbey Gardens, London SW1, separate from but adjacent to Westminster Abbey itself and close by the main building of the House of Lords.

---

[36] It is perhaps worth noticing that the final cost of the Lloyd inquiry is believed to have been less than £60,000, compared with the £1.68 million spent on the then very recent Hutton inquiry, and the £130 million on the Savile inquiry into the Bloody Sunday shootings.
[37] Personal letter, 24 June 2004.

There they heard and had expertly recorded the testimony of, among others, a range of Gulf War veterans and of widows of those who succumbed to their illnesses; eminent scientists; doctors and researchers from both sides of the Atlantic; parliamentarians from both sides of both Houses of Parliament; United States Congressmen and leaders of US Federal Agencies; senior former defence chiefs, including two former Chiefs of the Defence Staff, Field Marshal Lord Bramall and Marshal of the Royal Air Force Lord Craig, and General Sir Peter de la Billière, who commanded British forces in the field during the Gulf War. Some witnesses were suggested by the Royal British Legion; others volunteered to appear having learned of the inquiry in the press or on the internet.

One of the most impressive witnesses was again Flight Lieutenant John Nichol, President of the Gulf War Branch of the Royal British Legion, who had previously addressed and been cross-examined, also at Westminster, by the US Congressional Committee. He referred to the apparently unheeded fax cautioning against using anthrax and whooping cough vaccines in combination, sent from the Department of Health to the MoD a month before the war started, and the telephone calls to three members of the MoD's staff which no one could now recall. Was this, he asked, "cock-up or conspiracy?" Describing Alf as "the architect of this independent inquiry", Nichol thanked him for the way in which he had "tirelessly pursued the cause of Gulf veterans" and his "unshakeable commitment" to them. By contrast, he criticised the level of the MoD's spending on research into Gulf War illnesses, which had amounted to £8.5 million since 1997. That averaged some £1.2 million a year or £200 annually for each sick veteran. John Nichol compared that "miserly figure to the billions of pounds wasted in badly managed defence projects", to the £161 million the Government spent on its advertising budget, and the nearly £8 million spent every year on the MoD's entertainment budget. He summed up the feelings of the veterans with stinging sincerity. They had been made by the MoD, he told the inquiry, to feel that they were the enemy.

Another important witness was Robert Haley, professor of medicine at the University of Texas, who had led research into the effects of nerve agents on troops involved in the first Gulf War. He told the inquiry that research by his team, which had both examined veterans and studied animal experiments, indicated that low-level sarin nerve gas released during the conflict could have caused brain cell damage. The US Government had changed its attitude to his work when other distinguished scientists, replicating his studies, had also found brain damage in veterans.

Veterans' Minister stays away

The MoD submitted eleven files of written evidence to the inquiry, almost the whole of which had simply been downloaded from its website. Conspicuous by their absence, however, were Defence Ministers, none of whom was willing to co-operate. Indeed according to James Meikle in *The Guardian* of 16 July 2004, the MoD had even gone to the length of pressurising scientists and other advisers to "observe confidentiality" by boycotting the inquiry. And when Ivor Caplin, Joint Parliamentary Under Secretary of State at the MoD – even though described as the 'Minister for Veterans' – was asked to reconsider his position, he again declined. *"Using the department's all-purpose word for dodging the column, Caplin said it was not 'appropriate' to do so. This was a disastrous misreading of the mood of afflicted veterans and the bereaved families, which the report of the inquiry, with studied politeness, was to call a missed opportunity to begin a process of reconciliation with them."*

In fact all the signs pointed to a hardening of the MoD's attitude. On 4 November 2004 – only days before the inquiry's report – the department published a new report entitled *The 1990/1991 Gulf Conflict: Health and Personnel Related Lessons Identified*, in which MoD officials continued to argue that there was "no clinical evidence to suggest that the known effects of the suspected exposures have affected the health of veterans" and that "the vast body of research undertaken has found no link between specific causes and the symptoms".

"Coming as it did 14 years after the war, experienced MoD watchers saw the timing of this publication as every bit as crass as its contents which, as parliamentary questioning soon revealed, contained no crucially important

information held by the MoD. In fact its 'new' report was even more stale than its files sent to the Lloyd inquiry."

Lord Lloyd would soon publish his report and, even more embarrassingly for the MoD, publication of that of the US Federal Joint Research Advisory Committee on Gulf War Veterans' Illnesses was also imminent.

A report from the USA

The United States report appeared on 12 November. Its conclusions contrasted with those of previous US studies which had found that scientific evidence did not support a causal link between veterans' symptoms and chemical exposures in the Gulf and that stress was likely to have been an important contributing factor to the conditions veterans were presenting. One of the key findings of this new report was that psychiatric illness did not explain ill health in the "vast majority" of the 100,000 sick US Gulf veterans. On the contrary, it found that evidence supported a "probable" link between exposure to neurotoxins and the development of illnesses in Gulf War veterans, and that other wartime exposures may also have contributed to their ill health. Many troops had been exposed to substances – organophosphates heavily used as an insecticide and pyridostigmine bromide in the medication given to coalition troops – that affected the central nervous system and "a growing body of research" indicated that sick veterans differed from healthy ones "on objective measures of neuropathology and impairment".

Anthony Principi, secretary of the US Veterans Affairs Department, promptly made the highly important announcement that the Department would set aside a further $15 million for Gulf War illness research, and that none of it must be used to pay for studies that proposed stress as the only explanation for the mysterious ailments afflicting veterans of the 1991 Gulf War.[38]

The Lloyd Report

Lord Lloyd's report followed five days later. If the MoD publication of 4 November had been intended to pre-empt and defuse its impact, their hopes were shattered. In a work of sustained forensic brilliance,

---

[38] Associated Press, 12 November 2004.

Lord Lloyd emphatically rebutted the MoD's entrenched stance. His main finding was that sick Gulf War veterans were entitled to an admission by the MoD that they were ill because of their service in the Gulf. All epidemiological studies commissioned both in Britain and the US agreed that Gulf veterans were at least twice as likely to suffer ill health as they would have been if they had been deployed elsewhere, for example, Bosnia, or had remained in the UK.

One of the explanations often advanced for ill health among veterans was that it resulted from stress or psychiatric illness. In the years after the war, sick veterans were told, in Britain and the US alike, that they were not physically ill. By implication, their illnesses were 'all in the mind'. This was emphatically rejected by Lord Lloyd. While there had indeed been a very high level of stress, that alone could not explain Gulf War illnesses.

The report of the Lloyd inquiry, written before the American report appeared, was in almost complete agreement with it. If the 'jury was still out' on the precise causes of the illnesses presented, it was no longer enough for the MoD to say: "Yes, you are ill; but since we do not know which of the possible causes has caused your particular illness we are not going to admit that your illness is due to your service". A small proportion of those who were ill had the classic symptoms of post traumatic stress disorder, but this could not account for the great majority of those who were ill and felt let down and rejected. Having listened to the evidence of a wide range of veterans and of bereaved relatives, each of them representative of many others, together with much other evidence besides, the Lloyd inquiry considered their complaints justified.

Lord Lloyd also dealt with the term 'Gulf War Syndrome'. This, he noticed, was what the veterans had always called it and was the name under which they had made 1,388 claims for war pensions. It was also the name used by the public. But it was a name, Lord Lloyd found, that was "just a label" and the inquiry had been unable to see why the MoD had such difficulty in accepting it as an 'umbrella' description. The definition offered at paragraph 201 of the report was simply: "A collection of symptoms and signs which tend to occur together, and form a characteristic pattern, but which may not necessarily always be due to the same pathological cause". The inquiry recommended that since the definition was no more than a convenient label, favoured by the veterans, for wrapping the symptoms from which they were undoubtedly suffering, the MoD should accept it.

The question of compensation did not figure largely in the evidence presented to the inquiry by veterans themselves. For them the issue was not primarily one of money, but clearly any financial recompense would mark an acceptance of a link between their illnesses and the extraordinary – in many respects unprecedented – hazards to which Gulf veterans had been exposed.

"They were defending their honour, for in their eyes the MoD's stance clearly meant that, having first been hailed as brave and heroic for liberating Kuwait, they were now being characterised as hypochondriacs, lead swingers and even would-be benefit cheats".

Nonetheless, the issue of financial compensation featured conspicuously in the evidence of others, notably that of Marshal of the Royal Air Force Lord Craig of Radley, Paul Tyler MP, Michael Mates MP, Major General (Peter) Craig, Colonel Terence English of the Royal British Legion and others. Lord Craig told the inquiry that the absence of closure after so many years was now indefensible. "A little magnanimity" and an "imaginative one-off approach" was now called for. The Lloyd Inquiry asked the MoD to pay heed to these views. The veterans deserved no less. It recommended that the MoD should set up a fund out of which *ex gratia* payments should be made on a *pro-rata* basis to all veterans who had made successful claims, while the claims that had been rejected should be reviewed in the light of the inquiry's report.

Military chiefs call for action

When the Lloyd report was published on 17 November, Ministers did not immediately rush to air their views. Alf's reaction was soon made plain and, when it came, maintained the momentum created by its publication. Moreover, he had the support of some of the most respected soldiers of the time: two former Chiefs of the Defence Staff – Lords Bramall and Craig – and no less a figure also than the

Commander in the Field of British Forces during the 1990–91 conflict, General Sir Peter de la Billière. Together, on the 30 November 2004, all three joined with Alf in a letter to *The Times* that recalled the Duke of Marlborough's comment after Blenheim. Speaking in the House of Lords, Marlborough had said that the best way to celebrate the great victory there was to do right by the soldiers who had fought so bravely with him. The Lloyd report was in that proud tradition. Surely the time had come, they wrote, for Her Majesty's Government now to acknowledge that its endless procrastination, the inconclusive trials it had instigated and the expensive litigation on all sides should be brought to an end by agreeing to make *ex gratia* payments in full and final settlement. An acknowledgement by the Government to the men and women who had been struck down that their illnesses were due to their service in the Gulf would also be welcome and do some good in reversing the sense of rejection so many veterans now felt.

Alf's view was that not to have given evidence to an independent tribunal with the unimpeachable credentials of the Lloyd inquiry team was a crass blunder by a department of state claiming to pride itself on political transparency, and was now widely seen as such: *"What could have been more opaque than to hide from open questioning by a lawyer of Lord Lloyd's eminence and men of such distinction as Sir Michael Davies and Dr Jones? People on the Clapham omnibus – not to mention Gulf War veterans – were bound to see the MoD as defensive and so fixated by its own perspective that it had to go to any lengths to dodge the light of scrutiny. To veterans' organisations this obliterated the claim to political transparency and laid bare a total lack of commitment to finding a just solution"*.

In the Lords, just before the 2004 Christmas recess, Alf kept up the pressure by securing and leading a debate on the report of Lord Lloyd's independent inquiry. It had been hailed by stricken veterans and the bereaved families, he said, as "a triumph of social concern over official indifference: a treatise of transparent integrity and humanity". Yet the MoD was as apathetic in responding to its recommendations as it had been in failing to co-operate with the inquiry.

Alf was supported by Lady Park of Monmouth. Having taken part in no less than eight full debates on the issue, starting in 1996, she pointed to Annex D of Lord Lloyd's report listing ten pages of reports written and research projects undertaken from 1994 to 2004, some of them still proceeding. The Government apparently took the view, she said, that nothing definitive could be done until its research programme had been completed, thus making it impossible for anyone to know when closure of the veterans' claims could be completed. In the meantime "men sicken and die or become more ill". No government, she insisted, could afford to be seen to be unable or unwilling to act in the face of the evidence, nor to be seen to be careless of the well-being of our service men and women.

Air Vice-Marshal Lord Garden, a former Deputy Chief of the Defence Staff,[39] speaking as a recent insider, added his voice to the assault on the MoD. He confessed to finding it a little embarrassing to admit to having worked until recently in its "Kremlin-like" headquarters. But he could not fail to notice "a real paradox" between the ethos of the MoD and the individual armed services. The latter were trained to look after their people in both peace and war. A duty of care extended from the top to the bottom. Britain had such good armed forces because everyone knew they could rely on their comrades and their leadership. By contrast, he said, the MoD had a reputation of "cover-up, lack of transparency and unwillingness to support the troops when they are in distress". The MoD, he concluded, needed to take a more enlightened view of its responsibilities for its people.

Among others supporting Alf, the distinguished medical expert Lord Turnberg[40] concurred in commending Lord Lloyd's report. He regarded it as a very good summary of what was, to many, a very confusing picture. It had made a very good contribution to delineating what was fact and what was opinion. He accepted that more research was necessary if the mistakes made during the first Gulf War were not to be repeated, but meanwhile, despite the

---

[39] Formerly Sir Timothy Garden CB. Also RAF Air Vice-Marshall (retired), Director of the Royal Institute of International Affairs and Visiting Professor at the Centre for Defence Studies at King's College, London.

[40] Professor the Lord Turnberg, KBE MD FRCP. Professor of Medicine from 1973-97. His many distinguished appointments have included Presidency of the Royal College of Physicians and Scientific Advisor to the Association of Medical Research Charities. He has published four books and some 150 learned articles on medical and scientific research.

difficulties in making a clear-cut definitive diagnosis, the veterans who were suffering should receive some compensation. Lord Turnberg hoped the Minister replying to the debate (Lord Bach) would recognise that not to do so would increasingly be seen as not only unwarranted but uncaring.[41]

In the Commons, the call for magnanimity was taken up on 18 January 2005 by Brian Donohoe (Labour, Ayrshire Central), followed a week later by Tam Dalyell (Labour, Linlithglow), the 'Father of the House'. As a Labour Member of Parliament who had been there for a long time, said Dalyell, "I am ashamed of the seven years of Conservative lack of action but even more ashamed of seven years' inaction by a Labour Government". The Government's response was one of repetitive rebuttal.

Ivor Caplin, however, declared that the Government saw no case why one group of veterans should be singled out for "preferential treatment" by way of an *ex gratia* payment on top of the pensions they already received. As to where the Government intended to take the matter, he persisted that they still wanted, almost 15 years on, to "find out why some veterans from the first Gulf conflict are ill". To that end, he went on, the research programme would, at completion, have cost £8.5 million, while MoD officials were working closely with their US counterparts to ensure that the UK had "full visibility of all American research into Gulf health issues".[42]

"By now, veterans were grossly sceptical that 'visibility' of anything could move the Government toward a just solution. Their feeling was that the Government's mindset was that thousands of stricken veterans and bereaved families alike – and Air Vice-Marshal Lord Garden – were misguided and the MoD all-knowing and faultless. They could be forgiven for thinking that, on the pattern of its record since 1997, ministerial promises to give the issues renewed attention would come to nothing and that they were unmoveably resolved to go on ad infinitum, ignoratio elenchi, in pursuit of no useful conclusion".

---

[41] *Hansard*, Lords, 21 December 2004, cols.1717-1740.
[42] *Hansard*, Commons, 18 January 2005, cols. 235-237WH.

Time for a change of direction

With the Government under concerted criticism from seasoned parliamentarians and arguably the most eminent of the Law Lords, it was not unreasonable for the veterans to insist that the time had come for a reappraisal of its strategy. Inflexibility and lack of respect for the most distinguished of critics was doing nothing to assuage the anger and contempt of sick veterans who were wearied and felt demeaned by the attitude of successive administrations toward them. Ministers, they argued, had to recognise a need for reconciliation and a genuine resolve to find a solution, rather than continue to consign the issues to the long grass of research.

Their illnesses, so visibly afflicting the veterans – previously A1 – were undeniable. And while some of those illnesses may have been entirely unrelated to war service and experiences, the overwhelming evidence pointed to the hazards of the Gulf War being largely responsible. This was a situation similar to that faced by Alf when he had to try to resolve the cases on the thalidomide 'Y List' (see page 217), and it called for a similar generosity of spirit. Thus in pressing the Government to accept the Lloyd recommendations, Alf's stance was not 'do as I say' but 'do as I did'.

The American exemplar

Although Ivor Caplin had declined to participate in the Lloyd inquiry, he nevertheless visited the United States during Remembrance Week 2003. Reporting back in *The House Magazine*,[43] he wrote that the main purpose of his visit had been "to see how the Americans look after their veterans". In that context, as Alf could have predicted, his findings were remarkable. The US Veteran Affairs Department, he reported, was "the largest single provider of health professional training in the world, providing medical care to nearly five million veterans through 162 hospitals, 850 clinics and 135 nursing homes". The hospitals, founded in 1946, were the only free health providers in the USA, free at the point of delivery and across the country. "The numbers," wrote Caplin, "are staggering – almost three million veterans receive some form of financial support, totalling almost $23 billion a year". He was particularly interested to

---

[43] 'Veteran Traveller', 24 November 2003, pp.4-5.

discover that the US Department of Defense "doesn't get sued", whilst in Britain "we are paying out an increasing [but still undisclosed] amount in compensation and legal costs". Despite this, Caplin failed to draw the inescapable conclusion that it would be preferable to settle rather than continue to resist British veterans' claims in a climate of endless bitterness. Nor did he comment on the remarkable disparity of approach to the claims of sick veterans in the two countries. He might also have added that, having set up a Presidential Commission of Inquiry into Gulf War Illnesses soon after the war, the US Government had, by 1999, already come to accept that their veterans' illnesses were mostly due to Gulf service. Of some 700,000 US troops who served in the Gulf, 83 per cent became eligible for benefits through their equivalent of the Veterans Agency and 45 per cent had by then sought medical care there. The US Government had also accepted that 100,000 American troops were exposed repeatedly to low levels of chemical warfare agents; that more than 250,000 received pyridostigmine bromide, which the Pentagon could not rule out as being linked to Gulf illnesses; that 150,000 received the highly controversial and hotly-debated anthrax vaccine; that more than half their deployed troops entered or lived for months in areas contaminated by more than 315 tonnes of depleted uranium and radioactive toxic waste; and that thousands of them lived outdoors for months near to 700 burning oil wells that belched fumes and toxic particles day and night.[44] And finally, that the United States Government, by the end of 2004, had already spent or committed 280 million dollars on research, compared to our £8.5 million.[45]

A bid for closure

On 12 April 2005, a further attempt to resolve the claims of our Gulf War veterans was made in the rarely used but perhaps most distinguished meeting place in the House of Lords – the Queen's Robing Room, a venue made available only by Black Rod by consent of Her Majesty the Queen. The occasion, chaired by Alf, brought together Lord Lloyd of Berwick, Marshal of the Royal Air Force Lord Craig of Radley, Dr Jack Melling, formerly Director of

---

[44] *Hansard*, Lords, 26 January 2000, col.1648 (The Countess of Mar).
[45] *Hansard*, Lords, 21 December 2004, col. 1739.

the Microbiology Research Authority at Porton Down and Consultant to both the US Government Accountability Office (the investigative arm of Congress) and the US Research Advisory Committee on Gulf War Illnesses, Professor Simon Wesseley, Susan Freeth, Director Welfare for the Royal British Legion, and veterans Flt. Lt. John Nichol, Chairman of the Gulf War Veterans' Branch of the Legion, Dr Nigel Graveston, Chairman of the Gulf War Veterans and Families Association and Major Christine Lloyd, a severely disabled veteran of the conflict. The report of Lord Lloyd's inquiry, said Alf in opening the proceedings, offered an honourable way of achieving closure. Although it had been summarily discounted by the MoD, the report had been informed by a perspective notably absent from the MoD's thinking, which had been characterised by chronic procrastination and grave misunderstanding of what US research had achieved. Alf cited examples of a huge disparity between recent parliamentary replies and the findings of earlier US reports. Ministers here, for example, had grossly understated the tonnage of sarin and cyclosarin involved in the fall-out from the bombings at Khamisiyah and had assumed, contrary to the findings in the US, that exposure to low levels of nerve agents produces no long-term consequences. Moreover, human epidemiological studies from Japan, undertaken there after terrorist incidents in Tokyo in the 1990s, also showed chronic symptoms and/or alterations in brain chemistry after low-dose exposure to sarin.

Lord Lloyd was the next speaker. If anyone had felt a scintilla of doubt following his earlier inquiry report, then his resume and update on this occasion was such as to remove any possible ambiguity. It not only set the inquiry and its recommendations in context, but also dealt point by point with the Government's "worse than negative" response and the criticisms they had made of its findings. Lord Lloyd said that the Government had "made no attempt to answer any of the important issues" that had been raised. They had concentrated on "trivial" and "peripheral" points, such as the anonymous financial backing for his inquiry. He told the meeting that two facts emerged from all the evidence: first, that large numbers of troops returning from the Gulf were ill, both here and in the United States, very many of them with still medically unexplained illnesses; and secondly, that those who served in the Gulf were twice as likely to become ill as personnel who served in Bosnia or had remained at home. These two facts were indisputable and required a positive response from the Government. What veterans and those working to help them wanted was an end to the delay after now more than 14 years.

Lord Lloyd had been encouraged by a recent letter from the Rt. Hon. Charles Kennedy MP, then Leader of the Liberal Democrats, expressing his unequivocal support and welcoming Lord Lloyd's findings as the way forward to closure on an issue "that should have been resolved long, long ago". He noted that the inquiry had been funded by a number of charitable trusts and members of the public, all of whom wished to remain anonymous, and none of whom, as Lord Lloyd had made clear, had any axe to grind. The inquiry had been held in public, he continued, open to all who wished to be there, and the assistance of such distinguished and unquestionably independent assessors as Sir Michael Davies and Dr Norman Jones "explained the wide acclaim won by the report both here and abroad". In contrast, wrote Kennedy, while paying lip service to 'transparency', the MoD refused even to disclose the legal and other costs to taxpayers of contesting the war pension claims of Gulf veterans. They had failed to give Lord Lloyd access to MoD officials during his inquiry, Kennedy continued, "at a time when Gulf veterans with terminal illnesses were travelling from all over Britain to do so". They had also failed to honour undertakings to inform Parliament by given dates of the outcome of Porton Down's work on the health effects for British troops of the multiple immunisation programme and of fallout from the Khamisiyah bombings of March 1991 that included huge amounts of sarin and cyclosarin.

Charles Kennedy's damning critique ended with a call for all political parties to join in achieving a settlement on the basis recommended by Lord Lloyd. And were Liberal Democrats to be successful in the impending General Election, he said, they pledged to implement the report; meanwhile he was grateful "not only for its scrupulous fairness and clarity, but also for its humanity".[46]

---

[46] Letter released by Lord Lloyd and dated 23 March 2005.

Ministers continue to prevaricate

On 21 July 2005, Alf brought the issue back to the House of Lords, asking in the broadest possible terms what further consideration the Government had given to the problems and needs of veterans of the 1990/91 Gulf conflict with medically unexplained illnesses, and the dependants of those who had died. The Government's response, which followed another success in the General Election, was assigned to Lord Drayson, a new and it seemed more conciliatory Parliamentary Under-Secretary at the MoD. He said the Government remained "determined to address the medical concerns of Gulf veterans".

But was it not disturbing, Alf asked, that 14 years on from the conflict the House was still awaiting the outcome even of the Porton Down study of the effects of vaccines used on our troops? Moreover, was Drayson aware that US Government spending on research into Gulf War illnesses has now reached $316 million, while we had committed only £8.5 million; and of the Royal British Legion's statement that Gulf War widows would have been better treated had their husbands been in the United States and not the British Army?

Lord Drayson pointed to the "real challenge" often faced by science in coming to a conclusion as to the basis and cause for disease. He told the House that the complexity of factors within this whole area should not be underestimated. This response, in Alf's view, could only serve to consolidate the scepticism of those who took the view that research could not yield effective results within a meaningful time frame. He recalled that delay in the publication of findings from Porton Down had been raised as far back as October 2002, when Baroness Crawley, speaking for the Government, had said that it was hoped to have the final completed report by the end of 2003,[47] since when no more had been heard of making it available to the House.

Ecclesiastical interventions

The Lord Bishop of Norwich had joined the debate to comment that the Government's failure to recognise Gulf War illnesses simply

[47] *Hansard*, Lords, 7 October 2002, col.3.

added to the psychological distress of those who suffered from them.[48] And shortly afterwards, not content with this parliamentary foray, he took the remarkable step of addressing an open letter to the Prime Minister, now supported by the Roman Catholic Bishop of East Anglia, the Chair of the East Anglia Methodist District and the Bishops of Oxford, St. Edmundsbury & Ipswich, Portsmouth and Truro. The letter referred back to the early retirement of the Rev. David Peachell, pointing out that his distressing condition mirrored that of many others among whom he had served in the Gulf. They argued that the official failure to recognise their condition added to their distress and wished to add their voice to the rapidly increasing chorus imploring the Government to bring closure to an issue that should have been settled long ago. They felt that Lord Lloyd's inquiry had demonstrated conclusively that the veterans' illnesses were linked to Gulf War service. That they were not some figment of anyone's imagination but a terrifying reality that should be recognised by Ministers, and adequate compensation and support should now go to the victims and bereaved families.[49]

The Prime Minister responded on 17 October 2005, insisting that, while neither he nor the Ministry of Defence thought that the ill-health reported by the veterans was a figment of their imagination, the overwhelming weight of opinion of the scientific and medical community was that there were "too many different symptoms reported for this ill-health to be characterised as a syndrome in medical terms". He made no attempt to document this statement or to justify the huge gap between spending on research in Britain and the United States, but reiterated, nevertheless, that health and welfare support to veterans and their families was a top priority and always would be for this Government.

The Lord Bishop was unimpressed. He and his co-signatories were deeply disquieted by the Prime Minister's response, which they saw as "little more than a rehash of dated and discredited arguments used again and again by the MoD". In particular, those who had drafted his response had dismissed in disparaging terms Lord Lloyd's scrupulously fair and balanced findings and had ignored

---

[48] *Hansard*, Lords, 21 July 2005, cols. 1593-95.
[49] Open letter dated 25 September 2005, copied to Alf, Lord Lloyd and political leaders.

both the case of the Rev. David Peachell – of which they must have been aware, since it had been raised orally by Alf in the House of Lords – and also the views of the eminent military chiefs who had joined in calling for an end to the MoD's "endless procrastination, inconclusive trials and expensive litigation".

This was strong stuff, given further weight by a joint letter to all Scottish MPs and MSPs sent by the Rt. Rev. David Lacy, Moderator of the Church of Scotland, and Cardinal O'Brien, the Archbishop of St Andrews and Edinburgh, stressing the urgency of the need for closure of the controversy on the basis of the findings of Lord Lloyd's report. This, the Moderator and the Cardinal concluded, was not an issue for party animus but one on which Scotland's public representatives and churches should work together to achieve a humane settlement with no further delay.

Breakthrough

The MoD was now under the severest pressure and, behind the scenes, its case was beginning to crumble. Crucially, on the morning of 19 September 2005, the Veterans Agency submitted a response to the argument brought on behalf of Guardsman Daniel Martin in a test case heard by the Pensions Appeal Tribunal (PAT). At paragraph 11 of this seminal document, pregnant with consequences, the Veterans Agency at last accepted that 'Gulf War Syndrome' was a valid term to be used as an umbrella description for a variety of different conditions that had arisen. To quote from that key paragraph: "If the label is no more than that, a label, then the Secretary of State would concede that the appellant would be entitled to succeed. 'Gulf War Syndrome' is a label that is used by some persons, doctors and lay people, to refer to a broad range of symptoms suffered by certain servicemen and women who were connected with the 1991 Gulf War".

As we have seen, the US National Institute of Health Workshop had found, back in April 1994, that no single disease or syndrome was apparent, but rather multiple illnesses with overlapping symptoms and causes. The wheel had now turned full circle. In its finding of 31 October 2005 on the appeal of Guardsman Martin, the Tribunal commented: "Thus, 14 years after the end of the Gulf War, the Veterans Agency has finally conceded the validity of the label 'Gulf War Syndrome'. In that time many applications for such a condition were rejected, there have been numerous and expensive court cases and there are at present a number of ex-servicemen [at least 1,500] awaiting the result of this hearing. It is not for this Tribunal to ascertain why such a late concession was made but the kindest comment that can be made is that the lateness of this concession was unfortunate".

After assessing the evidence the Tribunal concluded, in total vindication of Lord Lloyd, that while the appellant had failed to show that 'Gulf War Syndrome' was a discrete pathological entity, Lord Lloyd in his report and Professor Simon Wesseley were correct when they said that "veterans of the Gulf War later developed an excess of symptomatic ill-health over and above that to be expected in the normal course of events" and that there was, retrospectively, "a Gulf War Health effect". In further endorsement of Lord Lloyd, the Tribunal found that the term 'Gulf War Syndrome' was the appropriate medical label to be attached to this excess of symptoms and a useful umbrella for that label. "It was," the Tribunal declared in withering criticism of defence ministers, "highly regrettable that there was such a delay in the Ministry of Defence accepting this approach. One wonders whether the acceptance might have been earlier by at least one year if they had attended and given evidence at the Lloyd Inquiry. The need to marshal one's arguments can frequently clarify one's views". In conclusion the Tribunal found that the appellant suffered a number of conditions that fell under the umbrella of 'Gulf War Syndrome'. To that extent the appeal was allowed.

Alf quickly recognised that this ruling – reported without exception by the mass media as a crushing defeat for the MoD – marked a turning point in the campaign he had led for more than a decade. "This landmark judgment," he told the press, "will hearten the many thousands of Gulf War veterans now in broken health, who still have undiagnosed illnesses. Their persistence in calling for a total review of MoD policy towards Gulf War illnesses is now seen to have been wholly justified". Lord Lloyd and Dr Norman Jones reinforced the finding by pointing out in a letter to *The Times*[50] that the use of the word 'syndrome' in medicine does not require the features involved to be caused by a single disease. The report of the Lloyd enquiry had stated the advantages of 'Gulf War Syndrome' as an umbrella label, while in no way implying either a single cause, or a uniform cluster of symptoms. Dr Jack Melling, a distinguished scientist and former Chief Executive Officer of the UK Microbiological Research Authority at Porton Down, weighed in with his support in a further letter to *The Times* on 23 November,[51] which, like the letter of Lloyd and Jones, remains unanswered. Melling pointed out that, even though it was not yet possible to prove a causal relationship between the specific toxic insults to which veterans were exposed and each illness symptom, once there is acceptance that service in that theatre of war is linked to a heightened risk of illnesses coming under the 'Gulf War Syndrome' umbrella label, the burden of proof on the veteran for the cause of their illness is lightened. "Is this why," asked Melling, "the Ministry of Defence so resists the term 'Gulf War Syndrome'?"

Denunciation in the USA

If criticism of the MoD establishment here was legitimately fierce, it paled alongside that of Dr James Binns, Chair of the US Government's Research Advisory Committee on Gulf War Veterans' Illnesses, in his testimony before a House of Representatives subcommittee on 15 November.[52] Binns recalled that in 1998, under direction from Congress, the Department of Veterans Affairs (VA) entered into a contract with the National Academy of Sciences. The Academy's Institute of Medicine (IOM) was tasked to review the scientific literature regarding substances to which troops were exposed in the Gulf to determine if they could have been linked to an increased risk of illness. These reports were to be used in determining whether such an illness should be presumed service-connected and thus trigger veterans' benefits. However, Binns now told the Congressional hearing, "for seven years VA and IOM staff

---

[50] 12 November 2005.
[51] *The Times*, 23 November 2005.
[52] US House of Representatives Committee on Government Reform Subcommittee on National Security, Emerging Threats and International Relations.

have subverted the will of Congress and misled the Secretary of Veterans Affairs". They had, he said, "shaped the methodology of the reports so that scientists who served on IOM committees were not permitted to consider an essential category of research mandated by law". They had, said this highly distinguished expert, deliberately failed to allow proper consideration of animal studies in determining whether an association existed between exposure and illness. "This fraud," said Binns, "has gone on since 1998 and continues to go on. It has defied the will of Congress. It has distorted the workings of the Institute of Medicine. It has denied the Secretary of Veterans Affairs accurate information on which to determine benefits due [to] ill veterans. It has misled veterans and their doctors. Most tragically, it has misdirected researchers down blind alleys and away from paths that might have led to treatments for these debilitating illnesses".

Binns came to a crushing climax: "I ask myself in what kind of a country we are living where we send men and women to war, and government officials treat them like this when they return...I urge Congress to use every power at its command to investigate this matter and ensure that the persons responsible are removed from positions of authority and punished".

Yet Binns' denunciation was not over. Notwithstanding a direction of law, he asserted, the IOM reports had never addressed undiagnosed illnesses: the "constellation of symptoms commonly referred to as 'Gulf War illnesses' or 'Gulf War syndrome' that are the central reason why this legislation exists and which affect at least 25 per cent of those who served in the Gulf War, as shown by multiple studies". Nor, again in contravention of the law, had account been taken of "exposure to multiple agents". Finally, in considering possible association between illness and exposure, Binns testified that the IOM had placed a substantially higher level of proof than that required by a specific statute.[53] Crucially, this ruled that "an association between the occurrence of an illness in humans or animals and exposure to an agent, hazard, or medicine or vaccine shall be considered to be positive...if the credible evidence for the association is equal to or outweighs the credible evidence against

---

[53] 38 USC Sec.1118(b)(3).

the association". In summary, said Binns, "VA and IOM have repeatedly and deliberately disregarded explicit statutory direction in implementing the law".

Surely time for the final curtain

In Britain, although no comparable statute existed, there was now no hiding place for the MoD. Here, in the light of the judgement on Daniel Martin's appeal, the next step – the final step if the MoD could bring itself to accept the logic and full implication of that judgement – was to take the issue back to Parliament. After tabling a couple of questions for written reply to clarify the Government's reaction to the judgement, Alf faced a conciliatory Lord Davies of Oldham, now speaking for the MoD, for oral exchanges on the floor of the House of Lords on 24 November. What action was the Government taking, Alf asked, in regard to the implications for other veterans of the 1990–91 Gulf War of the Pensions Appeal Tribunal decisions in the case of Guardsman Daniel Martin? To the relief, even the astonishment of the House, Lord Davies revealed that the Minister for Veterans had that very morning issued a statement welcoming the Pensions Appeal Tribunal's decision. The Government hoped it would address the concerns of Gulf veterans on this issue. This was encouraging, but Alf went on to suggest that it was now imperative, 15 years on from the conflict, to review very urgently every case affected by the judgment and bring closure to the whole sad story. The position established by the Tribunal, Lord Davies claimed, would give the Ministry a chance to move forward and enable progress to be made.

It was for Baroness Gardner of Parkes, a Conservative peer and a vice-president of the Royal British Legion branch in her locality, to remind Lord Davies of Alf's central role in this long and wearing campaign. Lord Davies welcomed the opportunity. We all, he said, recognise the significant role that he has played towards this landmark. It was a step forward, recognised as such by the Government. The Tribunal had not described 'Gulf War Syndrome' as a discrete medical illness and that remained the basis of the Government's position. Nevertheless, he concluded, the Tribunal's decision in the Martin case enabled the Ministry to go forward under the umbrella term, and that was their intention. This was the "germane and important point he made to the House and to the country".[54]

After the debate, Baroness Park of Monmouth wrote to Alf. She congratulated him on securing "the right result" and in a postscript added: "It is <u>entirely</u> thanks to you that so much has been achieved. Lord Lloyd did an excellent job but you have been the unremitting advocate, the driving force for the campaign".[55]

Justice delayed

In practical terms, however, the outcome remained unclear. Even now, the opportunity to "go forward" had not been matched by action. By the end of January 2006 there was still no sign of significant progress; nothing to justify the Prime Minister's assertion that the "support of veterans and their families is a top priority for this Government". On 2 February 2006, speaking as Chief of the Defence Staff throughout the first Gulf War, Lord Craig of Radley rose to ask, yet again, what steps the Government had taken in response to the Lloyd Inquiry.[56] Paying tribute to Alf, who had been "so energetic and resolute in his efforts to help veterans" and "a fine example to us all", he once more asked whether the time had not now come to settle the claims of stricken veterans. Lord Drayson, he said, had recognised the need to bring an "element of closure", but it was anything but clear that this would amount to full closure. Lord Craig hoped the Government's approach to veterans and their representatives would be less confrontational than it had been in the past. The basic question now was not why veterans were ill, but what to do to help them. A fund for *ex gratia* payments to successful claimants, as the Lloyd Inquiry had recommended, would help to address the many years of distress, even of rejection, to which the veterans had felt so exposed.

These were powerful words from a man of Marshal of the Royal Air Force Lord Craig's standing. Speaking next, Alf said that no one could be more eminently well placed than him to have led the debate or to assess the value of the Lloyd Inquiry. And to Lord

---

[54] *Hansard*, Lords, 24 November 2005, cols. 1723-26.
[55] Personal letter, 4 November 2005.
[56] *Hansard*, Lords, 2 February 2006, cols. 392-414.

Craig's name he proceeded to add an illustrious roster of those who had joined him in calling for closure of this now 15-year-old controversy. Since the successful pension appeal of Lifeguard Daniel Martin, there had been further identical decisions in favour of Gulf veterans Mark McGreevy and Richard Hilling. "No juggling with words," said Alf, could detract from the historic importance of the Tribunal's decisions in these cases, which so explicitly vindicated the stance taken by Lord Lloyd in his report. "Already gossamer thin," he continued, "the MoD's original case for seeking to discount the Lloyd report had now shrivelled to the most immodest of fig leaves". And even that had now been exposed as almost threadbare. The veterans, he concluded, needed more now than an 'element of closure'. Their aim was full and final closure and it needed to be fully understood in Whitehall that, if their striving for that outcome had to go on, then go on it would until right was done.

Even now, however, there was no sign of magnanimity from the MoD. The claims allowed by the Pensions Appeal Tribunal were subjected to detailed medical reappraisal. In the case of Daniel Martin this extended over four months. Indeed, it was only after a sharp parliamentary question from Alf that the three successful appellants eventually received entitlement and assessment notifications. The opinion of one eminent medical expert consulted by Alf in relation to the case of Mark McGreevy was that the behaviour of the MoD through the Veterans' Agency was "inexcusable". Their request for more and more information, he felt, appeared to indicate that the MoD still did not accept the medical basis for the verdict of the Tribunal and needed explanation.[57] Indeed, when Mr McGreevy finally received the agency's decision it was in terms that differed from the PAT's finding, a fact that drew a sharp rebuke from Harcourt Concannon, the distinguished president of the Tribunal, expressed in stinging language, accusing the Veterans' Agency of reinterpreting, manipulating and tampering with the terms of the Tribunal's decision.[58]

Alf also questioned what action the MoD had taken to make the Tribunal's decisions known to every veteran of the conflict they

---

[57] Personal letter, 6 March 2006.
[58] David Hencke, *The Guardian*, 13 June 2006.

could help. Lord Drayson's response was that there were no proposals to do so, but soon afterwards the veterans' organisations acted. They began contacting every veteran known to them who could benefit from the Tribunal's decisions. The number of cases previously rejected by the MoD going to appeal, and the PAT's awards for 'Gulf War Syndrome' steadily increased.

"Amazement is not too strong a word to capture the incredulity of veterans brought down by medically undiagnosed illnesses and bereaved families that neither the Ministry of Defence, its Ministers, nor the Prime Minister had yet perceived the need to repair the damage done over so many years; to accept the injustice felt by veterans; to answer the searing criticisms of the Pensions Appeal Tribunal; or even to apologise for the gravely serious failings that its criticisms addressed."

Alf could only reflect on a long and melancholy story, convinced that the MoD's unremitting resistance to the claims of Gulf War veterans had been founded on a fundamentally bogus premise. The hurdle of needing to prove the existence of a medical condition known as 'Gulf War Syndrome', in his view, had never been anything more than a bureaucratic creation and smokescreen. No thinking person – least of all Lord Lloyd – had ever contended that the illnesses experienced by Gulf War veterans – over 40 of them – amounted to a discrete pathological entity.

Equally inescapable, Alf felt, were the parallels between the Government's treatment of Gulf War veterans and its reluctance to compensate people with haemophilia infected with hepatitis C from contaminated blood products:

"In neither of these misfortunes, although mistakes were made, was there any question of malicious intention to harm those affected. Indeed, in the first Gulf War, on all fours with the supply of blood products to people with haemophilia, the intention had been to provide protection against illness: in the Gulf, quickly to guard against a range of possible dangers.

"Resentment was generated not by the origins of the consequent illnesses but by the bureaucratic response to those afflicted and bereaved when they were presented. Over many years civil servants and politicians alike persisted, in the face of every moral claim, in their demand for proof

positive of both legal liability and official negligence. Very few of them with any experience of active service or even of being in the armed forces at all. Their cold-blooded strategy was to refuse a public inquiry and to take advantage of veterans' difficulties in fulfilling the strict rites of law. One House of Commons Defence Committee report unequivocally described their attitude to Gulf War veterans as a 'culture of resistance' in which there seemed to be a deep-seated reluctance to respond positively to external stimuli and a blithe assumption that everyone else was wrong. When the full history of the campaign to recognise Gulf War illnesses in Britain is written, say campaigning veterans, the bureaucrats of the MoD – operating in the safety and comfort of their London bunker – may well be judged as even more culpable than their American counterparts, meriting criticism such as to make the bitter recriminations of Dr Binns in the USA seem modest. Meanwhile, however, the MoD still dodged every attempt to establish the costs to taxpayers of their clearly huge spending of taxpayers' money having fought veterans' and widows' pension claims with such unsuccess in courts and tribunals all over the UK."

A supreme achievement

Faced by years of procrastination and parsimony, Alf had led the campaign for the veterans with consummate parliamentary skill. When he instituted an independent public inquiry, ensuring that its members were of the highest standing, he decisively turned the tables on uncharitable governance. His brilliant coup irrevocably shifted the balance of power between the aggrieved citizen and executive government. It was an historic breakthrough. Never again could central government rely on a power of veto over independent public inquiries.

This was surely one of Alf's supreme achievements. Many others, although arduous and intense and of wider benefit, were but a sprint. The campaign to secure justice for Gulf War veterans was the full marathon, consistently uphill, in which Alf, by common consent, outmanoeuvred the mandarins of Whitehall. For 15 years, with unflagging conviction and commitment – in addition to all his other preoccupations, often severe spinal pain and the need, now and then, to take breath, not to say come up for air – he had given devoted parliamentary support to the Royal British Legion. So of the many letters of gratitude and congratulation he received after the PAT decision none was more apt than that from Brigadier Ian Townsend, the Legion's Director General. "I speak for the thousands of ill Gulf veterans whom we assist," he wrote, "when I say that we are heartened by your relentless pursuit for justice and recognition".[59] And that was 12 years <u>after</u> already having given him the Legion's coveted award of Life Membership.

Though, in Alf's view, it was unlikely that the MoD would ever openly to admit defeat, effectively their long and obdurate resistance had been broken. MoD watchers of long experience have concluded that all that is left to them now, having missed even the opportunity of graceful retreat, is damage limitation. Moral decency had prevailed.

The Rt. Hon. Lady Helene Hayman, Speaker of the House of Lords, Alf and Dame Vera Lynn on the occasion of her 90th birthday.

---

[59] Personal letter, 8 February 2006.

Chapter 16

THE WORST EVER
TREATMENT DISASTER
IN THE NHS

1989— 2007

"Never take no for an answer".

title of a 1951 film based on Paul Gallico's 'The Small Miracle'.

– The tragedy of haemophilia – A campaign for compensation
– The disaster escalates – Alf heads a new campaign – A change of Government
– Hepatitis C widows short-changed – The case for a public inquiry

The tragedy of haemophilia

An hereditary bleeding disorder, haemophilia has been a scourge immemorially. Though women can carry the disease and pass it on, almost all of those affected are males. As recently as the early 60s there was little or no treatment for the disorder. The parents of newly diagnosed children with haemophilia could not expect them to live beyond their teenage years, and had to watch them suffer the terrible pain of bleeding into joints and muscles.

There is still no cure, but by the beginning of the 20th century scientists had worked out that the condition was caused by problems in blood clotting. The introduction of manufactured clotting factors in the early 1970s brought a transformation that allowed people with haemophilia to live almost normal lives. But with that treatment – in many cases the injection two or three times a week of a clotting factor concentrate derived from human blood plasma – came tragic consequences. Some of the donated units of blood used to manufacture the clotting factor carried deadly contaminants, including the HIV and hepatitis C viruses. And because the clotting factors, known as Factor VIII and Factor IX, were made from the blood of thousands of donors,[1] the treatment carried a risk of infection. During the 1970s and the first half of the 1980s nearly 5,000 haemophiliacs and people with other clotting factor deficiencies were exposed to hepatitis C before, in 1985, safety measures were introduced to destroy viruses in NHS blood and blood products. Around a quarter of these were also infected with HIV, and still more with HIV alone by the same blood-borne route. Contamination, of course, was not confined to people with haemophilia; but because of the frequency of their treatment and heavy dependency on clotting factors derived from pooled blood donations they were at very substantially greater risk than the rest of the population.

When the awful truth about the scale of the disaster came to light, nobody would admit responsibility. Much of the blood had been imported from the United States, having been bought there from companies who are alleged to have paid for blood donations – some would say indiscriminately and as cheaply as possible.

But the counter argument has run that, because before 1985 there was no means of identifying the presence of the HIV and hepatitis C viruses, there was no negligence by, and therefore no liability attributable to, the National Health Service. The UK Government had a policy commitment to work towards self-sufficiency in blood products, but in the meantime supplies could not have been maintained without imported blood. The risks associated with the use of imported blood products had to be balanced against the need to provide life-saving treatment. Patients, it is argued, needed blood and had received the only products available at the time.[2]

A campaign for compensation.

When the effects of the contamination with HIV first became known, the Haemophilia Society began a vigorous campaign for financial help for members affected. Remarkably, in the light of subsequent events, the Conservative Government responded with something approaching alacrity. The issue having been raised by Labour and Liberal Democrat MPs in the early months of 1987, Parliament was

---

[1] According to *The Observer*, 16 April 2006, as many as 25,000.

[2] *Self-sufficiency in blood products in England and Wales: a chronology from 1973 to 1991* (Department of Health report, 27 February 2006).

lobbied by the Haemophilia Society that October – when Alf addressed the lobbyists in Westminster Hall – and on 16 November Tony Newton, Minister for Health, announced that the Government accepted the "wholly exceptional position of haemophiliacs" and that they should be treated on that basis. MPs were told that, having considered all the circumstances – and perhaps crucially the risk of successful legal action against them – Ministers had concluded that it would be right to make an *ex gratia* grant of £10 million to establish a trust fund. It would be empowered to make payments to infected patients and dependants throughout the United Kingdom, and to do so with greater flexibility than could readily be achieved in any other way.[3] The fund, which initially excluded non-haemophiliacs infected with NHS blood, was to be administered by the Macfarlane Trust, and payments to individuals would be ignored in the assessment of income support, family credit and housing benefit. They would, moreover, be entirely confidential and beneficiaries need not declare them either to the Department of Health and Social Security or their local authority.

Criticising the level of payments, some in the haemophilia community persisted, however, in seeking redress through the courts. Alf put the issue on the parliamentary agenda with a question to the Secretary of State for Health on 23 October 1989. Throughout that year, as before, he had consulted people who were HIV-positive about the problems they confronted and the treatment they were receiving. He now asked the Minister what representations had been received about settling out of court the legal actions of haemophiliacs contaminated with HIV by the injection of blood products supplied under the NHS, and with what result. At that stage, it emerged, 21 representations had been received – 19 from MPs and two from the Haemophilia Society – to which replies were in the process of being sent. Forging on from this opening, Alf then asked the Minister on 1 November if he would facilitate an out-of court settlement, since no one was in any doubt, in Whitehall or anywhere else, that the virus had been transmitted by NHS treatment. By then, 30 further representations had been received and a legal action had been brought that was being

[3] *Hansard*, Commons, 16 November 1987, col.767.

433

contested by the Government. The Minister could now take refuge, therefore, in the issue having become *sub-judice*, making further comment 'inappropriate'.

Reflecting the concern widely shared on both sides of both Houses of Parliament, Alf informed the Commons of "deeply moving correspondence" from HIV-infected haemophiliacs in all parts of Britain. It was "a dossier of despair", he said, that made the case for an out-of-court settlement overwhelming. Many victims of the disaster had already died. Many more knew that they had little prospect of living to see a settlement in court and rightly insisted that posthumous justice was no justice at all. Why could the Government not accept that they were just as deserving as those damaged by thalidomide had been and, in this case, by contaminated NHS blood? Haemophiliacs had been dealt "the cruellest possible hand".[4] They now had to live not only with a genetic disorder but life-threatening HIV as well. They were doubly stricken, he said, with visible effect across the House, and in double despair.[5]

Later that month, the Government, while not conceding liability, gave the Macfarlane Trust a further *ex-gratia* payment of £24 million. But even then the Trust's resources were sufficient to pay only £20,000 each to HIV-infected haemophilia patients. In May 1990, David Watters, then general secretary of the Haemophilia Society, wrote to inform Alf that a large number of his members who did not qualify for legal aid were being forced to use money from the Macfarlane Trust to fund their court actions. Would not the dispute be settled more quickly, and at less cost to the Government, by means of an inquiry of the kind that Alf himself, as the then Minister, had set up in 1978 under Sir Alan Marre to conclude the thalidomide dispute? On that basis, Alf appealed to Margaret Thatcher, the Prime Minister, making the case for treading the path of compromise, but she was unresponsive.[6]

Nor was the Government prepared to change course when on 26 June 1990 Mr Justice Ognall appealed to both sides in the legal case brought by haemophiliacs to give "anxious consideration" to a

---

[4] Not to mention partners infected by sex with a man with haemophilia.

[5] *Hansard*, Commons, 13 November 1989, cols.155-6w.

[6] *Hansard*, Commons, adjournment debate, 23 May 1990, cols.297-9.

compromise solution, offering to arbitrate to reach a settlement. In a long written answer to a question from Alf, the Secretary of State for Health, Kenneth Clarke, recalled that a total of £34 million had already been made available to the Macfarlane Trust to mitigate the effects of "this tragedy". He proposed to keep the sums available under regular review, and emphasised that the £34 million had been paid on an *ex gratia* basis. Help from it was not intended to subsidise litigation.

Mr Justice Ognall had suggested that there were court actions that could perhaps be settled not by a strict assessment of legal liability but on the basis of moral obligation. But Clarke's position was that he had already recognised the moral argument and the strong compassionate case by setting up the Macfarlane Trust and providing it with further resources to help those infected and bereaved. There were strong public policy reasons too for resisting the claims, in that for Ministers to concede that they owed a duty of care in circumstances like these would lead to large numbers of other costly and time-consuming claims and encourage more and more expensive litigation.[7] Two months later, however, a steering committee of solicitors representing the HIV/haemophiliac plaintiffs proposed a settlement of their litigation. This would result in the Government providing a further £42 million to the Macfarlane Trust for distribution to all haemophiliacs with HIV and their families according to their individual circumstances. Both sides then agreed that this would provide a fair, reasonable and proper way to resolve the plaintiffs' claims and end the litigation.[8]

The disaster escalates

The battle for a wider settlement with the haemophilia community, however, had scarcely yet begun. By the early months of 1993, it was clear that large numbers of haemophilia patients treated under the NHS had contracted hepatitis C before 1985, often as well as HIV. The life-threatening hepatitis C virus was identified only in 1989 and a wholly reliable test for it in blood was not developed until 1991. The infection had a longer incubation period than HIV

---

[7] *Hansard*, Commons, 15 October 1990, cols.659-62w.
[8] *Hansard*, Commons, 11 December 1990, cols.364-64w, in response to a question from Harriet Harman, Labour MP for Peckham.

and the first cases among haemophiliacs were only just coming to light.

This finding devastated a haemophilia community already trying to cope with crushing adversity. But they knew that Alf was on their side and that they could count on more than his understanding: his practical help was also guaranteed. Chris Hodgson, Chairman of the Haemophilia Society from 1997 to 2003, recalls that he was, above all, a great listener. "He responded instantly to the plight of patients who had suffered so much and talked with them, often very angry people who saw no hope for the future. Many of them could not begin to come to terms with the realisation that HIV and hepatitis C infection would mean early death. He used examples of their suffering in taking the issue to Ministers and raising parliamentary and public awareness in an arduous succession of Commons debates".[9]

Money could not end suffering from the new scourge, Alf told Ministers, but it could help. He wanted urgently to hear what financial provision they would be making to compensate the victims, only to be told with equal persistence that the Government had "no plans to make payments to haemophilia patients who may have been infected with hepatitis C".[10]

Alf heads a new campaign

In response, in March 1995, the Haemophilia Society launched a four-point campaign to focus public attention on the plight of its members. It sought urgent financial and medical help for increasing numbers of them now found to be infected with hepatitis C; provision of synthetic 'recombinant' clotting factors (safer than plasma-based products); a public inquiry to establish all the facts about the causes and course of the disaster; and in-depth research into the needs of those infected but not yet seriously ill.

The campaign centred on the medical, social and financial problems of whole families hit by sickness, loss of jobs, loss of income and loss of independence. Individuals with the disease, while trapped in an uphill struggle to maintain their families, had to live day by day with what they knew could soon become a terminal illness. One of

[9] Personal letter, 29 May 2005.
[10] *Hansard*, Commons, 21 November 1994, cols.29-30w.

the most pressing needs was for financial help to make up for reduced earnings and increased costs, and then secure funding for appropriate care, counselling and guidance.

Alf and his allies in the Commons pressed the Society's case there. Before the end of 1995, there had been seven more parliamentary questions on the issue, as well as five early-day motions – one of them, sponsored by Alf, backed by 269 other MPs of all parties – plus an adjournment debate and 291 letters to Ministers about the rapidly rising toll of hepatitis C infection.[11]

By the following February, it was estimated that 3,100 people with haemophilia had been infected with the hepatitis C virus from contaminated NHS blood products. Medical opinion was that up to 80 per cent of them would develop chronic liver disease. Of these, some 20 per cent would develop terminal disease with cirrhosis and liver cancer. More than 50 haemophilia patients infected with hepatitis C had already died and the death rate was accelerating. On 12 March, Alf again pressed the case for compensation.

In response, John Horam, Under Secretary of State for Health, explained the official line with calculated clarity. The Government, he said, had great sympathy with those who may have been inadvertently infected with hepatitis C through NHS treatment, but as no fault or negligence on the part of the NHS had been proved, they had no plans to make special payments. Their view remained that the best way for the Government to help was to encourage research and best treatment for those infected, as well as supporting voluntary groups working with patients infected. This they were already doing.[12]

This stance appeared not only stubborn and insensitive, but manifestly unjust and illogical. How could the Government make payments to a trust for haemophiliacs infected with HIV, yet refuse it for those infected with hepatitis C by precisely the same route and from the same source? On 22 May 1996, Alf led off in a further Commons debate.[13] This was not, he said, an issue between right and left in the House, but between right and wrong. His purpose in

---

[11] *Hansard*, Commons, 5 December 1995, cols.130-31.

[12] *Hansard*, Commons, 12 March 1996, cols.589-90w.

[13] *Hansard*, Commons, 22 May 1996, col.210.

calling for the debate was "to draw attention to a grave injustice and to secure for its victims the humane ministerial response they crave". The case for providing the help he was seeking for the victims of hepatitis C infection had to be seen in the context of what was already done to assist the 1,200 haemophilia patients infected with HIV. The hepatitis C infection had taken place at the same time as the HIV infection. The cause was the same. Yet those infected with hepatitis C and their dependants received nothing from a Government that had now provided £70 million in financial support for the HIV-infected and instituted a hardship fund to give them continuing support.

To underline the iniquity of the Government's stance, Alf cited the case of three brothers who had haemophilia. Two were infected with HIV by NHS treatment and the other with hepatitis C. All had subsequently died from their NHS treatment. The brothers with HIV received financial help from the Macfarlane Trust and so were able to make some provision for their families. But the brother who died from hepatitis C went to his grave having been denied any financial help. The Haemophilia Society's modest and, in Alf's submission, unexceptionable claim was that the terms of reference of the Macfarlane Trust should now be extended to include those contaminated with hepatitis C.[14]

Tony Newton, the Lord President of the Council and Leader of the House of Commons replied, quickly making it clear that there was little he could add to what Ministers had said on previous occasions. There had been a recent meeting with the Haemophilia Society and discussions were continuing about developing good practice in the treatment of patients and ensuring ready access to treatment centres.

Undeterred by Newton, one of his successors as Minister for Disabled People, Alf pressed the case with renewed energy and total conviction. In a further debate on 24 July 1996 he referred again to the "very deep sense of injustice" among people with haemophilia and their families. One of the arguments against compensating for hepatitis C infection was that it would take money away from patient care in the NHS. "To say that," said Alf, "is to get not just

---

[14] *Hansard*, Commons, 22 May 1996, cols.210-11.

the wrong end of the stick but the wrong stick". The Haemophilia Society simply wanted the terms of reference of the Macfarlane Trust – whose funding came from contingency monies, not from NHS budgets – to be extended to include patients infected with hepatitis C. "In none of the many campaigns in which I have been closely involved in this House in my 32 years here," he told the Commons, "have I had such a strong sense that it should not be necessary to campaign to right such an obvious wrong".[15]

Alf then decided to vent his sense of injustice in the national press, immediately finding a sympathetic reception in the broadsheets. "The Government knows we are right," he wrote in a feature for *The Times*, "and that our campaign is entirely free from party animus. In this final lap of the last parliamentary session before an election, the Government's legislative programme is gossamer thin and time [in the Commons] could unquestionably be found". If Ministers failed to act, and the campaign had to go on, he concluded, then go on it would until right was done.[16]

Alf followed up with a cross-party Early Day Motion signed by over 300 MPs and thus by a majority of MPs outside the Government. It called on the Government to acknowledge that over 3,000 people with haemophilia had been infected with the hepatitis C virus as a result of NHS treatment, 60 of whom had since died from liver disease contracted as a result. The motion asked the Government also to consider giving financial assistance for hepatitis C infection equal to that already granted for infection with HIV.[17] The emphatic success of this further motion visibly increased the build-up of pressure on the Government from both outside and inside Parliament and, on 11 December 1996, the Haemophilia Society again lobbied the House of Commons and presented a petition. On the same day, his time as an MP now drawing to its close, Alf spoke powerfully in a debate secured by John Marshall (Conservative, Hendon South). The achievement of elementary justice, he said, was at the heart of a campaign that was about morality: "It is morally wrong to deny the victims of this appalling further tragedy in the haemophilia community the modest help they

---

[15] *Hansard*, Commons, 24 July 1996, col.265.

[16] *The Times*, 6 June 1996.

[17] EDM 4, 23 October 1996.

seek". What was morally wrong ought no longer to be tolerated by parliamentarians Given the nod by Ministers, he was "sure the House would approve within the hour the help we seek".[18]

Under Secretary John Horam, however, again made it clear that no such nod would be forthcoming. There had been no test for detecting hepatitis C in blood donations until 1991, he said, and haemophiliacs had received the best treatment available at the time. It had been essential to their survival and no alternative was available. Having carefully considered representations from the Haemophilia Society in June 1996, he did not accept their proposals but "remained open to further arguments". The Society was not arguing that the NHS had necessarily been negligent and the Government took the view that compensation would be appropriate only where there had been negligence. This notwithstanding the same Government's decision to give financial help, without proof of negligence, for HIV infection. If payment was to be provided on the basis of non-negligent harm in this case, said Horam, "it would very quickly develop into a general no-fault compensation scheme, which would be both unworkable and unfair". This had been considered in relation to HIV cases, but on that occasion Ministers had been persuaded to set up a payments scheme by the very special nature of the disease (in particular, the expectation of most, if not all, that they had been delivered a death sentence) and the public reaction to it. They were not convinced that hepatitis C fell into the same special category. All the proposals for payment schemes involved the expenditure of substantial sums of public money which, as a Health Minister, Horam had to set against other claims on health service expenditure. The responsibility for other funding possibilities, he told the House, lay elsewhere.

A change of Government

The dissolution of Parliament in March 1997 brought an end to Alf's thirty-three years as the Member for Wythenshawe. His best efforts had still not overcome the Conservative administration's illogical and plainly unjust refusal to extend compensation to haemophilia patients infected with hepatitis C. Nevertheless, the Haemophilia Society's

[18] *Hansard*, Commons, 11 December 1996, col.256.

campaign went on and, very soon, Alf's entry to the House of Lords returned him to the fray. Even when he had contemplated retirement, Alf had not intended to cut his ties with the disability organisations with which he had been so irrevocably associated. There was far too much unfinished business for that to happen and further help for the haemophilia community was one of his priorities. There was, moreover, renewed hope. He would now be knocking on the door of a new administration of his own party (if not in every respect entirely of his own persuasion) and one in which most of the Ministers had been among the more than 300 signatories to his Early Day Motion of the previous year. As an experienced parliamentarian, however, he did not expect his objective to be swiftly achieved. Shortly after his introduction to the Lords, officials of the Department of Health again met the Haemophilia Society and listened to its arguments for a special payments scheme for hepatitis C infection, similar to that in place for HIV. But it was later announced that "after long and careful consideration" the new Labour Government had concluded that no further scheme should be established. They reiterated the Conservative line that compensation or other financial help to patients should be paid only when the NHS or individuals working in it were proved to be at fault. It was never explicitly stated, but there was here the very clear implication that the setting up by John Major's Government of a special payments scheme for HIV infection was seen by the new Government as unfortunate and an embarrassment, since that had been conceded without any admission of fault. The line had been broken and new Ministers (like the old) were driven to adopt the totally unconvincing argument that the impact of hepatitis C was fundamentally different than that of HIV, notwithstanding the fact that people were dying from both conditions.

By July 1998, ninety victims of the fatal hepatitis C infection had succumbed to liver failure. In silent tribute to their memory the haemophilia community delivered a poignant reminder to the Prime Minister by taking 90 white lilies to the steps of 10 Downing Street. Writing in *The Observer*, Alf remarked that more would die with every passing month and go to their graves with a deep sense of injustice.[19]

---

[19] *Observer*, 5 July 1998.

He was already a longstanding and steadfast champion of the Haemophilia Society, now led by Karin Pappenheim, but in 1999 his role as the pre-eminent parliamentary campaigner on their behalf was recognised and strengthened by his appointment to succeed Catherine Cookson as President of the Society. This was marked by a renewal of his parliamentary campaigning for what seemed to many in both Houses – and the wider public – an unanswerable case on moral if not also on legal grounds. Meanwhile the Government remained obdurate, consolidating its refusal to bend in replies to a series of questions and debates. Department of Health Minister John Denham – who had supported Alf's Early Day Motion in support of the Haemophilia Society's campaign when in opposition – now unequivocally confirmed the new Government's line that haemophiliacs infected with hepatitis C should not receive special payments. He insisted that the needs of people whose conditions resulted from "inadvertent harm" must be met by benefits available to the population in general, and added that he had seen "no evidence" to justify a public inquiry.[20]

The technology to make blood products free from hepatitis C in sufficient quantities to treat all haemophiliacs in the UK, Lord Hunt of Kings Heath told the House of Lords three months into a new century, was simply not possible prior to 1985. It had not been until 1987 that there had been proof positive of the means of eliminating the virus from NHS blood products. "It must be a matter of deep regret that before this," he said, "many haemophiliacs were inadvertently infected by treatment designed to improve their quality of life. But this is not of itself considered a justification for special payments". Comparisons between this decision and the scheme established for haemophiliacs infected with HIV were inevitable, but the Government's view was that there were significant and real differences between the two situations.[21]

Inevitably the Haemophilia Society's new President was in the vanguard of those taking a contrary view and was not disposed to take no for an answer. Irrefutably he had the moral high ground. The Government, he said, was peddling a fallacy that, unlike HIV,

[20] *Hansard*, Commons, 7 March 2000, col.138wh.
[21] *Hansard*, Lords, 30 March 2000, cols.992-93.

hepatitis C did not involve social stigma; they had simplified the previous government's reasons for compensating only for HIV infection "to the point of crude inaccuracy".[22] Raising his game, Alf bombarded the Government with a barrage of questions and speeches of compelling logic. His demeanour, as anyone who has had any meaningful contact with him knows, is both gentle and genuinely kind. But if anyone supposes that this makes his parliamentary approach muted or non-confrontational, they should read some of these speeches. Even so, and depressingly for the stricken community he was campaigning for, the Department of Health's response had now become a mantra: expressions of limitless sympathy, but no financial help or even – as had been conceded in other countries such as France and Canada – a public inquiry.

In February 2001, Dr Peter Jones, executive member of the World Federation of Haemophilia, speaking as an expert witness at a tribunal in Dublin, supported the call for a public inquiry in the UK. Other countries had launched investigations into the use of imported blood products and Dr Jones now called on the UK government to do the same. There remained, he said, serious public concern about how people became infected and the consequences for those afflicted. Dr Jones had particular cause to urge the case for an independent inquiry. Of 105 haemophilia patients under his care at the Royal Victoria Infirmary in Newcastle, 95 had become infected with HIV and hepatitis C and 77 of them had died.

The depth of despair into which people with haemophilia had fallen had left some of them prepared to risk their lives by refusing treatment with Factor VIII, the clotting agent derived from human blood and still used by the NHS, knowing that a safe – but more expensive – synthetic alternative could be made available. Modern screening and deactivation techniques had eliminated infection with hepatitis C and HIV, but two other infective agents, parvovirus B19 and hepatitis A, could still infect supplies, and – still more alarming – it now emerged that a "theoretical" risk of variant CJD (vCJD) infection among haemophilia patients could not be ruled out.

[22] *Hansard*, Lords, 23 April 2001, col.67.

On 23 April 2001, Alf led a Lords' debate on hepatitis C infection with his most intense and vehement assault yet on the Government's policy. He reminded the House that this small and stricken community – "in sorrow and acquainted with grief: recurrent and often abject grief and already disabled by a rare, lifelong bleeding disorder requiring continuous medical treatment" had now twice been infected *en masse* by unclean NHS blood and blood products. Of its 6,000 people, some 4,000 had now been infected with hepatitis C, of whom 1,240 had also been infected with HIV. Of the latter, 818 were now dead and well over 100 of those infected with hepatitis C alone had died of related cirrhosis of the liver and cancer. The further risk now identified and officially described as "theoretical" raised the possibility that hundreds of haemophilia patients had been infected with vCJD by blood donors who had since died of the disease and were unknowingly carrying it when they donated their blood. Even among those as yet unaffected by blood-borne viruses, there was the daunting worry of not knowing whether they would develop this life-threatening illness.

None of those infected, regardless of their current health, could obtain life insurance except at prohibitive rates, while more and more of them were becoming unemployable. Yet there was still no positive response from Ministers to the Haemophilia Society's calls for an independent public inquiry. This compounded their sense of injustice. They saw themselves as cast aside and forgotten: too small and powerless to be treated as politically important, notwithstanding the Government's Green Paper on Welfare Reform and Ministers having told both Houses of Parliament that its "commitment to the vulnerable is non-negotiable".

The argument that payments could be made only on proof of medical negligence, said Alf, was plainly at odds with several precedents. There had been schemes for vaccine damage and for the British survivors of Japanese POW camps, to name but two examples, the first of which was introduced during his time as Minister for Disabled People. In truth, the issue was not one of inflexible rule but of political will and priorities.

His ammunition by no means exhausted, his armoury was now significantly strengthened by a new development. This was a landmark judgement handed down by Mr Justice Burton in the High Court on 26 March 2001 in a case brought by 114 claimants infected by the virus. He ruled that under the product liability provisions of the Consumer Protection Act 1987, the National Blood Authority had been culpable in supplying blood contaminated with hepatitis C. This was not a finding of negligence; simply that the product had been defective. The judgment was 320 pages long and closely argued, but its main point, conceded by Lord Hunt speaking for the Department of Health in the House of Lords, was that the public had a right to expect that blood they received from the NHS was 100 per cent safe. The knowledge of the medical profession was not relevant in determining that legitimate expectation, nor was it relevant that the effect could not have been avoided. The judge's conclusion was that, once the risk is known about, the product is legally defective even if the risk could not be identified in the product.[23]

Alf naturally seized on these findings. The policy – in David Owen's time as Health Minister – of seeking 'self-sufficiency' suggested that that, even then, there had been some concern over imported supplies even if that risk could not be identified. Clearly any risk had applied to haemophiliacs far more than to patients given only a one-off blood transfusion. In response to questions from Alf, the Government admitted that they had decided not to seek leave to appeal against Mr Justice Burton's judgment.[24] But they argued that this did not affect their position on financial help on the pragmatic – some would say studiously cynical – ground that the Consumer Protection Act had not come into force until March 1988.[25] To which Alf's response was that any attempt to deny its benefits to the haemophilia community on that argument would provoke moral outrage. The Government, since coming to power, had never suggested repeal of the product liability provisions of the 1987 Act and now had no justification in principle for denying their application for the benefit of patients damaged by defective NHS products.

His final shot was to draw attention to what had happened in France, where two senior officials had been convicted, sentenced to four

---

[23] *Hansard*, Lords 29 March 2001, col.411.
[24] *Hansard*, Lords, 23 April 2001, col.204wa.
[25] *Hansard*, Lords, 29 March 2001, col.409.

years in prison and ordered to pay the sterling equivalent of £1.2 million on charges of "distributing tainted blood" that had infected more than 1,250 French haemophilia patients. A third senior health official had been given a four-year suspended sentence – but he too was heavily fined – and the Health Minister had resigned "in disgrace". Alf was not asking for that in Britain, but he urged Ministers not to demean the House and "another place" by making legal action the only way to resolve an issue that was so obviously one of social decency and moral right.[26]

Of all Alf's virtuoso performances, this was perhaps supreme. Even so it appeared to fall on deaf ears as Lord Burlison, deputising for Lord Hunt, responded with all the old familiar arguments. But close reading of the parliamentary record suggests that the Government's ground might have been subtly shifting. Knowing him well, Lord Burlison predicted that Alf, as president of the Haemophilia Society, would feel honour bound to pursue the issue "in dogged fashion" until he made progress generally on behalf of the haemophilia community.[27] So much for any thought there may have been that going to the House of Lords might have curbed Alf's commitment to social fairness.

And pursue it he did, pressing again for a public inquiry, while supporting the Haemophilia Society's campaign for treatment with the safer recombinant clotting factors to be made available to all haemophilia patients irrespective of age and regardless of where they lived in the UK.[28] Speaking at the Haemophilia Society's AGM in June 2001, Alf repeated his statement to the Lords, backed by medical experts, that the infection of the haemophilia community with HIV and hepatitis C had been the worst-ever treatment disaster in the history of the NHS, to which the Government – unlike others in Europe and North America – had been slow to respond. Its failure amounted to a denial of justice and was a moral disgrace. A succession of former Health Secretaries had been petitioned by the Haemophilia Society but had failed to act. The

---

[26] *Hansard*, Lords, 23 April 2001, cols.64-70.

[27] *Ibid*, col.75.

[28] 'Recombinant' clotting factors avoid the need for large quantities of human plasma. From 1998 the Department of Health issued instructions that recombinant clotting concentrates should be used to treat all children in England under the age of 16. In 2003, this policy was extended to adults, and by March 2006 all who wished to receive recombinant treatment had made the change.

haemophilia community was now being put at further risk by want of access to a safer form of treatment and, in the absence of an independent inquiry to bring out the facts and achieve wider public recognition of the disaster, redress for the afflicted and bereaved was being cruelly obstructed. The families affected were being left to fend for themselves in the face of a life-threatening illness. The new Labour Government, Alf pointed out, was then in its second term. It had promised greater stress on a higher standard of public services, including the NHS; but while issues of such deep concern to the haemophilia patient group remained unresolved, that pledge could not be kept.

The gauntlet had been well and truly thrown down. Even so, this did not present the full extent of the tragedy. The possibility now that vCJD might be transmitted in blood products was further increasing the stress imposed on the haemophilia community. Alf having again taken up the cause by parliamentary questioning, Lord Hunt replied that by 6 February 2002 eight people with vCJD were known to have been blood donors, that twenty two people had been identified as having received transfused blood from donors who later died of vCJD and that the total number of deaths from vCJD was 106.[29] It was not known how many haemophilia patients had received blood from donors who had since died of vCJD.[30] Alf also teased out the fact that there was no screening test for vCJD, although now as a precautionary measure all blood used in transfusions had the white cells removed and plasma from outside the United Kingdom was no longer used in the manufacture of blood products.[31]

Alf now initiated a further debate, the fourth in as many years. Lord (David) Owen, a health Minister at the time when many of the infections occurred, had written to him disclosing that monies allocated – and announced to Parliament – for making NHS blood products safer by ceasing to import blood from high-risk donors abroad had not been used for their stated purpose. His policy of

[29] *Hansard*, Lords, 6 February 2002, col.631.

[30] *Hansard*, Lords, 25 February 2002, col.192wa.

[31] *Hansard*, Lords, 25 February 2002, col.193wa. The first case of probable vCJD transmission by blood transfusion was announced by then Health Secretary John Reid in December 2003. Two further cases are known of recipients of blood diagnosed with vCJD who had received whole blood from donors who subsequently developed the disease. It is widely thought that the infection must have arisen from blood transfusion rather than the dietary route.

self-sufficiency was thus obstructed, but this had not been reported to Parliament. Moreover, to make matters worse, Lord Hunt had now admitted that nor had this been considered by the Department of Health's internal inquiry in 1997. All of which, Alf told the Lords, compounded the disquiet felt by the haemophilia community about the "grossly unjust" treatment of its members infected with hepatitis C and the Government's treatment of Mr Justice Burton's ruling against the National Blood Authority. For the logic of that ruling not to be applied to people with haemophilia who were undoubtedly infected by unclean NHS blood was "wrong in principle, cruelly discriminatory and morally perverse". Notwithstanding the new threat from vCJD, only 43 per cent of patients over 20 were receiving the safer recombinant treatment; 57 per cent were still forced to use blood products by which they could be infected and some had resorted to treatment strikes.[32]

Responding on behalf of the Secretary of State for Health, Lord Filkin began by marking Alf's contribution on this issue over many years. By his count, since the session of 1997/98 there had been four significant debates of his on the subject in the House of Lords and 45 parliamentary questions. Nevertheless, despite "continuing concern in the Government and across the House for the affliction of people who suffer haemophilia and hepatitis C or HIV",[33] the Government still held its line on refusing a public inquiry.

Unmistakably, however, the tide was now turning against the Government. In November 2002, an expert group, headed by senior former judge, Lord Ross, was appointed by the Scottish Executive to examine the issue. As a former Minister for Disabled People and President of the Haemophilia Society, Alf was invited by Lord Ross to give evidence, spending a full day with the expert group in Edinburgh. The group's eventual recommendation was that people who had contracted the hepatitis C virus from blood or blood products from the NHS in Scotland – and thus for whom the Executive had responsibility – should now be compensated. Alf promptly asked Lord Hunt what implications followed for NHS patients identically infected in other parts of the UK. Was it not

---

[32] *Hansard*, Lords, 12 March 2002, cols.764-72.
[33] *Ibid*, cols.778-79.

much to the honour of the Scottish Executive that the case for compensation had been independently examined "by an eminent Scottish judge, not as in Whitehall by an in-house inquiry behind closed doors at the Department of Health?" Was not the Haemophilia Society now seen to have been "eminently justified in insisting that to deny parity of treatment in this case would diminish the NHS to a two-tier, two-class and two-faced system of health care for the British people".[34] Faced with this onslaught, Lord Hunt was bound to sound pusillanimous: he could only repeat that as soon as the technology to make blood products free from hepatitis C became available, the NHS introduced it. On that basis, he said, there was no legal liability to justify compensation for people with haemophilia and hepatitis C.[35]

For the next nine months Alf kept up the assault, persisting in seeking financial redress and safer treatment for the haemophilia community. The Government's eventual surrender, though recognised as an historic breakthrough, was in some respects as illiberal and circumscribed as it was belated. This was implicitly acknowledged by timing the announcement in the still days of high summer, when Parliament was in recess, senior parliamentary journalists thin on the ground and even spin doctors lost in the long grass far from Westminster. It was on 29 August 2003, within months of his appointment as Secretary of State for Health, that the shrewd Dr John Reid, having looked, he said, at the history of the issue, quietly signalled that an *ex gratia* financial assistance scheme would now be introduced throughout the UK at an estimated cost of £85 million.

When, nearly three weeks later, Baroness Andrews, a Government Whip, reported to the House of Lords a change of heart that left several hapless Ministers there eating their own words, Alf described it as a deeply evocative moment for everyone who had campaigned for so many years – not least from both sides of the Lords – to achieve "this major and welcome change of policy". But could the House be assured that the scheme would cover dependants of the 212 haemophilia patients who had already died

[34] *Hansard*, 21 November 2002, col.506.
[35] *Ibid*, col.507.

of hepatitis C infection, as well as the 2,800 still living with the virus; and that it would take fully into account what other schemes provided, such as those in Canada and Ireland?

Baroness Andrews began by warmly congratulating Alf on his "outstanding record of promoting this socially just cause for haemophiliacs infected with blood products". Since the early 1980s, she said, he had consistently played an "outstanding role". She could not yet give details of the scheme, nor the assurance that Alf sought, but she was at pains to point out that it would be one of *ex gratia* payments not compensation, because, she said, there was no legal liability. "Given the knowledge and techniques available to the National Blood Service at the time, everything was done as it should have been".[36]

Hepatitis C widows short-changed

When, several months after it was announced, the details of the scheme were worked out, it was confirmed that its cost would be some £85 million (petty cash compared to the cost of any of the reforms introduced while Alf was Minister for Disabled People but still an important success). The scheme would be administered by a new agency, the Skipton Fund, and would provide £20,000 each for people with hepatitis C infection – even if it had been cleared by treatment – plus £25,000 for people with cirrhosis of the liver or liver cancer. Bereaved widows and dependants, however, were to be excluded from the scheme. While the Government had "great sympathy for the pain and hardship suffered by widows and other dependants of those inadvertently infected with hepatitis C", the purpose of new funding was not to compensate for bereavement but to help alleviate the suffering of people still living with hepatitis C infection.[37]

This settlement was similar to that suggested (but not formally agreed) in Scotland. It fell well short of what was called for and what was needed, providing barely a tenth of the compensation paid in the Republic of Ireland and well short of the settlement in Canada. Alf saw the fine print of the scheme not only as ungenerous to people living with haemophilia, but cruelly unjust to

---

[36] *Hansard*, Lords, 16 September 2003, 758-60.
[37] *Hansard*, Lords, 5 February 2004, col. 800, 12 January 2006, cols. 298/9.

widows. Their exclusion was both irrational and indefensible, he said, ignoring the extent to which their lives had been devastated by the disaster. They were now left not only in mourning but also financial hardship in the fourth richest country in the world.

On 25 March 2004, Alf pressed the point again, specifically asking the Government whether they would reconsider their decision to exclude widows from the scheme. But Lord Warner, newly appointed Minister of State at the Department of Health, could offer only renewed sympathy. There were no plans to reconsider the decision to restrict help to infected patients still living. Under pressure from a succession of peers supporting Alf from all across the House, Warner repetitively restated his sympathy but remained obdurate. Questioned by Earl Howe on the more generous schemes in Ireland and Canada, the Minister explained that the situation in those countries was different than in Britain. The Irish Government had set up their hepatitis C compensation scheme after a judicial inquiry there found that "wrongful acts were committed". There had been evidence of negligence by the Irish Blood Transfusion Service. The awards in Canada followed a class action brought against the Canadian Government. Subsequent inquiries found that "wrongful practices had been employed" and criminal charges had followed. Lord Warner stressed that the blood services in the UK had not been found to be similarly at fault. Compensation abroad, therefore, was being given in specifically different circumstances that did not apply in the UK.[38] Just how the "wrongful acts" found in other countries had differed from practice in the UK was not explained.

Notwithstanding the breakthrough he had achieved, Alf had no intention of giving up on his fight for a more generous and inclusive scheme. By May 2005, infected blood had caused the deaths of 1,137 haemophilia patients, 896 after being infected with HIV and 241 with hepatitis C. The cause, as Lord (Robert) Winston, a distinguished doctor and broadcaster, had pointed out some years earlier, was the same – a virus – and had come from the same source:

---

[38] *Hansard*, Lords, 25 March 2004, col. 796. According to press reports, an inquiry in Canada went on for five years and cost £1.24 million. It found that this "national – public health disaster" had been caused by systemic failure. Those infected received awards averaging £750,000. Although charges of criminal negligence were dropped as part of a deal with prosecutors, there was an admission of guilt to distributing contaminated blood that infected some 20,000 Canadian people, including many with haemophilia, with HIV or hepatitis C.

contaminated blood products.[39] For the wives of those who had died, said Alf, the result was also the same: devastated lives and widowhood. Why were the hepatitis C widows denied financial help available to HIV widows? What social justice or morality was there in denying parity of treatment to widows in identically the same tragic position? As before, however, Lord Warner now expressed yet more sympathy but was unwilling to relent.[40]

The Government's invariable line on the wider question of liability was that infection in this country had been "inadvertent". This had never seriously been doubted, but was hardly to the point. It was not suggested that organisations in Ireland, Canada and other countries deliberately infected people with hepatitis C. Their failings, whether or not the same, were no doubt equally "inadvertent". The principle established here was clearly set out in the High Court ruling of 2001: namely and essentially that people needing blood through the NHS were entitled to expect that it would be clean blood, and that entitlement was not met.

When Alf returned to the issue on 12 January 2006, Lord Warner continued to insist that while the Government had great sympathy for the pain and hardship suffered by the widows and dependants of those "inadvertently" infected with hepatitis C, the *ex gratia* payments scheme was designed to alleviate the suffering of people infected with hepatitis C and not to compensate for bereavement.[41] Appalled by this implacable formula, Alf asked Lord Warner whether he was aware that the ministerial decree to deny hepatitis C widows the financial help available to HIV widows was widely seen as blatantly unjust and utterly indefensible.[42]

The case for a public inquiry

In the same exchange on 12 January, Lord Warner said that the Government did not consider a public inquiry to be justified because they did not believe that any new light would be shed on this issue

---

[39] *Hansard*, Lords, 5 June 1998, col. 672. Lord Winston is a vice-president of the Haemophilia Society.

[40] *Hansard*, Lords, 26 May 2005, col. 567.

[41] *Hansard*, Lords 12 January 2006, col.299.

[42] Just how iniquitous is evoked by a recent letter sent to Alf by Harriet Bullock, who poignantly expresses both the sorrow and resentment occasioned by inflicted illness and ultimate bereavement: "It is now seven years since my husband died and I feel such anguish that his death and our great loss is still not seen as worth even acknowledging by those in power. There are, it seems, so few of us widows excluded from recognition by the Skipton Fund and still no-one will say why this is so...I am a victim as are my children and grandchildren. I despair".

as a result. In reality, the need for an independent inquiry was now compelling. In the summer of 2005, a press report based on documents obtained by the BBC under the Freedom of Information Act claimed that the Scottish Blood Transfusion Service, after discussing the risk of HIV infection with doctors, had decided not to put a warning on the clotting agent Factor VIII. The Service had come to the astonishing conclusion, it was revealed, that a warning "was likely to cause unnecessary stress to patients".[43]

More disturbing allegations were to follow, when a number of patients who had received infected blood used the Freedom of Information Act to request sight of critical documents from the 1970s and 80s relating to the use of contaminated NHS blood products. They were told that the papers had been "accidentally destroyed". Inevitably, despite official denials, there were suspicions of a cover-up. In response to a question by Lord Jenkin of Roding (a former Secretary of State for Health), Lord Warner assured the House that there had been no deliberate intention to destroy the papers. This mishap too had been inadvertent.[44]

Alf pressed the matter through a series of parliamentary questions. On what date or dates were the papers destroyed, he asked, and by whose decision? And, pointedly, whether these were the only documents that the Department of Health had destroyed in error. Lord Warner explained that during litigation many papers were recalled. The understanding of the Government was that these papers were not adequately archived and were "unfortunately" destroyed in the early 1990s. Further documents relating to the minutes and papers of the Advisory Committee on the Virological Safety of Blood between 1989 and 1992 had been destroyed between July 1994 and March 1998. "A decision, most probably made by an inexperienced member of staff," said Lord Warner, "was responsible for the destruction of these files".[45]

On the same day as this written answer (27 February 2006), the Department of Health published a report *Self-sufficiency in Blood Products in England and Wales*. This document, the outcome of an

---

[43] Louise Gray in *The Scotsman*, 1 and 2 June 2005.
[44] *Hansard*, Lords, 12 January 2006, col.300.
[45] *Hansard*, Lords, 27 February 2006, WA26.

internal inquiry, had begun four years earlier. It gave a long and detailed account of the circumstances leading to the infection of NHS patients with HIV and hepatitis C. Its most obvious defects were that it was not an independent study, that it took place behind closed doors and could not possibly have taken account of the documents destroyed by the department in the 1990s. The report was promptly condemned by many interested parties, not least the Haemophilia Society, which said that it was "a blatant attempt to gloss over the details of the events of the time and even to lay blame at the door of the patients themselves".

In fact, those patients who had managed to survive their malign infection were by now increasingly restive. The compensation they had received, they argued, had been based on an assumption that they faced early death. Although they were glad to still be alive, their funds were now acutely low, existing as they were on modest payments from the trust funds and state benefits. Margaret Unwin, the new chief executive of the Haemophilia Society, said that they had been treated "disgracefully and with a lack of respect"[46] They were living with unpleasant illnesses, she went on, because of an NHS blunder. There had never been an apology and to add insult to injury they were increasingly living in hardship. Alf's view, similarly, was that a grave injustice had been committed. He urged the Government to act with "decency and humanity" to alleviate the survivors' suffering. The money they had received so far had gone nowhere near compensating them for the damage inflicted on them by the NHS.[47]

Lord Jenkin of Roding returned to the issue of NHS culpability in the House of Lords on 19 April. Bearing in mind that the Department of Health had "inadvertently" destroyed all its own files on contaminated blood products and that much new information had recently come to light in the USA, Canada, Ireland and Scotland, was there not now an unanswerable case for a full and impartial public inquiry into what had been one of the major medical disasters in the NHS? Lord Warner would have none of this. While he continued to have "enormous sympathy" with the haemophilia

---

[46] *The Observer*, 16 April 2006.
[47] *Ibid*.

community, the Department had reported fairly and accurately on what it had been asked to do: namely "to identify many of the events and chronology in that period, which were quite complex, and the extent to which the policy of self-sufficiency would have avoided contaminated blood being used by haemophiliacs". The report, he said, made it very clear that the self-sufficiency policy would not have achieved that objective.[48]

In truth, the report may have identified "many" of the factors involved in the disaster, but manifestly did not reveal them all. This was not 'the full Monty' and if the Minister's response failed to satisfy many of the noble Lords, much less did it appease the media. On 23 April, *The Observer*, under the headline 'Tainted blood victims allege official cover-up', published a caustic article by its staff writer Lorna Martin. Letters seen by the newspaper had revealed that only senior officers, who would have known that the sensitive files should have been stored for at least 25 years, would have been in a position to retain or destroy them. Moreover, *The Observer* had learnt that the shredded documents were the same ones the Conservative government had gone to extreme lengths to suppress in 1990. "When a judge ruled that they must be released," wrote Ms Martin, "ministers, in an apparent attempt to avoid handing them over, announced a spectacular U-turn, offering an immediate out-of-court settlement to around 1,200 victims".

Invited to comment, Alf was quoted as saying that in other countries the disaster had been investigated properly out in the open. In Canada there had been legal action. In Ireland, victims had been adequately compensated and in France government officials had been sentenced to imprisonment for their part in the disaster. "But here in the UK," he told the paper, "the Government treats the victims with remarkable arrogance and disregard".

Any imputation of mischief that might have been read into the allegations reported in the press was somewhat obscured by events that unexpectedly embroiled Home Secretary Charles Clarke and Deputy Prime Minister John Prescott, leading to Clarke's removal from office and Prescott's demotion. Yet the fact remained that never had there been a clearer case of the need for an independent

---

[48] *Hansard*, Lords, 19 April 2006, cols.1054-6.

inquiry to satisfy the unease of the remaining survivors of this terrible calamity, many of whom were now living in poverty.

Supported throughout his long campaign by colleagues on all sides of both Houses and at every turn by the redoubtable Haemophilia Society – notably by Chris Hodgson, Roddy Morrison, Karin Pappenheim and her successors Graham Whitehead and Margaret Unwin – Alf's legendary persistence, sheer determination and relentless pressure had drawn important concessions from a reluctant Government that had come to seem quite out of reach. Its handling of the whole issue was seen by the haemophilia community as inept, unfair and indefensible. By 2007, 1,757 haemophilia patients who were exposed to HIV and/or hepatitis C by contaminated NHS blood and blood products had died since being infected and many more were now terminally ill. Of 4,670 patients who were infected with hepatitis C, 1,243 were infected also with HIV; and notwithstanding improvements in treatment for both viruses, only 2,552 patients with hepatitis C and just 361 with HIV were still alive. Nobody thought that the NHS Blood Service had contaminated people deliberately, but the aftermath of its handling of the disaster had left a bitter sense of injustice.

The Haemophilia Society had first called for a public inquiry in December 1988. It did so because, as in the cases of thalidomide and vaccine-damaged children, there was scant if any prospect of legal action being able to achieve an independent review of the causes and effects of the disaster or of the problems and needs of patients afflicted and the bereaved families. Even so, successive Governments had resolutely resisted a public inquiry, preferring in-house inquiries at the Department of Health into narrowly defined aspects of the disaster. Only officials had been involved, allowing no opportunity to hear evidence from infected patients and the dependants of those who had died, or even from former Ministers. Thus with the legal road closed and, after over 18 years on from the original call for a public inquiry, any hope of the Government conceding one immovably blocked, an open and independent inquiry held in public seemed to be the only way forward if the voices of those most affected were ever to be heard; the only way too of restoring public confidence in the safety of blood supplies and of Whitehall's ability to react to new viruses.

In recognition of this reality and the added anguish caused by the disclosure that haemophilia patients had been treated with blood from donors who had since died of vCJD, Alf now determined – as he had done in the case of the veterans of the first Gulf War with medically unexplained illnesses – that his only recourse was to consult widely on the possibility of taking a personal initiative to set up an inquiry independent of Whitehall and of finding a lawyer of the highest standing to conduct it.

On 19 February 2007, Alf announced that the former Solicitor General, The Rt. Hon. (Peter) Archer of Sandwell QC, would head an independent public inquiry. His terms of reference would be: "To investigate the circumstances surrounding the supply to patients of contaminated NHS blood and blood products; its consequences for the haemophilia community and others afflicted; and further steps to address both their problems and needs and those of bereaved families".

Lord Archer would call on patients, bereaved dependants, former Health Ministers and other witnesses to assist the inquiry, and would hope to receive the co-operation of relevant Government departments. He would be joined by colleagues of the highest professional standing: Lord Turnberg, immediate past President of the Royal College of Physicians, as medical assessor, and Dr Judith Willetts, Chief Executive Officer of The British Society for Immunology. Dr Norman Jones, Emeritus Consultant Physician at St Thomas's Hospital would also assist the inquiry as a consultant.

The story had not yet reached its denouement, but already the campaign stood as a testament to the resolve and skill of a man who believes passionately in the pursuit of what is right. Alf's parliamentary contribution had already earned abiding gratitude. The whole of the haemophilia community, said Graham Whitehead, CEO of the Haemophilia Society, had benefited from "his total commitment and enthusiasm for the haemophilia patient cause".[49]

---

[49] Personal letter, 8 June 2005.

POSTSCRIPT

In May 2007, there was one more, and surely decisive, twist in this sorry tale. *The Guardian* (25–26 May) reported that documents produced to the Archer inquiry showed that as long ago as 12 February 1979 the Medical Research Council had discussed the possible contamination of US blood products with a then new strain of hepatitis. Council members had expressed concern about the continued use of commercial plasma products. Other documents obtained by *The Guardian* contained minutes of the Committee on the Safety of Medicines from 13 July 1983, revealing that the committee was aware that patients who repeatedly received blood clotting-factor concentrates appeared to be at risk of AIDS, and knew that those risks "were highest if the blood products came from the blood of homosexual and IV [intravenous] drug users in areas of high incidence – e.g. New York and California". The possibility of withdrawing US preparations from the UK was considered, but the committee concluded that this was "not feasible on grounds of supply" and that the perceived level of risk did not "at present justify serious consideration of such a solution". The risk of contracting AIDS, the committee concluded, must be balanced against the "life-saving" benefits of their use to haemophiliacs. No one appears to have had regard to the *life-threatening* consequences of AIDS.

There were two particularly disturbing aspects of this decision. First, again according to *The Guardian*, that haemophiliacs were normally not told of the risk; secondly and crucially that Dr Spence Galbraith, head of the communicable disease surveillance centre at the Public Health Laboratory Service, had specifically warned the Department of Health and Social Security that, in the light of 14 known cases of people with haemophilia contracting AIDS after receiving Factor VIII concentrate, US blood products made in the affected period should be withdrawn. His warning was ignored.

It would be wrong to anticipate the final report of Lord Archer's inquiry, but this evidence has inevitably reinforced the sense of protracted and calculated injustice among people with haemophilia and the loved ones of both dead and living victims. Equally clearly, the evidence has emerged as a direct consequence of Alf's dogged and determined persistence in creating the Archer inquiry. It is a fitting climax to perhaps the final movement of the concerto of Alf's distinguished parliamentary career, part of a legacy, free of dubiety, for which so many people have cause to be grateful.

Chapter 17

REFLECTIONS

"So many issues have been swept under the carpet by successive governments, you no longer walk the carpets of Westminster: you have to climb them".

Alf Morris

In 1972, I was invited to address the annual conference of the Libraries Association in Hastings. It came as a surprise that they would want me as a keynote speaker. Before accepting, I asked them about it and they said it was because of the library legislation I had put on the statute book in section 2 of the Chronically Sick and Disabled Persons Act. They wanted me to explain the Act's philosophy and provisions in relation to libraries. Although I had consciously included library facilities for housebound disabled people in section 2, and libraries in its requirements on access to the built environment, this invitation brought home to me, perhaps for the first time, just how wide-ranging the policy areas covered by the new legislation were being seen. For here was a service of fundamental importance to the population at large that the Act was making as available to disabled people as to everyone else. It taught me, moreover, that there were pro-active campaigners in the community ready to run with my ideas: all they had needed was a prompt. Here was an early reminder that the Act had reached people who I had never specifically expected to reach and who were glad to be involved with me.

I didn't enter Parliament with the intention of specialising on disability. As we've seen, my first three years were spent with Fred Peart at the Ministry of Agriculture, Fisheries and Food. Fred's parliamentary antecedents were deep-rooted. His father, Colonel Peart, had been Emanuel Shinwell's agent when he returned to Parliament in 1935 having defeated Ramsey MacDonald at Seaham Harbour. When I entered Parliament in 1964, Mannie chaired the Parliamentary Labour Party (PLP) and was Father of the House – he had first been elected in 1922 – and closely bonded with Fred. Vicariously, I benefited from this link in that in Mannie's eyes I could do no wrong. Woe betide the hapless Member who challenged me in debate or contradicted my merest contribution to PLP proceedings. Mannie even asked me to address the General Management Committee of his Constituency Labour Party – a singular honour for so junior an MP. I was incredibly lucky also to find myself – after Fred's move from MAFF in 1968 to become the Leader of the House of Commons and to a great extent his principal assistant in what was a very close relationship – I found myself working with the key figure in managing the parliamentary machine. It was from him that I learned the intricacies of Commons procedure that were to prove so crucially important in all my future work.

Harry Truman once said of Washington DC, "If you want a friend here, buy a dog". That this was not true of Westminster first became crystal clear to me by the abiding friendship I had with Fred Peart. His death in 1988 was one of the saddest moments of my parliamentary life.

Inevitably the extent of my work with him meant that, although I had a close personal acquaintance with disability in my own and Irene's families and raised many issues of concern to disabled people, this was not initially my main political preoccupation. Rather than my having chosen to specialise on disability issues, I would say that disability chose me. Yet I understood how profoundly important it was as a policy area and knew that disabled people in sixties' Britain were its most neglected citizens. At variance with the Beatles no. 1 hit, they had no reason to 'believe in yesterday'. I knew too that disability was a family affair – so that the child of a disabled mother is as much involved in the problems of disability as the mother of a disabled child – and that estimates of its incidence would always be a misleading guide to the total number of people affected by the problems of disabled living. When you put disabled people in the context of family, as the BBC did in 1981 (in a profile of disability to mark the International Year of Disabled Persons), you find you're talking about roughly a third of the population. The BBC's survey found, if I remember aright, that 32 per cent of respondents said that their lives were significantly affected by disability: either as disabled people or the close relatives of a disabled person. By definition, where one member of a family is disabled, the family as a whole is likely to be involved in the problems of disabled living.

Nevertheless, as a newly elected MP I never dreamt – nor surely did anyone else – that I had any realistic chance of being able to legislate on disability, even when after five years in Parliament I won first place in the annual ballot for private members' bills in 1969. What I decided then was that I would at least try to get the issue on the parliamentary agenda – that would be achievement enough – but even this limited objective was perceived in some reaches of the corridors of power as incredibly ambitious. I had absolutely no expectation that my Bill would take off and become law. In fact if you'd told me then that, ascertainably, over 20 million people in the UK alone would benefit individually from its enactment, and moreover, that in the 35 years since the Chronically Sick and Disabled Persons (Scotland) Act became law, the number of individual beneficiaries there would exceed the current population of Scotland, I'd have thought you were ascertainably in cloud cuckoo land at its cloudiest. Yet take off the Bill did – achieving almost vertical ascent – and thereafter my parliamentary destiny was decided. For against incalculable odds I had enacted legislation that ranged widely over policy areas involving the departmental responsibilities of over a dozen secretaries of state: access to the built environment, local social services, healthcare, outdoor mobility, education, employment, transport, libraries and housing, to name but a few. The Act amended 39 existing other Acts of Parliament including such major statutes as the Public Health Act 1936, the Education Act 1944, the National Assistance Act 1946 and the National Health Act 1948, as well as legislating in areas – like access to the built environment, the problems and special needs of autistic, dyslexic and deaf/blind children – where previously there was no legislation of any kind to amend, either here or anywhere else in the world.

From then on, I was inevitably locked into seeking to ensure that this plethora of new legislative provisions was humanely implemented. I was assailed on all sides by organisations of and for disabled people who saw me as being able to advance their causes, many of them conflicting with each other. And since the mission that had fallen to me could never be fully achieved, with myriad aspects of age-old disadvantage and neglect, I have simply gone on seeking to do all I could to help, while emphasising the priority of the need at all times to work further to raise the status and well-being of disabled people and their families.

The task is unfinished. Most recently, the passage into law of the Disability Discrimination Bill 2005, a further lineal descendant of CORAD and Civil Rights (Disabled Persons) Bill, in which I was able to play some part, again improved the rights of disabled people; but we are still nowhere near the end of the road in securing full equality. Moreover if that is the picture in Britain, the scene is dramatically worse in many other countries where enhanced human and civil rights for disabled people are, as yet, scarcely on the agenda. And it was in responding to that daunting challenge that I was to become more and more deeply immersed.

Seven years ago I had the honour to be invited to chair the World Planning Group appointed by Rehabilitation International (RI) to draft its 'Charter for the Third Millennium' for disabled people world-wide. As these pages show, RI is the umbrella body for organisations of and for disabled people in over 100 countries. The new charter concentrates on basic human and civil rights: those of the more than 600 million people with physical, intellectual and sensory disabilities across the world. Today millions of them, children and adults alike, more especially among the poorest of the world's poor, still have to live with the effects of disabilities that were easily preventable at minimal cost. Failure to protect them was a problem not of resources but of political will and priorities. In the same way, purposeful action to reduce the handicapping effects of disability remains pitiably inadequate in large parts of the world. Indeed, and particularly in the poorest countries, the problems of disabled living, far from being reduced, are gratuitously multiplied by wholly unmerited but still lawful discrimination against disabled people there.

RI's updated charter presaged new hope and a new vision for a new century; one of full empowerment and genuine social inclusion for disabled people everywhere. Its emphasis is on value as well as cost and its plea to governments is for acts not of compassion but of enlightened self-interest and moral right. The charter's message to world leaders on discrimination against disabled people is unequivocal and strong: it is that what is morally indefensible ought no longer to be legally permissible.

The knowledge and skills now exist to enable all countries to remove the barriers that exclude people with disabilities from the life of their communities. It is possible now for every country to open all of its institutions and systems to all of its people. Here again what is too often lacking is the political will to proclaim and translate into action the policies necessary to bring this about. And, says the 'Charter for the Third Millennium', a nation that fails to respond to this challenge is failing to realise its true worth.

The new charter insists on the same human and civil rights for disabled people as for everyone else. It insists also that organisations working to help disabled people should be empowered with the resources necessary to share responsibility in national planning for rehabilitation and independent living. It calls on: "Every nation to develop, with the participation of disabled people's organisations, a comprehensive plan with clearly defined targets and timetables for implementing the aims set out in this Charter".

Other principal aims of the new charter included securing a UN Convention on the Rights of Disabled People as a key strategy, something that has finally come to fruition as I write these reflections. Documenting the case for the 'Charter for the Third Millennium' posed the question why so many people still acquire preventable disabilities and why the handicapping effects of their disabilities are so widely ignored. Its authors share the view of UNICEF's report on 'The State of the World's Children' which states: "When so much could be done for so many at so little cost, then one central, shameful fact becomes unavoidable; the reason that these problems are not being overcome is not that the task is too large or too difficult or too expensive. It is that the job is not being given sufficient priority because those most severely affected are almost exclusively the poorest and least politically influential people on earth". That shameful but inescapable fact demeans and diminishes us all.

The concept of equality is a difficult one since it is obvious that people are not, in a thousand and one ways, equal to each other. I can do no better than to quote Prince Ra'ad bin Zeid of Jordan, one of the members of my World Planning Group, speaking in Athens in support of the UN Convention on the Rights of Disabled People:

> "Human equality is central to the system of basic freedoms postulated by human rights law. Its core premise is that all persons not only possess inestimable inherent self-worth but also are inherently equal in terms of self-worth, regardless of their differences. Thus differences based on arbitrary factors from a moral point of view over which a person has no control, are considered invalid. This is not to say that there are no differences between the people; but in the realm of disability rights our struggle in helping to draft the Charter for the Third Millennium was to call for a genuinely egalitarian society, one that has a

positive and just approach to human differences. The disability rights debate is not about the enjoyment of specific rights, but about ensuring the effective enjoyment of all human rights".

The UN's founding principles recognised the inherent dignity, the equal and inalienable right of all humankind to freedom and justice. Again the UN has, in the universal declaration and the international covenants on human rights, recognised that everyone is entitled to all the rights and freedoms set forth, without distinction of race, colour, gender, language, religion, political or other opinion, national or social origin, property, birth or status. There was, as yet however, no specific reference there to the world's over 600 million disabled people who had waited far too long for their rights to be fully recognised and promoted as they would surely be by the Convention proposed by the charter. That was the next step for humankind.

One of the advantages of being in Parliament for 43 years is the development of a sense of perspective. Churchill, who served, with the exception of a two-year interval, from 1900 to 1964, once remarked, "The longer you can look back here, the farther you can look forward". The difficulty about that is just what the future can be seen to hold in a House of Commons of declining power. One change, which has been mentioned in an earlier chapter, is the curtailment of debates by the timetabling of more and more legislation in the Commons. When I first entered Parliament use of the 'guillotine' was rare; now the way that debates are cut is more akin to the use of a circular saw. In 1964, young new MPs, as before and since, argued for more 'family-friendly hours'. Open-ended debates could be arduous. I recall one morning, at around 5 a.m., when Joe Godber, then Opposition spokesman on agriculture, buttonholed me as Parliamentary Private Secretary to the Minister in the corridor outside the chamber and said, "Tell Fred [Peart] that if he will accept the substitution of 'may' for 'shall' in the next amendment I will withdraw all my others and he can go home"! Today the Government is free of any such pressure to compromise. Now the Bill would be guillotined and all uncompleted business would fall when time was up. I once put the case for 'family-friendly hours' to Manny Shinwell and he said,"When you get into Opposition you'll take a different view, Alf". And I did. Parliament is gravely weakened if you can lock the doors at 10 p.m. – often even earlier than that today. There is then less opportunity to scrutinise the actions of Ministers, who can avoid opposing arguments simply by the strategy of denying time. A good example of this was the Bill that became the Railways Act 2005, provisions of which were crucially important to Greater Manchester MPs. Yet time was inexorably called for the axe to fall on their amendments to the Bill, and MPs of all parties had later to troupe across to the Lords to hear their guillotined amendments debated there.

The most remarkable transformation in parliamentary convention is that which has resulted in an unshakeable reluctance to resign. In earlier days, the classic case was that of Sir Thomas Dugdale, who in 1954 resigned in the wake of the Crichel Down Inquiry even though it had exonerated him from any personal responsibility. Honour nevertheless persuaded him that, as the Minister in charge, he should stand down. More recently it sometimes became open to question just when, if at all, anyone would resign over anything. More than ever is done to uphold parliamentary standards, but Dugdale's approach is no longer even considered.

What we do have now, however, is an alarmingly high mobility of ministers <u>between</u> departments, so that incumbents rarely have long enough to get to grips with the full range of their responsibilities. This means that the bureaucracies of the Civil Service are strengthened, sometimes – as we have seen – with disastrous results. Within three months in 2006, there were three Ministers for Veterans, making it for one observer the most casualty-prone job in Whitehall. Alongside this there has been a parallel trend in the operation of select committees, whose members are now closer to the apparatchiks of Whitehall than to the generality of MPs, a danger discussed in my 1970 book 'The Growth of Parliamentary Scrutiny by Committee'.

MPs themselves tend in general to have less experience of work outside Parliament. There is a growing triumph of youth over experience. While something has been done to redress the gender imbalance of the House of Commons, age imbalance is now taking hold. This is unfortunate because Parliament needs to be seen and in fact to be representative of all sections of society.

Similarly, when I first became an MP, most of my colleagues and almost every Minister had served in the armed forces. Now the reverse is true, so that – as I have found over and over again as honorary parliamentary adviser to the Royal British Legion – there is a disturbing distance from and lack of understanding of the ex-service, and indeed the serving, community.

Apparent also is an increasing unwillingness to stand out of line in any way and to oppose conventional party wisdom. Too many MPs are now averse to raising their heads above the parapet. Indeed, in some cases, there is seemingly no parapet too low for them to get their heads under. Yet, refreshingly, there are still some for whom there is no obstacle too high if the cause is one worth fighting. Quintessentially Parliament is about holding the Executive to account. Anything that frustrates that purpose diminishes our democracy.

No job in my life has been accomplished without help from others; and no one has helped more and more often than my wife, Irene. Too often people expect her to achieve the impossible; yet uncannily she always exceeds expectation.

Alf Morris
April 2007

TRIBUTES

"...an excellent and genuine man. One of the few MPs and ministers who genuinely cares about people, and especially the disabled. The exact reverse of most politicians in fact – no vanity, and concerned with the real issues and not just the image and the packaging."

Bernard Donoughue, Downing Street Diary

"For me, Alf Morris is the champion of disabled people, not just because of the Chronically Sick and Disabled Persons Act, but for the whole of his parliamentary endeavour. It is an example of what can be achieved by gentle persuasion. While it is right to honour practical achievements – such as those in the areas of access and mobility – I think that Alf's outstanding contribution has been to raise awareness of the worth of disabled people, not only in the eyes of a largely uncaring society, but even more in terms of their own self-image. The triumph of his quiet crusade has been the empowerment of the powerless. He has made it more difficult for architects, planners and legislators to ignore disabled people, and in turn helped them to stop apologising for themselves and to claim a fulfilling place in society."

Claire Tomalin

"...there were a small number of people I could always rely on, no matter how great the difficulties. Alfred Morris stood out as the most considerate man in the House of Commons...[He] proved to be a man with quite exceptional understanding of my problem; we soon formed a warm personal relationship which I value highly...Working on the [Chronically Sick and Disabled Persons] Bill pulled me out of the isolation of deafness; it was a psychological tonic." *Jack Ashley, from Journey into Silence (1973)*

"The Joint Committee on Mobility for Disabled People applauds the successful endeavours that led to the 1970 Act and Alf Morris's subsequent and tenacious efforts for disabled people...the Act was a charter for disabled people. It gave them a realistic sense of their importance and an understanding of their right to be citizens and participate fully in society." *The late Sir Peter Large CBE*

"[Alf Morris] will go down in history as the supreme champion of disabled people." *The late Lord Longford, in the House of Lords*

"The All-Party Disability Group had its origins during the preparation of the Chronically Sick and Disabled Persons Bill. It brought together a dedicated team whose concern for disabled people transcended their political differences: a spirit that has continued to mark the work of the Group. I am delighted to have the opportunity to pay tribute to the outstanding work of Alf Morris. One of his great strengths has been his ability to win support from every part of the political spectrum to achieve an end that looks to improving the quality of life for all disabled citizens." *Sir John Hannam*

"In British society, there has always been unfairness and injustice, and those with physical, sensory or mental disabilities have had more than their share. Our social history is studded with failed attempts to treat disabled people with any degree of sympathy or equity because until my fellow co-operator Alf Morris piloted his landmark Bill through Parliament they did not have a champion. And what a champion! Born out of his family's experiences, he vowed to use his every parliamentary opportunity to right glaring wrongs. His Bill, which brought practical help and meaningful hope to tens of millions of disabled people, here and across the world, is his personal testament to the very essence of the spirit of co-operation. A cause he has espoused and adorned all his life.

"With his colleagues in the Co-operative Parliamentary Group, he has campaigned over many years to turn co-operative precepts into practice, more especially to the benefit of people in the greatest need. His distinguished work has earned him not only national but international acclaim. All Co-operators salute the advances that Alf has achieved for Britain's disabled people and their families, and we are proud that they were won in the name of the Co-operative Movement he loves." *Lord Graham of Edmonton*

"[The Labour Government] showed imagination and concern in bringing into being a Minister for Disabled People, and wisdom in choosing Alf Morris to fill the role.

"Alf is widely known and highly regarded throughout the UK and abroad, and his contribution to the cause of disabled people cannot be overstated. With his deceptively quiet voice and manner, he has proved himself more than a match for those who blocked the path towards the realisation of his goal: a new deal for disabled people.... He has skilfully succeeded in raising the profile of disabled people, in order to secure their rightful place in society."

George W Lee

"Alf has been one of the greatest allies we have had in Westminster in raising awareness of the prevalence and, more frequently than many think, the severity of the various forms of arthritis. He regularly reminds Rt. Hon. and Hon. members that arthritis is the biggest cause of physical disability in the UK, affecting around one in five of the population."

Neil Betteridge, Chief Executive, Arthritis Care

"Your public work for disability is without equal because you, in office and out of office, led the way. You are part of British Social History. Tens of thousands owe you much. Other Ministers *followed* you in their decency. The Aussies were right to honour you. Irene has been your rock.

Lord (Barry) Jones

"Alf Morris's support of disabled people is legendary. History has seldom produced a more compassionate man; I know that still now he will not rest, but continue the battle to secure the well-being of those dealt a poor hand in life and secure their fair and just recognition."

Chris Hodgson, former chair of the Haemophilia Society

APPENDIX

ALF MORRIS, CHARITY CHAMPION:
A LIST OF HIS OFFICES

Alzheimer's Society	Vice President
ASPIRE	Patron
Ataxia UK	Patron
Axess Information Association	Patron
British Polio Fellowship	Vice Patron
Children's Research Fund	Trustee
Council for the Advancement of Communication with Deaf People	Patron
Crisis	Vice President
Crossroads Association	Patron
Disabled Living	Vice President
Disabled Living Foundation	Vice President
Greater London Action on Disability	Patron
Haemophilia Society	President
Hallé Orchestra	Trustee
Manchester Dogs' Home	President
Manchester United Supporters Trust	Patron
Mobilise Organisation	Vice President
Motability	Founder Patron
National Information Forum	Patron
North Regional Association for Sensory Support	President
PHAB	Vice President
Rehabilitation International	Life Vice President
Royal Schools for Deaf Children	Patron
St. Dunstan's	Governor
Skill	Vice President
Snowdon Award Scheme	Vice President
Society of Chiropodists and Podiatrists	President
The Dame Vera Lynn Trust for Children with Cerebral Palsy	Patron
The Royal British Legion	Hon. Parliamentary Adviser
United Co-operatives Charitable Foundation	Patron
Vitalise	Vice Patron
War Widows' Association	National Vice President

INDEX

471

473